Signs, Wonders, and Gifts

Signs, Wonders, and Gifts

Divination in the Letters of Paul

JENNIFER EYL

OXFORD
UNIVERSITY PRESS

OXFORD

UNIVERSITY PRESS

Oxford University Press is a department of the University of Oxford. It furthers
the University's objective of excellence in research, scholarship, and education
by publishing worldwide. Oxford is a registered trade mark of Oxford University
Press in the UK and certain other countries.

Published in the United States of America by Oxford University Press
198 Madison Avenue, New York, NY 10016, United States of America.

© Oxford University Press 2019

CIP data is on file at the Library of Congress
ISBN 978–0–19–092465–2

1 3 5 7 9 8 6 4 2

Printed by Sheridan Books, Inc., United States of America

For my parents, Pat and Tony Eyl

Contents

Acknowledgments

IT IS THRILLING to refine a project and watch it flourish, expand, and take new, unexpected directions. I owe a debt of gratitude to numerous people for invigorating conversations, mentorship, and encouragement throughout the process of thinking through many of my ideas. First, I woud like to thank Ross Kraemer whose inspiring influence drew me from Classics to Religious Studies and taught me always to inquire, "What is at stake, and for whom?" I thank Stanley Stowers for guiding my interest in this project, which was originally a PhD dissertation. I am also grateful to Bill Arnal, Debra Scoggins Ballentine, Willi Braun, Barry Crawford, Natasha Margulis, Craig Martin, Karin D. Martin, Paul Robertson, Emma Wasserman, Stephen L. Young, and Ophelia—many of whom read and offered excellent feedback on various stages of these chapters. Daily conversations—sometimes significant, sometimes in passing—with Robyn Faith Walsh, Erin Roberts, and Sarah Rollens (the Lady Cabal!) made this book much better and more interesting than it would have been otherwise. They certainly made it more compelling to write. Thank you to the American Academy in Rome for use of their library facilities throughout the Spring of 2017. I owe a debt of gratitude to the anonymous reviewers for their insightful comments and to my editor at Oxford, Steve Wiggins, for encouraging this project. I am forever indebted to my sister, Nancy Eyl, who has always inspired me to demand more of myself. Special thanks to Jessica Kim for her keen editorial eye and for enticing me to take breaks with adventurous fishing trips to Maine. In addition to those mentioned above, I thank the many other scholars whose intellectual bravery has opened new ways of seeing and understanding the world and the past.

Introduction

BY THE POWER OF SIGNS AND WONDERS

For I will not venture to speak of anything except what Christ has accomplished through me to win obedience from the gentiles, by word and deed, by the power of signs and wonders, by the power of the spirit [pneuma] of God, so that from Jerusalem and as far around as Illyricum I have fully proclaimed the good news of Christ.

—ROM 15:18–19 (NRSV)

In the end . . . classifications, like generic boundaries, run to the limits of their usefulness if they prevent us from seeing the cross-fertilization of ideas and intellectual practices from one field to the next.

—PETER STRUCK, *Birth of the Symbol**

THE FIRST PREMISE of this book is that the apostle Paul engaged in numerous forms of divination and claimed to possess divine powers. While Paul undoubtedly taught ethics and preached the resurrected Christ to gentiles, he did so while *also* claiming to read divine signs and perform miracles. The second premise is that Paul's divinatory practices are best understood within a framework of reciprocity that dominated human–divine relations in the ancient Mediterranean. Insofar as Paul extends divine abilities to his gentile followers, such abilities come in exchange for followers' unwavering *pistis*, or faithfulness, to Christ and to the Judean deity. This book, then, is largely a project of redescription, comparison, and taxonomy. I redescribe, reclassify, and recontextualize Paul's repertoire of divinatory and wonderworking practices vis-à-vis other widespread, similar practices, and, furthermore, I reexamine how New Testament scholars have dismissed

---

* Peter Struck, *Birth of the Symbol: Ancient Readers at the Limits of Their Texts* (Princeton, NJ: Princeton University Press, 2004).

the importance of reciprocity in Paul's teachings. Such an endeavor necessarily involves "a radical alteration of the habitual terms of description"[1] because Paul's divinatory practices have traditionally received their own unique categories to make them appear distinct from the practices of others around him. Instead of maintaining the illusion of uniqueness, this book resituates Paul's practices in the wider world of ancient Mediterranean religiosity and wider relations of mutual beneficence. My goal in such a project is threefold: (1) to extract Paul from the Christianity that unfolded in his wake and to resituate him in the only milieu he knew—the first-century Mediterranean world; (2) to contribute to the scholarly body of knowledge regarding divinatory and wonderworking practices in antiquity; and (3) to understand how Paul utilizes the ethic of faithfulness vis-à-vis his followers' cultivation of their own divinatory powers.

Paul's performance of wonders, his interpretation of signs, and his engagement in practices of prophecy and speaking in tongues, constitute a significant and legitimating aspect of his teaching. Contrary to what some other scholars have argued—that Paul did not want to draw attention to his wonderworking and divinatory practices—I argue that such practices were crucial to Paul, even when they do not constitute the primary focus of his letters. As this study will demonstrate, such practices are variations of widely recognized and deeply rooted methods of communicating information from gods (projections of the future, endorsements, desires, and will) and of demonstrating superhuman power channeled through a human agent. It should go without saying that Paul practiced forms of divination and wonderworking that would have been intelligible to others around him. He was not wildly unlike his contemporaries and he did not "make up" what he was doing from whole cloth. Even when he engaged in practices and made statements that may have been perceived as exotic and mysterious, he did so in a cultural arena where exoticism and secrecy held discernible functions and values. Even when he innovated, he innovated upon the cultural practices familiar to him and to his peers. To be clear—Paul was not a stranger "borrowing" practices from the world around him; rather, his choices were constituted by and intelligible in that world.

Eschewing specialization in one domain, Paul's array of divinations and miracles run the gamut of divinatory practices of the first-century Mediterranean. He prophesies, he uses ancient books to explicate mysterious and divine knowledge, he channels forms of divine speech (which he calls *glōssai*), he provides demonstrations of miraculous power imbued to him through the Judean deity,

---

1. Jonathan Z. Smith, "*Dayyeinu.*" In *Redescribing Christian Origins*, edited by Ron Cameron and Merrill P. Miller (Atlanta, GA: Society of Biblical Literature, 2004), 484.

he performs miracle healings with no medical training, and he refers to a host of unnamed signs, wonders, and "mighty works." Related to these practices, he also claims to have been singled out for this role by his god, that he has had epiphanic visitations by Christ, and that he traveled, involuntarily, to heavenly realms. Like other divinatory–wonderworkers, Paul is clear that these powers and miracles do not originate with him; rather, they are examples of a deity working through him. In addition to his expertise in such practices, Paul presents himself as the arbiter, administrator, and educator to his followers who have been endowed with divinatory powers, which he calls *charismata pneumatika*. He shares such benefits with them (Rom 1:11), instructs them on the nature and use of their benefits (1 Cor 12:1–14:40), and hierarchically arranges the value of each benefit (Rom 12:6–8; 1 Cor 12:27–31).

But Paul is not alone in his divinatory and wonderworking expertise. Greek and Latin writers such as Plato, Juvenal, Lucian, the author of the *Didache*, Josephus, and Philostratus ridicule and warn of itinerant wonderworkers and prophets, most of whom are accused of being quacks, phonies, and charlatans. Paul himself refers to "false brothers" and "super-apostles" who claim powers similar to his. That so many writers allude to an anxiety over the authenticity of traveling preacher–teacher figures points to their prevalence and the uncertainty of their authority. In Greco-Roman antiquity, interpreting divine information and exhibiting strange powers endowed by a god were the markers that rendered some religious specialists intelligible as such, regardless of "official" credentials or sincerity.

There is a lacuna in Pauline scholarship, however, regarding Paul's divinatory and wonderworking practices. This lacuna appears to be the result of New Testament scholarship's historically intimate relationship with academic Christian theology.[2] More clearly, things like wonderworking, speaking in tongues, and prophesying have long been viewed as antithetical to the sobriety of Western Christian rationalism, and have therefore been swept under the rug or dismissed in pursuit of preserving a myth of "rational" Christian beginnings,

---

2. This problem is not relegated to the world of New Testament studies, exclusively. Daniel Ogden's informative *Magic, Witchcraft, and Ghosts in the Greek and Roman Worlds* (Oxford: Oxford University Press, 2009) examines magicians, miracle-workers, sorcerers, and prophetic *daimones* of every stripe. Yet, there is no significant attention to figures who are foundational in Christianity (Jesus, Peter, Paul, etc.). Chapter 3 includes Persians, Egyptians, Chaldeans, and Syrians as "Alien Sorcerers" but does not include anyone from Judea. Chapter 4 is titled "The Rivals of Jesus" but does not consider Jesus himself as a magician or wonderworker.

and thus a "rational" essence to Christianity itself.[3] Scholarship that examines the divinatory practices and miracle-workings of Paul in Acts of the Apostles and other later texts is fairly extensive (for helpful bibliographies, see Praeder 1983; Schreiber 1996; and Reimer 2002). Yet, when it comes to examining Paul's self-presentation as a divinatory specialist, evidenced by his own first-person accounts, the scholarship becomes noticeably sparse. Three general strategies characterize how scholars have addressed Paul's references to divination and wonderworking: to fully ignore Paul's involvement in such activities, to give a cursory nod to Paul's mention of such practices but then deny or excuse his involvement, or to classify his practices as unique or distinct from the divinations and miracleworkings that Paul's ancient contemporaries practiced across the Mediterranean. Most scholarship comes down on the side of denial or taxonomic uniqueness.

For example, one scholar has argued that later apocryphal characterizations of Paul as wonderworker are *unpauline*[4] and that the apostle mentions such powers, begrudgingly, simply to compete with his opponents. Another scholar suggests that Paul's special powers and gifts merely "provide a sense of excitement and empowerment."[5] Bert Jan Peerbolte has noticed this absence of scholarly attention: "In many studies Paul is depicted as a preacher, a theologian or a missionary manager who started and organized new congregations . . . . Rarely, however, is Paul treated from the perspective of the performance of miracles."[6] The present study seeks to resolve such an oversight.[7]

---

3. This has been true among scholars, theologians, and lay Christians alike. See the editorial of Chris Lutes, "First Church of Signs and Wonders: Do We Want Magic or God?" *Christianity Today* 45.1 (2001): 81. Bernd Kollman discusses this in "Images of Hope: Towards an Understanding of New Testament Miracle Stories." In *Wonders Never Cease: The Purpose of Narrating Miracle Stories in the New Testament and Its Religious Environment*, edited by Michael Labahn and Jan Liertaert Peerbolte (New York: T & T Clark, 2006), esp. 244–248. With specific regard to prophecy versus rationalism, see Laura Nasrallah, "*An Ecstasy of Folly:*" *Prophecy and Authority in Early Christianity* (Cambridge, MA: Harvard University Press, 2003), esp. 1–15.

4. Dennis MacDonald, "Apocryphal and Canonical Narratives about Paul." In *Paul and the Legacies of Paul*, edited by William Babcock (Dallas, TX: Southern Methodist University Press, 1990), 55–69. E. Haenchen argues similarly in his *Apostelgeschichte*, 100–101. For a response to MacDonald's argument, see Stanley Stowers, "Comment: What Does *Unpauline* Mean?" In *Paul and the Legacies of Paul*, 70–78.

5. Richard Horsley, *1 Corinthians* (Nashville, TN: Abingdon, 1998), 54–55.

6. Bert Jan Lietaert Peerbolte, "Paul the Miracle Worker: Development and Background of Pauline Miracle Stories." In *Wonders Never Cease: The Purpose of Narrating Miracle Stories in the New Testament and Its Religious Environment*, edited by Michael Labahn and Jan Liertaert Peerbolte (New York: T & T Clark, 2006), 180–99..

7. One of the most vocal scholars to argue that Paul was hesitant to perform miracles or demonstrate powers of the spirit is Dieter Georgi in his lengthy and detailed *The Opponents of*

The studies that do examine Paul's claims to divinatory practices are few in number and of limited help in this study. John Ashton's *The Religion of Paul the Apostle*,[8] whose title nods to Albert Schweitzer's *The Mysticism of Paul the Apostle*,[9] undertakes a comparative analysis between Paul's religiosity and shamanism. Yet the grounds for comparison are limited almost exclusively to ancient Jewish evidence, neglecting the rest of the Greek and Roman world of which Paul was likewise a product. While Ashton smartly critiques the scholarly habit of examining Paul solely as a theologian, his study does not aim for the broader theoretical and historical framework of the present study, in locating Paul's divinatory expertise within deep traditions of reciprocity.

Colleen Shantz's 2009 study, *Paul in Ecstasy*, applies knowledge of neurobiology to a study of what happens in the brain during Paul's "religious experiences" such as possession, trances, visions, and glossolalia.[10] Although some scholars have questioned the legitimacy of measuring brain activity in relation to spiritual experiences,[11] Shantz offers a much needed corrective to what she calls

---

Paul in Second Corinthians. Georgi challenges the long-standing scholarly notion that Paul's opponents in 1 and 2 Cor are the same, by arguing that 1 Cor is written against Gnostics and 2 Cor targets other itinerant Jewish–Christian preachers like Paul himself. In so doing, Georgi claims that Paul's opponents in 2 Cor trade on the performance of miracles, signs, wonders, and dramatic shows of power. Paul, however, demonstrates the authenticity of his calling and apostleship by distancing himself from such showy practices, emphasizing instead the power of the gospel and the lack of need to prove himself. According to Georgi, Paul reluctantly engages in divinatory practices only as a desperate last resort to vie with his errant but convincing competitors. In *Signs of an Apostle*, C. K. Barrett suggests that Paul "could even appeal to visions and revelations, all the apparatus of *Schwarmerei*, 'enthusiasm' in the bad sense, but he knew as he did so that he acted like a fool." In reference to Paul's use of *terata* and *dunameis* in 2 Cor 12:12, Barrett suggests, "To appeal to them is part of the folly which Paul permits himself to indulge in this chapter." The sentiments of Georgi and Barrett are echoed in Dennis R. MacDonald. F. F. Bruce ignores the issue altogether in his "Is the Paul of *Acts* the Real Paul?" Bruce examines a number of inconsistencies between Paul as he presents himself in the letters and Paul as he is presented by the author of Acts, suggesting that elaborations in Acts exaggerate or "fill in the gaps" left by the epistles. Yet, he does not examine Paul's miracles and wonderworking in Acts vs. the letters—a strange oversight given the prominence of showy miracles in Acts and scholars' dismissal of Paul's claim to miracles in the letters. See Dieter Georgi, *The Opponents of Paul in Second Corinthians* (Philadelphia: Fortress Press, 1986); C. K. Barrett, *The Signs of an Apostle* (Philadelphia: Fortress Press, 1972), 42; Dennis MacDonald, "Apocryphal and Canonical Narratives About Paul," 55–70.

8. John Ashton, *The Religion of Paul the Apostle* (New Haven, CT: Yale University Press, 2000).

9. Albert Schweitzer, *The Mysticism of Paul the Apostle* (New York: Holt, 1931).

10. Colleen Shantz, *Paul in Ecstasy: The Neurobiology of the Apostle's Life and Thought* (New York: Cambridge University Press, 2009).

11. For example, Ann Taves writes, ". . . scholars and researchers, including a number of self-identified neurotheologians, most of whom lack training in theology or religious studies, have enthusiastically embraced the challenges of identifying the neural correlates of religious

"the scholarly construction of what amounts to be a disembodied Paul."[12] She reminds us that not only did Paul live, *embodied*, in a world—his readers did as well. Understanding Paul in this sense, Shantz argues that, "ecstasy is actually a significant feature of Paul's life and impetus to his thought."[13] While Schantz's study focuses on neurobiology, its first premise is that Paul indeed participates in practices of divination, wonderworking, and ecstatic possession.

Stefan Schreiber (1996)[14] and Bert Jan Lietaert Peerbolte (2006)[15] both address Paul as a miracle-worker in the letters and in later depictions of the apostle. Schreiber echoes Dieter Georgi's earlier suggestion that Paul's hand was almost forced in resorting to miracles in 2 Cor 12:12 (albeit, Schreiber is more open to that simply as a possibility, whereas Georgi argues it definitively), and Schreiber emphasizes Paul's insistence that divine power does not originate with him, but with God. Yet Schreiber, too, does not endeavor to explain Paul's disinterest in power in terms that extend beyond traditional theological explanations or to connect Paul's divinations and miracles to reciprocity. Only in the last few pages of "Paul the Miracle Worker" does Peerbolte look specifically at Paul's self-presentation as a wonderworker: ". . . Paul speaks of 'signs of an apostle' as *actions* that Paul himself had *performed*" (197). Yet Peerbolte's examination is not intended to be extensive, and in its brevity reiterates Paul's own claims without offering the explanatory context the present study strives for. For example, Peerbolte (like Schreiber) recognizes that Paul attributes his miracles to a divine source and not to himself (199), but he suggests that, "by ascribing the origins of his deeds to Jesus Christ, the miracle worker referred to a transcendent source for his power and presented the gospel not only in words, but also in deeds" (199). Thus, Peerbolte tends to describe Paul's claims rather than contextualize or explain his practices.

Graham Twelftree's *Paul and the Miraculous* seeks to address the curious rift between the miracle-laden practices of Jesus in the canonical gospels and what

---

experience without engaging the critiques of the concept that led many scholars of religion to abandon it." See Ann Taves, *Religious Experience Reconsidered: A Building Block Approach to the Study of Religion and Other Special Things* (Princeton, NJ: Princeton University Press, 2009), 8.

12. Shantz, *Paul in Ecstasy*, 3.

13. Ibid., 13.

14. Stefan Schreiber, *Paulus als Wundertäter: Redaktionsgeschichtliche Untersuchungen zur Apostelgeschichte und den authentischen Paulusbriefen* (New York: de Gruyter, 1996).

15. Jan Lietaert Peerbolte, "Paul the Miracle Worker: Development and Background of Pauline Miracle Stories." In *Wonders Never Cease: The Purpose of Narrating Miracle Stories in the New Testament and Its Religious Environment* (London: T&T Clark, 2006), 180–199.

most theologians have presumed to be a miracle-free Paul. Twelftree is correct that "the critical study of Paul has been dominated by an interest in him as an intellectual and theologian, not as a person involved in the miraculous or performing miracles."[16] While he succinctly identifies a number of Paul's references to the miraculous, he denies that Paul would have personally engaged in all such practices (which I address in Chapters 3 and 4). His project is one of synthesis and of saving: synthesizing the various portraits of Paul as a miracle-worker in Acts and Paul of the letters, and "saving" Paul from looking like a magician. Paul is saved from this image by means of framing the book through experiencing the miraculous. By that, I mean that Twelftree investigates Paul's passive encounter with God's miracles, but denies Paul's active participation in the kinds of wonderworking practices that this book investigates. Twelftree's overall approach considers Paul as an inheritor of Jewish tradition of miracles, rather than an inhabitant and an example of a type of religious actor in the early Roman Empire. Perhaps most important, none of the aforementioned studies consider the way Paul ties wondrous powers and divinations to *pistis* and human–divine reciprocity.

In a sense, it comes as little surprise that Paul's numerous divinatory and wonderworking practices have enjoyed special categorization that distinguishes them from ancient comparanda: Such unique classification begins with Paul himself. That is, the apostle devises his own taxonomy for identifying his repertoire of skills—they are simultaneously "pneumatic things" [*ta pneumatika*; typically translated as "spiritual"][17] and "gifts" [*charismata*].[18] The two have long been elided into "spiritual gifts." As I will demonstrate, Paul's contemporaries (supporters and detractors alike) would have understood his practices as types of *mantikē, teratoskopia, goēteia*, or even *mageia*, but Paul innovatively repackages them as *charismata pneumatika*. Although divinatory abilities were widely understood to be gifted by gods, Paul redraws the boundaries, dividing legitimate from illegitimate as well as insider from outsider practices. His innovative terminology designates his own practices (and those of his followers) as legitimate and insider.[19] These distinctions have persisted over time; scholarly inheritance and

---

16. Graham Twelftree, *Paul and the Miraculous: A Historical Reconstruction* (Grand Rapids, MI: Baker Academic, 2013), 4.

17. For example, Rom 1:11, 15:27; 1 Cor 9:11, 12:1, 14:1, 14:37.

18. For example, 1 Cor 1:7, 12:4, 12:9, 12:28, 12:31; Rom 1:11, 11:29, 12:6.

19. For example, in his list of condemned "works of the flesh" in Gal 5:19–20, Paul includes *pharmakia*, a combination of medicinal concoctions and divine power used for healing or casting spells. The New Revised Standard Version of the Bible (NRSV) translates this as *sorcery*.

perpetuation of Paul's innovative classification is, to some degree, culpable for the taxonomic problems I address in Chapter 1.

Indeed, for Greek or Latin speakers, a wealth of terminology was available to identify and locate a diverse array of divinatory and so-called magical practices and practitioners. Such terms include *prophētes, astrologos, mantis, vates, haruspex, augur,* and *goēs* as well as the practices of *mageia, teratoskopeia,* and *mantikē* previously mentioned. Such terminology, while dizzying to a modern reader, conveyed the necessary information to allow a Greek or Latin speaker to "locate" a practice or practitioner somewhere in the larger field of legitimacy, authority, class, ethnicity, gender, etc. This is true today for English speakers as well: Implicit cultural information is encoded in designations such as Jesuit priest, astrologer, palm reader, snake oil salesman, Santero, tarot reader, Indian yogi, occultist, yoga instructor, witch doctor, psychic medium, cult leader, Unitarian Universalist (UU) minister, shaman, Satanist, New Age herbalist, televangelist, Wiccan witch, and Pentecostal preacher. This is not to correlate the specifics of the former list with the latter, but to point out that all such terms convey information that is simultaneously vague yet precise enough for us to make determinations about a person's authority, trustworthiness, authenticity, practices, beliefs, and legitimacy, and sometimes their ethnicity, social class, and sex. We make such determinations regardless of whether the encoded "information" is correct or not.

It is not the work of this book to disentangle the encoded cultural information regarding the various religious practitioners of the early Roman Empire,[20] but to reorganize the divinatory and wonderworking practices of Paul so that we may make sense of them. These practices are an important feature of Paul's overall schema, and would be intelligible across the Empire as variations of things people already do. Because these practices are so numerous in Paul's letters and because they have long enjoyed unique classification, I propose a taxonomy that contextualizes and "naturalizes" them according to ancient Greek, Roman, and Judean thinking and practice. Furthermore, because all such practices are intertwined and co-implicated in his letters, the taxonomy proposed herein carefully separates the practices, to make sense of them. Figure I.1 illustrates my recategorizing of Paul's divinations, divine powers, and discursive claims.

Yet, Paul himself claims the ability to heal by harnessing or channeling divine power. When he does so, he calls it a "gift," thereby sheltering his practices from accusations of *pharmakia.*

20. Heidi Wendt's 2016 study, which devotes a chapter to Paul, successfully articulates how such a wide array of practitioners compete with one another in the first and second centuries. See Heidi Wendt, *At the Temple Gates: The Religion of Freelance Experts in the Roman Empire* (New York: Oxford University Press, 2016).

Divinatory Practices	Wonderworking Practices	Discursive Claims to Divine Authority
• Interpretation of non-verbal divine signs or communications • Channeling information from a divine source through speech or verbal sound of a human agent • Use of literary texts or written symbols to discern divine information or disposition	• Performance of un-identified wonders, powers, and abilities through the human agent of a god • Healings through the human agent of a god • Transformation of material bodies into different material bodies	• Claims to have epiphanies or visitations by a god • Claims to possess secrets, mysteries, and special knowledge from a divine source • Claims to be commanded by a deity

FIGURE I.I Broad taxonomy for Paul's divinatory–wonderworking practices.

Parameters of Study

In order for us to shift how we understand Paul's divinatory and wonderworking practices, we must first consider the intellectual dispositions and traditions that impede such a shift. Chapter 1, then, looks at three primary reasons why Paul's practices have been interpreted and classified in ways that occlude their historical milieu. In short, these reasons are (1) the problematic myth of Christian uniqueness, (2) the use of an ideologically grounded monothetic model of classification, and (3) a mode of religiosity traditionally favored by New Testament scholars, which looks askance at practical and literal demonstrations of divine power. Disentangling the various strands of such habits allows for fuller and more nuanced redescription.[21]

Because Paul's divination and wonderworking have been ascribed unique categories for themselves, a practice such as speaking in tongues has been treated as a separate type of thing, as opposed to being one example of the widespread practice of channeling divine speech. Chapter 1 offers an approach to categorizing and comparing Paul's practices that contextualizes them historically—an approach

21. My notion of redescription is borrowed from Ron Cameron and Merrill Miller who suggest, "Redescription is a form of explanation that privileges difference and involves comparison and translation, category formation and rectification, definition and theory." See Ron Cameron and Merrill P. Miller, "Introducing Paul and the Corinthians." In *Redescribing Paul and the Corinthians*, edited by Ron Cameron and Merrill P. Miller (Atlanta, GA: Society of Biblical Literature, 2011), 1.

brought to the study of religion initially through the work of Jonathan Z. Smith. Additionally, this chapter explicates the value of thinking in terms of *modes of religiosity* to understand our evidence. I argue that Paul moves in and out of various modes of religiosity that include a primary mode pertaining to practical, mundane understandings of the gods, as well as a secondary mode that favors the conceptual, counterintuitive, and more cognitively strenuous. Paul operates in these modes of religiosity simultaneously, and the seamless overlap broadens his ability to reach his audience. Academic theologians themselves usually operate in the secondary mode of religiosity, which further explains why practices of divination and wonderworking have been disparaged, rejected, or ignored. Addressing these pervasive issues in taxonomy is hardly immaterial insofar as it lays the foundation for shifting how we categorize and contextualize Paul's practices and teachings.

While Chapter 1 addresses how we think about categories, Chapter 2 examines how ancient people conceptualized the presence of gods. Chapter 2 demonstrates the ubiquity of divinatory practices in antiquity that, in turn, indicates a widespread religious and epistemological disposition best expressed by Xenophon: "They [the gods] know all things, and warn whomsoever they will in sacrifices, in omens, in voices, and in dreams."[22] Thus, the religious disposition is that gods and other nonobvious, divine beings are present in the world and take an interest in human affairs. The epistemological disposition holds that there is important knowledge to be gained from observing and interpreting gods' physical impact on the world. This chapter explores a wide range of methods for Greeks, Romans, and Judeans to ascertain information from gods and provides the larger context for how Paul conceptualizes the palpability of the Judean deity. The chapter examines the ubiquitous interpretation of oracles, seers, dreams, animal behavior, and meteorological events, as well as the more peripheral practices of reading signs in sneezes, hiccups, and random bizarre occurrences. Uniting all such practices is the Greek notion of a divine *sēmeion*, or sign.

Chapters 1 and 2 lay the necessary groundwork for Chapter 3, which turns our attention to the various divinatory practices that Paul discusses with his readers and in which he claims expertise. Three broad categories account for Paul's array of skills: (1) the interpretation of nonverbal divine signs or communications [*sēmeia*], (2) the channeling of divine information through the speech faculty of a human agent, and (3) the use of literary texts or written symbols to discern divine messages. These categories include what Paul calls the interpretation of signs, speaking in tongues, and (oral and literacy-based) prophecy. On a

---

22. Xenophon, *On the Cavalry Commander*, 9.9. Xenophon in Seven Volumes (Vol 7), trans. E. C. Marchant and G. W. Bowersock (Cambridge, MA: Harvard University Press, 1925).

fundamental level, each of the practices claims to express and assert the desires and intentions of a deity, yet they have been typically organized according to later Western Christian categories. This chapter cuts across later Christian categories to redescribe Paul's practices in a way that normalizes them in their historical environment. I draw on widely available ancient comparanda to show that Paul shares the same epistemological disposition of his contemporaries regarding the palpability of his god(s), and that, furthermore, he engages in similar kinds of divinatory practices as his peers. Paul does not invent his practices from whole cloth, but repackages and innovates upon practices that have long been part of ancient religiosity.

While divination and miracle-working are not twin practices, they are brought into close relationship in Paul's letters. Thus, Chapter 4 examines the array of wonders that we see him claim, mention, or describe. Such practices include multiple references to unnamed "wonders" [*terata*] and "powers" [*dunameis*]. These vague references span the majority of the undisputed letters. This necessarily includes his claim to heal the sick or injured through an ability to channel divine power vis-à-vis other healer–wonderworkers. Additionally, the chapter demonstrates, aspects of Pauline baptism overlap with this genre of wonderworking practice; I suggest that the most frequently overlooked feature of Pauline baptism is his claim to transform the material nature of his followers' bodies into new, divine bodies. Instead of viewing baptism solely through a lens of initiation or purification, I suggest that we also consider Pauline baptism in light of ancient rituals that transform materials of one kind into materials of a different kind.

Chapter 5 considers Paul's numerous claims to be a handpicked mediator between the Judean deity and the world of gentiles—a claim that further authorizes his divinatory and wonderworking expertise. The chapter contextualizes his many and varied claims within widespread rhetorical practices of divine authorization, seen in the Septuagint (LXX) and in numerous Greek and Latin texts and inscriptions. Furthermore, it highlights what I call Paul's "divinatory pedagogy," in which he teaches his followers how to value and appropriately use their own divinatory and wonderworking skills. Thus, it is not just Paul's repertoire of divinatory practices that bolster his authority and prestige; it is also his evaluating, sharing, and teaching of such practices to others.

Chapter 6 demonstrates how Paul relates this rich array of divine abilities to the ethic of *pistis*, or faithfulness. I argue that Paul's divinatory and wonderworking powers, as they are extended to his gentile followers, are best understood within the framework of reciprocity that defines human–divine relationships in antiquity. In essence, Paul suggests that such skills and powers are extended in proportion to gentile faithfulness. The apostle does not say that such gifts are offered "in exchange for," but rather, "in proportion to" faithfulness. The reciprocal relationship between *pistis* and his divinatory powers hinges on the mechanism of empowerment—that is, the *pneuma* of Christ. The chapter explores forms of reciprocity thought to be critical to religions in the ancient Mediterranean and challenges scholarship that reduces ancient religiosity to *do ut des* [I give so that you will give].

Notes About Terminology

Steve Mason has argued convincingly that *Ioudaios* is a term that first and foremost denotes ethnicity, not religion; it refers to a member of the ethnic group whose roots lie in Judea. The word denotes, "precisely the same relationship to the name of the homeland that Ἄραψ, Βαβυλώνιος, Αἰγύπτιος, Σύρος, Παρθυαῖος, and Ἀθηναῖος have to the names of their respective homelands."[23] As was the case for Greeks, Egyptians, or members of other ethnic groups who live away from their homeland, *Ioudaios* applies to Judeans living in Rome, Ephesus, Alexandria, Athens, or anywhere in the diaspora.[24] Following Mason's example, the book uses "Judean" as a translation for Ἰουδαῖος and *Iudaeus*, except when citing other sources who use the more traditional Jew/ish.[25] Like Mason, I am interested in the ethnic categories that were current in antiquity. His study details the parallel construction of ethnic terminology for a range of ancient *ethnē* whose religious practices and beliefs are aspects of the *ethnos*, but whose nomenclature ("Egyptian," "Greek," et al.) does not refer primarily or exclusively to those practices and beliefs. "Jew" and "Jewish," as markers primarily of religion (which also continue to suggest ethnicity), are misleading in that they obscure the fundamental ethnic nature of the Greek word and category.[26] In the few instances when

---

23. Steve Mason, "Jews, Judeans, Judaizing, Judaism: Problems of Categorization in Ancient History," *Journal for the Study of Judaism* 38 (2007): 457–512.

24. Ibid., esp. 483 and following.

25. Ibid., 457–512.

26. Scholars do not agree on this issue. For example, Mason, "Jews, Judeans, Judaizing, Judaism," 493, critiques Daniel Schwartz's argument that *Ioudaios* transitioned from ethnos to religion as early as the Babylonian exile. Further, he addresses Shaye Cohen's position that this transition from ethnicity to religion happened during the Hasmonean period (494). A 2011 issue of the *Journal of Ancient Judaism* is devoted almost entirely to the problem of terminology and the historical accuracy and usefulness of terms such as Jew, Judaism, Jewish, or Judean. See Daniel Schwartz, *Studies in the Jewish Background of Christianity* (Tübingen, Germany: Mohr Siebeck, 1992); Shaye Cohen, *Beginnings of Jewishness: Boundaries, Varieties, Uncertainties* (Berkeley: University of California Press, 1999); Daniel Boyarin, *Border Lines: The Partition of Judeo-Christianity* (Philadelphia: University of Pennsylvania Press, 2006); Cynthia Baker, "A 'Jew' by Any Other Name?" *Journal of Ancient Judaism* 2.2 (2011): 153–180; Beth Berkowitz, "A Short History of the People of Israel From the Patriarchs to the Messiah," *Journal of Ancient*

I use the term Israelite, I do so in reference to biblical-era figures such as Moses, Elijah, and Abraham.[27]

In a field that has no consistent or unanimous definition of religion, it is imperative for any study to define how the term is used. Some scholars have argued that "religion" is a third-order conceptual tool invented by other scholars.[28] We now have a healthy bibliography of studies that investigate the invention of religion as a specifically Western and, more important, colonialist category.[29] To be sure, religion is not a native category to people in the ancient Mediterranean—not to Greeks, Romans, Judeans, Egyptians, etc., and if we are to rely on the vocabularies of Latin, ancient Greek, or Hebrew, we are stuck without a word that correlates to religion. Greeks have words like *thrēskeia*, *thusia*, and *eusebeia* to identify specific practices or to denote appropriate respect toward gods. Also, Greeks occasionally used the phrase *ton peri theōn* [τὸν περὶ θεῶν], "things pertaining to the gods," to describe practices and discourses pertaining to such beings.[30] Still, none of these terms or phrases can rightfully be translated as religion. The Latin *religio*, whose etymology is uncertain, is most frequently used to describe precision in

---

Judaism 2.2 (2011): 181–207; Seth Schwarz, "How Many Judaisms Were There?: A Critique of Neusner and Smith on Definition and Mason and Boyarin on Categorization," *Journal of Ancient Judaism* 2.2 (2011): 208–238. See also the numerous scholarly positions expressed in a special issue of the *Marginalia Review of Books*, "Jew and Judean: A Forum on Politics and Historiography in the Translation of Ancient Texts." August 26, 2014, available at https://marginalia.lareviewofbooks.org/jew-judean-forum/.

27. It is not the task of my study to pin down the date at which *Israelite* transitions to *Judean*, nor for when *Judean* transitions to *Jew*. These questions are beyond the scope of my study and are treated in detail by other scholars.

28. For systematic treatment of various approaches to this question, see Kevin Schilbrack, *Philosophy and the Study of Religions: A Manifesto* (Malden, MA: Wiley Blackwell, 2014), esp. 83–110.

29. See Daniel Duboisson, *The Western Construction of Religion: Myths, Knowledge and Ideology*, trans. William Sayers (Baltimore: Johns Hopkins University Press, 2003); Tomoko Masuzawa, *The Invention of World Religions* (Chicago: University of Chicago Press, 2005).

30. The phrase occurs hundreds of times in Greek texts as early as the seventh century BCE. Such a phrase is routinely translated as "religion," as in the example of Polybius 6.56, where the translator attributes the superiority of Romans over Greeks to Roman "religious convictions": "But the quality in which the Roman commonwealth is most distinctly superior is in my opinion the nature of their religious convictions [ἐν τῇ περὶ θεῶν]. I believe that it is the very thing which among other peoples is an object of reproach, I mean superstition, which maintains the cohesion of the Roman State." See *The Histories of Polybius*. Translated by W. R. Paton. Loeb Classical Library (Cambridge, MA: Harvard University Press, 1927), vol. 3. For the difficulty of speaking in terms of religion in antiquity, see Steve Mason's discussion, "Jews, Judeans, Judaizing, Judaism," 480–488; also Jonathan Z. Smith, "Religion, Religions, Religious." In *Relating Religion: Essays in the Study of Religion*, edited by Jonathan Z. Smith (Chicago: University of Chicago Press, 2004), 179–196.

degree and performance of cultic veneration.[31] In that sense, *religio* and *pietas* are related, but again, do not correlate to what those in the contemporary West typically call religion. While such observations ought not to be ignored, this study stands on a few indispensable tenets: (1) people in the ancient Mediterranean overwhelmingly participated in practices of veneration toward gods, *daimones*, ancestors, etc.; (2) most people appear to have thought that such beings had an impact in the world; and (3) such beings communicated with humans and would even imbue select humans with special capabilities not naturally available to mortals. Thus, for the purposes of this study, I use the word religion but in a fairly minimalist sense that adheres closely to the Greek phrase *ton peri theōn*, that is, practices and discourses pertaining to that class of beings who share the qualities of being divine, nonobvious, and often immortal. This also conforms to Cicero's understanding of *religio* as *cultus deorum*—concern for the gods.[32] Such a minimalist approach does not address the larger issue of defining religion overall, but alerts the reader to the narrowed scope of the book. In addition to this clarification, it is important to note that the many things pertaining to the gods did not constitute a separate, independent sphere of human activity. Religious practices and beliefs, rather, were deeply embedded in and widely dispersed across all facets of daily life. The modern concept of "secular" simply did not exist.

A consistent problem appears in almost all studies that address Paul's "mysticism," "ecstasy," "shamanism," "miracles," et al., namely, reliance on *experience* as a category for analysis. The category of *experience* tiptoes perilously close to a *sui generis* notion of religion—an approach that has been heavily criticized in the past forty years. Robert Sharf observes that experience is used rhetorically to, "thwart the 'objective' and the 'empirical,' and instead to valorize the subjective, the personal, the private."[33] Experience is ill-defined, and, even more so, *religious experience* provides "new grounds upon which to defend religion against secular and scientific critique."[34] This book seeks to identify and contextualize a range of divinatory practices promoted by the apostle Paul; it does not seek to dismiss historical context in favor of the timeless, ahistorical, or subjective. Thus,

---

31. The meaning of *religio* changes over time, from Plautus to Augustine. For a useful investigation of its nuances, see Brent Nongbri, *Before Religion: A History of a Modern Concept* (New Haven, CT: Yale University Press, 2013), esp. 26–34.

32. Cicero, *De Nat. Deo.* 2.3.9.

33. Robert Sharf, "Experience." In *Critical Terms for Religious Studies*, edited by Mark C. Taylor (Chicago: University of Chicago Press, 1998), 94–116, esp. 94.

34. Ibid., 98.

my methodological affinity for practice theory and consistent interest in social practices over and against religious experiences.

Getting inside Paul's head is a notoriously fraught enterprise. It comes as no surprise that scholars (and theologians) who attempt to parse Paul's meaning frequently discover a Paul who bears an uncanny resemblance to the scholars (and theologians) themselves. With that in mind, this study approaches Paul in terms of his practices that are rooted in his environment, rather than his thoughts that are too easily and unconsciously rooted in the scholar's environment. This is not to suggest that the book never speculates on or examines what Paul appears to be expressing or thinking, but rather, that we may make greater headway in contextualizing Paul by looking at how particular kinds of actions function in a larger field of actions. Putting aside the unnecessary locating of ideas and practices as "above" or "below" one another, Ann Swidler helpfully assesses the value of practice theory: "[It] moves the level of sociological attention 'down' from conscious ideas and values to the physical and the habitual. But this move is complemented by a move 'up,' from the ideas located in individual consciousness to the impersonal arena of 'discourse.' "[35] Like all people, Paul was engaged in social activities. Because the social "is a field of embodied, materially interwoven practices centrally organized around shared practical understandings,"[36] we must look at those shared practical understandings as they exist among people in the first-century Mediterranean. The notion of *practice* draws our attention toward the extent to which experiences are the result of human agency, labor, and intentional conditioning.

How to call the Judean books that Paul so regularly quotes is neither obvious nor straightforward. Paul himself uses the term *graphē*, or Writings. Philo and Josephus, on the other hand, both use *ta hiera grammata*, or sacred scripture or sacred Writings.[37] Typically, this study will draw upon Paul's term, Writings. The designation Septuagint/LXX operates as a placeholder for the Greek translation(s) Paul had access to, even if that translation does not exactly match the Septuagint that has survived. When necessary, I am more specific and refer to Torah or the Prophets. Most important, however, retaining Paul's term *graphē* underscores the literary–textual nature of Paul's interpretive practices. That is,

---

35. Ann Swidler, "What Anchors Cultural Practices." In *The Practice Turn in Contemporary Theory*, edited by Theodore Schatzki et al. (New York: Routledge, 2001), 75.

36. Theodore Schatzki, "Introduction: Practice Theory," In *The Practice Turn in Contemporary Theory*, edited by Theodore Schatzki et al. (New York: Routledge, 2001), 3.

37. See, for example, Philo's *Life of Moses* 2.290, 292; *Special Laws* 2.159; *De Vita Contemplativa* 78.2.

undergirding much of his career lie literary–interpretive practices put toward divinatory uses.

Paul's Teachings Tied to His Divinatory Expertise

Paul's divinatory and wonderworking practices are part of his overall preaching career and, as such, ought not to be divorced from that context. That teaching career includes exegesis of the Septuagint, preaching gentile participation in the *pneuma* of the resurrected Christ (which draws directly from his interpretation of the Septuagint),[38] intellectualist discourse on ethics and morality in which he is clearly a sort of literate "philosopher" of his time, and finally, expertise in a wide range of divinatory and wonderworking abilities. Scholars have had no discomfort with the first two of these components. The third, the philosophical, aspect has been contested, but recent scholarship has argued convincingly for the influence of Greek philosophy on Paul's thought.[39] Yet, the fourth part of Paul's activities—the divinatory and wonderworking expertise—has been overlooked so consistently that most do not generally recognize Paul's divinatory or wonderworking practices as such. Yet, his divinations and wonderworkings are tied intimately to the three other "components" of his career.

Paul's strident ethic of self-mastery, *enkrateia*, dominated philosophical discourse of his day.[40] A central concern in both middle Platonism and Stoicism, *enkrateia* and its opposite, *akrasia*, are the precise terms that Paul uses to describe moral dispositions of gentiles after and before Christ, respectively.[41] As Stanley

---

38. For a closer examination of these aspects to Paul's career, see Stanley Stowers, "What is Pauline Participation in Christ?" In *Redefining First-Century Jewish and Christian Identities: Essays in Honor of Ed Parish Sanders*, edited by Fabian E. Udoh (Notre Dame, IN: University of Notre Dame Press, 2008), 352–371; John Gager, *Reinventing Paul* (Oxford: Oxford University Press, 2000); Caroline Johnson Hodge, *If Sons, Then Heirs: A Study of Kinship and Ethnicity in the Letters of Paul* (Oxford: Oxford University Press, 2007).

39. Troels Engberg-Pedersen, *Paul and the Stoics* (Louisville, KY: Westminster John Knox Press, 2000); Stanley Stowers, "Did Pauline Christianity Resemble a Hellenistic Philosophy?" In *Paul Beyond the Judaism/Hellenism Divide*, edited by Troels Engberd-Pedersen (Louisville, KY: Westminster John Knox Press, 2001); Emma Wasserman, *The Death of the Soul in Romans 7: Sin, Death, and the Law in Light of Hellenistic Moral Psychology*. (Tübingen, Germany: Mohr Siebeck, 2008); Emma Wasserman, "Paul Among the Philosophers: The Case of Sin in Romans 6–8," *Journal for the Study of the New Testament* 30.4 (2008): 387–415.

40. Jean-Baptiste Gourinat, "*Akrasia* and *Enkrateia* in Ancient Stoicism: Minor Vice and Minor Virtue?" In *Akrasia in Greek Philosophy: From Socrates to Plotinus*, edited by Christopher Bobonich and Pierre Destrée (Leiden: Brill, 2007), 215–248.

41. Paul writes of *enkrateia* in 1 Cor 7:9, 9:25, and Gal 5:23. Lack of self-control, *akrasia*, is referred to at 1 Cor 7:5. Likewise, Paul teaches about the passions [*pathē*]: Rom 1:26, 7:5; Gal

Stowers has pointed out, Philo and Josephus bill Judaism as akin to a philosoph-ical school for self-mastery.⁴² Philo refers to synagogues as schools that open every seventh day where Judeans and gentiles alike can learn "practical wisdom (*phronēsis*), self-restraint (*sophrosunē*), courage (*andreia*), justice (*dikaiosunē*), and all the other virtues."⁴³ In his *Against Apion*, Josephus essentially argues that, "Judaism is a philosophy for the masses and that gentile religious practices lead to a lack of self-control."⁴⁴ Given the prominence of self-mastery as a cen-tral concern in first-century philosophical discourse, it comes as no surprise that Josephus and Philo render Judaism as appealing to those who might feel the pull of this ethic. Stowers writes, "If one understands the enormous attraction exerted by the ideal of self-mastery and the powerful interpretation of the Jewish law as a means to it, then the popularity of Jewish practices becomes understandable. The Jews were set apart from all the other peoples of the empire in certain way, giving the appearance of a uniquely disciplined nation of philosophers to many pagans."⁴⁵ As much as Philo and Josephus bill Judaism as a philosophical school where one learns *enkrateia* and other virtues, Paul likewise offers the same ethic to gentiles who follow his understanding of Judean teachings.

In his letter to the Romans, Paul engages in innovative mythmaking regarding the history of gentiles, as he explains to his readers why gentiles are in a state of abhorrent *akrasia* prior to participation in Christ:

> Claiming to be wise, they became fools; and exchanged the glory of the im-mortal God for images resembling a mortal human being or four-footed animals or reptiles. Therefore God gave them up in the lusts of their hearts [ταῖς ἐπιθυμίαις τῶν καρδιῶν αὐτῶν] to impurity . . . . For this reason God gave them up to degrading passions [πάθη ἀτιμίας] . . . . And since they did not see fit to acknowledge God, God gave them up to a debased mind and to things that should not be done. They were filled with every kind of wickedness, evil, covetousness, malice. Full of envy, murder, strife, deceit,

---

5:24. His use of desire [*epithumia*] dominates this moral discourse, however: Rom 1:24, 6:12, 7:7, 7:8, 13:9, 13:14; 1 Cor 10:6; Gal. 5:16, 5:17, 5:24; Phil 1:23; 1 Thess 2:17, 4:5.

42. Stanley Stowers, "Paul and Self-Mastery." In *Paul in the Greco-Roman World: A Handbook*, edited by J. Paul Sampley (Harrisburg, PA: Trinity Press International, 2003), 524–550.

43. *Spec. Laws* 2.62.

44. Josephus, *Ag. Ap.* 2.193; Stowers, "Paul and Self-Mastery," 533.

45. Stowers, "Paul and Self-Mastery," 533.

craftiness, they are gossips, slanderers, God-haters, insolent, haughty, boastful, inventors of evil, foolish, unfaithful, heartless, ruthless.[46]

Participation in Christ, whose salvific arrival in the world was predestined in Paul's holy books, redeems the gentiles and renders them just and good in the eyes of Paul's Judean deity.

The ethic of self-mastery, then, was not only likely to be familiar to many of his listeners, but Paul promised a specific way for gentile initiates to cultivate this ethic, namely, through participation in the *pneuma* of the resurrected Christ. For Paul, the means to gentile *enkrateia* and salvation come through receiving Christ's *pneuma*, which confers to gentile initiates inclusion in the family of Abraham and inheritance to all the promises made to Abraham and his descendants.[47] Furthermore, as an interpreter of the Septuagint, Paul claims that all of this has long been predicted in and intended by the holy books of Moses and ancient Israelite prophets. Again, I point to Rom 3:21–22: "... the justice of God has been disclosed, and is attested by the law and the prophets, the justice of God through the faithfulness of Jesus Christ for all who entrust." Elsewhere he reinterprets Hosea to include gentiles in the plan of the Judean deity, "Those who were not my people I will call 'my people,' and her who was not beloved I will call 'beloved.' And in the very place where it is said to them 'You are not my people,' there they shall be called children of the living God" (Rom 9:25–26).

Paul's notion of *pneuma* links his ethical teachings, his certainty that gentiles are to be included in the family of Abraham, and his divinatory and wonder-working expertise. It is through participating in the pneuma of Christ that gentiles are able to develop and wield special skills that pertain specifically to the Judean god. This is where Paul's taxonomy—*charismata pneumatika*—becomes important. For Paul, these practices are not *mantikē, mageia, goēteia,* or even *pharmakeia;* they are a separate, legitimate set of abilities bestowed on the follower, in direct proportion to the person's degree of *pistis*. But such abilities, as we will see, are in fact examples of divinatory skills that set the practitioner apart from other humans, both delineating and demonstrating a specialized relationship to a divinity. Paul's "native" category has been misinterpreted by scholars insofar as they have reinscribed the uniqueness that his terminology presumes, by virtue of adopting his emic classification.

---

46. Rom 1:22–31.

47. For a study of Paul's use of kinship language and gentile inclusion in the family of Abraham, see Hodge, *If Sons, Then Heirs.*

If we compare 1 Cor 12:4–11 and Gal 5:22–26 we find that *pneuma* is the link between Paul's ethical teachings and divinatory practices. Whereas he calls the specific skills imparted by the *pneuma* "gifts" [χαρισμάτα], he titles the moral and ethical benefits of the *pneuma* "fruit of the pneuma" [καρπὸς τοῦ πνεύματός]. Thus, the same substance enabling him and his gentile followers to channel divine speech, heal, and perform wonders also has a lasting and beneficial effect on the ethical and psychological disposition of gentile followers:

> By contrast, the fruit of the pneuma is love, joy, peace, patience, kindness, generosity, faithfulness, gentleness, and self-control [ἐγκράτεια]. And those who belong to Christ Jesus have crucified the flesh [τὴν σάρκα] with its passions and desires [τοῖς παθήμασιν καὶ ταῖς ἐπιθυμίαις]. If we live by the pneuma, let us also be guided by the pneuma. Let us not become conceited, competing against one another, envying one another.
>
> (Gal 5:22–26)

Contrast this with 1 Cor 12:4–10:

> Now there are a variety of gifts [χαρισμάτων], but the same pneuma, and there are varieties of services [διακονιῶν] but the same Lord . . . . To each is given the manifestation of the pneuma for the common good. To one is given through the pneuma the utterance of wisdom, and to another the utterance of knowledge according to the same pneuma, to another *pistis* by the same pneuma, to another gifts of healing by the same pneuma, to another the working of miracles, to another prophecy, to another discernment of spirits [*pneumata*], to another various types of tongues, to another the interpretation of tongues.

For Paul, the ability to divine information from the realm of the gods and to perform strange, miraculous wonders, is tied to his teachings regarding Christ's *pneuma* as well as salvation and ethical improvement for gentiles. This should be kept in mind lest the reader prioritize one aspect of his teaching at the expense of another.

I

Taxonomy and Pauline Uniqueness

THE PROBLEM OF CATEGORIES AND MODES

TO DEMONSTRATE THAT Paul engaged in numerous forms of divination and wonderworking and to further demonstrate that such practices were not unique vis-à-vis Paul's contemporaries, it is helpful to first understand why and how Paul's activities have come to be viewed as special and distinct. How has Pauline prophecy been made to appear totally unlike anything that came before it? Why is "speaking in tongues" viewed as radically unlike other, similar practices of channeling divine voices, even though we see these other practices described in numerous Greek, Roman, and Judean sources? How have Paul's divine gifts been divorced from the context of widespread understanding of reciprocity with gods? The process of answering these questions sheds light on our own practices of classification and the ways in which we confer legitimacy on some religious practices but not others. This chapter explores two methodological problems that get in the way of understanding Paul's divinatory and wonderworking practices. First, traditional practices of classification have created a silo of uniqueness for things pertaining to Paul and early Christianity.[1] I offer a corrective to that problem by suggesting we take seriously polythetic classification as a methodology. Second, thinking in terms of *modes of religiosity*, as formulated by Harvey Whitehouse and adapted by Stanley Stowers, elucidates how an intellectualist mode of religiosity consistently outshines the practices that do not rely on literacy or the interpretive strategies of intellectuals. Recognizing many ancient authors' preferences,

---

1. This silo of uniqueness obtains even at the level of translation. See Ross Kraemer and Jennifer Eyl, "Translating Women: The Perils of Gender-Inclusive Translation of the New Testament." In *Celebrate Her for the Fruit of Her Hands: Studies in Honor of Carol L. Meyers*, edited by Charles Carter (Winona Lake, IN: Eisenbrauns, 2015), 295–318.

as well as our own, for the literate and intellectual, at the expense of the mundane and practical, allows us to address that bias in our analyses.

Understanding Paul as Unique

Traditionally, scholars and theologians have constructed the image of an early Christianity constituted by beliefs and practices that defy taxonomy. Simply put, taxonomy is the practice of naming and ordering things in relation to other things.[2] The taxonomic uniqueness conferred upon early Christianity sets it apart as a *tertium quid*, distinct from Judean practices and teachings (which it simultaneously draws from and must surpass), and from Greek and Roman religious practices and beliefs (lumped together into the anachronistic and unvariegated category of paganism). In his groundbreaking study of the gospel of Mark, Burton Mack assesses this traditional way of thinking about early Christianity: "The fundamental persuasion is that Christianity appeared unexpectedly in human history, that it was (is) at core a brand-new vision of human existence."[3] Because this incomparably distinct Christianity defies taxonomy, one is hard-pressed to undertake careful, detailed comparative work (one cannot compare that which is incomparable). Furthermore, to compare something understood to be unique can be perceived as an affront. J. Z. Smith has argued as much: "'Unique' becomes an ontological rather than a taxonomic category; an assertion of a radical difference so absolute that it becomes 'Wholly Other', and the act of comparison is perceived as both an impossibility and an impiety."[4] Under the model

---

2. To borrow Bruce Lincoln's definition, " . . . taxonomies are regarded—and announce themselves—as systems of classifying the phenomenal world, systems through which otherwise indiscriminate data can be organized in a form wherein they become knowable." Bruce Lincoln, *Discourse and the Construction of Society: Comparative Studies of Myth, Ritual, and Classification* (Oxford: Oxford University Press, 2014), 7.

3. Burton Mack, *A Myth of Innocence: Mark and Christian Origins* (Minneapolis: Fortress Press, 1988). Mack adds, "The code word for serving as a sign for the novelty that appeared is the term unique (meaning singular, incomparable, without analogue)" (4).

4. "On Comparison." In *Drudgery Divine*, 38. Smith points out that the notion of being "unique" does not have to imply incomparability. The problem is the special way in which the idea has been used to conceptualize early Christianity. He writes, "There is a quite ordinary sense in which the term 'unique' may be applied in disciplinary contexts. When the historian speaks of unique events, the taxonomist of the unique *differentium* that allows the classification of this or that plant or animal species, the geographer of the unique physiognomy of a particular place, or the linguist of each human utterance is unique, he or she is asserting a reciprocal notion which confers no special status, nor does deny it—indeed it demands—enterprises of classification and interpretation. *A* is unique with respect to *B*, in this sense, requires the assertion that *B* is, likewise, unique with respect to *A*, and so forth" ("On Comparison," 37). Thus, uniqueness in itself is not a problematic assertion, given that all things are unique in

of Christian uniqueness, the ancient Mediterranean world becomes little more than a backdrop—the nearly inconsequential scenery behind the culmination of a grand play whose script was written ages earlier.

The argument for early Christian incomparability takes many forms. Rudolph Bultmann described gospels as "a unique phenomenon in the history of litera-ture, and at the same time . . . symbolic of the distinctive nature of the Christian religion as a whole."[5] In his critique of the incomparability of the *Christ-event*, Burton Mack observes that the events pertaining to the death and resurrection of Jesus are "those events at the beginning where, according to Christian teaching, God entered into human history. . . . Insofar as Christianity actually is peculiar as a religion . . . it is certainly due to just this notion of an event within history that interrupted the normal course of human social activity and created a new kind of time and society."[6] James Dunn, while allowing for Paul's indebtedness to Jews and Greeks for the majority of his ideas and language, further argues that scholars must acknowledge "the creative power of his own religious experience—a furnace which melted away the many concepts in its fires and poured them forth into new molds."[7] The implication here is that Paul's "new molds" are themselves unprec-edented and incomparable, rather than a reiteration or recombining of practices and teachings that would have been widely recognized by many people in the ancient Mediterranean. Instead of being symptomatic or emblematic of religious innovations of the early Roman Empire, the "creative power of Paul's religious

the sense that all things have particular properties and characteristics which distinguish them from other things. Or as Smith would have it, "the affirmation of individuality" is still subject to "the probity of class" ("On Comparison," 37). Jonathan Z. Smith, "On Comparison." In *Drudgery Divine: On the Comparison of Early Christianities and the Religions of Late Antiquity* (Chicago: University of Chicago Press, 1990), 36–53.

5. Rudolph Bultmann, "Evangelien." In *Religion in Geschichte und Gegenwart*, 2nd ed. (Tübingen: Mohr Siebeck, 1928), vol. 2, 419, trans. JZ Smith in "On Comparison," 39. Smith, "On Comparison, 40, offers a good critique of the notion that the gospel genre is unique: "Scholarship has related the gospel to many forms of contemporary literature, from biography to aretology, but none of them seems precisely the same. However, this is a quite or-dinary statement of difference which need not be raised to the language of the 'unique' except when under the influence of a nostalgia for the 'specialness' conceded to early Christianity." For a counterargument to idea that gospels are unique specimens, see Robyn Walsh and David Konstan, "Civic and Subversive Biography in Antiquity." In *Writing Biographies in Greece and Rome: Narrative Technique and Fictionalization*, edited by K. de Temmerman and Kristoffel Demoen (New York: Cambridge University Press, 2016), 26–43.

6. Mack, *A Myth of Innocence*, 8.

7. James Dunn, *Jesus and the Spirit: A Study of the Religious and Charismatic Experience of Jesus and the First Christians as Reflected in the New Testament* (Grand Rapids, MI: Eerdmans, 1997), 4.

experience" is understood to be radically unlike the creative power of other self-appointed religious authorities and religious entrepreneurs.

Additionally, some scholars and theologians have stipulated that Christianity innovatively introduced "belief" onto the stage of human religiosity. Charles King offers an insightful critique of this position, in which he points out that nearly everybody in antiquity held religious beliefs: that the gods exist, that the gods hear prayers, that the gods participate in reciprocal relations with humans, etc. The difference, according to King, was not that early Christians had "belief" and non-Christians had only empty rituals, but rather, that Christian orthodoxy will eventually insist upon strict adherence to doctrinal positions versus the, "essentially polythetic nature of Roman [and Greek, I would add] religious organization, in which incompatible beliefs could coexist simultaneously . . . without conflict."[8] Rather than inventing and subsequently cornering the market on religious belief, early Christian leaders simply came to organize and prioritize "correct" belief.[9]

The extent to which Paul's expertise in divination and wonderworking has been overlooked pertains directly to the assertion of Christian (and thus, Pauline) uniqueness. Without question, the ability to properly and successfully read divinely sent signs, to translate divinely inspired speech, to facilitate divine healings, and to demonstrate other divine wonders, were skills claimed by many religious actors in antiquity. These kinds of practices were widespread and, as such, would have been recognizable to Paul's followers and detractors alike. By "recognizable" I mean that observers would have understood that miracles and sign reading belong to a larger class of activities that mediate information and powers from strange, sometimes unknown, divine sources. This is the case whether a practitioner's legitimacy was acknowledged by the state, acknowledged by local groups, or self-appointed and entrepreneurial. There is no explanation for why Paul's practices should be viewed as radically different, other than the

---

8. Charles King, "The Organization of Roman Religious Beliefs," *Classical Antiquity* 22.2 (2003): 275–312, esp. 275.

9. I refer specifically to beliefs about gods. Correct "belief" was also characteristic of philosophical schools, as King points out. Such emphasis on correct belief among philosophical schools resulted in competition for students and conflict between schools. This, however, did not preclude the combining of beliefs. For example, Seneca is widely viewed as a first-century Stoic, though his sexual ethics are clearly Neopythagorean. For the importance and caveats in comparing early Christianity and philosophical schools, see Stanley Stowers, "Does Pauline Christianity Resemble a Hellenistic Philosophy?" In *Redescribing Paul and the Corinthians*, edited by Ron Cameron and Merrill Miller (Atlanta, GA: Society of Biblical Literature, 2011), 219–244. The centrality of "belief" in Christianity should not be conflated with the importance of *pistis* [faithfulness] in Paul's letters. This latter topic will be addressed in Chapter 6.

theologically interested assertion that Paul is radically different. The creation of taxonomic categories that maintain an ontological division between the divinatory practices of Judeans and Christians, on the one hand, and those of everyone else in the ancient Mediterranean, on the other, depends on a theological interest in uniqueness.

As a preliminary example, let us look at the scholarly approach to prophecy in Paul's letters. A wealth of studies examines the significance of prophecy to Paul's teaching, as well as studies that approach Paul specifically as a prophet.[10] Yet, studies linking Paul to divinatory expertise are difficult to find. How can this be, if prophecy is itself a divinatory practice?[11] Furthermore, when scholars do link prophecy and divination (or even so-called magic) to one another, the subject of Paul is rarely found.[12] Because the Hebrew Bible (and thus the Greek

---

10. See Pamela Eisenbaum, "Paul as the New Abraham." In *Paul and Politics: Ekklesia, Israel, Imperium, Interpretation*, edited by Richard A. Horsley (Harrisburg, PA: Trinity Press International, 2000), 130–145; N. T. Wright, "Paul, Arabia, and Elijah (Galatians 1:17)," *Journal of Biblical Literature* 115.4 (1996): 683–692; Andrzej Jacek Najda, *Der Apostel als Prophet: Zur prophetischen Dimension des paulinischen Apostolats* (Frankfurt: Lang, 2004); David Hill, *New Testament Prophecy* (Atlanta, GA: John Knox Press, 1979); W. A. Grudem, *The Gift of Prophecy in 1 Corinthians* (Washington, DC: University Press of America, 1982); David Aune, *Prophecy in Early Christianity and the Ancient Mediterranean World* (Grand Rapids, MI: Eerdmans, 1983); T. W. Gillespie, *The First Theologians: A Study in Early Christian Prophecy* (Grand Rapids, MI: Eerdmans, 1994); T. W. Gillespie, "A Pattern of Prophetic Speech in First Corinthians," *Journal of Biblical Literature* 97.1 (1978): 74–95; Joseph Verheyden et al., eds., *Prophets and Prophecy in Jewish and Early Christian Literature* (Tübingen, Germany: Mohr Siebeck, 2010); E. Earle Ellis, *Prophecy and Hermeneutic* (Tübingen, Germany: Mohr Siebeck, 1978). As demonstrated in my Introduction, one is hard-pressed to find a study with the words "Paul" and "divination" in the title.

11. I am not the first to make this observation. See, for example, JoAnn Scurlock, "Prophecy as a Form of Divination; Divination as a Form of Prophecy." In *Divination and Interpretation of Signs in the Ancient World*, edited by Amar Annus (Chicago: University of Chicago Press, 2010), 277–316; Anne Marie Kitz, "Prophecy as Divination," *Catholic Biblical Quarterly* 65 (2003): 22–42.

12. For example, Paul does not appear in the essays contained in the recent studies that look at prophecy, divination, magic, and religion in antiquity, such as, David Aune, ed., *Apocalypticism, Prophecy, and Magic in Early Christianity* (Tübingen, Germany: Mohr Siebeck, 2006); Robert M. Berchman, ed., *Horizons of Prophecy, Divination, Dreams, and Theurgy in Mediterranean Antiquity* (Atlanta, GA: Scholars Press, 1998); Amar Annus, ed., *Divination and Interpretation of Signs in the Ancient World* (Chicago: University of Chicago Oriental Institute, 2010); Leda Ciraolo and Jonathan Seidel, *Magic and Divination in the Ancient World* (Leiden: Brill, 2002). This list could be much longer, but suffice to say that Paul is comfortably linked with prophecy but rarely with divination. And when prophecy and divination are linked to one another, Paul's practices are not considered in light of that relationship. Two important exceptions include David Aune's earlier *Prophecy in Early Christianity and the Ancient Mediterranean World* (Grand Rapids, MI: Eerdmans, 1983) and Heidi Wendt, *At the Temple Gates: The Religion of Freelance Experts in the Roman Empire* (New York: Oxford University Press, 2016).

translation used by Paul) makes prohibitive claims against specific types of divinatory practices (explored briefly in Chapter 2),[13] and because many scholars have argued for an exclusively "Jewish" pedigree for Christianity,[14] the resulting picture is that the revered figureheads of early Christianity did not engage in divinatory practices.

Yet, the structure of this argument does not pass muster. If we were to cast this topic in different terms—say, dietary restrictions—one would not claim that ancient Judeans and early Christians simply refrained from eating. Rather, we are equipped to recognize that some foods were considered clean and others unclean, but regardless of which was which, they are all classifiable in a larger group of "things people eat" or "food." Likewise in the case of divinatory practices, some practices might be considered acceptable and others derided or forbidden. Yet, all such practices were, in fact, divinatory in nature. By arguing that Paul did not engage in divinatory practices, one adheres to the Hebrew Bible's assumption of radical difference between Israelites and their neighbors, and one furthermore adheres to long-standing Christian claims that Christians, too, were radically different. In this sense, "divination" is used as a polemical title much in the same way "magic" was used by early anthropologists: to denote practices that are ritualistic, devoid of meaningful content, false, inferior, inaccurate, ineffectual, prerational or nonrational, and demonstrative of pseudo-science.

To return to the example of prophecy, we need not look hard to see how Judean and Christian prophecy has been distinguished, qualitatively, from "pagan" divination. For example, J. H. Bernard's 1905 essay "Prophets and Prophecy in New Testament Times" distinguishes the speech of apostolic-era prophets (modeled on biblical prophets) from heathen (read: pagan) practices: "Their utterances were not the mere rhapsodies or expressions of frenzied ecstasy, like the utterances of heathen oracles. But they were inspired by a spirit not altogether their own, and their words were greater than they knew."[15] He concludes his study by asserting " . . . the [Christian] office of prophet was emphatically Jewish in its conception and in its origin"(123). Thus, Judean prophecy was ontologically unique compared with pagan oracles, despite that both practices claim divine inspiration and

---

13. Exod 22; Deut 18; Lev 19 and 20, specifically.

14. By exclusively "Jewish" pedigree, I mean the assumption that there was a pure Judaism uncontaminated by the practices or beliefs of other peoples and in which all Jews adhered to the behaviors prescribed in the Hebrew Bible or LXX.

15. J. H. Bernard, "Prophets and Prophecy in New Testament Times," *The Biblical World* 25.2 (1905): 121.

deliver a divine message.[16] Judean prophecy is legitimate, while heathen oracles are "mere rhapsodies." Furthermore, New Testament–era prophecy is modeled on Judean prophecy, exempting it from accusations of meaningless frenzy. In the late nineteenth century, R. V. Foster distinguished true Hebrew prophets from the false by asserting that false prophets "spoke lying divination, after the manner of the heathen" (169–170).[17] This sentiment certainly persists and informs how many people have classified and understood true versus false prophecy by using the distinctions of Christian and pagan.

That ancient Israelite and early Christian figureheads have not been associated with divination or wonderworking is somewhat of an exaggeration, of course. A number of studies have examined Moses' wondrous powers, Jesus has been considered in light of his wonders and miracle working, and the apostles in canonical Acts and Apocryphal Acts have received such attention as well.[18] We have generally accepted that such figures are indeed depicted as divinatory experts who go so far as to possess magical powers. The operative verb in this observation, however, is *depict*. All such figures are shielded by prehistory or third-person accounts of them. Thus, divinatory and magical portrayals of sages, wise men, heroes, prophets, or soteriological figures are understood today in light of how ancient authors typically portray such figures or in light of how later generations exaggerated and mythologized their skills.[19] But in the case of Paul (of the epistles, not the Paul of Acts), we have the boon of first-person claims to

---

16. To be clear, I am not arguing that Israelite prophecy and non-Israelite oracles are identical. As Smith, "On Comparison," 43, has pointed out, the comparative enterprise can be as fraught with assumptions of utter difference, as it can by "a parataxis of likeness." We ought not swing far in the opposite direction and assert that prophecy and oracles are *exactly* the same. Rather, as Smith suggests, we need a "discourse of difference" in which negotiation, classification, and comparison are invited. Without claiming that prophecy and oracles are merely "the same," we can certainly claim that they are not entirely dissimilar and that both belong to a larger taxonomic category.

17. R. V. Foster, "Hebrew Prophets and Prophecy," *The Old Testament Student* 6.6 (1897): 166–170. Here, Foster alludes to biblical prohibitions and 2 Kgs 17:17; Jer 14:14; and Ezek 13:7.

18. See John Gager, "Moses the Magician: Hero of an Ancient Counter-Culture?" *Helios* 21 (1994): 179–188; John Gager, *Moses in Greco-Roman Paganism* (New York: Abingdon, 1972); J. Van Seters, "A Contest of Magicians? The Plague Stories in P." In *Pomegranates and Golden Bells. Studies in Biblical, Jewish, and Near Eastern Ritual, Law, and Literature in Honor of Jacob Milgrom*, edited by D. P. Wright, D. N. Freedman, and A. Hurvitz (Winona Lake, IN: Eisenbrauns, 1995), 569–580; T. Römer, "Competing Magicians in Exodus 7–9: Interpreting Magic in Priestly Theology." In *Magic in the Biblical World. From the Rod of Aaron to the Ring of Solomon*, edited by T. Klutz (New York: T & T Clark International—Continuum, 2003), 12–22; Morton Smith, *Jesus the Magician* (Berkeley, CA: Ulysses Press, 1998).

19. Pál Herczeg observes as much in his analysis of the apostles John and Peter in the Apocryphal Acts. Pál Herczeg, "*Theios anēr* Traits in the Apocryphal Acts of Peter." In *The Apocryphal Acts of Peter: Magic, Miracles, and Gnosticism*, edited by Jan Bremmer (Leuven, Belgium: Peeters,

such expertise and power. Paul alone "depicts" himself; he speaks for himself, he describes many of his divinatory practices, he teaches his readers to hierarchically organize divinely bestowed *charismata*, and he refers to his own performance of wonders. Such a first-person account of divinatory expertise and teaching has hardly been mined by scholars for the wealth of information it offers.[20] But for those who find discomfort in the notion that Paul personally claimed divinatory expertise, there is no "literariness" to hide behind; no narratological scapegoat for denying Paul's self-portrayal. This is perhaps why Paul (of the letters) is missing from such studies.

The traditional approach in the study of early Christianity is to examine prophecy as a unique practice, which is shared in some respects with "pagan" prophecy, but is mostly traceable to Israelite or Judean prophecy. But as Martti Nissinen warns: "Prophecy should not be contrapositioned with divination, but should be seen as one form of it."[21] Although prophecy is a subtype of divination, this hypotactic relationship is reorganized, such that Christian prophecy is legitimized by its pedigree with prophecy in the Hebrew Bible, and all other ancient divinatory practices are classified together and subsequently dismissed.[22]

1998), 29–38; Pál Herczeg, "Sermons in the Acts of John." In *The Apocryphal Acts of John*, edited by Jan Bremmer (Kampen, The Netherlands: Kok Pharos Publishers, 1995), 153–170.

20. An exception to this, James Tabor (*Things Unutterable: Paul's Ascent to Paradise in Its Greco-Roman, Judaic, and Early Christian Contexts* [Lanham, MD: University Press of America, 1986], 1, 57), points to the significance of Paul's first-person account. Also, although she focuses primarily on a class of religious actors she calls freelance experts, Heidi Wendt, *At the Temple Gates*, 146–147, notes that Paul offers rare first-person evidence for such actors.

21. Martti Nissinen, "Prophecy and Omen Divination: Two Sides of the Same Coin." In *Divination and Interpretation of Signs in the Ancient World*, edited by Amar Annus (Chicago: Oriental Institute of the University of Chicago, 2010), 341–347, esp. 342.

22. Such a distinction between the legitimacy of divinatory practices persists today: Palm readers, astrologers, and clairvoyants are disparaged, while the pope of the Catholic Church is widely accepted by Catholics as the legitimate mediator between the divine and mortal realms. Indeed, he is called the Holy See, and the Vatican gets its name from Lat. *vaticinium* [prophecy]. We understand a strong distinction between the prestige of papal practices (specifically, those practices that claim the pope can determine and enact the will of a god) vs. the practices of lesser divinatory specialists; to suggest that a television astrologer ought to receive the same degree of respect and deferment as the pope would be understood by many people as improper. Yet, when retroactively ascribing to Paul an extraordinary amount prestige and authority, Christians and scholars throughout history have failed to realize that in his own day, Paul was not a head priest at the Jerusalem temple, nor pontifex maximus at Rome, nor any sort of established religious figure who received general acceptance from wide populations of people. Rather, Paul and self-appointed religious specialists of his genre were disparaged and satirized in a similar way that astrologers, so-called cult leaders, and other self-appointed divination specialists are disparaged today. We see such criticism, for example, in Lucian's *Alexander the Quack Prophet*.

Because most Christians (Marcion of Sinope notwithstanding) have claimed a "Jewish" pedigree for their religion, prophecy is therefore a legitimate means for Christians to receive information from the Christian deity. Yet, the differences between prophecy and other divinatory practices are not ontological. Rather, the differences exist to differentiate categories of people, in this case Judeans and (early) Christians from "pagans" or "heathens." The truth of the matter is that both prophecy and other types of divinatory practices share some things in common and do not share others. As J. Z. Smith has pointed out, the enterprise of comparison is really a matter of weighing similarity and difference in terms of "less" and "more," rather than reducing the objects of comparison to absolute likeness or otherness.[23] Or as M. David Litwa notes, "Comparison never means identity."[24]

Peter Struck suggests that a significant difference between Greek divination and prophecy of the Hebrew Bible (and thus, LXX) is that Greek prophetic practices operate incrementally, providing insights that amount to "small bore."[25] Struck understands prophecy in the Hebrew Bible (and later apocalyptic texts) to be, "quite different phenomena," in which prophets offer "large judgments about the alignment of the universe, or have revelatory visions that open a vantage to the underlying structure of the cosmos."[26] Greek divination, on the other hand, typically addresses immediate concerns related to military tactics, financial decisions, and political strategies. Armin Lange, prior to Struck, distinguishes between the two types of divinatory practices insofar as Near Eastern (and thus, Israelite) prophets preferred intuitive "divine revelation" over deductive divinatory skills more common among Greeks.[27]

It would seem hard to argue with the assessments of Struck and Lange, given the abundance of evidence we have for the type of deductive divination that does address the tactical, financial, and politically strategic among Greeks. Additionally, the prominence of intuitive cosmic-order prophecy among Israelites is equally abundant. Yet, I would redraw the lines of comparanda. That is, the conclusions

23. See Jonathan Z. Smith, "On Comparison." In *Drudgery Divine: On the Comparison of Early Christianities and the Religions of Late Antiquity* (Chicago: University of Chicago Press, 1990), 36–53.

24. M. David Litwa, *Iesus Deus: The Early Christian Depiction of Jesus as a Mediterranean God* (Minneapolis, MN: Fortress Academic, 2014), 33.

25. Peter Struck, *Divination and Human Nature: A Cognitive History of Intuition in Classical Antiquity* (Princeton, NJ: Princeton University Press, 2016), 11.

26. Ibid.

27. Armin Lange, "Greek Seers and Israelite-Jewish Prophets," *Vetus Testamentum* 57 (2007): 461–482.

of Struck and Lange are possible only if we ignore numerous other examples of necromancy, divination using lots (ummim and thurim), "magical" practices, astrology, dream incubation, and the like among Israelites, while also ignoring the Greeks (and Romans) who link cosmic ideas to divinatory practices and forego the use of tools. We find this in the early Stoics, and as late as the second century. In his *Life of Sulla*, for example, Plutarch describes a series of ominous signs that foretell the civil wars. The Tyrrhenian/Etruscan specialists are consulted, who function similarly to Israelite prophets in this passage:

> The Tuscan wise men [Τυρρηνῶν] declared that the prodigy foretokened a change of conditions and the advent of a new age. For according to them there are eight ages in all, differing from one another in the lives and customs of men, and to each of these God has appointed a definite number of times and seasons, which is completed by the circuit of a great year. And whenever this circuit has run out, and another begins, some wonderful sign is sent from earth or heaven, so that it is at once clear to those who have studied such subjects and are versed in them, that men of other habits and modes of life have come into the world, who are either more or less of concern to the gods than their predecessors were. All things, they say, undergo great changes, as one again succeeds another, and especially the art of divination; at one period it rises in esteem and is successful in its predictions, because manifest and genuine signs are sent forth from the Deity; and again, in another age, it is in small repute, being off-hand, for the most part, and seeking to grasp the future by means of faint and blind senses. Such, at any rate, was the tale told by the wisest of the Tuscans [οἱ λογιώτατοι Τυρρηνῶν], who were thought to know much more about it than the rest.[28]

Certainly, there are obvious and notable differences between divinatory practices that deliver grand cosmic messages (i.e. Israelite prophets) versus the information concerning the immediate and practical (i.e. Greek necromancers, seers, and lot drawers). But a more productive comparison is to be found among Israelite necromancers, seers, and lot drawers with their Greek, Roman, and Etruscan equivalents. Non-Judeans, too, had figures with grand prophetic visions tied to time and cosmology, but they often came in the field of philosophy—a taxon not native to ancient Israel. As Martti Nissinen again points out, "it would be wrong

---

28. Plutarch, *Life of Sulla* 7.3–5. Translated by Bernadotte Perrin. Loeb Classical Library (Cambridge, MA: Harvard University Press, 1916), vol. 4.

to separate prophecy from omen divination in a way that suggests a fundamental disparity in their conceptual, intellectual, and ideological basis."[29]

Prophecy is but one example of Paul's many divinatory and wonderworking practices that have been classified as taxonomically unique, despite functional similarity and family resemblance. This same problem extends to the full repertoire of Paul's divinatory and wonderworking practices: channeling other types of divine speech, interpreting signs and wonders, claiming to have visions of and visitations from gods, the working of miracles, the miraculous power to heal, etc. What I suggest is a useful and careful taxonomy of divinatory practices that properly contextualizes Paul and his divination and wonderworking within the larger frame of mediating *god-to-human* communication and demonstrating *god-to-human* power. Insofar as these practices are understood to be god-to-human, we see that they constitute part of an implied reciprocal relationship with deities, which will be addressed in Chapter 6. Such a taxonomy cuts across emic distinctions (both ancient and modern) and claims to uniqueness, while not losing sight of how ancients themselves categorized such practices.

The Problem of Monothetic Classification

Much of the difficulty in demonstrating how Paul's practices relate to the wider world of divinatory practices in antiquity derives from the lack of a useful theoretical model that examines the full range of practices. To some degree, we have traditionally imported ancient polemical distinctions between "insider" (or correct or legitimate) practices and "outsider" (or incorrect or ineffective) practices, thereby reinscribing such divisions as modern scholarly categories, or taxa. The long-standing assertion of Christian uniqueness has lent itself to a monothetic taxonomy that is the tacit methodology in much of the analysis of Paul's practices and teachings.

In the natural and social sciences the traditional way of classifying things into groups (or sets or classes) has been to suppose that all members of the group or class must possess the same defining features of the class in order to belong. This way of classifying things is known as monothetic, and it dominated systems of classification until the past one hundred years.[30] The boundaries of monothetic

---

29. Nissinen, "Prophecy and Omen Divination," 345.

30. Sokal and Sneath define monothetic classification: "The ruling idea of monothetic groups is that they are formed by rigid and successive logical divisions so that the possession of a unique set of features is both sufficient and necessary for membership in the group is thus defined" (13). In Robert Sokal and Peter Sneath, *Principles of Numerical Taxonomy* (San Francisco: Freeman, 1963).

classification are rigid and can appear arbitrary, such that objects, animals, or plants that differ in only one or two aspects must be classified differently, though they have much more *in* common than not. Monothetic classification results in hundreds of discreet classes or groups that do not overlap; nonetheless, their constituent members often resemble one another in many ways or are clearly linked.

In 1763 French botanist Michel Adanson commented that in order for an individual plant to belong to a specific class of plants, it did not have to possess every defining feature of that class.[31] Instead, a class could be defined as having a range of properties or qualities, and its constituent members could share many or most of those qualities, but certainly not all. Furthermore, it is not necessary that a single defining feature be held in common by all members of the class.[32] Biologist Morton Beckner utilized this concept in the mid-twentieth century under the title "polytypic" classification,[33] until microbiologist Peter Sneath suggested the title "polythetic," which natural and social scientists have been using ever since.[34]

---

31. Michel Adanson, *Familles des plantes* (Paris: Vincent, 1763). That the concept of polythetic classification first develops in the natural sciences in not germane to my argument. However, it is meaningful to note that the sciences and humanities often have more to offer one another than scientists and humanities scholars suspect. For more on this mutually enriching relationship, see: Edward Slingerland, *What Science Offers the Humanities: Integrating Body and Culture* (Cambridge: Cambridge University Press, 2008); and Slingerland's follow up study, *Creating Consilience: Integrating the Sciences and the Humanities* (New York: Oxford University Press, 2011).

32. Wittgenstein's famous example is that of the fibers of a rope: "the rope consists of fibres, but it does not get its strength from any fibre that runs through it from one end to another, but from the fact that there is a vast number of fibres overlapping." See: Ludwig Wittgenstein, *Preliminary Studies for the "Philosophical Investigations," Generally Known as The Blue and Brown Books* (Oxford: Blackwell, 1958), 87.

33. Beckner provides the first full definitions of polytypic and polythetic, which scholars continue to rely on. See Morton Beckner, *The Biological Way of Thought* (New York: Columbia University Press, 1959). He writes, "A class is ordinarily defined by reference to a set of properties which are both necessary and sufficient (by stipulation) for membership in the class. It is possible, however, to define a group K in terms of a set G of properties $f_1, f_2, \ldots f_n$ in a manner. Suppose we have an aggregation of individuals (we shall not as yet call them a class) such that:

   1) Each one possesses a large (but unspecified) number of properties in G.
   2) Each f in G is possessed by large numbers of these individuals and
   3) No f in G is possessed by every individual in the aggregate.

By the terms of (3), no f is necessary for membership in this aggregate; and nothing has been said to warrant or rule out the possibility that some f in G is sufficient for membership in the aggregate" (22).

34. Peter Sneath, "The Construction of Taxonomic Groups." In *Microbial Classification*, edited by G. C. Ainsworth and P. Sneath (Cambridge: Cambridge University Press, 1962); For a brief history of the term, see Rodney Needham, "Polythetic Classification: Convergence and Consequences," *Man* 10.3 (1975): 349–369, esp. 353–357.

Category "123"

	i	*ii*	*iii*	*iv*
A		X	X	
B		X	X	
C			X	X
D	X			X
E	X	X		

FIGURE 1.1 The hypothetical category "123" using polythetic classification.

Sneath, working with biostatistician Robert Sokal, provide the present definition of polythetic classification in their text on numerical taxonomy: "A polythetic arrangement . . . places together organisms that have the greatest number of shared features, and no single feature is either essential to group membership or is sufficient to make an organism a member of the group."[35] Such a method greatly expands our ability to remain sensitive both to difference and similarity in the process of identification and classification. To illustrate, Figure 1.1 provides five hypothetical samples (A, B, C, D, E) with a range of four characteristics (*i, ii, iii, iv*) within a larger class called 123. It is possible, with a polythetic understanding of classification, to group all five samples together, though characteristics *i, ii, iii,* and *iv* are not distributed consistently or evenly among them:[36]

Notably, Samples A and B do not overlap with D in the sharing of their characteristics, nor do C and E overlap. Furthermore, out of the four characteristics of the class, none appears ubiquitously, such that the class is defined ultimately by that single, ubiquitous quality or characteristic. Yet the samples may be classified together because they pertain to the larger category "123" in ways that link them together and to the category. For example, Needham cites Beckner's application of the polythetic concept with the larger category of *escape reactions*, "such

---

35. Sokal and Sneath, *Principles of Numerical Taxonomy*, 14.

36. This model is admittedly simplified. As Kenneth Bailey points out, "Typologies with only a few variables are often theoretically irrelevant" (31). See Kenneth Bailey, "Constructing Monothetic and Polythetic Typologies by the Heuristic Method," *The Sociological Quarterly* 14.3 (1973): 291–308. The problem of classification arises, to begin with, because of the abundance and range of variables that simultaneously suggest similarity and difference. The distribution of four characteristics across five samples does not reflect how many variables and samples are often under examination. These numbers ought, really, to be multiplied fiftyfold.

as heading for the rocks, withdrawing into a shell, running, and so on. It would be very difficult . . . to attempt to specify a set of characteristics, other than this functional one, which all these responses, and no others, possess. 'The class of escape reactions . . . is fully polytypic [or polythetic] with respect to those features of observable behavior in the single response, and with respect to movements in relation to any environmental coordinate system, e.g. movements toward or away from particular things'" (354). As opposed to a monothetic type, in which all members must possess identical features, and each feature is a necessary requirement for membership in the class, the polythetic type allows for greater breadth and attention to variegation in how things relate to one another, as well as how they relate to the larger category of which they are ostensibly a part.[37]

Kenneth Bailey emphasizes the importance of polythetic classification in the sciences: "The polythetic typology has been heralded as a breakthrough in biology. If restricted to monothetic typology, a biologist would have to place in different cells two animals that displayed 999 points of similarity but differed on the thousandth variable. These two animals clearly belong in the same group. The polythetic typology allows this. The monothetic does not" (295).[38] Polythetic taxonomy has been used in biology, zoology, botany, microbiology, and bacteriology

---

37. There are both benefits and drawbacks to polythetic classification. It demands more complex thinking about how (potential) members of a class relate to one another, which makes the resultant category less arbitrary and more attuned to how things relate. As Sokal and Sneath, *Principles of Numerical Taxonomy*, 15, suggest, polythetic taxa "have a high content of information." It is driven more by empirical evidence than by a priori conceptualization, and is thus "truer to ethnographic materials" (Needham, "Polythetic Classification," 358). Furthermore, the class in a monothetic typology is a priori; that is, the limits and qualities of the class are set when constituent members are sought. On the contrary, polythetic classification so carefully considers the members and how they pertain to one another that the members themselves set the limits and qualities of the class. Yet, there are challenges and complications to using a polythetic model of classification. Because boundaries are less arbitrary and more complex, there are always borderline cases. Furthermore, polythetic classes may (and often do) overlap, as they are not mutually exclusive. Finally, the project of comparison is rendered more complex, since comparison itself depends on boundaries between those things intended for comparison.

38. Bailey, "Constructing Monothetic and Polythetic Typologies by the Heuristic Method," 291–308.. Sokal and Sneath, *Principles of Numerical Taxonomy*, 14, developed the concept further, to distinguish between generally polythetic and *fully* polythetic classifications. Because many taxa or classes do appear to have at least one quality or characteristic that is shared by most or all of its members, such classes do not seem to be fully polythetic. Yet, because there is always the possibility of a hitherto undiscovered member that lacks the common feature, classes are understood to be fully polythetic at least in theory. For example, they point out that possessing red blood corpuscles was a confirmed and definitive characteristic of all vertebrates until some species of fish were discovered lacking them (13). Clearly, these fish were also vertebrates, and thus the characteristics of vertebrates were expanded, as was the notion that we cannot say for sure when a class is generally or fully polythetic.

for several decades. It has been employed in anthropology since the 1970s,[39] but has made little headway in the field of religious studies. Its most vocal proponent in the latter field has been Jonathan Z. Smith, whose own background was—not coincidentally—in the classification and typology of botany.[40]

Charles King applies a polythetic taxonomy model in his study on the organization of Roman religious beliefs. As he suggests, the model ought not to be applied blindly, as there are some weaknesses, such as the assumption that "every element in any given set has equal weight and equal probability of occurring in the set."[41] To demonstrate how this supposition can be inaccurate, he provides the following example: "All birds may not fly, and everything that flies is not a bird, but the ability to fly is still a more frequently occurring characteristic of membership in the set 'bird' than having webbed feet" (287). Rather, he argues, the model is most useful if "refined so as to accommodate clusters . . . of varying intensity and distribution." In our case, this would refer to clusters of divinatory practices. Thus, the use of objects or "tools" (lots, drums, ummim and thurim, ostraka, burning embers) may be more or less common at times and for specific reasons, than the observation of animal behavior (flight of birds, whinny of horses, barking dogs, etc.). Furthermore, some in antiquity may insist that the use of tools in divinatory practice is less legitimate or less prestigious than inspired speech, yet the practices are linked by accomplishing feats through special powers bestowed by gods, ascertaining messages from gods and expressing that information in "human" terms. Paul himself points to this in Rom 6:19 when he tells his readers "I am speaking to you in human terms [*anthrōpinon*] because of your natural limitations [lit. *because of the weakness of your flesh*]."

King uses the notion of "fuzzy" or "graded" sets to account for the uneven, or clustered, distribution of characteristics of a class or set (288). The graded set remains polythetic, yet allows for the possibility that some types of divinatory practices in antiquity were widespread while others were anomalous or rare. Likewise, it accounts for the fact that some practices are clustered in certain periods of time, among certain areas, or in certain forms. For example, channeling communications from gods, ancestors, or daemons may come more often in the form of intelligible speech that needs only a modicum of interpretation. Yet, it

---

39. Needham brought polythetic classification, as a concept and methodology, to the social sciences. See Rodney Needham, "Polythetic Classification: Convergence and Consequences," *Man* 10.3 (1975): 349–369.

40. Smith discusses his arrival at and use of this approach throughout the essays of *Relating Religion*, but especially in "When the Chips Are Down" (1–60).

41. Charles King, "The Organization of Roman Religious Beliefs," *Classical Antiquity* 22.2 (2003): 275–312.

may also come in the form of *un*intelligible speech entirely dependent upon inter-pretation. We will see this in Chapter 3 when we encounter how Paul's speaking in tongues has been traditionally classified as a unique kind of practice.

The study of early Christianity has long maintained several, simultaneous monothetic models of what constitutes divination, wonderworking, prophecy, or even so-called magic. These categories are, admittedly, unwieldy; they overlap in theory and in practice, their boundaries are frequently indistinct. It is important for this study, however, to consider how the multiplicity of monothetic taxa has shaped our understanding of Paul's claims to divinatory expertise, as well as our understanding for how such diverse practices relate to one another in antiquity. Rather than classifying practices as divinatory (or not) based on (1) who practices them and who forbids them, (2) whether they employ tools or not, or (3) whether they are in relation to Yahweh, Christos, Zeus, dead ancestors, Apollo, etc., we ought to look instead at how the range of practices pertain to one another, how they function, and what they seek to accomplish. Needham insists on the impor-tance of polythetic classification in comparative work: "Comparative studies are likely to be defective and unproductive so long as they continue to be carried out within conventional, i.e., monothetic, taxonomies and by reliance on substan-tive paradigms" (365). A polythetic approach to classification allows for dynamic, nuanced avenues for comparing intraclass divinatory practices, somewhat syn-chronically, and to better understand how Paul's practices fit into the larger class of Mediterranean divination and wonderworking.

Modes of Religiosity and Paul

In addition to adopting a polythetic approach to classification, we can more thor-oughly redescribe Paul's divinatory and wonderworking practices by thinking in terms of *modes of religiosity*. A modal approach allows for a flexible, polythetic ap-proach to religion generally,[42] but, more important, it allows us to (1) redescribe Paul's diverse practices in relation to their historical milieu and (2) to understand the resistance toward understanding Paul in this way. Understanding the persist-ent scholarly resistance to normalizing and contextualizing Paul's practices is as compelling and important as redescribing those practices. The work of Harvey Whitehouse, modified and applied by Stanley Stowers, is instrumental to the project of reenvisaging Paul in such a manner.

---

42. Bruce Lincoln also notes the importance of polythetic approaches to how we define and classify religion. See Bruce Lincoln, *Holy Terrors: Thinking About Religion After September 11* (Chicago: University of Chicago Press, 2006), 5.

Harvey Whitehouse offers two modes of religiosity, which he grounds in studies of human cognition: the imagistic mode and the doctrinal mode.[43] The imagistic mode of religiosity includes practices that tend to be emotionally or psychologically jarring (and therefore memorable to the participant). Examples of this include rituals that involve cutting, branding, or burning parts of the body, the ingestion of drugs that alter perception or mood, rituals in which one feels the spirit of another being enter the body, and rituals of ecstatic speech or uncontrollable bodily movements. Jarring practices "tend to trigger a lasting sense of revelation and to produce powerful bonds between small groups of ritual participants" (63). This mode of religiosity tends to involve "high levels of arousal" (71) and requires little cognitive labor for memorizing complex ideas or interpretations. Thus, the imagistic mode is not the mode in which one develops doctrine, cosmological theories, or complex theology. Rather than developing "why-type" knowledge, the imagistic mode calls upon implicit "how-type" knowledge.[44] Implicit knowledge is typically encoded and procedural, and draws on bodily fluency insofar as knowledge does not have to be weighed, considered, examined, recollected, or recalled. It is fast and lacks hesitation because of cognitive assumptions, habitual practice, and deep internalization. It does not ask why. The imagistic mode of religiosity operates in the realm of human cognition that Whitehouse calls the "cognitive optimum:" that is, the zone in which an idea or practice may be just counterintuitive enough to be flagged by the memory (and thus, easily recalled), but not so counterintuitive as to require extensive thinking or memorization.

The doctrinal mode of religiosity, however, is cognitively costly. That is, the doctrinal mode requires extensive cognitive labor and intellectual investment, and it facilitates "the storage of elaborate and conceptually complex religious teachings in semantic memory." (65). Whitehouse claims that this mode of religiosity is often linked to hierarchical social arrangements and centralized institutions—a claim that requires modification if we are to apply it to Paul. The doctrinal mode attracts and cultivates commitments to "correct" thinking (i.e.

---

43. Harvey Whitehouse, *Modes of Religiosity: A Cognitive Theory of Religious Transmission* (New York: AltaMira Press, 2004).

44. As Whitehouse observes, implicit knowledge is bracketed off from other domains of knowledge—it is default, knee-jerk, unreflective, and automatic. We implicitly know that we cannot walk through walls or cannot breathe under water. Other forms of implicit knowledge become incorporated into our minds and bodies—how to ride a bicycle, how to tie our shoes, how to brush our teeth. We also have implicit ideas about gods—that they exist and that we can communicate with them and that they communicate with us. Implicit knowledge is not always correct. Likewise, explicit knowledge is not wrong simply because it is counterintuitive (calculus is counterintuitive, but not "wrong").

orthodoxy), symbolism, and interpretation. Cosmological theories too complex to comprehend at first glance demand repetition, teaching, and memorization. The doctrinal mode is bolstered by literacy and is often linked to a class of literate specialists charged with learning complex ideas and teaching them to nonexperts. Whitehouse observes, "a great deal of religious knowledge consists of cognitively costly concepts" (25). For Paul's gentile followers, it is cognitively costly to re-member all the details of story of Abraham, Isaac, and Ishmael; costly to recall how the faithfulness of Christ reiterates the faithfulness of Abraham and how their own faithfulness pertains to that; costly to comprehend that with baptism comes the receiving of the *pneuma* of a divine being named *Christos* (as opposed to the imagistic ritual of actually receiving that *pneuma*); costly to understand why the Judean god is the answer to one's ethical and moral failings; still more costly to retrain the mind into thinking that the gods honored by you and eve-ryone you have ever known are not gods at all.

According to Whitehouse, "Modes of religiosity constitute attractor positions around which ritual actions and associated religious concepts cumulatively tend to cluster" (74). This is an important point since modes "do not specify a set of law-like rules for building individual behavior" (75). Thus, a moving back and forth between modes is possible, as is the likelihood that many religious practices may fit somewhere between, or tend more strongly in one direction or another, while not being entirely situated exclusively in one mode. These modes are distri-butive, flexible, and intersect or overlap, especially in large, complex populations of people with disparate interests and claims. The plasticity of this approach, like polythetic classification, renders the scholar beholden to the data instead of the other way around. Modes of religiosity identify and describe tendencies to-ward attractor positions, instead of squeezing practices and beliefs into discretely bounded boxes for the comfort of the person trying to make sense of it all.

The salient differences between Whitehouse's imagistic mode and the doc-trinal mode are that the former is simple, vague, and riddled with contradictory ideas about gods and other such divine beings. Contradictions are generally ir-relevant to practitioners, since practical ritual performance takes precedence over theory, and the mode itself makes use of implicit, practical knowledge. This explains Charles King's observation that in traditional Greek and Roman religions, "incompatible beliefs could coexist simultaneously."[45] The latter mode, to the contrary, generates complex, intellectual, counterintuitive ideas that re-quire great effort for their transmission and retention: "The resulting bodies of esoteric knowledge contain concepts and systems of interlocking connections

---

45. See Charles King, "The Organization of Roman Religious Beliefs," 275.

that are just about as far from natural cognition as possible" (56). There is nothing intuitive or even sensible in thinking that a man executed by the state has come back to life, and if my body is infused with the breathy substance of his divine spirit I will be adopted into the lineage of his ancient, foreign people, and I too will come back to life after I am dead and I will subsequently live forever in the sky with his father–god, the creator of the cosmos. These few details alone require a scratching of the head, a bending of the mind, and memorization. The two modes do not exist in isolation; any given "religion" may incorporate both modes. But as is often the case, the specialists of the doctrinal mode disparage the imagistic mode as shallow, empty ritualism. The tendency for literate, intellectual theologians to disparage other modes of religiosity is an issue that reappears throughout this book.

There are challenges in using Whitehouse's theory of two modes to examine Paul and his followers. First, the specifics of his modes are influenced by the pervasiveness of religious ideologies that appear to generate wars and other forms of resolute conflict. Whitehouse is interested in the connection between human cognition and intensity of religious fervor on a grand scale as seen in the Crusades or, more recently, between Western (largely Christian) powers and various conservative, reactionary (Muslim and Jewish) groups in the Middle East.[46] We do not see wars fought in antiquity in the name of religion; indeed, we do not even see a word for religion. But perhaps more important for this project, two modes cannot sufficiently account for all human religiosity. This is where the modifications introduced by Stanley Stowers become pertinent.

Stowers brings the discourse of "modes of religiosity" to the study of the ancient Mediterranean in a way that helps our understanding of the function and

---

46. This is not to suggest that the Crusades or the problems of so-called terrorism of today (including conflicts with the Taliban, Al-Qaeda, or ISIS) are actually about "religion" (as opposed to control of medieval trade routes, Middle Eastern oil supplies, patriarchal control of women, resistance to Western imperialism, Zionist policies toward Palestine, populist pressures in favor of democracy, etc.). Rather, whereas the interests at stake in modern conflicts are often masked as "religious" in essence, such discourse did not predominate in antiquity. Gods were inevitably involved in wars, insofar as gods were involved in everything. But the spread of a religious ideology was not the most (or the sole) salient feature of conflict. Whitehouse's concerns clearly lie with conflicts over religious ideologies: "Notions of telepathy and love magic are no more or less intrinsically believable than notions of redemption and spiritual salvation. There is nothing to choose between these two sets of concepts with regard to relative degrees of inherent plausibility and absurdity. One set of concepts may be more complex and harder to acquire than the other, but that alone cannot explain why those concepts attract more fanatical commitment than the ragbag of supernatural beings, rituals, and folktales that cluster around the cognitive optimum position. Some people are prepared to die in the name of abstract theological or cosmological principles, whereas hardly anybody would lay down their lives to defend a belief in horoscopes and homeopathy" (Whitehouse, *Modes of Religiosity*, 119).

place of divinatory and wonderworking practices. Stowers' modes are more nuanced than those of Whitehouse in their application to premodern and pre-Christian worlds. Using the case study of animal sacrifice, he delineates four modes of religiosity, two of which are significant in an examination of Paul: the *religion of everyday social exchange* and the *religion of the literate cultural producer.*[47] The religion of everyday social exchange describes "practices of the family and household"[48] that respond to everyday concerns and reproduce the everyday hierarchy of relationships. As with Whitehouse's imagistic mode, these practices are not governed by systematic, theologized ideas that provide or discern their own meaning. Rather, the "deeper meanings" of such practices come later, as a result of the intellectualized religious practices and concerns of literate producers. Thus, offerings to Zeus of the Pantry address and alleviate concerns for the everyday (specifically, the contents of the pantry), and, subsequently, literate specialists may imbue such behavior with allegorical, symbolic, or metaphorical meaning. We see this very clearly, for example, throughout the writings of Philo of Alexandria, who "reveals" the deeper symbolic meaning of ancient Israelite practices and attitudes through the lens of highly literate middle Platonism.

Like Whitehouse, one of Stowers' intentions is to push beyond long-standing binary categories used to discuss religions, such as routinized and charismatic,[49] great and little traditions, urban and rural, private and public, literate and nonliterate, or elite and mass. These categories are filled with "unworkable difficulties" that unintentionally fail to account for the religious practices and beliefs of all sorts of people and also imply institutionalism where it may not exist or sheer individualism where it also does not exist. These "unworkable" categories have distinct boundaries, and simple questions disrupt their usefulness: How to describe the religious practices of a rural person who moves to the city? What do we make of the religious practices of a highly literate person who practices something "typical" of the illiterate masses? Not only do slaves, women, foreigners, etc. fall through the cracks with such categories, but so does the realization that

---

47. Stanley Stowers, "The Religion of Plant and Animal Offerings Versus the Religion of Meanings, Essences, and Textual Mysteries." In *Ancient Mediterranean Sacrifice*, edited by Jennifer Wright Knust and Zsuzsanna Várhelyi (New York: Oxford University Press, 2011), 35–56. These two modes overlay with what he calls *civic religion* and the *religion of literate specialists and political power.* These two additional modes are modifications of the two primary modes, and of less importance in this book. For further explanation, see Stowers, "The Religion of Plant and Animal Offerings," 49–51.

48. Ibid., 36.

49. I would argue that Whitehouse does not go far enough in critiquing the model of routinized vs. charismatic. Stowers' modification of Whitehouse does this work.

practices and people are linked in more intricate ways. To reiterate Whitehouse, modes are "attractor positions" around which certain types of practices and mental dispositions tend to congregate.

Stowers suggests that the "dominant epistemological mood in the religion of everyday social exchange was uncertainty."[50] This uncertainty he compares to being in a "many-windowed house with curtains up after dark:"[51] Those inside sense they can be seen but have little knowledge regarding the intentions of who is watching them, except that those watching also possess mind, desire, intention, and have superior knowledge and power compared with those inside. Appeasement and communication are central to this reciprocal relationship that may at first blush appear to reproduce the dynamic of patron–client or king–subject, but Stowers suggests that the gods are better understood as "interested parties."[52] He describes four characteristics of conceiving gods (and similar beings) in this mode of religiosity: "People interact with them as if they were persons; they are local in ways that are significant for humans; one maintains a relationship to them with practices of generalized reciprocity; and humans have a particular epistemological stance toward them."[53] The religious social formations with gods as lawgivers, moral exemplars, and cosmic principles tend to be divorced from location and often derive from "institutionalized literate elite" (here we see indebtedness to Whitehouse's doctrinal mode).[54]

Because gods are interested parties, because they possess greater knowledge and power, and because they participate in the events of daily life, the most common default position, both cross-culturally and trans-historically, is the religion of everyday social exchange. Stowers suggests that the religion of everyday social exchange includes three families of practices: divinatory practices; "speaking practices" like prayer, blessings, or curses; and "practices of social reciprocity" such as animal and plant offerings (38). I would like to complicate this network of practices by noting that one person may simultaneously offer gifts to a deity or *daimon* while speaking a prayer and reading and interpreting the

---

50. Stowers, "The Religion of Plant and Animal Offerings," 39.

51. Ibid. Part of this uncertainty is not always knowing the precise identity of the deities to appease or venerate. For example, a second-century herm (Inv 3892 T) in the Istanbul Archaeological Musuem reflects this epistemological uncertainty: "To the gods who ward off evil and protect us from catastrophe" [*theois apotropaioi kai aleskakooi*]. The generic plural term, gods, allows for a kind of divine anonymity with regard to protective chthonic deities, without causing the mortal subject to be offensive or irreverent.

52. Ibid., 37.

53. Ibid., 37.

54. Ibid., 37.

resulting signs. That is, divinatory practices and speaking practices take place within a larger framework of reciprocity with gods.

The propensity toward symbolic and metaphorical interpretation is an example of the secondary mode of religiosity, the religion of the literate cultural producer.[55] I say "secondary" because, as Stowers points out, this mode is parasitic upon the religion of everyday social exchange. Everyday social exchange is a mode of practical know-how, with regard to navigating relationships between humans and deities. The secondary mode depends upon the primary mode of everyday social exchange as the object of its intellectual interpretation, allegorizing, and theorizing. The religion of the literate cultural producer depends on that first, more fundamental mode, so that practices such as animal sacrifice, divination, and various other forms of reciprocity are, as Aristophanes comically put it, "enigmatized."[56] This secondary mode takes the literalness and self-evident practicality of various religious practices, and massages them into mysteries, obfuscations that must be explained, paradoxes that bend the mind, and grandiose cosmic truth claims that must be contemplated, debated, and defended. The communicative symbol delivered by a lightning strike is reconfigured in an intellectualized practice that uses written symbols called "letters." Literacy becomes a cornerstone in practices of enigmatizing and mystifying.

Although the modes are attractor positions, and therefore social conditions produce demographics of people who tend toward one mode or the other, the same person may operate in one mode at one moment and in another mode at another moment. This is not unlike shifting gears in a manual transmission, depending on the interests and demands of a given context. For example, as a priest of Apollo at Delphi, Plutarch would have overseen ritual sacrifices or offerings and mediated visits to the oracle, but he was also a highly literate intellectual who produced numerous treatises on morality and ethical development. In Plutarch, we can see how one mode expounds on another mode: The sacrifices and oracular utterances replicate practical reciprocal relations in a ritualized manner (the body is positioned just so, gifts are offered, requests are made, communication is reciprocated or not, food is eaten, songs are sung, etc.). In short, relationships are built or maintained in practical ways, for practical purposes. Plutarch's own assessment of such practices, however, belies intellectual interests dependent on literacy, philosophy, and cognitively costly interpretation.

---

55. Ibid., 46. Like Whitehouse, Stowers does not argue that these are discreet, mutually exclusive realms of religiosity, but account for tendencies.

56. *The Birds* 959–990.

Stowers' modification of Whitehouse's modes includes the distinction among different types of literate specialists. Figures such as Cicero, Seneca, or Plutarch are at the opposite pole from Paul insofar as the former derive their legitimacy from a widely recognized system of authorization and therefore have specific relations to power. Cicero and Seneca are intimately tied to state authority. Plutarch was a priest of Apollo for thirty years at the most historically revered oracular site. Paul's claim to legitimacy does not derive from widespread, culturally acknowledged sources such as a ritual of investment or initiation, specialized training with a priest,[57] connection to imperial or local power, etc. Rather, he usurps the authority of any traditional body (the authority of a local synagogue or ruling body of priests in Jerusalem) and claims God as his direct source of ordination and calling. The bypassing of these avenues of authorization, which Heidi Wendt details in her rubric of "freelance expert," is also characteristic of one type in Stowers' mode of the literate cultural producer: independently authorized, at odds and in competition with socially recognized bodies of power and legitimacy.

While Stowers uses animal sacrifice to demonstrate these modes of religiosity, the present study brings a modal understanding to an analysis of divinatory practices, wonderworking, reciprocity, and Paul. There is no doubt that Paul can be understood as one of many independent specialists operating in the mode of the literate cultural producer, but I would add that he participated in dual modes, often simultaneously. He moves between modes of religiosity such that the overlay, sometimes seamless, likely attracted a range of potential followers. He provides practical demonstrations of divine power and sign-reading abilities in which his followers may witness the palpability of the Judean deity, but he also teaches esoteric knowledge pertaining to meanings, essences, metaphors, and mysteries. Like Philo, who interprets earthquakes as divine intervention and also allegorizes multiple myths from early Israelite history, Paul operates in and out of modes. He casts his religiosity net wide: His primary goal may be preaching gentile salvation and inclusion in the family of Abraham through gentile participation in the *pneuma* of the resurrected Christ, but he also presents ethical teachings and interpretations of the Septuagint, often through the lens of Stoicism and middle Platonism. In addition to this, he is equally invested in, not to mention legitimated through, practical wonderworking abilities that address practical concerns such as healing the sick and divining the direct will of his deity through speech and the interpretation of divine signs.

---

57. In my view, Acts' claim (22:3) that Paul studied under Gamaliel is unreliable. Paul makes no mention of Gamaliel nor of studying in Jerusalem.

Key to this endeavor is an examination of practices that interpret information and demonstrate empowerment from gods to mortals. As we will see in the following chapters, divinatory and wonderworking practices claim to interpret information from a divine source or to channel divine power—but usually with regard to practical aspects of living. The flight of birds, for example, may determine the outcome of a financial transaction. A thunderbolt may convey whether a military invasion is encouraged. The proclamation of a soothsayer may influence whether two people marry. Or gods may act through mortals to "miraculously" heal deafness, skin conditions, or breast cancer. Gods may also implant egregious knowledge or wisdom in the minds of mortals. The "miraculous" aspect to such claims is that the human in question can do or perform things beyond the normal capabilities of mortals. Mortals have universal limitations that gods can choose to extend, defy, or temporarily suspend. But divinatory practices can also employ texts, allegory, or discourses of mystery and essences, as in the case of prophets who claim to discern ultimate things about humanity's place in the cosmos through holy books or secrets imparted from a god.

One caveat: Insofar as the ability to be "intellectualized" is concerned, there exists an important distinction between animal sacrifice and practices of divination or wonderworking. Animal sacrifice is a practical, ritualized slaughter that must be performed in specific ways, according to local traditions; it entails the din of human voices and dying animals, the spilling of blood, disemboweling the *splanchna*, skinning, carving up meat, and the general exposure to disarticulated body parts (head, hooves), blood, and gore. On the one hand, inventing or reinventing the "meaning" of such a ritual is a separate type of practice—an intellectual practice that is not at all gory[58]—and those who interpret and imbue ritual slaughter with "meaning" simultaneously ascribe a type of worth to the practice through their own distinct practices of interpretation, allegorizing, and theorizing.[59] The practical know-how of ritual slaughter is supplied various interpretive frameworks after the fact. Practices of divination and wonderworking, on the other hand, are not typically imbued with deeper meaning. They are not allegorized or turned into metaphors. After all, what is the "deeper meaning" of asking a god, "Should we launch our ships?" or, "Show me a sign." When the sky suddenly shudders with sonorous thunder and someone claims to understand its meaning, a second person does not subsequently ask, "What is the deeper meaning of reading the sky in this way?" To be clear—practices of

---

58. Stowers, "The Religion of Plant and Animal Offerings," 47–49.

59. For an excellent analysis of this, see Daniel Ullucci, *The Christian Rejection of Animal Sacrifice* (New York: Oxford University Press, 2011).

divination demonstrate the cognitive propensity toward reading the world for symbols and data couched cryptically, but ancients did not ask "What is the *meaning* of interpreting divine signs?" Instead, some asked, "Does this work? Is this the correct reading? Do gods actually communicate this way?" Divination and the working of wonders provide solutions to practical problems, direction to the uncertain, and authority to those who claim the skills to interpret or work miracles. The *tools* of the literate cultural producer are turned toward divination or wonderworking— for example, using a collection of old texts to divine the near future (Sibylline Oracles; prophetic interpretations of Homer; Paul's use of Gen 15–21), or using mysterious written incantations to open avenues for divine power (for healing disease, transforming substances, causing someone to fall in love, influencing a court case, etc.). But the goals are practical, literal, and pertain to the visible–visceral–palpable. Divination and miracles are not easily translated into the mode of the literate cultural producer so much as the skills of that mode are applied toward practical ends. Instead, the practices typical of everyday social exchange are critiqued and disparaged by specialists invested in the secondary mode—the mode of the theoretical, counterintuitive, and cerebral.

Conclusion

A book that redescribes and contextualizes the divinatory and wonderworking practices of Paul must first contend with the problems of how Christianity and its figureheads have enjoyed radically unique categories and interpretations. It is not enough to simply point and claim, "See how Pauline *glôssa* is similar to other examples of channeling the speech of deities in antiquity." In addition to noting how supposedly unique practices were widespread and therefore recognizable to many people in antiquity, it is important to understand how categorical difference emerges. Rather than defending monothetic classification, which results in like things being routed into classificatory silos of uniqueness, I argue that a more nuanced and polythetic approach to classification better serves us in examining historical data pertaining to Paul and the emergence of Christianity. This includes any analysis of his divination and miracles.

Furthermore, by employing a framework of modes of religiosity, we can account for how and why some religious practices take precedence over others. There is no doubt that the mode of the literate cultural producer retools the practices of everyday social exchange, such that the primary mode (the everyday) is rendered inferior, shallow, and rudimentary (negatively inflected) when compared with the ethereal, cerebral, and cognitively costly mode of the literate producer. Yet, as we will see with Paul, a toggling between modes extends the breadth of a religious specialist's ability to reach a larger audience. Paul is not solely delivering a cognitively costly, intellectualist message of ethics, primordial history of the nations, and personal salvation. He is also demonstrating practical powers, addressing practical concerns, and teaching his followers how to communicate with the supreme (Judean) creator–God. We see these distinctions, for example, in Rom 7:14–20 and 1 Cor 12. In the Romans passage, Paul makes use of the long-standing image of a person struggling with the magnetic pull of wrong-doing (the prototype for which is the figure of Euripides' Medea, later used by Platonists and Stoics to discuss the problem of anger, vengeance, and *akrasia*).[60] 1 Corinthians 12 details a list of practical divinatory and wonderworking skills that include miraculous healing from sickness. By disarticulating the various limbs of classification and modality, Paul's practices may be demystified, normalized, and "naturalized" as types of practices we see across the ancient Mediterranean.

---

60. Epictetus, *Discourses* 1.28.9–10. Seneca will reuse her in his own tragic version of *Medea* (circa 50 CE). For more on the figure of Medea as a trope for philosophers in discussing anger and the passionate emotions, see Kathryn Gutzwiller, "Seeing Thought: Timomachus' Medea and Ecphrastic Epigram," *American Journal of Philology* 125.3 (2004): 339–386; Richard Joyce, "Early Stoicism and *Akrasia*," *Phronesis* 40.3 (1995): 315–335; Stanley Stowers, "Paul and Self-Mastery." In *Paul in the Greco-Roman World: A Handbook*, edited by J. Paul Sampley (New York: Bloomsbury T & T Clark, 2016), vol. 2, 270–300.

2

Divinatory Practices and Palpability of the Gods

IN HIS FOURTH-CENTURY BCE *Anabasis*, Xenophon of Athens describes
the extended military campaigns and travails of ten thousand Greek mercenaries
fighting in Persia. Throughout the lengthy story of harrowing escapes and nail-
biting adventures, the Hellenes are frequently dependent on the cryptic advice
and directives of gods. At Socrates' urging, Xenophon first consults the oracle at
Delphi before joining Cyrus' expedition (3.1.5–8). Soon after arriving in Cilicia
(via Sardis), he receives a startling dream in which Zeus' lightning bolt strikes his
father's house in Athens. Xenophon frets over how to interpret this sign, clearly
of divine origin (3.1.11–13). He observes a divine sign in a sneeze that confirms his
impulse to continue onward (3.2.8–9). Pressed to accept command of the army in
Book 6, he first offers sacrifices to Zeus and then recalls having heard, at Ephesus,
an eagle scream to his right. The seer [ὁ μάντις], whom he had been consulting at
the moment, alerted him to both his impending suffering and glory (6.1.21–23).
Throughout the seven books of the *Anabasis*, the mercenary army regularly finds
and interprets divine information in sacrificed animals.

Xenophon's story is one of countless examples of Greeks understanding themselves to be in meaningful communicative relationships with gods, *daimones*,
ancestors, spirits, or the dead. But Greeks were hardly alone in the breadth and
creativity of their divinatory practices. Indeed, divinatory practices stand at the
heart of ancient Mediterranean religiosity from Roman Palestine, Egypt, and
the Near East, to Anatolia, Greece, and the Iberian Peninsula. Inhabitants of
the ancient Mediterranean ubiquitously depended on and engaged in multiple
strategies of communication with gods and other such beings in order to discern
divine will, to implore the gods to ensure a particular outcome in a given situation, and to convey to other mortals what the gods have to say. Such strategies of
communication reflect implicit understandings of reciprocal relations between

gods and humans as well as the palpability of gods' presence in human life. This chapter demonstrates such palpability insofar as it was imagined and felt in both stark and subtle ways in every arena of daily living. To make sense of Paul's divinatory and wonderworking practices, we must understand the breadth and pervasiveness of this sentiment and accompanying practices. The most common Greek word to indicate divine communication is *sēmeion*, or sign. *Sēmeia* [signs] and *terata* [wondrous or terrifying things] were means by which such beings contacted mortals to demonstrate this presence and convey privileged information.[1] *Sēmeia* and *terata* were, furthermore, the very terms favored by Paul in noting his ability to interpret information from his Judean deity, as well as the terms he uses to denote the divinely endorsed miracles he has performed in front of his followers.

Generally speaking, divinatory practices were not heavily theorized or theologized in antiquity, nor were they governed by a clearly articulated logic. Rather, the existence of the gods and their interest in communicating with mortals were simply taken for granted. Practices were either passed down with an unclear folk history or altered by means of innovation to suit the interpreter or the outcome of a particular situation. In fact, the practices themselves likely preceded their explanations: Studies in the cognitive science of religion have argued persuasively that cognitive evolution contributes to humans' reading the world for signs, warnings, dangers, and independent, invisible agents.[2] It is likely that explanations for divinatory practices (understandings of how and why they worked) were developed in response to the existence of such practices that were already in place. This is characteristic of the mode of religiosity in which the

---

1. An extensive bibliography exists on "signs and wonders." See, for example, Walter Burkert, "Signs, Commands, and Knowledge: Ancient Divination Between Enigma and Epiphany." In *Mantikê: Studies in Ancient Divination*, edited by Sarah Iles Johnston and Peter Struck (Boston: Brill, 2005), 9–49; Vernon S. McCasland, "Signs and Wonders," *Journal of Biblical Literature* 76.2 (1957): 149–152; Steven J. Scherrer, "Signs and Wonders in the Imperial Cult: A New Look at a Roman Religious Institution in the Light of Rev 13:13–15," *Journal of Biblical Literature* 103.4 (1984): 599–610; Ulrike Riemer, "Miracle Stories and Their Narrative Intent in the Context of the Ruler Cult of Classical Antiquity." In *Wonders Never Cease: The Purpose of Narrating Miracle Stories in the New Testament and Its Religious Environment* (New York: T & T Clark, 2006), 32–47; G. H. Twelftree, "Signs, Wonders, Miracles." In *Dictionary of Paul and His Letters* (Downers Grove, IL: InterVarsity Press, 1993), 875–877.

2. See Justin Barrett, *Why Would Anyone Believe in God?* (Walnut Creek, CA: AltaMira Press, 2004); Ilkka Pyysiäinen, *Supernatural Agents: Why We Believe in Souls, Gods, and Buddhas* (Oxford: Oxford University Press, 2009); Scott Atran, *In Gods We Trust: The Evolutionary Landscape of Religion* (Oxford: Oxford University Press, 2002). For a useful application of cognitive studies to the study of Greek religion, see Jennifer Larson, *Understanding Greek Religion: A Cognitive Approach* (New York: Routledge, 2016).

practical, mundane practices of communication between mortals are ritualized
and replicated between mortals and divine beings.

Michael Schwarz refers to divination as one of the "first forms of hermeneutics" and a "hermeneutics of the natural world." He writes, "Divination
techniques reflect a particular worldview . . . . [It] is a system in which every
detail of the environment is filled with meaning. To the diviner the world is inherently semiotic" (165).[3] While I would hesitate to describe divination as a co-
hesive "system," Schwartz accurately captures the sense that the world was read
for divine information. Indeed, Plotinus likens divination through augury to
reading the letters of an alphabet: " . . . they [the gods] furnish the incidental
service of being letters [γράμματα] on which the augur, acquainted with that
alphabet [τοιαύτην γραμματικὴν], may look and read [εἰδότας ἀναγινώσκειν] the
future from their pattern—arriving at the thing signified by such analogies as
that a soaring bird tells [σημαίνει] of some lofty event" (Ennead 3.6).[4] Plotinus
argues that the gods supply this service out of concern for the whole [σωτηρία
τῶν ὅλων]. Cicero understands such practices as so common that he begins his
De Divinatione by stating, "Now I am aware of no people, however refined and
learned or however savage and ignorant, which does not think that signs are given
of future events, and that certain persons can recognize those signs and foretell
events before they occur."[5] Pliny the Elder provides some examples: "warnings
drawn from lightning, the forecasts made by oracles, the prophecies of augurs,
and even considerable trifles—a sneeze, a stumble—counted as omens."[6] Pauline
Ripat echoes their sentiments: "The anecdotal evidence makes it clear that the
purported divine responses to anxious individuals virtually formed the white

3. Michael Schwartz, "Divination and Its Discontents: Finding and Questioning Meaning
in Ancient and Medieval Judaism." In Prayer, Magic, and the Stars in the Ancient and Late
Antique World, edited by Scott Noegel, Joel Walker, and Brannon Wheeler (University
Park: Pennsylvania State University Press, 2003), 155–168.

4. Plotinus, Enneads, translated by Stephen MacKenna and B. S. Page. Mesopotamian divination was often understood in terms of writing and reading: The position of the stars was likened
to "sky writing" that Babylonian astrologers "read," and cuneiform omens were understood to
be the writing of the gods. See Giovanni Manetti, Theories of the Sign in Classical Antiquity,
translated by Christine Richardson (Bloomington: Indiana University Press, 1993), 4–6.

5. "Gentem quidem nullam video neque tam humanam atque doctam neque tam immanem
atque barbaram, quae non significari futura et a quibusdam intellegi praedicicue posse ceneat."
De Div. 1.2. Cicero, De Divinatione. Translated by William Armistead Falconer. Loeb Classical
Library (Cambridge, MA: Harvard University Press, 1923).

6. "Ecce fulgurum monitus, oraculaorum praescita, haruspicum praedicta, atque etiam parva
dictum in auguris, sternumenta et offensiones pedum." Nat. Hist. 2.24, Rackham trans.

background noise of [Rome]."[7] Divinatory practices do not pertain to prognostication alone; while anxiety over the future may have dominated the list of reasons why people turn to invisible, divine beings for information, the reasons also included inquiries regarding the past or for validation of the present course of action.

Ancient Mediterranean religiosity was largely organized around an understanding of reciprocity between gods and humans. This was the case among Judeans, Greeks, Romans, Egyptians, Persians, Macedonians, etc. Through ritual veneration, temple *cultus*, vegetal offerings, and animal sacrifice, human beings offered the proper amount and quality of *pietas* (to borrow the Romans' term) that the gods deserved by virtue of being godly. In return for this, the gods watched over humans. They provided good crop years, healthy children, protection to the city, safety against those who would do one harm, and longevity for the paternal line. I will look closely at reciprocity in Chapter 6, but for now it should suffice to say that providing signs was one of the means by which gods demonstrated their concern for mortals. They dropped hints, warned of danger, expressed approval or disapproval, and provided guidance. Sometimes this information was unreservedly delivered, such as in the case of a startling eclipse or a bizarre dream. In other instances, information had to be sought out. Here, we can point to oracles, the casting of lots, the reading of birds in flight, or channeling forms of speech of divine origin. Gods also imbued some mortals with the power to heal or to facilitate divine healing, and they could communicate verbally by overtaking the speech organs of select mortals. These mundane concerns and the divinatory practices that address them fall into the mode of everyday social exchange.

Sarah Iles Johnston is correct to observe that divination surrounds us even today.[8] Astrologers, tarot readers, and psychic mediums can easily be found in any modern city or town. Joseph Smith invented the Church of Jesus Christ of Latter-Day Saints by divining the Book of Mormon through "peep stones"—rocks he kept at the bottom of a hat through which he could visualize the translation of the mysterious golden plates delivered to him by the angel Moroni.[9] Televangelist Pat Robertson determined that the 2010 earthquake in Haiti came as God's

---

7. Pauline Ripat, "Roman Omens, Roman Audiences, and Roman History," *Greece and Rome* 53 (2006): 156.

8. Sarah Iles-Johnston, *Ancient Greek Divination* (Oxford: Wiley-Blackwell, 2008), 1–3.

9. The use of "seer stones" was also practiced by nineteenth-century Americans in search of buried treasure. See Ronald W. Walker, "The Persisting Idea of American Treasure Hunting," *BYU Studies* 24 (1984): 429–459; David Persuitte, *Joseph Smith and the Origins of the Book of Mormon* (Jefferson, NC: McFarland, 2000).

punishment for Haitians' rumored eighteenth-century pact with "the devil" [i.e. native Haitian gods] to free themselves from French colonialism.[10] News media frequently run stories about the face of Jesus (or the Virgin Mary, or even popularly sainted Michael Jackson) that an unsuspecting suburbanite discovers on her piece of toast or that mysteriously appears on a neighborhood tree trunk. When this happens, the likeness of the god/saint/hero/ancestor is posited by some to be a "sign." In a Stockton, CA, neighborhood in 2009, observers could not decide if the miraculous face discovered in a birch tree stump was Michael Jackson *or* Jesus; both were equally famous and Michael Jackson, according to one interviewee, was capable of the same salvific work as Jesus.[11] Such examples remind us that reading the world for signs and the implicit assumption that the dead or deified continue to present themselves to the living, are neither foreign nor defunct ideas.[12] These latter examples may strike some readers as having nothing to do with religion; because "religion" deals only with the lofty and transcendent, the Virgin Mary would never appear on a piece of toast. Yet, for those who understand gods as both palpable and present, there are few places or manifestations that exclude such beings.

Survey of Divinatory Practices and Techniques

Centuries after Xenophon's *Anabasis*, the central concerns in Cicero's *De Divinatione* indicate that the variety of divinatory practices have not changed dramatically. What follows is an exploration of the multitude of ways in which gods were imagined to make contact with humans and disclose privileged information. Ancient evidence for such practices is so abundant that the survey here can only pale in comparison with the thoroughness of other studies, beginning

---

10. James Wood, "Between God and Hard Place," *New York Times* (January 23, 2010). URL: http://www.nytimes.com/2010/01/24/opinion/24wood.html?scp=4&sq=pat%20 robertson%20haiti%20earthquake&st=cse. A similar sentiment was expressed by the governor of Tokyo, who suggested the March 2011 tsunami was divine punishment. See Justin McCurry, "Tokyo Governor Apologises for Calling Tsunami 'Divine Punishment,'" *The Guardian* (March 15, 2011). URL: http://www.guardian.co.uk/world/2011/mar/15/ tokyo- governor-tsunami-punishment.

11. CBS-Affiliate KOVR, Stockton, CA, published July 6, 2009. Accessed Dec 17, 2018. YouTube video: https://www.youtube.com/watch?v=L_fQ6SK7Aoc.

12. Cognitive scientists and developmental psychologists have explored the reasons why humans tend to imagine the persistence of consciousness after death, both in relation to oneself and to others. See Jesse Bering, "Intuitive Conceptions of Dead Agents' Minds: The Natural Foundations of Afterlife Beliefs as Phenomenological Boundary," *Journal of Cognition and Culture* 2.4 (2002): 263–308; Shaun Nichols, "Imagination and Immortality: Thinking of Me," *Synthese* 159.2 (2007): 215–233.

with Bouché-Leclercq's four-volume study from the late nineteenth century.[13] The sheer breadth and diversity of such practices, which extend diachronically, geographically, and socioeconomically, are self-evident for those who have spent time reading ancient poets, dramatists, historians, biographers, paradoxographers, philosophers, and rhetoricians. Gods may have received veneration at specific locales, but it was assumed that a being from the divine world could be anywhere at any given time. Thus, random parts of world could suddenly come alive with messages and meaning, confirming Pliny's opinion that "the gods exercise an interest in human affairs,"[14] and that humans could, with correct interpretation, understand divinely sent *sēmeia*. While the apostle Paul does not engage in each of these practices, this survey lays the groundwork for understanding the epistemological disposition shared by Paul and his followers. Despite the supposed remoteness of the Judean deity in some LXX texts, we will see that he too was thought to have his hand immediately in the world. Paul cannot be understood outside the context of this way of thinking or outside of such practices. This analysis also includes ancient voices critical of such practices—almost all of whom are to be found among the intellectual literate elite.

Oracles and Oracular Sites

Institutional oracular shrines punctuated the Mediterranean geography, where visitors approached with questions beyond the capacity of human knowing and received answers from Zeus/Jupiter, Apollo, Asclepius, Demeter, and other gods or goddesses.[15] The most famous and long-standing of such oracles were found at Delphi, Dodona, Clarus, and Didyma. Yet lesser oracles functioned at Siwa,[16] Apamea,[17] and Oinoanda.[18] The rituals in preparation

---

13. See A. Bouché-Leclercq, *Histoire de la divination dans l'antiquité* (Paris: E. Leroux, 1879), vols. 1–4.

14. Pliny, *Nat. Hist.* 2.26 Translated by H. Rackham. Loeb Classical Library 330 (Cambridge, MA: Harvard University Press, 1938), vol. I, books 1–2.

15. Occasionally, the oracular pronouncements of one god demanded piety toward another god. An inscription from Anatolia quotes Apollo as saying that proper worship of Artemis will deliver the town from the plague it currently suffers. See Fritz Graf, "An Oracle Against Pestilence From a Western Anatolian Town," *Zeitschrift für Papyrologie und Epigraphik* 92 (1992): 267–279.

16. Robert Jackson, *At Empire's Edge: Exploring Rome's Egyptian Frontier* (New Haven, CT: Yale University Press, 2002); Klaus Kuhlmann, *Das Ammoneion: Archäologie, Geschichte und Kultpraxis des Orakels von Siwa* (Mainz: P. von Zabern, 1988).

17. Jean Balty, "Apamea in Syria in the Second and Third Centuries A.D.," *Journal of Roman Studies* 78 (1988): 91–104.

18. N. P. Milner, "Notes and Inscriptions on the Cult of Apollo at Oinoanda," *Anatolian Studies* 50 (2000): 139–149.

for oracle seeking, as well at the details of how oracles were delivered, varied from site to site,[19] yet the goals and results of oracle-seeking were the common across the Mediterranean: powerful and/or wealthy individuals and representatives of governments sought to determine the gods' opinion regarding the best course of action and how to avert disaster.

At Delphi, for example, Apollo sent oracles delivered in garbled speech by the Pythia.[20] The Pythia's words, in turn, were "translated" by a *prophetēs* to the visitor.[21] The translation was characteristically ambiguous, leaving correct interpretation up to the questioner.[22] Interpretation was frequently wrong, such as when Croesus famously sent delegations to question the oracles at Delphi and Thebes about attacking Cyrus and was told that if he attacked the Persians he would destroy a great empire. Croesus attacked, not realizing that the fallen empire would be his own (Herodotus 1.53–56.). Cicero points to the significance of consulting oracles before any major undertaking: "And, indeed, what colony did Greece ever send into Aeolia, Ionia, Asia, Sicily, or Italy without consulting the Pythian or Dodonian oracle, or that of Jupiter Hammon?" (*de Div.*1.1).[23]

---

19. For a description of the variety of preparation rituals and pronouncement traditions, see Iles-Johnston, *Ancient Greek Divination*, 2008.

20. A host of myths bolstered the importance of each oracular site (and the oracles were always tied to location). For example, Delphi billed itself as the center of the world, and even had on display a large "navel" stone that Zeus had placed there (see Pindar, frag. 54). Didyma, likewise, claimed to be the site where Apollo met and fell in love with Branchus, Apollo's first prophet (see Callimachus, frag. 229). Oracles had a significant economic impact on their surrounding communities. Such importance has been evinced through archaeology. Delphi, for example, was the regular recipient of expensive gifts from visitors. Oracle sites also hosted games and festivals and often created an ever-expanding compound of buildings to house visitors.

21. By all accounts, it is clear that the gods spoke from within the oracle. The Pythia, for example, spoke always in the first person as Apollo. It is clear that a theory of possession was at work; the Greek words usually used to describe Pythian activities include *empimplemi* [to fill up], *enthousazo* [inside of her], *katecho* [held her]. This "possession" of the oracle further points to the semiotics of the mundane and the intimacy of contact with gods.

22. Heraclitus, frag.18, claims that the god whose oracle is at Delphi neither speaks nor conceals, but gives signs [*sēmainei*]. William Harris explains the problematic translation of the Greek *sēmainein*: "The Oracle responds with indirect information rather than words, he intimates things rather than indicating them. So going to ask the oracle a question will give you a puzzle of some sort, relevant indirectly rather than a response to your question (Harris, "Heraclitus," 9). N. P. Milner, "Notes and Inscriptions," 143, clarifies, "To Zeus belong the most important sign-oracles, to Apollo the speaking oracles; the will of Zeus is made known by signs and portents, but Apollo speaks through the mouth of the prophet inspired by him."

23. Translated by William Armistead Falconer. Loeb Classical Library (Cambridge, MA: Harvard University Press, 1923).

Oracles could also be drawn by lot.[24] Archaeological evidence supports this especially at Dodona.[25] Beans or pebbles marked "yes" or "no" were placed into a jar, and the petitioner asked a specific question, often inscribed on a rolled-up lead tablet. More than 1,400 of these tablets have been excavated from Dodona alone.[26] The inspired priestess then drew the answer from the jar, which was understood to be the god's answer. David Potter suggests that this type of oracle would be more popular among the poor, since visits to important oracular shrines were out of their reach, both financially and physically. Even many of those who managed to travel to places like Dodona or Delphi used lot oracles as cheaper and more immediate means of gaining the opinion of the gods, since only the wealthy could afford to consult with the priests directly. As Potter explains, "The spoken responses of the gods were essentially the words of the gods for the rich. The procedures for consulting the gods mirrored the social stratification of society as a whole."[27]

Living oracles affixed to specific geographical locations such as Delphi, Dodona, and Apamea responded, however vaguely, to specific questions posed by enquiring visitors. Yet, obscure and mysterious oracular pronouncements were also collected for future use.[28] Sibylline prophecies, for example, offered "discursive pieces of verse addressed to the world in general rather than to any particular enquirer" (Parke, 7).[29] While it seems that the Sibyl was originally linked to an actual Greek oracle at Cumea,[30] the name itself eventually suggests a title for a female prophet. We know of Sibyls in as disparate places as Cumae, Cimmerium,

---

24. This seems to be scholarly consensus on how to understand ancient Israelite Urim and Thummim. See Cornelis Van Dam, *The Urim and Thummim: A Means of Revelation in Ancient Israel* (Winona Lake, IN: Eisenbrauns, 1997).

25. For a good discussion of this, see Iles-Johnston, *Ancient Greek Divination,* 68–70; Eric Lhote, *Les lamelles oraculaires de Dodone* (Geneva: Droz, 2006).

26. For a catalogue of some of the specific questions asked at Dodona, see Esther Edinow, *Oracles, Curses, and Risks Among the Ancient Greeks* (New York: Oxford University Press, 2007), 72–124. Cicero gives a description of lots worked in *de Div.* 1.34.76.

27. David Potter, *Prophets and Emperors: Human and Divine Authority From Augustus to Theodosius* (Cambridge, MA: Harvard University Press, 1994), 49.

28. Such collections should be distinguished from collections of prodigies, such as the Roman *Annales Maximi.* See Robert Drews, "Pontiffs, Prodigies, and the Disappearance of the *Annales Maximi,*" *Classical Philology* 83.4 (1988): 289–299.

29. For an examination of the history of the many Sibyls and the development of Sibylline Oracles, see H. W. Parke, *Sibyls and Sibylline Prophecy in Classical Antiquity* (London: Routledge, 1988).

30. See Parke, *Sibyls and Sibylline Prophecy,* 71–99.

Phrygia, Samos, and Tivoli. Her original oracular site at Cumae waned in popularity by the early Roman Empire, and what remained were the oracular books.[31] The original *Libri Sibyllini* were destroyed in the fire in the temple of Jupiter Optimus Maximus in 83 BCE, and what was compiled as the *Oracula Sibyllina* in the centuries that followed appeared to be largely Judean and, later, Christian uses of the Sibyl to foretell disasters and plagues.[32] Oracles of Bacis were also collected and consulted,[33] as were collections of the later Chaldean oracles,[34] the Egyptian Oracle of the Potter and Oracle of the Lamb.[35] Paul uses the LXX in a comparably oracular way, which I will consider in Chapter 3.

Insofar as oracles had long been sought by political parties and heads of state to answer political questions concerning policy and warfare, the political control of oracles also figured in their functioning. Augustus transferred all the Sibylline Oracle books to the temple of Apollo on the Palatine near his new palace at the same time that he banned the public circulation of such oracles.[36] Pauline Ripat examines the sudden and thorough shift from Demotic to Greek, as the language used in oracular inquiry of Egyptians, as soon as the province was annexed as part of the Empire.[37] She argues persuasively that such a shift can be explained only by insistence of the new Roman administration, to ensure that Rome was not excluded from understanding and being privy to popular oracular activity in its newest province. As part of solidifying political control over Egypt, Roman policy toward Egyptian oracles was such that the powerful priesthood could not

---

31. L. Richardson describes later Cumae as "a paradigm of vanished greatness, the harbor so silted up that it was unusable, the forum beginning to crumble into ruin." See L. Richardson Jr., "Trimalchio and the Sibyl at Cumae," *The Classical World* 96.1 (2002): 77. The Sibyl can actually be traced to Asia Minor, but her earliest presence in Italy appears to have been at Cumae.

32. See Parke, *Sibyls and Sibylline Prophecy*, 152–173, esp. 137. Parke suggests that the vague and ominous nature of the Sibylline Oracles predisposed the genre to later use among apocalyptic-minded Judean and Christian writers.

33. When Bacis is discussed by ancient writers, he is mentioned usually in tandem with the Sibyl. See, for example: Herodotus 8.20, 9.43; Lucian, *de Mort Peregr.* 30.15; Plutarch, *de Pyth. Or.* 10.399a; Cicero, *de Div.* 1.18; Plato, *Theages*, 124d8; Callimachus, *Iambi.* frag 195.31; Aelius Aristides, Πρὸς Πλάτωνα περὶ ῥητορικῆς 12.19.

34. R. Majercik, *The Chaldean Oracles, Text, Translations, and Commentary*. Studies in Greek and Roman Religion v (Leiden: Brill, 1989).

35. Frankfurter, *Religion in Roman Egypt*, 1998.

36. See J. L. Lightfoot, *The Sibylline Oracles, With Introduction, Translation, and Commentary on the First and Second Books* (Oxford: Oxford University Press, 2007), 89.

37. See Pauline Ripat, "The Language of Oracular Inquiry in Roman Egypt," *Phoenix* 60.3 (2006): 304–328.

be allowed to engage in popular religious activity in a language unfamiliar to Roman administrators.

Dreams and Dream Interpretation

While ancients did not uniformly agree on the nature and significance of dreams,[38] literary and epigraphical evidence suggests the practice of reading dreams for information from the gods was a pan-Mediterranean phenomenon that cut across economic, geographic, and educational divisions. If interpreted correctly, dreams provided useful information regarding the dreamer's health, family, enemies, and future.[39] Dream books and manuals abounded; we have recovered numerous inscriptions advertising the services of *oneirokritai* [dream-judges] or Roman *coniectores* [interpreters],[40] dream narratives often legitimated the authority of new political, religious, or both, figures, and "incubation" centers offered opportunities for visitors to receive direct visions of and healing from gods.

Unlike a modern Western understanding of dream activity, which posits that the human brain generates dreams during rapid-eye-movement (REM) sleep as part of a nightly maintenance process of compressing information or memories, many ancients thought the sleeping person was responsible for neither the content nor form of her dreams.[41] Greek poetry, tragedy, and history

---

38. Dreams were sometimes thought to be the result of the material conditions of sleep, such as Aristotle's suggestion that faint noises near the sleeper may infiltrate dreams as loud thunder (*On Divination Through Sleep* 463a3). Heraclitus, for example, thought dreams were nonpredictive and simply carried over into the dream state the concerns and anxieties of daily life. See H. D. Rankin, "Heraclitus on Conscious and Unconscious States," *Quaderni Urbinati di Cultura Classica*, New Series 50.2 (1995): 73–86.

39. Scholars have often asserted that a revelatory belief in dreams was virtually unanimous in antiquity. William Harris takes issue with such a blanket assertion, arguing instead that most people believed *some* dreams *could* be revelatory. In such instances, "The gods communicated, and one way they did so was by sending dreams" (123). See William Harris, *Dreams and Experience in Classical Antiquity* (Cambridge, MA: Harvard University Press, 2009), 123–228, in which he explores in detail ancient ideas regarding the truthfulness and trustworthiness of dreams.

40. For example, stele 27567 in the Egyptian Museum, Cairo, is a Hellenistic advertisement for a professional dream interpreter from Crete, who operates in Memphis. Standing only thirty-six cm tall, its inscription reads, "I interpret dreams, having a command from the god. With good fortune. The interpreter is Cretan." See Harris, *Dreams and Experience in Classical Antiquity*, 137.

41. This is perhaps an incomplete picture of contemporary approaches to dreams. The notion that dreams are predictive certainly persists in the modern West, and one can find any number of dream interpretation books and websites available. But most contemporary work on dreams ranges from cognitive–scientific to psychoanalytic. For a helpful bibliography, see

continually demonstrate that dreams are thought to originate externally.[42] For the less skeptical, dreams literally entered the sleeping mind from outside the body as messages, warnings, exhortations, and even attempts to deceive.[43] *Epiphany* or *theophany* dreams can be found diachronically from the eighth century through Augustine.[44] In Plato's *Crito*, Socrates claims that a female dream vision dressed in white announced to him the date of his execution (44ab). He claims in the *Apology* that dreams [ἐξ ἐνυπνίων] are one means by which god commanded him to "cross examine those who think they are wise but are really not so" (*Apol.* 33c).[45] And in the *Phaedo* he claims that his sudden endeavor at creating music and poetry comes from commands received in dreams (61b). Cicero's fictional *Somnium Scipionis* is certainly the most extended description of ancient epiphany dreams.

William G. Domhoff, *The Scientific Study of Dreams: Neural Networks, Cognitive Development, and Content Analysis* (Washington, DC: American Psychological Association, 2003); Rachel B. Blass, *The Meaning of the Dream in Psychoanalysis* (Albany: State University of New York Press, 2002).

42. A few examples include Pindar, *Pythian Ode* 4.163, *Olympian Ode* 13.66–80; Aeschylus, *Prometheus Bound* 645–660; Euripides, *Hecuba* 70–97; Sophocles, *Electra* 460, 645; Herodotus 1.34–36. The earliest Greek attestations to this are found in Homer. Here, Zeus has summoned a "dire dream" [οὖλον ὄνειρον] to visit the sleeping Agamemnon. To be clear, Agamemnon is not understood to "have a dream" in the sense that it is generated by his mind; rather, he is passively visited by a dream-figure while he sleeps. The poet recounts how a personified dream approaches: "He found him sleeping within his shelter in a cloud of immortal slumber. Dream stood then beside his head in the likeness of Nestor, Neleus' son, whom Agamemnon honored beyond all elders beside. In Nestor's likeness the divine Dream spoke to him: 'Son of wise Atreus breaker of horses, are you sleeping? He should not sleep night long who is a man burdened with counsels and responsibility for a people and cares so numerous. Listen quickly to what I say, since I am a messenger of Zeus, who far away cares much for you and is pitiful" (*Iliad* 2.18–27, Lattimore trans.). Harris, *Dreams and Experience in Classical Antiquity*, 24, has identified this passage as the earliest dream description in Greek literature. However, it is not the earliest mention of dream interpretation: Achilles suggests earlier in book 1 that they consult a dream interpreter [ὀνειροπόλον] to discover why Apollo is angry with the Achaians (1.63).

43. There are a number of literary instances in which the gods send intentionally misleading information by dreams. See, for example, *Iliad* 10.496; Herodotus recounts that in his dreams, the gods instructed Xerxes not to cancel his campaign against the Greeks. Xerxes was deceived by his dreams and lost the war, of course (7.12–19). In other instances, trusting dreams in general has proved misguided: A letter from one Apollonios to his brother Ptolemaios at the Memphis Serapeum survives in an archive of *ostraka*. Apollonios writes, "We have failed, being misled by the gods and trusting dreams." See Harris, *Dreams and Experience in Classical Antiquity*, 169.

44. The bones of St. Stephen, for example, were said to be revealed to the monk Lucian in a dream visit by the Rabbi Gamaliel in 415 CE. Lucian does not trust the dream initially. Gamaliel appears to him in three separate dreams, finally becoming angry and insisting that Lucian recover the bones. See Charles Freeman, *Holy Bones, Holy Dust: How Relics Shaped the History of Medieval Europe* (New Haven, CT: Yale University Press, 2011).

45. Harris, *Dreams and Experience in Classical Antiquity*, 25.

In Athenaeus' *Deipnosophistae* the painter Parrhasius claims to have been visited by Herakles in his dreams, so that he would know precisely how to depict the hero in a portrait (12.62).[46]

Because only some dreams were thought to be sent to the sleeper with cloaked information to be deciphered, skillful dream interpretation proved invaluable. Not only must one be able to distinguish a sign-bearing dream from a nightmare caused by indigestion, one must also be able to read the sign-bearing dream properly. Misinterpreting or ignoring a dream could spell disaster: Valerius Maximus recounts the death of the *equus* Haterius Rufus in a gladiatorial fight at Syracuse. In the previous night's dream Haterius had foreseen his death in the arena, and had even seen the face of his killer. When encountering his killer in real life the next day, he ignored the previous night's dream and indeed met his demise (*Memorable Deeds and Sayings*, 1.7.8).[47] Artemidorus' second-century *Oneirokritika* provides

---

46. Divine dreams were such a reliable trope that they were frequently used as propaganda in legitimating the power and authority of political and religious figures. Robin Wildfang examines the propagandistic qualities of dreams concerning the birth of Augustus, as found in Suetonius and Dio. The details—that his mother Atia dreamed of intercourse with a serpent and that her intestines were raised to the stars—echo the birth and conception dream narratives pertaining to Alexander the Great and even lesser Greek heroes such as Aratus and Aristomenes. Wildfang argues aptly that these dream sequences would have resonated successfully among subjects in the eastern areas of the empire. See Robin Lorsch Wildfang, "The Propaganda of Omens: Six Dreams Involving Augustus." In *Divination and Portents in the Roman World*, edited by Robin Lorsch Wildfang and Jacob Isager (Odense, Denmark: University of Odense Press, 2000), 43–56. Conversely, another dream sequence found in Suetonius would have provided better propaganda at Rome, as it relied on "conveniently dead" republican stalwarts (Quintus Catulus and Cicero) and the grand figure of Jupiter Optimus Maximus. In a dream of Quintus Catulus, the god chooses a boy with remarkable similarity to Augustus to safeguard the *signum rei publicae*—a clear endorsement of Augustus' right to rule. The next day Cicero is recounting his own dream in which a boy was let down from heaven on golden chains after which Jupiter handed the boy a whip. Cicero then sees Augustus in the flesh and confirms that he is indeed the divinely authorized boy. Compare the passages in Suetonius (*Divus Augustus* 94) and Dio (45.1.2) with those of Plutarch (*Alexander* 2.4–3.2), Lucian (*Dial Mort.* 13 and *Alexander* 7), Pausanias 4.14.4–7, and Justin 11.11.3–6. Also see Sulochana R. Asirvatham, "Olympias' Snake and Callisthenes' Stand: Religion and Politics in Plutarch's *Life of Alexander*." In *Between Magic and Religion: Interdisciplinary Studies in Ancient Mediterranean Religion and Society*, edited by Sulochana R. Asirvatham et al. (New York: Rowman & Littlefield, 2001), 93–125. The writer of the canonical gospel of Matthew does precisely the same thing in Jesus' birth narrative. Matthew 1.20–25 demonstrates Jesus' status as a divinely authorized figure by using a dream-figure messenger of God who informs Joseph of Mary's impending divine pregnancy. See Derek S. Dodson, *Reading Dreams: An Audience-Critical Approach to the Dreams in the Gospel of Matthew* (New York: T & T Clark, 2009).

47. Valerius Maximus is rather fond of the dream prediction. Of the eighteen dreams he recounts, almost half concern the narrow escape of death through correct interpretation of a dream or death as a result of ignoring a dream. Still others concern the confirmation of an impending, unavoidable death foretold in a dream.

five volumes of information on how to interpret one's dream visits and visions.[48] And Artemidorus is hardly the first specialist to publish his knowledge: he asserts that he has consulted the earlier work of Antiphon of Athens (2.14),[49] Aristander of Telemessus in Lycia (1.31), Panyasis of Halicarnassus (1.2, 1.64, 2.34), Nicostratus of Ephesus (1.2), Apollonius of Attalia (3.28), Alexander of Myndus, and Phoebus of Antioch (2.9). He tells us that Demetrios of Phaleron wrote five books on dreams, Geminus of Tyre wrote three, and Artemon of Miletus wrote twenty-two books on dreams (2.44).[50]

Through ritual incubation, mortals actively solicited dream visits from gods.[51] Most commonly attested is the practice of visiting the healing centers of Asklepius at Epidauros, Pergamon, Corinth, Athens, Kos, Lebena, and even Rome.[52] At an Asklepieion, the sick or injured visitor slept overnight in an *abaton* with the hope that the god would visit and cure his or her ailment in a dream. After being cured of an affliction ranging from paralysis, gout, and intestinal worms to chronic headaches and blindness, the healed person purchased and dedicated ceramic votive offerings in the shape of the healed body part. In other instances, public inscriptions [*iamata*] were dedicated, with descriptions of the cured aliments and dream visions.[53] Incubation

---

48. Artemidorus and Daniel E. Harris-McCoy. *Artemidorus' Oneirocritica: Text, Translation, and Commentary* (Oxford: Oxford University Press, 2012).

49. Cicero also claims that Chrysippus wrote a book on dreams, for which he used Antiphon as an authority. See *de Div.* 1.20.34.

50. Artemidorus, however, avoids discussing the divine origin of dreams. Rather, he emphasizes that dreams ought to be examined and interpreted very carefully, since they do bear meaning. His approach is one of classifying and systematizing dream interpretation, rather than considering *oneirogenesis*.

51. "Sought dream" is a term used by Serenity Young in her study on dreams and Buddhism, yet the term is certainly apropos here. See Serenity Young, "Buddhist Dream Experience: The Role of Interpretation, Ritual, and Genderm." In *Dreams: A Reader on the Religious, Cultural, and Psychological Dimensions of Dreaming*, edited by Kelly Bulkeley (New York: Palgrave, 2001), 9–28.

52. See M. P. J. Dillon, "The Didactic Nature of Epidaurian Iamata," *Zeitschrift für Papyrologie und Epigraphik* 101 (1994): 239–260.

53. Such practices persist today. For example, Christians in contemporary Rome often leave thank you notes at the feet of paintings or statues of saints; small "thank-you" inscriptions to the Virgin Mary can also be purchased and installed in public walls attached to churches such as near the basilica of Sant'Agnese fuori le mura. Such votive offerings of gratitude are often in the shape of the afflicted body part: eyes, breasts, feet, lungs, etc. See also Chapter 6 on reciprocity.

dreams were also received from Apollo, Amphiaros, Serapis, and other gods and heroes.[54]

Throughout the Hebrew Bible and LXX, God repeatedly visits Israelites in dreams.[55] There is also evidence of theophanic incubation dreams in these texts.[56] 1 Kings 3:5 and 2 Chr 1:5 depict God appearing to Solomon, when he sleeps near the altar at Gibeon.[57] As a boy, Samuel is visited by God as he sleeps near the Ark of the Covenant. In that divine dream-visit, Samuel is given prophetic insight into God's plans for Eli (1 Sam 3:2–15). The narration of Jacob's dream of the ladder does not start as a typical incubation dream, yet Jacob reacts by exclaiming that the precise spot where he slept must be the house of God but he did not previously know it. He erects a stone pillar to commemorate its status as a site with great proximity to God (Gen 28:10–22). While not always associated with the practice of divine healing, then, it appears that sleeping in or next to the house or temple of a god renders some people more likely to have a dream-visit from those gods.[58]

In his treatise *de Somniis*, Philo writes, "…Deity [τὸ θεῖον] sent the appearances which are beheld by man in dreams in accordance with the suggestions of his own nature" (*de Somniis* 1.1).[59] The Alexandrian classifies dreams in three ways, which descend in clarity as they are determined to be less directly authored by God. The first kind of dream is that in which God himself is the direct author. Such

---

54. Some examples of incubation dreams include Pausanias 1.34.5, Lycophron, *Alexandria* 1047ff, Strabo 6.284 (Daunia and Calchas), Vergil, *Aeneid* 7.81–95, Ovid, *Fasti* 4.649–664. Both Ovid and Vergil stress the antiquity of incubation dreams among Romans. Harris, however, disputes the antiquity of dream interpretation in general among Romans. He argues, for example, that incubation dreams may not have been part of the ritual at the temple to Asklepius at Rome. See Harris, *Dreams and Experience in Classical Antiquity*, 184.

55. In many instances, God sends a messenger angel in his stead. For an examination of the importance of dreams in the Hebrew Bible, see Ann Jeffers, *Magic and Divination in Ancient Palestine and Syria* (New York: Brill, 1996), 44, 125–139. Also see Robert K. Gnuse, *Dreams and Dream Reports in the Writings of Josephus* (New York: Brill, 1996), 68–100.

56. Robert Gnuse argues that the deliberateness of the incubation in the Hebrew Bible is left ambiguous lest it appear that Yahweh is coerced into theophany. Josephus appears to preserve the ambiguity, whereas Philo and other pseudepigraphic authors do not. For treatment of this reluctance, see Robert Gnuse, "The Temple Experience of Jaddus in the Antiquities of Josephus: A Report of Jewish Dream Incubation," *The Jewish Quarterly Review* 83.3–4 (1993): 349–368.

57. C. L. Seow, "The Syro-Palestinian Context of Solomon's Dream," *Harvard Theological Review* 77.2 (1984): 141–152.

58. These biblical incubation examples are treated briefly in Frances Flannery-Dailey, *Dreamers, Scribes, and Priests: Jewish Dreams in the Hellenistic and Roman Eras* (Leiden: Brill, 2004), 52.

59. Yonge translation.

dreams, for Philo, cannot be misinterpreted. A subset of this type of dream, and equally comprehensible, is that which is delivered by one of God's messengers, angels, or interpreters (1.190). The second kind of dream comes as a result of the resting mind being in unison with the mind of the universe and is therefore susceptible to divine impulses and receiving information regarding the future. This kind of dream is indirectly of divine origin and is therefore prone to mis-understanding. The third type of dream results in the sleeping mind agitating itself into a kind of frenzy [κορυβαντιᾷ] and inspiration [ἐνθουσιῶσα] so that it is capable of prognostication. This class, while also ultimately of divine origin, is the most prone to misinterpretation, and can be understood only through "the science of the interpreter of dreams" [τῆς ὀνειροκριτικῆς ἐπιστήμης] (2.4). Philo's *de Somniis* is an extensive treatise not on the nature of dreams, for he elaborates on that only briefly and occasionally. Rather, the purpose of the text is to elabo-rate on the proper interpretation of dreams in the Sacred Writings. He himself interprets (often allegorically) the dreams that were themselves interpreted in the original text.[60]

The Behavior of Animals and the Appearance of Their Parts
Augury and Birds in Flight

The use of birds in divination hung "on a sense of harmony between gods and birds, whereby benevolent gods send true signs by means of compliant messenger birds" (165).[61] Across the Mediterranean swans, eagles, hawks, swallows, chickens, and doves were some of the many birds to communicate the will and opinions of the gods. Divination through avian activity was common among Greeks, Romans, Etruscans, and Egyptians, but the practice took center stage among the Romans. Steven Green refers to augury as "the oldest and one of the most prestig-ious forms of religious practice at Rome."[62] Green also points out that by the late Republic, Roman intellectuals categorized augury as one of the three significant

---

60. While hardly a professional dream interpreter, Josephus also claims impressive *oneirocritical* skills. For example, he claims to have ascertained in a dream the triumph of Rome over Judeans (*War* 3.8.351–354). He further identifies other skilled Jewish dream interpreters: Simon the Essene (*Ant.* 17.345; *War* 2.112–113), Menahem who foresees Herod's rise to power (*Ant.* 15.373–379), and Judas who foretells the death of Antigonus (*War* 1.78–80, *Ant.* 13.311–313). For a more thorough treatment of Josephus' position on dreams and dream interpretation, see Gnuse 5–33.

61. Steven Green, "Malevolent Gods and Promethean Birds: Contesting Augury in Augustus' Rome," *Transactions of the American Philological Association* 139 (2009): 147–167.

62. Ibid., 147.

manifestations of Roman religiosity managed by priesthoods (the other two being rituals/*sacra*, and prodigies/portents). Pliny tells us that Roman *haruspices* possessed illustrated books for the identification of various bird species used in augury (*Nat. Hist.*10.37). The traditional understanding of the founding of Rome supposes that augury played a central role, and that Romans made no important decisions without taking the auspices.[63] In the later Republic, augury is part of the college of *pontifices*—state supported and part of public office.[64] Given that *augustus* is linked etymologically to the Latin *augur* (both words pertaining, ultimately, to *auctoritas*), Octavian adopts the name as a means of linking himself to that age-old means of listening to the gods (Green, 150).[65]

Avian signs indicated fortune as often as misfortune. According to Dio Cassius and Plutarch, Cleopatra became focused on inauspicious signs just prior to the Battle of Actium, when swallows were seen nesting on her flagship, the *Antonias*. In Dio's account, swallows built a nest around her tent and on her ship.[66] According to Plutarch, who calls the presence of the birds a "terrible sign" [*sēmeion deinon*], a second group of swallows attacked the nest and killed the nestlings.[67] Suetonius (*Aug.* 95) and Dio (46.46.2) claim that when taking the auspices during his first consulship in 43 BCE, Octavian sees an omen of twelve vultures nearby. Not only does Octavian determine that the sign is auspicious, he also understands it as an allusion to Romulus' augural sign of twelve vultures during the founding of Rome (Livy 1.6.3–1.7.3). The authors of the canonical gospels claim that a dove descends on the newly baptized Jesus, in order to legitimate Jesus' status, as well as the authority of the gospels' accounts.[68]

63. Livy 6.41.

64. Mary Beard, John North, and Simon Price, *Religions of Rome: A History* (Cambridge: Cambridge University Press, 1998).

65. Rosalinde Kearsley, "Octavian and Augury: The Years 30–27 B.C.," *The Classical Quarterly* 59.1 (2009): 147–166; Harold Y. McCulloch Jr., "Literary Augury at the End of 'Annals' XIII," *Phoenix* 34. 3 (1980): 237–242. In the *Res Gestae*, Augustus claims the title of augur.

66. Dio Cassius, 50.15.1–2. Christopher McDonough suggests that Dio adds the tent detail to evoke bird's nest omens in the stories of Antiochus and Alexander, son of Pyrrhus, also found in Aelius Aristides' *Attic Nights* 10.34. See Christopher McDonough, "The Swallows on Cleopatra's Ship," *The Classical World* 96.3 (2003): 251–258.

67. Plutarch, *Antony* 60.7. Swallows in the autumn (the battle took place on September 2) would have been a very unusual sight, and swallows in general were sometimes associated with retreat and fair-weather friends. See *Ad Herennium* 4.48.

68. Mark1.10–11; Matt 3.16; Luke 3.22; John 1.32.

This makes sense, insofar as many people understood augural birds to be directed by gods.[69]

Extispicy

Plutarch recounts that when Aemilius Paulus prepared for battle against Macedonian King Perseus at Pydna, the Roman and Macedonian soldiers were startled by a lunar eclipse. Aemilius sacrificed eleven heifers to the moon, and the next day undertook multiple sacrifices to Heracles, in pursuit of a favorable sign. Over and over again the Romans slaughtered oxen and read the entrails, waiting for Heracles to indicate that an attack against Perseus was advisable. Plutarch writes, " . . . but with the twenty-first victim the propitious signs [τὰ σημεῖα] appeared and indicated victory if they stood on the defensive" (*Aem.* 17.11).[70] In gratitude, Aemilius promised a hecatomb and games in the god's honor. Plutarch's account captures the central role that extispicy (reading animal entrails) played prior to making significant decisions.[71] Like lot oracles, the reading of animal entrails was a binary practice, allowing "yes/positive" or "no/negative" answers. Also, like the use of oracles, the divinatory reading of sacrificial entrails was widespread and millennia old by the first century CE. Cicero observes that, "nearly everyone uses entrails in divination."[72]

Extispicy appears to have originated with Babylonians and Assyrians in Mesopotamia and spread westward through the Hittites, to Greece, Etruria, and Rome (320).[73] Livers, hearts, lungs, and intestines revealed favorable and unfavorable information to the petitioner, drawn typically from oxen, sheep, goats, heifers, and bulls. Unlike the generic interpretation of eclipses or earthquakes, entrail interpretation required specialists trained in the anatomy of inner organs as well as training in how to connect variations in size, shape, and color to divine intentions.

---

69. Xenophon and Cicero attest to the pervasiveness of this idea: Xenophon, *Memorabilia* 1.1.3; Cicero, *de Div.* 1.120.

70. Plutarch, *Lives*. Translated by Bernadotte Perrin. Loeb Classical Library (Cambridge, MA: Harvard University Press, 1914).

71. See also Herodotus 6.76–92; Xenophon, *Hellenica* 3.1.17; Arrian 4.4.3.

72. *De Div.* 1.10; Marie-Laurence Haack, *Les haruspices dans le monde romain* (Pessac, France: Ausonius, 2003).

73. Derek Collins, "Mapping the Entrails: The Practice of Greek Hepatoscopy," *American Journal of Philology* 129.3 (2008): 319–345; Ulla Jeyes, "The 'Palace Gate' of the Liver: A Study of Terminology and Methods in Babylonian Extispicy," *Journal of Cuneiform Studies* 30.4 (1978): 209–233.

Hepatoscopy, the reading of livers, has left ample evidence even in the archaeological record. Dozens of model livers excavated in Palestine, Syria, and Anatolia may have been used for instruction in the *technē* or as practical reference guides for use in the act of interpretation.[74] The best known of these models, the Piacenza Liver, dated to 100 BCE, is divided into sixteen sections, each featuring the inscribed name of a deity. Each section and deity correspond to a section of the sky, as divided by Etruscans, making the liver a map of the heavens. A *haruspex* held the liver up to the sky, oriented to a specific direction, and thus gauged the intentions of the gods who controlled the regions of the sky correlating to the matching animal liver.

Reading the entrails of animals is not entirely arbitrary. On the contrary, the practice reflects widespread ideas about anatomy, semiotics, and divine presence. We have extensive evidence especially in the case of hepatoscopy. For Plato, the liver mediated the struggle between the reasoning and appetitive parts of the soul. The liver kept the appetite in check by transforming intellect and reason into a commanding sensation of fear. Such sensations caused the liver to swell or shrivel, to bend or harden, to open its ducts or shut them—depending on the conflict between reason and appetite. In some sense, the appetitive part is constrained through fear and the "stick" for beating fear into that part of the soul is the liver (*Timaeus* 71a–d4). Derek Collins has called the liver the "divinatory viceroy" of the appetitive part of the soul (328). Platonists are not alone in theorizing the relationship between the liver and divine communication. The Stoic notion of *sympatheia* likewise coheres with hepatoscopy. *Sympatheia* is the notion that all things in the cosmos are suffused with divine logos and interpenetrated with pneuma and therefore all parts are interconnected insofar as they are all parts of the cosmic whole. Thus, animals (and their parts) can sympathetically reflect divine energy and be used to express divine dispositions. Even earlier than Plato, the Stoics, and Etruscans, however, the Babylonians appear to have thought a healthy liver indicated the presence of a deity as much as an unhealthy liver indicated the absence of a deity (Collins 324; Bouché-Leclercq 1.130).

Plutarch's account of the Battle of Pydna also exemplifies the role that extispicy has in reciprocal relations with gods. Within a twenty-four-hour period, Aemilius offers thirty-two animals to the gods (eleven to the moon and twenty-one to Heracles). Such offerings are simultaneously petitions for endorsement and demonstrations of piety. After receiving positive signs from the god, he promises to return the kindness with extensive sacrificial offerings

---

74. Collins, "Mapping the Entrails," 325.

(the hecatomb), followed by games in the god's honor. Reciprocal benefaction, as we will see in Chapter 6, frequently involves divinatory signs in relation to mortal piety.

Terrestrial and Celestial Signs
Eclipses and Stars

Herodotus' description of eclipses—when "day suddenly turns to night"[75]—captures the logic behind why many believed that anomalies pointed to the involvement of gods in the world. The reversal of the typical pattern of things, especially celestial bodies, was widely understood as message-bearing. Diodorus Siculus describes the general panic and anxiety that eclipses produced among the Agathocles' forces when fighting the Carthaginians near Italy: "On the next day there occurred such an eclipse of the sun that utter darkness set in and the stars were seen everywhere; wherefore Agathocles' men, believing that the prodigy portended misfortune for them, fell into even greater anxiety about the future."[76] Philo claims that celestial bodies were created by the Judean deity not only to send light upon the earth, but also to "display signs [σημεῖα] of future events. For either by their risings, or their setting, or their eclipses, or again by their appearance or occultations, or by the other variations observable in their motions, men oftentimes conjecture what is about to happen" (*On Creation* 58.3, Yonge trans). He reiterates this sentiment in *On Providence*: "For eclipses are natural consequences of the rules which regulate the divine natures of the sun and moon; and they are indications either of the impending death of some king, or of the destruction of some city, as Pindar also has told us in enigmatical terms, alluding to such events as the consequences of the omens which I have now been mentioning" (frag. 2.50).[77] Elsewhere, Philo recounts in *The Life of Moses* that Moses brings a terrifying eclipse down on the Egyptians.[78] Pliny stops short of arguing that eclipses are sent by the gods, but claims that they foreshadow future

---

75. Herodotus 1.74, 7.37. For examination of whether this first eclipse, which frightened the Lydians and Medes into a truce, is historically plausible, see Alden Mosshammer, "Thales' Eclipse," *Transactions of the American Philological Association* 111 (1981): 145–155. Mosshammer claims that Herodotus' chronology is incorrect, and he places the eclipse at the wrong battle, in the wrong decade.

76. 20.5.5. Diodorus Siculus, *The Library of History*. Translated by Russel M. Geer. Loeb Classical Library (Cambridge, MA: Harvard University Press, 1954).

77. Pindar, frag. 74 is in response to a solar eclipse.

78. *Life of Moses*, 123ff.

events: "Portentous and protracted eclipses of the sun occur, such as the one after the murder of Caesar the dictator and during the Antonine war which caused almost a whole year's continuous gloom."[79]

According to Pliny, it was commonly believed that a star is allotted to each human being, the quality and brightness of that star being proportionate to the importance of the person to whom it is attached. We come by this information in Pliny because he disputes the idea by claiming that stars are attached to the firmament and that they do not, in fact, "fall when someone's life is being extinguished."[80] Comets, apparently, are a different story for Pliny: While discussing their different types he claims that "'Javelin-stars' quiver like a dart; these are a very terrible portent [*atrocissimo significatu*]" (*Nat. Hist.* 2.89).[81] He continues to describe the comet that appeared in the sky for seven days at the outset of Augustus' rule. The comet, Augustus claimed, was interpreted by the common people [*vulgus*] as evidence that Julius Caesar has been received among the gods. Privately however, according to Pliny, Augustus understood the comet as having been born specifically for him, and portended favorably for his own nascent rule *(Nat. Hist.* 2.94). This was also a trope used for propaganda: The author of the Gospel of Matthew depicts three *magoi* traveling to Jerusalem because they have seen Jesus' star ["his star," αὐτοῦ τὸν ἀστέρα], indicating the birth of a king.[82] Despite supposed prohibitions against astrology in the Hebrew Bible/LXX, we see quite clearly in numerous ancient Judean authors the interpretation of astrological events. Even in Gen 1:14, God creates and affixes stars [φωστῆρες] to the firmament in order to illumine the earth at night, to separate night from day, to track the passage of days and seasons, but also to be used as signs.[83]

Earthquakes

Almost all ancient writers who mention earthquakes speak of them as divine signs, often as a god's strategy to punish specific people. This is true among historians and explicitly literary authors, alike. Sophocles' Oedipus states "And

---

79. *Nat. Hist.* 2.99. Rackham trans.

80. *Nat. Hist.* 2.28 Rackham trans.

81. "acontiae iaculi modo vibrantur, atrocissimo significatu." Rackham trans.

82. Matt 2.2.

83. Evidence for Judean/Jewish participation in astrology amasses especially in late antiquity, given the number of synagogues with astrological motifs represented in mosaic form. See Rachel Hachlili, "The Zodiac in Ancient Jewish Synagogal Art: A Review," *Jewish Studies Quarterly* 9.3 (2002): 219–258.

he went on to warn me that signs [σημεῖα] of these things would come, in earthquake, or in thunder, or in the lightning of Zeus. Now I perceive that in this
journey some trusty omen [πτερὸν, pteron, *lit.* "winged thing"] from you has
surely led me home to this grove."[84] Josephus recounts how the Israelites are
about to be attacked, unarmed and unprepared, by the Philistines:

> for, in the first place, God disturbed their enemies with an earthquake,
> and moved the ground under them to such a degree, that he caused it to
> tremble, and made them to shake, insomuch that by its trembling, he made
> some unable to keep their feet, and made them fall down, and by opening
> its chasms, he caused that others should be hurried down into them; after
> which he caused such a noise of thunder to come among them, and made
> fiery lightning shine so terribly round about them, that it was ready to
> burn their faces; and he so suddenly shook their weapons out of their
> hands, that he made them fly and return home naked. (*Ant. Jud.* 6.27)

In the *Judean War*, Herod emboldens the Judeans to conquer the invading
Athenio and his Arabians, despite a devastating earthquake that has destroyed
much of the city, but none of the army. Rather than allowing the Judeans to take
the earthquake as a sign that God is against them, he reinterprets the sign to
argue that God is laying a trap for the Arabian invaders (1.373). Diodorus Siculus
claims that Alexander was eager to besiege and control the Aornus Rock because
of Heracles' earlier desire to do so. Heracles refrained, however, because of "sharp
earthquake shocks and other divine signs," making Alexander all the more eager to
do so, in order to surpass the earlier hero's accomplishments (*Biblioteca Historica*
17.85). Dio Chrysostom (*Orations* 38.20) comments on the irony of "blaming"
gods for plaguing humanity with earthquakes, yet congratulating and honoring
humans for comparable amounts of human suffering they cause through war.
Pliny comments not on earthquakes as punishment, but as portents: "The city of
Rome has never shaken without this being a premonition of something about to
happen" (*Nat. Hist.* 2.200). In discussing the demise of the war-thirsty Phlegyans,
Pausanias claims they were "completely overthrown by the god with continual
thunderbolts and violent earthquakes" (9.36.3).[85] The author of the Gospel of
Matthew uses the divine earthquake as a literary trope, such as when claims that

---

84. Sophocles, *Oedipus at Colonus*, trans. Richard Jebb (Cambridge. Cambridge University
Press, 1889), 94–97.

85. Pausanias, *Description of Greece*. Translated by W. H. S. Jones. Loeb Classical Library
(Cambridge, MA: Harvard University Press, 1918).

at the moment of Jesus' death, "the earth shook and the rocks were split." This divine *sēmeion* is so clear that a Roman centurion and other bystanders in the text are convinced that Jesus was the son of a god (27.51–54).

Thunder and Lightning

Like other celestial and terrestrial events of great energy and gusto, thunder and lightning were often interpreted as being sent by a god or gods. Nestor interprets Zeus' message for the Achaeans in the *Iliad*: "For he flashed lightning on our right, showing signs of favor" (2.353).[86] Pliny, while criticizing the divinatory association between gods and severe weather, refers to actual records regarding such interpretations: "Historical record also exists of thunderbolts being either caused by or vouchsafed in answer to certain rites and prayers" (*NH* 2.140). When describing a battle between Spartans and Athenians, Pausanias writes, "But the god caused the rain to descend more densely, with loud claps of thunder, and dazzled their eyes with lightning flashing in their faces. All this put courage in the Lacedaemonians, who said that heaven itself was helping them and as the lightning was on their right, Hecas the seer [ὁ μάντις] declared the sign of good omen [τὸ σημεῖον]" (Pausanias 4.21.7).[87] In his first-century BCE *Roman Antiquities*, Dionysius of Halicarnassus provides a vivid description of thunder-and-lightning interpretation in a war between Romans and Tyrrhenians. The demonstrative value of the passage warrants full citation:

> The Tyrrhenians, being irked by the prolongation of the war, taunted the Romans with cowardice because they would not come out for battle, and believing that their foes had abandoned the field to them, they were greatly elated. They were still further inspired with scorn for the Roman army and contempt for the consuls when they thought that even the gods were fighting on their side. For a thunderbolt, falling upon the headquarters of Gnaeus Manlius, one of the consuls, tore the tent in pieces, overturned the hearth, and tarnished some of the weapons of war, while scorching or completely destroying others. It killed also the finest of his horses, the one he used in battle, and some of his servants. And when the augurs [λεγόντων δὲ τῶν μάντεων] declared that the gods were foretelling [προσημαίνειν] the capture of the camp and the death of the most important persons in it,

---

86. Zeus thunders as a sign to the Trojans at 8.170, and flashes on the right again for the Greeks at 9.236.

87. W. H. S. Jones trans.

Manlius roused his forces about midnight and led them to the other camp, where he took up quarters with his colleague. The Tyrrhenians, learning of the general's departure and hearing from some of the prisoners the reasons for his action, grew still more elated in mind, since it seemed that the gods were making war upon the Romans; and they entertained great hopes of conquering them. For their augurs [μάντεις], who are reputed to have investigated with greater accuracy than those anywhere else the signs that appear in the sky [τὰ μετάρσια], determining where the thunderbolts come from, what quarters receive them when they depart after striking, to which of the gods each kind of bolt is assigned, and what good or evil it portends, advised them to engage the enemy, interpreting the omen [σημεῖον] which had appeared to the Romans in this wise: Since the bolt had fallen upon the consul's tent, which was the army's headquarters, and had utterly destroyed it even to its hearth, the gods were foretelling to the whole army the wiping out of their camp after it should be taken by storm, and the death of the principal persons in it. "If, now," they said, "the occupants of the place where the bolt fell had remained there instead of removing their standards to the other army, the divinity who was wroth with them would have satisfied his anger with the capture of a single camp and the destruction of a single army; but since they endeavoured to be wiser than the gods and changed their quarters to the other camp, leaving the place deserted, as if the god has signified that the calamities should fall, not upon the men, but upon the places, the divine wrath will come upon all of them alike, both upon those who departed and upon those who received them. And since, when destiny had foretold that one camp should be taken by storm, they did not wait for their fate, but of their own accord handed their camp over to the enemy, the camp which received the deserted camp shall be taken by storm instead of the one that was abandoned." (*Roman Antiquities* 9.6)[88]

This passage in Dionysius of Halicarnassus demonstrates the inescapability of the gods' presence in the world. The Tyrrhenians' divinatory specialists take upmost care in analyzing celestial signs to the point of determining the identity of the god attached to individual lightning bolts and the quadrant of the sky whence each strike arrives. Both the Romans and Tyrrhenians understand the destructive bolt to come from a divine source yet the Romans make the mistake

---

88. Dionysius of Halicarnassus, *Roman Antiquities*. Translated by Earnest Cary. Loeb Classical Library (Cambridge, MA: Harvard University Press, 1950).

of thinking the god in question has been appeased by destroying one specific encampment. In moving the army to join a nearby regiment, the Tyrrhenian seers take this to mean that the entire Roman army will be punished with divine wrath. Gnaeus Manlius' mistake is in thinking he can elude the very real and very serious intentions of a god, but the Tyrrhenians understood that such maneuvering is not possible for mortals.[89] The gods are very real, very present, and have their hand in human affairs.

Sneezing

Greek and Roman interpretations of sneezing have not warranted much scholarly attention since Arthur Stanley Pease's 1911 essay "The Omen of the Sneeze."[90] Like many of the day-to-day methods of reading the world for divine signs, sneeze interpretation appears to have been both widely practiced and highly criticized.[91] Frontinus provides us with an example of how one person's impulse to interpret a sneeze is dismissed on the spot by another. According to Frontinus, an Athenian naval pilot heard one of his rowers sneeze as they set out to battle. Judging the sneeze a negative sign, he ordered a retreat, to which his General Timotheus exclaimed "Out of so many thousands, do you really think it strange that one has had a chill?" (*Stratagems*, 1.12.11).[92]

Most commonly, however, sneezing served as a positive sign for "ratification of the truth" of words or actions being spoken or undertaken at the precise moment of the sneeze.[93] Xenophon recounts in the *Anabasis* that just as he was calling for the Hellenes to fight their way home to Greece, a man in the assembly sneezed. Unanimously, the soldiers understood the sneeze as a sign from Zeus. Xenophon then tells us "'I move, gentlemen, since at the moment when we were talking about deliverance an omen from Zeus the Saviour [οἰωνὸς τοῦ Διὸς τοῦ σωτῆρος] was revealed to us, that we make a vow to sacrifice to that god thank-offerings for

---

89. The outcome of the battle was inconclusive in the end, with the Tyrrhenians abandoning their camp after hours of fighting and after heavy Roman losses (*Rom. Ant.* 9.10–13)

90. Arthur Stanley Pease, "The Omen of the Sneeze," *Classical Philology* 6.4 (1911): 429–443.

91. Both the practice and the criticism continued into late antiquity. John Chrysostom rails against interpreting sneezes in his twelfth *Homily on the Epistle to the Ephesians*. He lambasts such practices as slavish, womanly, and ignorant. Augustine speaks against it in his *de Doctr. Christ* 2.20, as does Ambrose in *Sermo* 24.6.

92. Charles E. Bennett trans.

93. See W. R. Halliday, *Greek Divination: A Study of Its Methods and Principles* (Chicago: Argonaut, 1967), 176.

deliverance as soon as we reach a friendly land; and that we add a further vow to make sacrifices, to the extent of our ability, to the other gods also. All who are in favour of this motion,' he said, 'will raise their hands.' And every man in the assembly raised his hand" (*Anab.* 3.2.8–9).[94]

Perhaps the most curious discussion of sneezes is to be found in Plutarch's *de Genio Socratis*. The dialogue, likely written at the end of the first century,[95] is set during the Theban struggle for independence from Sparta in the late fourth century BCE—a topic Plutarch discusses elsewhere in his *Life of Pelopidas*. With the subject of Socrates at the heart of the dialogue's discussion, Plutarch deliberates on the nature of human motivation and daimonic guidance.[96] All participants in the discussion agree that Socrates was led by some kind of inner divine guide that enabled him to discern and navigate the world. The figure of Theocritus reports that this *daimonion* was supposedly a sneeze. Yet Polymnis disagrees because Socrates' actions were too certain and right to be guided by as minor a sign as a sneeze. Galixidorus disagrees with Polymnis by pointing out that a seer can actually derive quite important information from small signs that elude most people (582A–582B). The question then comes down to this: Did Socrates' *daimon* communicate with him directly, or did it communicate in some manner that needed interpretation? It is understood in the dialogue that divine signs appear to humans, even in the guise of sneezes. The figure of Simmias concludes that Socrates was so predisposed to divine guidance that his particular *daimon* communicated directly to him, without the need to interpret obscure signs.

---

94. Xenophon, *Anabasis*. Translated by Carleton L. Brownson. Loeb Classical Library (Cambridge, MA: Harvard University Press, 1922). Pease, "The Omen of the Sneeze," 431, argues that, depending on context, circumstance, and physical position of the person sneezing, a sneeze could be understood as an auspicious or inauspicious sign. Sneezing to the left or to the right could tell different things, for example. This left–right distinction is often manipulated for literary purposes; Catullus capitalizes on an ambiguity in poem 45, when he leaves the reader wondering if Amor sneezes approval or disapproval at the love between Acme and Septimius. His clause *Amor sinistra ut ante dextra sternuit approbationem* (lines 17–18) still puzzles classicists. See Edward Frueh, "*Sinistra ut Ante Dextra*: Reading Catullus 45," *The Classical World* 84.1 (1990): 15–21. Frueh (18) points out that among Latin poets, sneezing is frequently how Amor demonstrates the approval of two lovers. Aristotle mentions that a midnight sneeze is understood more [positively?] than a sneeze at midday (*Prob.* 33.11). See also Theocritus 7.96 and *Odyssey* 17.541–547.

95. For the dating of the text see the Introduction in the De Lacy translation, 370.

96. Scholars have not taken a great interest in this dialogue. For recent treatment, see Mark Riley, "The Purpose of Plutarch's *De Genio Socratis*," *Greek, Roman, and Byzantine Studies* 18.3 (1977): 257–273. Also see W. Hamilton, "The Myth in Plutarch's *De Genio* (589F–592E)," *The Classical Quarterly* 28.3 (1934): 175–182. For how this dialogue pertains to Plutarch's general attitude to *daimones*, see Frederick Brenk, "'A Most Strange Doctrine.' *Daimon* in Plutarch," *The Classical Journal* 69.1 (1973): 1–11.

Multiple Simultaneous Sēmeia

Multiple divine communicative signs were sometimes ascribed by ancient historians to major political events and leaders. Such descriptions drew on several methods of divination and interpretation simultaneously, such as dreams, the behavior of animals, meteorological events, and monstrosities. By the first century, the ascription of such diverse omens likely resulted from the constraints and expectations of living under an imperial authority that, since Augustus' reign, was consciously tied to divinity and simultaneously demanded allegiance by its subjects of all social classes. Richmond Lattimore accounts for at least twelve different portents and signs pertaining to Vespasian's ascent to power and the divine authorization of his rule.[97] Such signs included the oak tree of the Flavians, which issued a new shoot at the birth of each of Vespasia's (Vespasian's mother) children. The quality of the shoot indicated the character of the child, and Vespasian's shoot became a complete tree. A dog brought him a human hand. An ox burst into his dining room and lay submissively at his feet. Nero was told in a dream to bring the sacred chariot of Jupiter Optimus Maximus to Vespasian's house. In the time of Galba a statue of Divus Julius turned, of its own accord, to the east (Vespasian was from the east).[98] Vergil,[99] Tibullus,[100] Ovid,[101] and Dio Cassius[102] described scores of signs that portended the death of Caesar.[103] Such portents included an eclipse, the howling of dogs, ill-omened birds, eruptions of Etna, earthquakes in the Alps, speaking cattle, rivers standing still, blood in well-waters, thunderbolts from a clear sky, and comets.

Prior to the imperial period, Rome saw multiple disturbing omens around the year 130 or 129 BCE: *parhelia* [two suns] or *anthelion* [an alternative sun] were recorded (Cicero, *de Div.* 1.97; *de Nat. deorum* 2.14; *rep.* 1.15), two black snakes entered the shrine of Minerva (Obseq, *Liber Prodig.* 28a), a rain of stones, and a statue of Apollo that wept (Dio 24, frag. 84.2). Because these events were understood to be foreboding, a nine-day period of ritual expiation was ordered in early

---

97. Richmond Lattimore, "Portents and Prophecies in Connection With the Emperor Vespasian," *The Classical Journal* 29.6 (1934): 441–449.

98. Suetonius, *Vesp.*

99. *Georgics* 1.466–488.

100. Tibullus, 2.5.71.

101. *Metamorphosis* 15.782–798.

102. Dio, 45.17.

103. For brief discussion of such portents, see Margaret E. Hirst, "The Portents in Horace *Odes* I.2.1–20," *The Classical Quarterly* 32.1 (1938): 7–9.

129.[104] The confluence of multiple signs demanded attention. In the case of multiple signs that promoted the power of a political figure, such signs worked to legitimate power more thoroughly. In the case of multiple signs that foreshadowed some future disaster, sustained public action from the top down was required.

Excessive Concern for the Palpability of the Gods

Divinatory sign reading could also be taken too far by some ancient standards. Among Theophrastus' fourth-century BCE collection of character types that includes such examples as "The Boor," "The Flatterer," and "The Late-Learner," we find a description of "The Superstitious Man" [ὁ δὲ δεισιδαίμων].[105] Theophrastus describes the *deisidaimoniac* as "cowardly in relation to daimonic things" [δειλία πρὸς τὸ δαιμόνιον]. Because the character type is relatively brief but quite descriptive, a full citation is helpful:

> The Superstitious man [*ho de deisidaimōn*] is one who will wash his hands at a fountain, sprinkle himself from a temple-font, put a bit of laurel-leaf into his mouth, and so go about the day. If a weasel run across his path, he will not pursue his walk until someone else has traversed the road, or until he has thrown three stones across it. When he sees a serpent in his house, if it be the red snake, he will invoke Sabazius,— if the sacred snake, he will straightway place a shrine on the spot. He will pour oil from his flask on the smooth stones at the cross-roads, as he goes by, and will fall on his knees and worship them before he departs. If a mouse gnaws through a meal-bag, he will go to the expounder of sacred law and ask what is to be done; and, if the answer is, "give it to a cobbler to stitch up," he will disregard the counsel, and go his way, and expiate the omen by sacrifice. He is apt, also, to purify his house frequently, alleging that Hecate has been brought into it by spells; and, if an owl is startled by him in his walk, he will exclaim "Glory be to Athene!" before he proceeds. He will not tread upon a tombstone, or come near a dead body or a woman defiled by childbirth, saying that it is expedient for him not to be polluted. Also on the fourth and seventh days of each month he will order his servants to mull wine, and go out and buy myrtle-wreaths, frankincense, and smilax; and,

---

104. Tom W. Hillard, "Scipio Aemilianus and a Prophecy from Clunia," *Historia: Zeitschrift für Alte Geschichte* 54.3 (2005): 344–348.

105. For commentary see J. M. Edmonds, ed. and trans., *The Characters of Theophrastus* (Cambridge, MA: Harvard University Press, 1961).

on coming in, will spend the day in crowning the Hermaphrodites. When he has seen a vision, he will go to the interpreters of dreams [*oneirokritas*], the seers [*manteis*], the augurs [*ornithoskopous*], to ask them to what god or goddess [*tini theōn ē thea*] he ought to pray. Every month he will repair to the priests of the Orphic Mysteries, to partake in their rites, accompanied by his wife, or (if she is too busy) by his children and their nurse. He would seem, too, to be of those who are scrupulous in sprinkling themselves with sea-water; and, if ever he observes anyone feasting on the garlic at the cross-roads, he will go away, pour water over his head, and, summoning the priestesses [*hiereias kalesas*], bid them carry a squill or a puppy around him for purification. And, if he sees a maniac or an epileptic man, he will shudder and spit into his bosom.[106]

For Theophrastus, the person who engages in one or two of these practices is not superstitious. Rather, he points to the absurdity of the person who is so obsessive about oracle-seeking and sign reading that he cannot put one foot in front of the other without checking first with the gods or local divinatory specialists.

Such a criticism is echoed hundreds of years later, in Plutarch's *Peri Deisidaimonias*, in which Plutarch understands *deisidaimonia* to be at the far pole opposite atheism—both of which stand in contrast to ancestral *eusebeia* handed down by the gods (166B). Whereas atheism, for Plutarch, is an example of falsified [*diepseusmenos*] reason, *deisidaimonia* is an emotion [*pathos*] generated by false reason [*logou pseudos*]. Thus, dread of deities, which most translators render as "superstition," is problematic not only because it results from false ideas and reasoning, but because its emotional toll is hateful and drives people to paranoia or suicide: "Of all kinds of fear the most impotent [*apraktotatos*] and helpless [*aporōtatos*] is superstitious fear" (165D).[107] Plutarch cites several examples of mortals who have met with disaster or taken their own lives because dread overwhelmed them after reading signs.[108] For the person who is bombarded

---

106. Edmonds trans. For an examination of each of these practices, see W. R. Halliday, "'The Superstitious Man' of Theophrastus," *Folklore* 41.2 (1930): 121–153. See also James Diggle, *Theophrastus: Characters*. Edited with Introduction, Translation, and Commentary. Cambridge Classical Texts and Commentaries 43 (Cambridge: Cambridge University Press, 2004); Hugh Bowden, "Before Superstition and After: Theophrastus and Plutarch on *Deisidaimonia*," *Past & Present* 199.3 (2008): 56–71.

107. Plutarch, *Moralia*. Translated by F. C. Babbitt. Loeb Classical Library (Cambridge: Harvard University Press, 1928), vol. II.

108. Such examples include Midas, who committed suicide after a series of disturbing dreams, Aristodemus, king of the Messenians, who committed suicide after his *manteis* showed alarm over bad signs, and the general Nicias, who kept his navy paralyzed with fear over a lunar eclipse

everywhere by divinatory *sēmeia*, even sleep is no solace since signs and messages arrive there as well (165E–166A).

Ancient Theories and Critics of Divination

Although the overwhelming majority of people in antiquity read the physical world for signs and communication from gods, and thus the divinatory use of texts appeared secondarily, divinatory practices were hardly relegated to the illiterate or subsistence-level poor. Participation in and defense of such practices were taken up by literate intellectuals with an interest in philosophy, epistemology, and even the natural sciences.[109] Indeed, as we will see in the next chapter, some divinatory practices—including Paul's prophetic reading of texts—were rooted in literacy and intellectualism. Plato's *Timaeus*, while critical of some types of divination, provides scholars with a picture of how divinely inspired communication was understood among some intellectuals in antiquity:

> A sufficient token [σημεῖον] that God gave [δέδωκεν] unto humanity's foolishness the gift of divination [μαντικὴν] is that no one achieves true and inspired divination when in their rational mind [ἔννους], but only when the power of their intelligence is fettered in sleep or when it is overcome by disease or by reason of some divine inspiration [ἐνθουσιασμὸν π αραλλάξας]. But it belongs to an individual when in their right mind to recollect and ponder both the things said in a dream or waking vision [ὄναρ ἢ ὕπαρ] by the divine and inspired nature [ὑπὸ τῆς μαντικῆς τε καὶ ἐνθουσιαστικῆς φύσεως], and all the visions [φαντάσματα] that were seen, and by the means of reasoning to discern about them all how they are significant and for whom they indicate [σημαίνει] evil or good in the future, the past, or the present. But it is not the task of the person who has been in a state of frenzy, and still continues so, to judge the apparitions and voices [τὰ φανέντα καὶ φωνηθέντα] which they saw or uttered; for it was well said of old that to do and to know one's own and oneself belongs

---

(168F–169A). He also points to Judeans who allowed Jerusalem to be attacked and captured, rather than transgress the prohibition against work on the Sabbath: " . . . and they did not get up, but remained there, fast bound in the toils of *deisidaimonia* as in one great net" (169C). It is unclear if Plutarch here refers to the attack by Antony in 38 BCE or Pompey in 63 BCE. Plutarch, *On Superstition*. Translated by Frank Babbitt. Loeb Classical Library (Cambridge, MA: Harvard University Press, 1928).

109. The fact that literate intellectuals also practiced and defended various types of divination is further evidence that Stowers is correct about "unworkable" categories such as rural–urban religion or elite–poor religion.

only to those who are sound of mind. It is therefore customary to set up the tribe of prophets [τὸ τῶν προφητῶν γένος] to pass judgment upon these inspired divinations [ἐνθέοις μαντείαις]; and indeed, these are sometimes named "diviners" [μάντεις] by those who are wholly ignorant of the truth, that they are but interpreters of the mysterious words pronounced by means of enigmas [αἰνιγμῶν] and of those visions [φαντάσεως], but by no means diviners (μάντεις). The most just thing is to call them prophets, that is interpreters of what has been divined [προφῆται δὲ μαντευομένων]. (71e–72a)[110]

Timaeus makes two distinctions here, pertaining to states of mind and roles of practitioners. First, he distinguishes between the state of *enthusiasmos*, during which one is weakened by sickness, unguarded during sleep, or for some other reason susceptible to divine inspiration, and the state of being *ennous*—clearheaded, rational, and able to interpret the divine voices and images. Second, he distinguishes between the people who are engaging in such practices—the *mantis* is the vehicle through whom divine messages, images, and powers are delivered, and the *prophetēs* interprets. This reflects the specialists' roles at many oracle sites, as well as Paul's understanding of the distinction between those who speak in tongues versus those who interpret.

Cicero's *De Divinatione*, written as a kind of supplement to the *De Natura Deorum*, is a two-book treatise that deals with divination practices and the arguments that rationalize and explain divination.[111] In book 1, Cicero's brother, Quintus, defends such practices particularly as they are justified by Stoics. Quintus explains *divinatio* to a depth that the average farmer or artisan likely never felt compelled to explain. Book 2 provides Cicero's rebuttal, criticism, and refutation.[112]

---

110. W. R. M. Lamb, trans., *Plato in Twelve Volumes* (Cambridge, MA: Harvard University Press, 1925), vol. 9.

111. Schofield suggests that the topic of *de Div.* attracted Cicero "by the special opportunities for philosophical rhetoric which it afforded him" (47). *De Div.*, to Schofield, was an ideal topic in which to present a pro–contra argument regarding something widely practiced and valued. This further permitted him to bring Hellenistic philosophical discourse into the Roman rhetorical environment. See Malcolm Schofield, "Cicero for and Against Divination," *Journal of Roman Studies* 76 (1986): 47–65.

112. Similar to Schofield, Mary Beard suggests that Cicero's persona in book 2 should not be taken for Cicero's personal skepticism (he himself was an augur), but ought to be understood in the wider context as assimilating Greek philosophy to Roman practices. According to Beard, Cicero is in keeping with the academic tradition of laying out both sides of the argument without drawing the conclusion for the reader. See Mary Beard, "Cicero and Divination: The Formation of a Latin Discourse," *Journal of Roman Studies* 76 (1986): 33–46.

Cicero begins his discussion of divination by pointing out the ubiquity of it: He names the Greeks, Assyrians, Chaldeans, Egyptians, Cilicians, Pisidians, and Pamphylians as having divinatory specialists and techniques. Among Romans, he traces divinatory practices back to Romulus and Remus, as well as the Etruscans. Among philosophers he counts Pythagoras, Democritus, Socrates, Zeno of Citium, Dicaearchus the Peripatetic, and Chrysippus as supporting the legitimacy of divination, to one degree or another. He tells us that several philosophers had written books dealing with this very subject: Chrysippus wrote two books on divination, one book specifically regarding oracles, and another regarding dreams. Chrysippus' student Diogenes published on divination, as did Antipater and Posidonius (1.3.6).

He identifies two types of divination: one dependent on craft [*ars*] and one dependent on nature [*natura*].[113] This echoes earlier Greek distinctions between natural divination and *technē*—the former happens "naturally" in the form of dreams or unsolicited means, and the latter requires some skill and often employs devices like lots, bowls, dice, or entrails. Plato and Quintus find natural divination superior to and more trustworthy than *ars/technē*: "The ancients, then testify that in proportion as prophecy [μαντικὴ] is superior to augury [οἰωνιστικῆς], both in name and in fact, in the same proportion madness, which comes from god [μανίαν σωφροσύνης τὴν ἐκ θεοῦ], is superior to sanity, which is of human origin."[114] From Quintus' defense of the Stoic position on divination, we can count Stoics as among the strongest supporters of such practices, especially when they fit the criteria of being "natural."

Stoic positions on divination were the result of "careful reflection on the nature and structure of the universe," (125)[115] which reflected Stoic ideas of Providence, Fate, and cosmic *sympatheia*. Furthermore, divination worked insofar as it depended on the repeated observation of outcomes. For Quintus, repeated observation verifies the legitimacy of divination, even if mortals do not understand why it works. Quintus articulates two primary reasons why divination ought to be trusted: the reliance on verifiable observation of outcomes even when the reasons are uncertain, and the belief that gods have concern for mortals. Peter Struck redescribes this succinctly:

---

113. *De Div.* 1.6, 1.18.

114. Plato, *Phdr.* 244d. *Plato in Twelve Volumes.* Translated by Harold N. Fowler (Cambridge, MA: Harvard University Press, 1925), vol. 9.

115. R. J. Hankinson, "Stoicism, Science and Divination," *Apeiron: A Journal for Ancient Philosophy and Science*, 21.2, *Method, Medicine and Metaphysics: Studies in the Philosophy of Ancient Science* (Summer 1988): 123–160.

From a perspective that is tone deaf to the divine, the coincidental event is a sudden intervention that we just happen to run across. It is an event that takes place in our own world, whose capacity to carry significance and whose status as an omen grows entirely from its origin with the gods, which is by definition hidden from us. A bird might just be a bird and a chance meeting becomes a coincidence with meaning only when a god's hand is behind it. In fact, a simple coincidence might be said to be the sine qua non of meaninglessness. The ancient habit of seeing just these crystallizations of randomness as the ultrasignificant language of the divine dramatically points to a certain willful resistance to nonsense, as assertion of sense where none is by any logical definition possible.[116]

As Struck observes, the distinction between meaningless coincidence and meaningful omen depends on the involvement of gods. I would add to Struck's observation that divinatory practices function according to a logic and sensibility on two fronts. First, people regularly examine the world around them and make accurate predictions regarding future events, particularly with regard to weather, health symptoms, and anticipating the behavior of others. That the world can be read and interpreted by the movement of trees, spots on the skin, or suspicious behavior lends to the practice of reading innumerable things for innumerable reasons. Second, we have all experienced ourselves as the possessors of secret knowledge regarding the future of others. Person A may know that Person B will be robbed at noon today. An army regiment may know that its enemy will be surrounded and attacked tomorrow in the middle of the night. The parents of a child may know their child will be spending the summer at grandma's, long before the child herself knows. If mere mortals can possess exclusive information about the futures of others, prior to others' knowing it for themselves, and if those same mortals are certain about the superior knowledge of gods, it makes sense that gods are imagined to be the purveyors of exclusive knowledge regarding all kinds of people and events. Humans themselves regularly possess privileged information about the past, present, and future; why not the gods, who are far greater?

Criticism and Prohibition

Imagining that gods, dead ancestors, and other such beings habitually communicated with humans did not go unscrutinized in antiquity. Criticisms ranged from defending the dignity of gods (perhaps gods are too lofty to leave

---

116. Struck, *Birth of the Symbol*, 95.

signs for humans in the guise of birds or dreams) to dismissing the validity or effectiveness of specific divinatory practices (dreams may be less reliable than the flight of birds). Others argued against divination by means of the observed laws of nature insofar as fate can neither be escaped nor tampered with. Some critics targeted divinatory practices when practiced by other ethnic groups. I focus my attention on two significant sources of criticism, namely, book 2 of Cicero's *De Divinatione* and the Greek translation of the Hebrew Bible. Cicero captures the range of reasons why some ancients—many of them philosophically minded— were skeptical about divinatory practices. The Septuagint, on the other hand, appears to embody a deep tension between official prohibitions against divinatory practices while simultaneously condoning and even promoting them. That tension, or contradiction, comes as a result of renouncing the divinatory practices pertaining to other gods.

In book 2 of *De Divinatione*, Cicero attacks divinatory practices on several fronts. He begins by asserting that divination offers no special skills to equip mortals with living, in the way that doctors, navigators, mathematicians, and music teachers do. When one is ill, one consults a doctor and not a dream interpreter. When one travels by sea, the navigator—and not a *vates*—guides the ship. Divination specialists cannot calculate the circumference of the sun, nor can they divine the skills to learn the harp, provide moral guidance, or counsel generals on the next course of military strategy (2.3.9–2.4.12).[117] After this initial assessment of the uselessness of divination, Cicero's unfolding attack addresses four discrete problems. First, he argues for a logical flaw regarding divination vis-à-vis chance [*fortuna*] and fate [*fatum*]. Second, he argues that the laws of nature, which pervade all things, cannot be broken to allow for divination. He challenges the ethics of gods who would send obscure and unhelpful messages to mortals. Finally, he argues that the regular habit of sending messages regarding petty concerns is below the dignity of gods.

Unpredictable events happen in life, and this sense of chance is a fact of the universe for both Quintus and Cicero. Thus, Cicero argues, the gods cannot know exactly what will happen at every given moment. If the gods know every event in advance, "then the event is certain to happen. But if it is certain to happen, chance does not exist. And yet, chance does exist, therefore there is no foreknowledge of

---

117. Cicero is wrong, of course, insofar as dreams were frequently thought to accompany healing by Asklepius, and divinatory signs were an indispensable part of military strategy. See above on "Dreams and Dream Interpretation," "Augury and Birds in Flight," and Chapters 3 and 4 for more on dreams and healing, respectively.

things that happen by chance" (2.6.18).[118] Cicero suggests that if Quintus should like to emend his definition to include foreknowledge of things that are fated to happen (rather than those things subject to *fortuna*), then there is no use for divination since fate cannot be dodged or diverted. Auspices, oracles, lots, and extispicy are all useless practices in guiding humans on a safe course of action since to ignore an oracle would result in the same outcome as to obey an oracle. He backs his brother into a logical quandary: Events are either subject to chance, and can therefore not be foreseen, or things are fated, in which case divination is impotent in protecting mortals from what awaits (2.8.21).

Cicero then argues that laws of nature [*natura rerum*] would have to break in order to accommodate divination. He demonstrates this using a hypothetical example of learning, by means of extispicy, that he is on the verge of significant financial gain. He writes, "Assuming that all the works of nature are firmly bound together in a harmonious whole . . . what connection can there be between the universe and the finding of a treasure?"[119] He continues, "What natural tie, or what 'symphony,' so to speak, or association, or what 'sympathy,' as the Greeks term it, can there be between a cleft in a liver and a petty addition to my purse? Or what relationship between my miserable money-getting, on the one hand, and heaven, earth, and the laws of nature, on the other?" (2.14.33–34). Cicero denies the possibility that the lobes of an animal liver change, depending on the questions or fate of the petitioner who has chosen that particular animal for sacrifice. He then derides his brother for using the example of Caesar's offering of a sacrifice and finding no heart in the bull's chest cavity: "How does it happen that you understand one fact, that the bull could not have lived without a heart and do not realize the other, that the heart could not suddenly have vanished I know not where?" (2.15.37). Such instantaneous changes are contrary to empirical knowledge of anatomy and physiology.

Cicero lambasts the notion that gods would be so maleficent as to send useless and intentionally obscure messages. He queries, "In the first place, why do immortal gods see fit to give us warnings which we can't understand without the aid of interpreters? In the next place, why do they warn us of things which we cannot avoid?" (2.25.54).[120] To his mind, even mortals with a basic sense of

---

118. " . . . certe illud eveniet; sin certe eveniet, nulla fortuna est; est autem fortuna; rerum igitur fortuitarum nulla praesensio est." Cicero, *De Divinatione*. Translated by William Armistead Falconer. Loeb Classical Library (Cambridge, MA: Harvard University Press, 1923).

119. Falconer trans.

120. "Quid autem volunt di immortals primum ea significantes, quae sine interpretibus non possimus intellegere, deinde ea, quae cavere nequeamus?"

decency would not warn their peers of inescapable harm, since the resulting dread would be tantamount to torture. Further, Cicero refutes the notion that gods would speak to mortals in garbled speech, riddles, or by means of easily misunderstood techniques: "If we had the right to know what was going to happen, it should have been stated to us clearly: or, if the gods did not wish us to know, they should not have told us—even in riddles [*occulte*]" (2.25.55). This is particularly true for Cicero in the case of dreams: "It would, therefore, have been more in keeping with the beneficence of the gods, in consulting for our good, to send us clear visions in our waking moments rather than unintelligible ones in our dreams" (2.60.126).

Cicero takes greatest offense at the notion that gods would resort to lowly means of communicating with mortals: "Do you really believe that Jupiter would have employed chickens to convey such a message to so great a state?" He also places dreams in the arena of the lowly: "Do the immortal gods, who are of surpassing excellence in all things, constantly flit about, not only the beds, but even the lowly pallets of mortals, wherever they may be, and when they find someone snoring, throw at him dark and twisted visions, which scare him from his sleep which he carries in the morning to a dream-expert to unravel?" (2.63). He answers his own question explicitly: "My conclusion is that obscure messages by means of dreams are utterly inconsistent with the dignity of the gods" (2.64.135).

Cicero's critique of divinatory practices provides an ideal example of the tension between modes of religiosity. His arguments, dependent on extensive reflection and philosophical interests, go against widespread assumptions about the degree and manner in which divine beings take an interest in human affairs and participate in reciprocal acts of communication. Cicero's argument is an example of the type of cerebral theologizing of the religion of the literate cultural producer; gods are "of surpassing excellence in all things" and would, therefore, never deign to send trifling messages about human fate. As is common in this mode of religiosity, the practices and default assumptions of the religion of everyday social exchange are critiqued or sometimes dismissed entirely. Yet, Cicero himself does not escape that default mode, insofar as he was a member of the college of augurs, as of 53 BCE—perhaps the most prestigious position in the Republic. His support for augury, however, derived from its value to the state, *rei publica causa* (*de Div.* 2.75).[121] One continues to engage in augury, that most venerable of Roman forms of divination, out of respect for tradition and stability of the social order. Contrary to Cicero's critiques, most people in antiquity would have agreed

---

121. C. Wayne Tucker, "Cicero, Augur, De Iure Augurali," *The Classical World* 70.3 (1976): 171–177.

with Plutarch's Galixidorus, who claims that a seer can read divine information in the smallest of signs, to which most people are oblivious (*De Genio Socratis*, 582A–582B). Thus, Cicero, Plutarch, and others like them are capable of engaging in different modes of religiosity to suit specific needs, but gravitate toward the deliberative, theoretical mode.

Prohibitions in the Hebrew Bible and Its Greek Translation

Despite the prohibition against specific types of divinatory and so-called magical practices in parts of the Hebrew Bible and its Greek translation(s), abundant evidence demonstrates that Israelites and later Judeans engaged in taxonomically similar practices of their immediate neighbors and, later, of those across the Roman Empire.[122] Armin Lange observes that a full monograph would be required simply to document the use of dreams in the Hebrew Bible, not to mention the many other divinatory practices described therein.[123] The excavation of magic bowls, curse tablets, incantations, and the presence of Near Eastern astrology from the Dead Sea Scrolls to the Talmud indicate that canonical proscriptions were often ignored.[124] This fact provides ample rebuttal to scholars who might argue that Paul eschews such practices because they are forbidden to his *ethnos*.

At first glance, several passages appear to prohibit divinatory practices altogether. Exodus 22:17 commands, "You shall not procure sorcerers [φαρμακοὺς]." Several passages in Leviticus outlaw the practices of bird augury and seeking the

---

122. Several studies have explored divinatory and magical practices among Israelites and later Judeans. See, for example, Frederick H. Cryer, *Divination in Ancient Israel and Its Near Eastern Environment* (Sheffield, UK: Sheffield Academic Press, 1994); Ann Jeffers, *Magic and Divination in Ancient Palestine and Syria*. For her understanding of the distinction between magic and divination, see pp.1–4.

123. Armin Lange, "The Essene Position on Magic and Divination." In *Legal Texts and Legal Issues: Proceedings of the Second Meeting of the International Organization for Qumran Studies*, edited by Moshe Bernstein et al. (New York: Brill, 1997), 392.

124. Dan Levene, *A Corpus of Magic Bowls: Incantation Texts in Jewish Aramaic From Late Antiquity* (New York: Keegan Paul, 2003); Robert M. Berchman, ed., *Mediators of the Divine: Horizons of Prophecy, Divination, Dreams, and Theurgy in Mediterranean Antiquity* (Atlanta, GA: Scholars Press, 1998). Helen Jacobus, *Zodiac Calendars in the Dead Sea Scrolls and Their Reception: Ancient Astronomy and Astrology in Early Judaism* (Leiden: Brill, 2014); Mark Geller, "Deconstructing Talmudic Magic." In *Magic and the Classical Tradition*, edited by C. Burnett, W. Ryan (London: Warburg Institute, 2006), 1–18; Gideon Bohak, "Prolegomena to the Study of the Jewish Magical Tradition," *Currents in Biblical Literature* 8 (2009): 107–150; Nissenin, "Prophecy and Omen Divination," 342.

services of a divinatory–ventriloquist (*lit.* "belly-talker").[125] Deuteronomy 18 is
the most thorough of such prohibition passages:

> There shall not be found among you one who cleanses his son or his
> daughter by fire [περικαθαίρων . . . ἐν πυρί), one who practices divina-
> tion [μαντευόμενος μαντείαν], one who acts as diviner [κληδονιζόμενος],
> one who practices ornithomancy [οἰωνιζόμενος], a sorcerer [φαρμακός,],
> one who casts spells [ἐπαείδων ἐπαοιδήν], a ventriloquist and one who
> observes signs [ἐγγαστρίμυθος καὶ τερατοσκόπος], and one who inquires
> of the dead [ἐπερωτῶν τοὺς νεκρούς]. (Deut 18.10–11, NETS)

This passage is part of Moses' instructions to the Israelites as they are about to dispossess the Canaanites of land after escaping Egypt and wandering through the
desert. Moses provides guidelines for determining legitimate Israelite authority
in the future, as well as the religious practices that will distinguish Israelites from
their gentile neighbors. Gideon Bohak observes that this list of prohibitions does
not target specific practices, but the practitioners themselves, "who are presented
as the exact opposite of the God-sent prophet. To him one may listen, to them
one may not."[126] Indeed, Moses continues in the Deuteronomy passage to claim
that God will raise up a prophet, and explains how to distinguish a God-sent
prophet from a false prophet.[127] This passage appears not to problematize the
practices because they pertain to divination or even "magic," but because they
"are the religious customs of the pre-Israelite dwellers of the land of Canaan"
(Bohak 16).

---

125. Lev 19.26: "You shall not practice bird augury [οὐκ οἰωνιεῖσθε] or interpret bird signs [οὐδὲ
ὀρνιθοσκοπήσεσθε]"; Lev 19.31: "Do not turn to mediums (*lit.* "belly-talkers" [ἐγγαστριμύθοις])
or enchanters [ἐπαοιδοῖς]; do not seek to be defiled by them."; Lev 20.6 and 20:27, likewise,
prohibit the ἐγγαστρίμυθος (*lit.* "belly-talker") and charmer [ἐπαοιδός], demanding that both
types of practitioners be condemned to death. See also Num 23:23: "There is no bird augury
[οἰωνισμὸς] in Jacob, no divination [μαντεία] in Israel."

126. Gideon Bohak, *Ancient Jewish Magic: A History* (Cambridge: Cambridge University
Press, 2008), 14.

127. In telling Moses of a future prophet, the Lord instructs him on how to determine a real
prophet from a fake: "Any prophet who speaks in the name of other gods, or who presumes
to speak in my name a word that I have not commanded the prophet to speak—that prophet
shall die. You may say to yourself 'How can we recognize a word that the Lord has not spoken?'
If a prophet speaks in the name of the Lord but the thing does not take place or prove true,
it is a word that the Lord has not spoken" (Deut 19.20–22). Paul echoes this sentiment when
discussing his competitors (1 Cor 14:37–38). Likewise, the second-century *Didache* is concerned with discerning a true from a fake prophet (*Didache* 11).

The proscribed divinatory practices are characteristic of outsider groups. Thus, such passages forbid them not because they do not work, but because Israelite participation in such practices would constitute disloyalty to the Israelite God: "For anyone who does these things is an abomination to the Lord your God, for it is because of these abominations that the Lord your God will destroy them utterly from before you. You shall be perfect before the Lord your God" (Deut 18.12–13, NETS).[128] Likewise, Leviticus 20:6–8 forbids bird augury and belly-talking prophecy in the same breath that it insists on loyalty to the Israelite god. The Deuteronomist insists on a clear distinction between Israelites and those whose land they are about to take, and such a distinction is found partly in the methods of communicating with gods: "For these nations that you are about to dispossess, these will hear omens and divinations [κληδόνων καὶ μαντειῶν], but as for you, the Lord your God has not granted you to do so." (Deut 18.14, NETS).[129] The text does not call into question the success of the divining or magical practices of nearby peoples because it is understood that gods *do* leave signs in the world and that humans have developed skills for discerning their gods' thoughts and intentions, as well as techniques for channeling divine powers. Furthermore, such prohibitions place divine communication in the hands of a local priestly elite. As Ann Jeffers suggests, "This is not so much a rejection of forms of magic and divination as a takeover by the priestly order with the aim to control the means of divine communication. This apparently successful takeover of magic and divination has resulted in both its assimilation into controlled forms and in unequivocal condemnations of the forms that could not be controlled" (634).[130]

If the seeking out and interpreting of *sēmeia* are not practiced in relation to the deity of the Israelites, such passages strictly forbid them.[131] Yet the Hebrew Bible and LXX provide extensive examples of the presence of divinatory specialists among Israelites, most especially Moses, but also Aaron, Elijah,

---

128. (12) ἔστιν γὰρ βδέλυγμα κυρίῳ τῷ θεῷ σου πᾶς ποιῶν ταῦτα· ἕνεκεν γὰρ τῶν βδελυγμάτων τούτων κύριος ἐξολεθρεύσει αὐτοὺς ἀπὸ σοῦ. (13) τέλειος ἔσῃ ἐναντίον κυρίου τοῦ θεοῦ σου.

129. (14) τὰ γὰρ ἔθνη ταῦτα, οὓς σὺ κατακληρονομεῖς αὐτούς, οὗτοι κληδόνων καὶ μαντειῶν ἀκούσονται, σοὶ δὲ οὐχ οὕτως ἔδωκεν κύριος ὁ θεός σου.

130. Ann Jeffers, "Magic and Divination in Ancient Israel," *Religion Compass* 1 (2007): 628–642.

131. This is true of divinatory practices, as well as so-called magic. As Stephen Ricks observes, "it is not the nature of the action itself, but conformity of the action (or actor) to, or deviation from, the values of Israelite society—as these values are reflected in the canonical text of the Bible—that determines whether it is characterized as magical." See Stephen Ricks, "The Magician as Outsider in the Hebrew Bible and the New Testament." In *Ancient Magic and Ritual Power*, edited by Marvin Meyer and Paul Mirecki (Boston: Brill, 2001), 131.

and Elisha.[132] Such practices even become stereotypical of Judeans, in the eyes of Romans. In his sixth *Satire*, for example, Juvenal lampoons a "palsied Jewess" who tells fortunes and interprets dreams for "the minutest of coins" (*Satire* 6.542–547).[133] Paul's immediate competitors, presumably Judeans whom he calls "super-apostles" [*huperlian apostoloi*], are clearly capable of the same divinatory and wonderworking feats as he.[134]

The practices we see proscribed in Exodus, Leviticus, Numbers, and Deuteronomy use polemical Greek terms that describe things Israelites and Judeans themselves did on a regular basis, but in orientation (at least, officially) to their sole prescribed deity. This is not unlike the author of Acts using the term *magos* in a derogatory manner to identify Peter's most stringent competitor, Simon, while Peter engages in identical feats of divination and wonderworking.[135] The "prophet" is the premier divinatory specialist sanctioned by the Hebrew Bible/LXX; such a figure can foretell the future, interpret signs, part waters, turns his staff into a snake, and deliver the very specific commands of a god. The title *apostolos* will come to occupy similar legitimacy and prestige in early Christianity. The ontological uniqueness applied to prophets of the LXX reflects the methodological problems of taxonomy discussed in Chapter 1.

Conclusion

This chapter demonstrates the breadth and pervasiveness of divinatory practices in antiquity. Such practices cohere with widespread ideas about gods and other divine beings: that they are interested in human affairs, that they are (usually) invisible but occupy a palpable presence in the world, and that they communicate to people using signs [*sēmeia*]. Through overtaking the speech faculty of mortals, appearing in dreams, effecting internal organs of animals or directing their behavior, and by generating a range of celestial, terrestrial, or involuntary bodily movements, gods were understood to exert themselves in the world. Indeed, I have examined here a small number of ways in which ancients sensed that palpability and presence. Paul does not appear to have engaged in every practice

---

132. 2 Kgs 2.14, 2.24, 3.14–20, 4.15–17, 4.32–34. Additionally, many instances of divination by means of Urim and Thummim are carried by the high priest in his breastplate or ephod. See 1 Sam 2:28, 14:18 (Ahijah wears the ephod with Urim and Thummim); 1 Sam 23:9–12, 30:7 (David frequently consults the oracle–prophet Abiathar, who dons the ephod for divination).

133. Loeb Classical Library edition, translated by G. G. Ramsay, 1928.

134. 2 Cor 11:5.

135. Acts 8:9–24.

examined here, but understanding the breadth of such practices helps us to contextualize Paul within his chronological and cultural milieu.

Divinatory practices are not theologically impoverished nor are they specifically "pagan" in any meaningful sense of the word. Such practices simply mediate information beyond the realm of possible human knowledge by extrapolating from clues left in the world, or, in other words, by "reading in" to the world. These practices make sense only in the context of reciprocal relations with gods and spirits who care to communicate with people to begin with. Not only did Greeks and Romans widely assume that such beings did care to communicate, but so did ethnic Judeans, including Paul. To Paul's mind, in fact, his god cares the greatest.

3

A *Taxonomy of Paul's*
Divinatory Practices

THE PREVIOUS CHAPTER demonstrated that Greeks, Romans, Judeans, and others in the ancient Mediterranean assumed the interest, palpability, and communicativeness of gods and other divine beings. Because gods took an interest in human affairs and because they had power and knowledge far beyond that of mortals, it was common to turn to them for aid and supplementary knowledge. The basic assumption that gods existed and participated in the world in practical ways is a fundamental aspect of the mode of religiosity that replicates features of everyday living. This includes reciprocal practices of communication and benevolence. Gods were regularly petitioned for information, and they frequently provided unsolicited information or endorsement.

Building on the ubiquitous and fundamental sense of divine palpability I have already explored, the following chapters will make sense of Paul's many divinatory and miracle-working practices. Far from being taxonomically unique or even specifically "Christian," such practices would be recognizable to his readers, followers, and others around him. This chapter examines Paul's divinatory practices, whereas Chapter 4 will examine Paul's wonderworking practices. I offer three primary categories for Paul's divinations, populated by constitutive examples from which the categories derive their distinctiveness, illustrated in Figure 3.1.

These three broad categories include numerous practices such as Paul's claim to recognize and interpret the meaning of *sēmeia*, a practice he calls *glōssai* (or, speaking in tongues), the practice of oral prophesying, and a form of prophecy grounded in literacy and allegorical interpretation. This chapter provides numerous *comparanda* that allow us to contextualize and make sense of Paul's divinations. Such contextualizing involves discovering the shared practical

Divinatory Practices
• Interpretation of non-verbal divine signs or communications
• Channeling information from a divine source through speech or verbal sound of a human agent
• Use of literary texts or written symbols to discern divine information or disposition

FIGURE 3.1 A taxonomy of Paul's divinatory practices.

understandings that Greeks, Romans, and ethnic Judeans would have held with regard to such activities and claims.

Paul's Divinatory Repertoire

Paul's divinatory practices fall into three types. First, he interprets nonverbal cues as encrypted messages from the Judean deity. Like other Greek speakers, he calls such things *sēmeia* [signs]. As we saw in Chapter 2, the range of things that counted as "signs" was indeed vast. Second, Paul channels divine messages by means of verbal communication. He does this in two distinct ways: through the utterance of unintelligible sounds or language, which he calls *glōssai*, and through intelligible sounds that he calls *propheteia*. Finally, Paul uses literary texts, written symbols, or both, to discern predictive information from the Judean deity. For Paul, as for other Greek speakers, interpreting texts in such an oracular way is also a kind of prophecy. These do not account for the full range of ways that Paul's contemporaries would engage in divination; we cannot say, for example, whether Paul used oracle pebbles, drew lots, or employed any other types of objects for discerning divine will. We can surmise that Paul did not interpret animal entrails, given that he never mentions the practice and his position on animal sacrifice is complicated at best. Among the innumerable approaches to divination in antiquity, the three broad categories I just outlined account for Paul's divinatory expertise for which we have incontrovertible evidence.

Interpretation of Nonverbal Divine Signs or Communications

In Rom 15:19 Paul writes, "For I will not dare to speak of anything except what *Christos* has accomplished through me to lead the gentiles to obedience by word and deed, by the power of signs and wonders [*en dunamei sēmeiōn kai teratōn*] by

the power of the pneuma" (NRSV, modified). What does Paul mean by *sēmeia* and *terata* [signs and wonders]? His terminology matches that used by Greek speakers to describe communication from gods and other divine beings, as well as the evidence of divine authorization or endorsement. As we saw in Chapter 2, the discernment and interpretation of *sēmeia* was perhaps the most widespread way to characterize divinatory practice in antiquity. A *sēmeion* was the means par excellence through which gods communicated to people, and we have an abundance of evidence suggesting that people spent a great deal of time and energy perfecting and disputing how to identify and interpret *sēmeia*. Paul uses variations of *sēmeion* six times in his undisputed letters: Rom 4:11 and 15:19; 1 Cor 1:22 and 14:22; twice in 2 Cor 12:12.[1] Not all of these uses pertain to a study of wonderworking and divinatory practices, but all uses demonstrate what Clifford Ando has called the empiricist basis of many religious practices in antiquity.[2]

James Allen draws attention to the two subtly distinct meanings of *sēmeion*: evidence or proof of something, or a cryptic message of divine origin.[3] More often than not, Paul uses *sēmeia* in the sense of "evidence." This is clear in 1 Cor 14:22 when he tells his readers "Tongues, then, are a *sēmeion* not for those who are steadfast [*pisteuousin*] but for the unfaithful [*apistois*]."[4] Likewise, in Rom 4:11 he claims circumcision is a kind of evidence [*sēmeion*] or marker indicating Abraham's righteousness, and in 2 Cor 12:12 he writes "The *sēmeia* of a [true] apostle were performed among you with utmost patience—signs and wonders and mighty works [σημείοις τε καὶ τέρασιν καὶ δυνάμεσιν]." What appears in 2 Cor 12:12 to be a sort of taxonomic tautology ("The signs performed among you were the signs and wonders . . . "), is in fact an example of the two different usages of *sēmeion*.[5] Paul's first use in 2 Cor 12:12 indicates empirical evidence or proof, while

---

1. *Sēmeia* is also used in the pseudo-Pauline 2 Thess 2:9, 3:14, 3:17; Heb 2:4.

2. While Ando makes a distinction between Roman and Greek religious sentiments, I think many of his ideas of Rome can, in fact, be extended to nearly all cultures of the ancient Mediterranean. He writes, "They [Romans] sought information through observation of the actions of the gods in the world . . . . And insofar as that information was acquired through sense perception, it was knowledge of a very particular kind." This, he calls an "empiricist epistemology" (Ando, Preface). I would argue that the Romans were no more or less empiricist than Greeks, Judeans, or Egyptians, but *how* they went about obtaining information may have been distinctive in the way that many cultural practices are distinctive.

3. James Allen, *Inference From Signs: Ancient Debates About the Nature of Evidence* (Oxford: Clarendon, 2001).

4. "ὥστε αἱ γλῶσσαι εἰς σημεῖόν εἰσιν οὐ τοῖςπιστεύουσιν ἀλλὰ τοῖς ἀπίστοις."

5. Both Harris, *The Second Epistle to the Corinthians*, 2005, and Lambrecht, *Second Corinthians*, 1999, agree with the two meanings of *sēmeia* in their commentaries on 2 Corinthians.

the second usage indicates cryptic information of divine origin that depends on the skills of a specialist to reveal and interpret.

This second usage of *sēmeia* is most pertinent. On two occasions Paul claims to not only discern what is and is not a sign, but he can also interpret the signs once he has identified them—two aspects of the divinatory practice of sign reading that are inextricably related. Paul first refers to this practice in 2 Cor 12:12. Just prior to the passage, he claims to have experienced divine visions that—at least on one occasion— include being swept up to the third heaven (2 Cor 12:1–10). It is then that he tells them the signs of a [true] apostle were performed among them ("signs, wonders, and mighty works").[6] The second passage is Rom 15:19 previously recounted.[7] Here, the indisputability of divine signs apparently carried a force so great that some gentiles became obedient to Paul's gospel message. In both passages Paul remains vague and refrains from naming specific signs or wonders. Were they lightning bolts that struck at the moment he made a grandiose claim? Were sick followers healed from the brink of death by means of his intercessory powers with God? Were various people suddenly overcome with indecipherable speech? If his claim is true—that such things were performed in front of his followers—then presumably he assumes some of them will recall it. Thus, while we cannot know precisely what Paul's *sēmeia* and *terata* were, the abundance of examples in Chapter 2 certainly provides us with possibilities.

Paul likely derives the phrase "signs and wonders" [*sēmeia kai terata*] from the Septuagint, although the words occur in close proximity to one another elsewhere in Greek texts. Polybius, Dionysius of Halicarnassus, Plutarch, Appian, and Artemidorus use *sēmeia kai terata* together as a unit, sometimes with minor variations.[8] In the LXX *sēmeia kai terata* occur most commonly in Exodus and Deuteronomy and refer to the events surrounding Moses, Aaron, and Pharaoh.[9] At Exod 7:9, the Lord says to Moses "And if Pharaoh should speak to you, saying, 'Give us a sign or wonder,' you also shall say to Aaron, your brother, 'Take the rod, and throw it upon the ground before Pharaoh and before his attendants,

---

6. "οὐδὲν γὰρ ὑστέρησα τῶν ὑπερλίαν ἀποστόλων, εἰ καὶ οὐδέν εἰμι. (12) τὰ μὲν σημεῖα τοῦ ἀποστόλου κατειργάσθη ἐν ὑμῖν ἐν πάσῃ ὑπομονῇ, σημείοις τε καὶ τέρασιν καὶ δυνάμεσιν."

7. οὐ γὰρ τολμήσω τι λαλεῖν ὧν οὐ κατειργάσατο Χριστὸς δι' ἐμοῦ εἰς ὑπακοὴν ἐθνῶν, λόγῳ καὶ ἔργῳ, (19) ἐν δυνάμει σημείων καὶ τεράτων, ἐν δυνάμει πνεύματος.

8. Polybius, 3.112.8; Dionysius of Halicarnassus, *Ant. Rom.* 12.11.3; Plutarch, *Alex.* 75.1, *Dion* 24.6, *Septem sapientium Convivium* 149C; Appian, *Bellum Civile* 2.5.36, 4.1.4; Artemidorus, 3.28; Philo, *Life of Moses* 1.95.6, 1.178.1; *Special Laws* 2.218; *On the Eternity of the World* 2.6; Josephus, *Ant* 20.168; *de Bello* 1.28.

9. Exod 7:3, 7:9, 11:9, 11:10; Deut 4:34, 6:22, 7:19, 11:3, 13:2, 13:3, 26:8, 28:46, 29:2, 34:11.

and it will be a dragon'" (NETS). Aaron does precisely this when called before
Pharaoh, and his staff turns into the promised serpent. Pharaoh summons his
wise men [τοὺς σοφιστὰς Αἰγύπτου καὶ τοὺς φαρμακούς] [spell casters or charmers]
and sorcerers [identified as the enchanters of the Egyptians—οἱ ἐπαοιδοὶ τῶν
Αἰγυπτίων] who perform the same feat. The source of their power to transform
objects, however, is derisively called *pharmakeia*. Aaron's abilities not only come
from the correct deity; they are also superior to the others' powers, and thus his
staff wholly swallows theirs.

It is possible that *sēmeia kai terata* is a hendiadys whose meaning is actually
wondrous signs. Yet, in many cases it is clear that *signs* and *wonders* are understood
to be two distinct things. In his commentary on Romans, Origen writes "They
are called 'signs' in which is indicated that there is something miraculous or something will be. Wonders, on the other hand, refer to those things in which merely
something miraculous is shown."[10] In different terms, Origen suggests that Paul's
sēmeia are predictive divinatory messages, whereas Paul's *terata* pertain to the immediate moment. Paul, of course, gives no such indication, but Origen's explanation indicates that even ancients sought to clarify the terminology. Paul does
not refer to *terata* elsewhere outside this phrase. The difference between the two
is negligible, since wondrous things [*terata*] were often understood to be divine
sēmeia. If that is the case, then 2 Cor 12:12 refers to two discrete means by which
Paul proves his legitimacy before observers, namely, wondrous signs and mighty/
powerful works. While this may be a more clear understanding of the Greek, the
modern reader is still left with no specific information regarding Paul's wondrous
signs or his works of power. Whether Paul names three types of evidence here
(signs, wonders, and mighty works) or two types of evidence (wondrous signs
and mighty works) bears no consequence on my argument. Although *sēmeia* and
terata are often understood to be two distinct things, the concepts' filial relationship is further demonstrated when paired adjectivally.[11]

If Paul does understand *terata* and *sēmeia* to be distinct things, we also
have abundant evidence for the reading and interpretation of *terata*. A *teras* is
a wonder, marvel, or terrifyingly strange thing, the appearance of which can
only be a message or portent from a god. Conjoined twins, statues that bleed, or

---

10. Origen, *Commentary on Epistle to the Romans* 10.12.4, in *The Fathers of the Church: A
New Translation*, trans. Thomas P. Scheck, vol. 104 (Washington DC: Catholic University of
American Press, 2002). Likewise, Servius attempts this distinction in his commentary on the
Aeneid: "*Prodigium, portentum,* and *monstrum* are separated by a fine line, but for the most
part they are used indiscriminately for each other." *Ad Aen.* 3.366.

11. Plutarch, *Dion* 24.6, speaks of many prodigious signs [πολλὰ τερατώδη σημεῖα], and Philo, *de
Vita Mosis* 1.178, mentions a most wondrous sign [σημεῖον τερατωδέστατον].

spontaneously combusting objects count as *terata*. Dionysius of Halicarnassus, for example, describes the javelin tips of an encamped Roman army that spontaneously burst into flames and burned like torches throughout most of the night. The *teratoskopoi*, or marvel-readers, understood this to convey the Romans' victory over the Sabines the next day.[12] A staff that transforms into a serpent is a *teras*. Although Paul uses *terata* and certainly claims the ability to interpret *terata* (and even perform *terata*), he refrains from calling himself a *teratoskopos*. Such a title might carry negative connotations for Paul, even when his actual practices are teratoskopic in nature. Philo, for example, uses *teratoskopos* in a derogatory manner to describe the false and wicked diviner–soothsayers of non-Judeans.[13] While Paul does not use *teras* outside the phrase *sēmeia kai terata*, and thus his phraseology likely derives from the magical wonders of the LXX, both he and his listeners would have been entirely familiar with the extensive associations with the word outside of Judean texts or traditions.

Channeling Information From a Divine Source by Speech or Verbal Sound of a Human Agent

In Paul's letters we find two speech practices that channel divine information through humans. Paul calls one of these practices *glōssai*, or tongues, and the other he calls *prophēteia*, or prophecy. The two practices are intertwined; in 1 Cor 14:5 he writes, "I wish all of you to speak in tongues, but more so to prophesy. For the one who prophesies is better than the one who speaks in tongues, unless he [the latter] interprets, so that the assembly may build itself up."[14] The two practices offer disparate degrees of accessibility to the listener, yet both practices find their wider context in among divinatory communication from gods and other such beings.[15] Paul's practice of *glōssai* is a kind of divinatory speech that is neither new

---

12. Dionysius of Halicarnassus, *Rom. Ant.* 5.46.

13. *De Somniis* 1.220; *On Special Laws* 4.48; *On the Confusion of Tongues* 159. The irony should not be lost on us that Philo uses *teratoskopos* disparagingly, despite the fact that he himself often discusses divine *terata*, and the LXX repeatedly uses *teras* and *terata*.

14. The translation in the text is from the NRSV. It translates into Greek as follows: "θέλω δὲ πάντας ὑμᾶς λαλεῖν γλώσσαις, μᾶλλον δὲ ἵνα προφητεύητε· μείζων δὲ ὁ προφητεύων ἢ ὁ λαλῶν γλώσσαις, ἐκτὸς εἰ μὴ διερμηνεύῃ, ἵνα ἡ ἐκκλησία οἰκοδομὴν λάβῃ."

15. Speech practices claiming to channel the voices or messages of gods and other such beings are found almost universally in human cultures. See Felicitas D. Goodman, *Speaking in Tongues: A Cross-Cultural Study of Glossolalia* (Chicago: University of Chicago Press, 1972); J. Gwyn Griffiths, "Some Claims of Xenoglossy in the Ancient Languages," *Numen* 33.1 (1986): 141–169; Newton H. Malony, *Glossolalia: Behavioral Science Perspectives on Speaking in Tongues* (New York: Oxford University Press, 1985); Carlyle May, "A Survey of Glossolalia and

nor unique in the ancient Mediterranean, although his specific terminology has
an impact on how such practices are evaluated and classified in the centuries after
him. [16] We have many examples of divinatory "esoteric speech acts"[17] that reflect
Paul's practices in key ways. Chapter 1 addressed the problematic history classifying prophecy, so its treatment here focuses on two issues: (1) the privileging of
prophecy over and against other forms of divination, and (2) the use of texts in
prophetic claims.

Related Phenomena in Non-Christian Religions," *American Anthropologist* 58.1 (1956): 75–
96; Watson E. Mills, *Speaking in Tongues: A Guide to Research on Glossolalia* (Grand Rapids,
MI: Eerdmans, 1986). The first serious study to develop a typology of glossolalia is Emile
Lombard's 1910 study, *De la glossolalia chez les premiers chrétiens et des phénomènes similaires*
(Lausanne, France: Bridel, 1910), to which contemporary linguists still respond.

16. Two issues have come to preoccupy scholarship about tongues, namely, whether Paul's
glōssai are unprecedented in history and whether Paul approves of the practice. That these two
questions have dominated scholarly discussions of tongues hints at anxieties about Paul (and
therefore Christians) "borrowing" from so-called pagans and whether glossolalia is an acceptable form of Christian worship today. Anthony Thiselton, for example, argues that tongues
were a gift only for the inarticulate or uneducated and that Paul disapproves of tongues in
public. See Anthony Thiselton, "The 'Interpretation' of Tongues: A New Suggestion in the
Light of Greek Usage in Philo and Josephus," *Journal of Theological Studies* 30 (1979): 15–36.
See also J. P. M. Sweet, "A Sign for Unbelievers: Paul's Attitude to Glossolalia," *New Testament
Studies* 13.3 (1967): 240–257; Gerald Hovenden, *Speaking in Tongues: New Testament Evidence
in Context* (London: Sheffield Academic Press, 2002). Dale Martin examines practices of
tongues from Greenland to South America to Ethiopia. He successfully challenges the notion, common among scholars such as Thiselton, that glossolalia was associated with low
status. On the contrary, Martin argues, the ability to speak in tongues can both confer and
reflect higher status, at least within the practicing group (and often beyond it). See Dale
Martin, "Tongues of Angels and other Status Indicators," *Journal of the American Academy
of Religion* 59.3 (1991): 547–589. Related to questions about Paul's approval of the practice,
several studies have also looked at gendered aspects of *glōssai* and Paul's conflict with female
authority in Corinth. Lee A. Johnson, "Women and Glossolalia in Pauline Communities: The
Relationship Between Pneumatic Gifts and Authority," *Biblical Interpretation* 21 (2013): 196–
214; Antoinette Clark Wire, *The Corinthian Women Prophets: A Reconstruction Through Paul's
Rhetoric* (Minneapolis: Fortress, 1990).

17. I borrow this term from Martin, "Tongues of Angels and Other Status Indicators," who
writes, "By 'esoteric' I mean a speech act whose meaning is closed to most members of the
group in which it occurs. The speech is taken by the participants to be a language (thus the
inappropriateness of 'glossolalia' as it is understood by most contemporary linguists and
psychologists), but not that of normal discourse. The acquisition of the 'language' is closed to
all but certain participants who acquire the ability to speak it in abnormal ways, by teaching
from spirits or gods, supernatural or unusual endowment, or training by other persons in se-
cretive, esoteric procedures" (548–549). Martin challenges scholars who conceive of glossolalia
as meaningless utterance of gibberish, citing the fact that most practitioners understand their
speech to be a language, even if it is a language they cannot identify.

Paul's explicit discussion of *glōssai* appears in 1 Corinthians, with concentrated attention in Chapters 12–14.[18] As special abilities gifted [*charismata*] by the Judean god through the pneuma of Christ, tongues are not a normal form of language. At 13:1 he distinguishes between the tongues of mortals [ταῖς γλώσσαις τῶν ἀνθρώπων] and the tongues of angels [καὶ τῶν ἀγγέλων]. At 14:2 he indicates that tongues are a conversation with God and that listeners cannot understand those who speak in tongues because, "they are speaking mysteries through the *pneuma*" [πνεύματι δὲ λαλεῖ μυστήρια]. As a sort of divine dialect, *glōssai* partake of the language of god, angels, and divine *pneuma*. We also know that Paul understands tongues to be unintelligible, as opposed to intelligible prophecy (which is delivered in speech clear enough for others to understand, although not entirely devoid of some obscurities and esotericism). Paul asks his readers at 14:9, "If in a tongue you utter speech that is not clear to understand [μὴ εὔσημον λόγον] how will anyone know what is being said?" Because the nonspecialist cannot understand this esoteric speaking, interpreters are necessary. Paul ranks the interpretation of *glōssai* as important as *glōssai* itself at 14:13: "Therefore, one who speaks in a tongue should pray for the power to interpret" [διὸ ὁ λαλῶν γλώσσῃ π ροσευχέσθω ἵνα διερμηνεύῃ]. In that sense, the interpretation of *glōssai* is a divinatory practice similar to the interpretation of *sēmeia*. Paul also indicates that while speaking in tongues, the mind [*nous*] is inactive: "If I pray in a tongue, my spirit [*pneuma*] prays, but my mind is barren" [*akarpos*] (14:14). As for Paul's expertise in tongues, he thanks God at 14:18 that he practices tongues more than all of his readers [εὐχαριστῶ τῷ θεῷ πάντων ὑμῶν μᾶλλον γλώσσαις λαλῶ].

Thus, we may make six claims regarding Paul's understanding of "tongues": (1) It is not a standard form of human communication; (2) it is a form of communication that derives from gods, angels, or *pneumata*; (3) it is incoherent, unintelligible, or both, necessitating an interpreter, (4) it ranks below prophecy, (5) the mind or *nous* is displaced or inactive, and (6) Paul's expertise surpasses that of his readers.

If Paul were supposing that the gods speak in a different language than humans, he would certainly not have been alone. Indeed, the language of gods was somewhat of a curiosity to many ancient writers. For example, *Poimandres* 26 refers to the beings of the eighth heavenly sphere who praise god, "in a language of their own."[19] Dio Chrysostom twice mentions the language of gods in his *Discourses*. At 10.23 he asks rhetorically, "Tell me—do you think Apollo

---

18. Gordon Fee has suggested that Rom 8:26 is also a reference to tongues. See Gordon Fee, *God's Empowering Presence: The Holy Spirit in the Letters of Paul* (Peabody, MA: Hendrickson, 1991), 581–584.

19. *Poimandres*, trans. G. R. S. Meade (London: Theosophical Society, 1906).

speaks Attic or Doric? Or do men and gods use the same language [διάλεκτ ον]?"[20] He then comments that Homer was safe from deception when visiting the oracle because he understood fully the utterances [τὰς φωνάς], unlike people who knew just a few words of Persian, Median, or Assyrian and were therefore functionally ignorant of other languages. But in criticizing the boldness of Homer's lies about the gods in book 11 (which he denies is a criticism), Dio remarks that Homer spoke as if he had been familiar with the language of the gods [ὡς ἔμπειρος ἧς τῶν θεῶν γλώττης]. The poet is accused of claiming that the gods had different names for things, which explains why he calls the Skamander River the Xanthus in his verse; on top of his exaggerations and disrespectful portrayals of gods, Homer commits the infelicity of freely mixing various Greek dialects to suit his metrical needs, and, worst of all, uses the dialect of Zeus [ἀλλὰ καὶ Διαστὶ διαλέγεσθαι].[21]

In addition to using the "language" of animals, wind, or thunder, gods also spoke using vocalizations that resembled human language. This happened by commandeering the voice of an actual human, giving us two commonly cited comparanda for Paul's tongues. In the first instance, gods enter or inspire humans so as to use their voices for speaking. In some of these cases, a god or spirit pervades the human body and wrests control over the ability to communicate, displacing the *nous*. This is seen, for example, in Plato's *Timaeus*, when he claims that *mantikē* cannot happen while one is *ennous*—in the mind. Discerning the meaning of divine communication comes through reasoning [*logismos*], which cannot be done while one is infused with divine inspiration.[22] Philo also writes of divine beings inhabiting humans and manipulating the organs of speech to communicate: "— for in real truth the prophet [ὁ προφήτης], even when he appears to be speaking, is silent, and another being is employing his vocal organs, his mouth and tongue, for the explanation of what things he chooses; and operating on these organs by some invisible and very skilful act, he makes them utter a sweet and harmonious sound, full of every kind of melody."[23] For example, Cicero describes Cassandra being overtaken by the god and used for speech: "Nunc non Cassandra loquitur, sed deus inclusus corpore humano" (*De Div.*1.67). Vergil's description of the

---

20. *Discourses* 10.23. Translated by J. W. Cohoon. Loeb Classical Library (Cambridge, MA: Harvard University Press, 1932).

21. *Discourses* 11.22–24.

22. *Timaeus* 71E–72A. See Martin, "Tongues of Angels and Other Status Indicators," 570–571. Socrates makes a similar claim in Plato's *Ion* 534c-d.

23. *Who is the Heir of Divine Things*, 266. Yonge trans.

Cumean Sibyl is one of a raving mad woman uttering incoherent exclamations.[24] Plutarch quotes Heraclitus as referring to the Sibyl's "frenzied lips" whose words last "a thousand years with her voice through god."[25] While Paul does not use the term *mania*, his assertion that the *nous* is inactive while one is speaking in tongues resonates easily with widespread ideas of possession by gods. Xenophon observes that the dramatic behavior of "all who are under the influence of any of the gods" renders such people "well worth gazing at." He proceeds to note that compared with those who are possessed by Love, those possessed by other divinities "have a tendency to be sterner of countenance, more terrifying of voice, and more vehement."[26]

In other instances, humans "learn" the language of gods such that select mortals can utter divine languages without explicitly being inhabited by the god, *daimon*, spirit, etc. The *Testament of Job* includes several examples of divinatory speech in which Job's daughters sing and speak ecstatically in divine languages, receiving as their inheritance precious cords or sashes that enable them to speak so. When each daughter dons her sash, she immediately sings and chants in an angelic dialect [τῇ ἀγγελικῇ διαλέκτῳ], takes on the dialect of the archons [τὴν διάλεκτον τῶν ἀρχῶν], and speaks in the dialect of those on high [ἐν τῇ διαλέκτῳ τῶν ἐν ὕψει] or in the dialect of the cherubim [ἐν τῇ διαλέκτῳ τῶν Χερουβιμ]. Each daughter utters apothegms and speaks ecstatically in her own extraordinary dialect [ἐν τῇ ἐξαιρέτῳ διαλέκτῳ].[27] We also see this in chapter 8 of the *Apocalypse of Zephaniah*, when the narrator encounters a group of angels in his travels: "I myself prayed together with them; I knew their language, which they spoke with me."[28] Thus, whether we look at accounts of divine "inhabitation" or of accounts

---

24. *Aeneid* 6.47–6.90. See also Euripides, *Bacchae* 298–301.

25. *Moralia* 397A: "Σίβυλλα δὲ μαινομένῳ στόματι᾽ καθ᾽ Ἡράκλειτον ᾽ἀγέλαστα καὶ ἀκαλλώπι στα καὶ ἀμύριστα φθεγγομένη, χιλίων ἐτῶν ἐξικνεῖται τῇ φωνῇ διὰ τὸν θεόν." That gods use the bodies of prophets through which to speak is a widespread notion that Plutarch elsewhere scoffs at: "Certainly it is foolish and childish in the extreme to imagine that the god himself after the manner of ventriloquists [τοὺς ἐγγαστριμύθους, *lit.* "belly-talkers"] (who used to be called 'Eurycleis,' but now 'Pythones') enters into the bodies of his prophets [τὰ σώματα τῶν προφητῶν] and prompts their utterances, employing their mouths and voices as instruments [ὀργάνοις]. (*De def. orac.* 414E). Plutarch, *Moralia*, with an English translation by Frank Cole Babbitt (Cambridge, MA: Harvard University Press, 1936). Plutarch, incidentally, offers a similar disdain for "belly-talking" that we see in Deut 18 (Chapter 2, "Prohibitions in the Hebrew Bible and its Greek Translation").

26. *Symposium* 1.9.10, trans. O. J. Todd.

27. Testament of Job, 48–52.

28. James H. Charlesworth, ed., *The Old Testament Pseudepigrapha* (London: Darton, Longman & Todd, 1983).

when mortals proficiently speak the dialect of gods, we have numerous examples from antiquity that parallel Paul's *glōssai*.[29]

In his cross-cultural examination of channeling communication from gods or the dead, James Jaquith observes that all such practices demand a performer, an audience, and nonlanguage verbalization by the performer.[30] The value of such speech, for Jaquith, is such that the "performer transmits culturally relevant information to an audience via nonlinguistic codes."[31] He describes such communication not exclusively in terms of religious practices, but rather, in terms of communicative performance. Cast in the terminology of linguistic anthropology, Jaquith queries, "What cultural factors allow, encourage, or even demand that in these, and other formal communicative behaviors, information transmission is relegated to low-capacity codes while the highest-capacity code available—the native language of the performer and the audience—is ignored or rejected?"[32] When we put this question to the evidence in Paul, we find that in the larger field of "low-capacity codes" (or, Dale Martin's "esoteric speech acts"), Paul's *tongues* are an example of the low*est*-capacity verbal code possible—not merely confusing or cryptic, but thoroughly unintelligible. Paul's tongues appear to take the factors of secrecy, ambiguity, and esotericism—characteristic of oracles, prophets, and necromancers—and "ratchet" those factors up a notch by drawing on widespread speculation that gods have separate languages and that people can channel their messages.

---

29. Paul's *glōssai* are subject to the problems of taxonomic uniqueness discussed in Chapter 1. For example, Christopher Forbes' 1995 study rejects all parallels, ensuring that Paul's divinatory speech practices constitute a distinct special category ("Christian glossolalia"). Forbes so constricts the criteria for comparison that all other evidence from antiquity is inadmissible. He claims in his introduction, "It is extremely difficult to parallel many of the features of early Christian enthusiasm *at all* within Hellenistic religion and culture" (5). If his strict monothetic approach to comparison were applied to the oracle at Delphi, oracular pronouncements delivered in verse and those delivered in unmetered speech would be classified in two distinct and unrelated categories. Differences between hexameter and unmetered speech are obvious, but such a distinction would not keep an ancient Greek or a modern scholar from understanding both as examples of oracular practice. Forbes' insistence that every single detail must be identical in order for two comparanda to match defies the very practice and purpose of comparison. See Christopher Forbes, *Prophecy and Inspired Speech in Early Christianity and Its Hellenistic Environment* (Tübingen, Germany: Mohr Siebeck, 1995).

30. James Jaquith, "Toward a Typology of Formal Communicative Behaviors: Glossolalia," *Anthropological Linguistics* 9.8 (1967): 1–8. Additionally, Evandro Bonfim examines tongues in light of the "ritual value of incomprehensible speech." See Evandro Bonfim, "Glossolalia and Linguistic Alterity: The Ontology of Ineffable Speech," *Religion and Society: Advances in Research* 6 (2015): 75–80.

31. Jaquith, 2.

32. Ibid., 2.

Clint Tibbs casts this practice in terms of spiritism, arguing that both glosso-lalia and prophecy are examples of communication not only with God, but also with the world of *pneumata* (i.e. spirits, *daimones*, dead ancestors, and angels).[33] Tibbs' argument rests on his understanding of *pneuma*, noting that Greek speakers used a host of words to describe and denote "spirit" beings but that among Hellenistic Jewish writers the word *pneuma* was sometimes used inter-changeably with *daimon*.[34] He cites Philo's *On the Giants*, which equates angels, *daimones*, and *psuchai*: "It is Moses' custom to give the names of angels [*angeloi*] to those whom other philosophers call demons [*daimones*], souls [*psychai*] that fly and hover in the air."[35] Philo then clarifies, "So if you realize that souls and daemons and angels are but different names for the same one underlying object, you will cast from you that most grievous burden, the fear of daemons or su-perstition [*deisidaimonian*]."[36] Elsewhere, Philo describes the nature [*ousia*] of angels as *pneumatikē*,[37] and associates angels with *pneumata*.[38] Tibbs also finds the overlapping of terminology in Ps 103:4 that is later quoted in Heb 1:7: ὁ ποιῶν τοὺς ἀγγέλους αὐτοῦ πνεύματα ["He makes his angels spirits"]. This is also seen in Job 4:15–18: "A spirit [πνεῦμα] glided past my face, and the hair on my body stood on end. It stopped, but I could not tell what it was. A form [μορφὴ] stood before my eyes, and I heard a hushed voice: 'Can a mortal be more righteous than God? Can even a strong man be more pure than his Maker? If God places no trust in his servants, if he charges his angels [ἀγγέλων αὐτοῦ] with error . . . ' "[39] Tibbs fur-ther argues that Josephus demonstrates "a commitment not only to a god [*theos*], i.e. the only 'true' God of the Jews, but also recognition of a multitude of angels [*angeloi*], spirits [*pneumata*], daemons [*daimones*] and unspecified powers such as *phantasmata*, 'visionary beings,' and *tuchē*, 'fate,' personified."[40]

---

33. Clint Tibbs, *Religious Experience of the Pneuma: Communication With the Spirit World in 1 Corinthians 12 and 14* (Tübingen, Germany: Mohr Siebeck, 2007).

34. "The term *daimōn* denoted 'a spirit' in pre-Christian Greek literature. The term *pneuma* indicated 'a spirit' in Hellenistic Jewish literature" (113).

35. *Gig* 1.6. Translated by F. H. Colson and G. H. Whitaker. Loeb Classical Library 227 (Cambridge, MA: Harvard University Press, 1929).

36. *Gig* 1.16.

37. *QG* [*Questions on Genesis*] 1.92.

38. *Moses* 1.274, 277.

39. Job 4:15–18.

40. Tibbs, *Religious Experience of the Pneuma*, 115.

Tibbs argues that in 1 Corinthians, Paul is talking to his readers about how to communicate with the "spirit" world. By his definition, tongues could include a Greek speaker suddenly channeling Aramaic, as well as a human suddenly channeling the language of gods, the dead, angels, *daimones*, etc. For Tibbs, those who speak in tongues and those who prophesy are mediums through whom various kinds of *pneumata* communicate. He translates 1 Cor 12:1, for example, as, "Now concerning spiritism [communication with the world of spirits . . .], brothers, I do not want you to be ignorant."[41] Tibbs' translation of 1 Cor 12:1 may not convince audiences resistant to the idea, but his argument correctly identifies the function and nature of prophecy and tongues as examples of channeling the speech of divine beings, with an appreciation for how the two practices differ.

Despite the significant role that tongues played as one of Paul's methods for channeling divine words and intentions, prophecy outranks it.[42] Compared with *glōssai*, which is named twenty-one times in one letter (1 Corinthians), Paul discusses prophecy twenty-nine times across six letters, and this latter figure does not account for the dozens of instances when Paul quotes or alludes to a prophecy.[43] Regardless of how Paul's readers may have estimated the two practices, Paul certainly devotes more attention to prophecy. Much of 1 Cor 14 explains to his readers the distinction between the two practices, which rests on the issue of intelligibility. Without interpretation, *glōssai* may communicate much in the way of affect but little in the way of content. Aside from performative affect, though highly compelling, what would be accomplished by delivering

41. For his translation of 1 Cor 12:1–11, 14:1–33, and 14:37–40, see Tibbs, *Religious Experience of the Pneuma*, 279–283.

42. The following studies represent just a fraction of the scholarship on Paul and prophecy: John Ashton, 179–197; Joseph Verheyden, Korinna Zamfir, and Tobias Nicklas, eds., *Prophets and Prophecy in Jewish and Early Christian Literature* (Tübingen, Germany: Mohr Siebeck, 2010); Stephen E. Witmer, *Divine Instruction in Early Christianity* (Tübingen, Germany: Mohr Siebeck, 2008); Pamela Eisenbaum, "Paul as the New Abraham." In *Paul and Politics: Ekklesia, Israel, Imperium, Interpretation*, edited by Richard A. Horsley (Harrisburg, PA: Trinity Press International, 2000), 130–145; N. T. Wright, "Paul, Arabia, and Elijah (Galatians 1:17)," *Journal of Biblical Literature* 115.4 (1996): 683–692; Andrzej Jacek Najda, *Der Apostel als Prophet: Zur prophetischen Dimension des paulinischen Apostolats* (Frankfurt: Lang, 2004); David Hill, *New Testament Prophecy* (Atlanta, GA: John Knox Press, 1979); W. A. Grudem, *The Gift of Prophecy in 1 Corinthians* (Washington, DC: University Press of America, 1982); David Aune, *Prophecy in Early Christianity and the Ancient Mediterranean World* (Grand Rapids, MI: Eerdmans, 1983); T. W. Gillespie, *The First Theologians: A Study in Early Christian Prophecy* (Grand Rapids, MI: Eerdmans, 1994); E. Earle Ellis, *Prophecy and Hermeneutic* (Tübingen, Germany: Mohr Siebeck, 1978). See also Chapter 1, n 63.

43. Compared with other letters, 1 Thessalonians depends more lightly on prophecy. Paul names the practice outright only once (1 Thess 5:20), but frequently refers to his duty to deliver "the word of the lord" and "the word of God" (1 Thess 1:8, 2:4, 2:13).

an oracle whose words and sounds are left unintelligible? Paul does not dismiss *glōssai* but indicates that such unintelligible speech profits no one but the speaker, who participates in some kind of communion with god.[44] I would add, however, that Paul's assessment of tongues as "lower" (or, more circumspect) in status compared with prophecy comes as no surprise, given the elevated divinatory role that prophecy has in Judean and earlier Israelite traditions. Prophecy is frequently constructed as the most legitimate Israelite and Judean divinatory practice.

Philo's *On the Special Laws* offers a meaningful glimpse into how prophecy is privileged above other forms of divinatory speech practices. In a larger discussion of the commandment against bearing false witness, Philo explains why colluding to offer testimony in support of a false accuser is more insidious than falsely accusing. Not holding back his disdain for dishonesty and its capacity to destroy relationships of mutual trust as well as civil society, he writes, "but some persons practise such an excess of wickedness that they not only accuse mortal men, but adhere and cling to their unrighteousness, so as even to raise their lies as high as heaven, and to bear their testimony against the blessed and happy nature of God."[45] Philo is not referring to your run-of-the-mill liars, but those who specialize in divinatory speech practices that do not qualify (for him) as "true prophecy." The extended passage warrants full citation:

(47) If, then, some persons, being assembled together in companies and numerous multitudes, attempt to make any innovations, one must not consent to them, since they are adulterating the ancient and approved coinage of the state; for one wise counsel is superior to many attempts, but ignorance, in conjunction with numbers, is a great evil; (48) but some persons practise such an excess of wickedness that they not only accuse mortal men, but adhere and cling to their unrighteousness, so as even to raise their lies as high as heaven, and to bear their testimony against the blessed and happy nature of God. And by these men I mean soothsayers [τερατοσκόποι, "wonder-readers"], and diviners [οἰωνοσκόποι, "dream-readers"], and augurs [θύται, "sacrifice-readers"], and all other persons who practise what they call divination [μαντικὴν] studying, an art without any art [κακοτεχνίαν], if one must tell the plain truth, a mere bare imitation of the real inspiration [ἐνθέου κατοκωχῆς] and prophetic gift [προφητείας]; (49) for a prophet [προφήτης] does not utter anything whatever of his own, but is only an interpreter [ἑρμηνεὺς], another Being suggesting to

---

44. 1 Cor 14:2–5.

45. *On the Special Laws* 4.48, Yonge trans.

him all that he utters, while he is speaking under inspiration, being in ignorance that his own reasoning powers are departed, and have quitted the
citadel of his soul; while the divine spirit [τοῦ θείου πνεύματος] has entered
in and taken up its abode there, and is operating upon all the organization
of his voice, and making it sound to the distinct manifestation of all the
prophecies which he is delivering. (50) But all those persons who pursue
the spurious and pretended kind of prophecy [βωμολόχον μαντικὴν] are
inverting the order of truth by conjectures and guesses, perverting sincerity, and easily influencing those who are of unstable dispositions, as
a violent wind, when blowing in a contrary direction, tosses about and
overturns vessels without ballast, preventing them from anchoring in the
safe havens of truth. For such persons think proper to say whatever they
conjecture, not as if they were things which they themselves had found
out, but as if they were divine oracles [θεῖα λόγια] revealed to themselves
alone, for the more complete inducement of great and numerous crowds
to believe a deceit. (51) Such persons our lawgiver very appropriately
calls false prophets [ψευδοπροφήτην], who adulterate the true prophecy
[τὴν ἀληθῆ προφητείαν], and overshadow what is genuine by their spurious devices; but in a very short time all their manoeuvres are detected,
since nature does not choose to be always hidden, but, when a suitable
opportunity offers, displays her own power with irresistible strength.
(52) For as in the case of eclipses of the sun the rays which have, for a
brief moment, been obscured, a short time afterwards shine forth again,
exhibiting an unclouded and far-seen brilliancy without anything whatever coming over the sun at all, but one unalloyed blaze beaming forth
from him in a serene sky; so also, even though some persons may deliver
predictions [χρησμολογῶσί], practising a lying art of prophecy [μαντικὴν
μὲν ἐπεψευσμένην], and disguising themselves under the specious name of
prophetic inspiration [ὄνομα τὸ προφητείας], falsely taking the name of
God in vain, they will be easily convicted.[46]

For Philo, the only true divinatory practice is called prophecy. A real/true/le-
gitimate/sincere prophet may have the ability to read marvels [terata], interpret
dreams [oneiroi], deliver predictions [chresmologia], and authentically engage in
other sorts of divination [mantikē], but the true specialist is called a prophētes;
he is not called a terataskopos, mantis, chresmologos, etc. Any sort of divinatory
specialist who goes by any other title is simply a pseudoprophētes. Additionally,

---

46. *On the Special Laws* 4.47–52, Yonge trans.

to invalidate a prophet one need only call him by another title. Thus, regardless of how extensive and diverse the divinatory and wonderworking practices were among Israelites and later Judeans, the qualification "prophecy" and "prophet" simultaneously reflected and conferred legitimacy. Given the prestige of such a designation, it is no wonder that prophecy emerges superior to tongues when Paul ranks his various *charismata*.

For most ancient people, prophecy was an oral and aural performance completely independent of the ability to read or write. Indeed, the majority of ancient prophets were illiterate, whether Greek, Roman, Judean, or Near Eastern.[47] Most of Paul's own followers were likely illiterate, yet 1 Corinthians suggests that quite a number of them prophesied. His discussion of their prophetic practice is concentrated in chapters 11–14 of 1 Corinthians, where he instructs them regarding proper etiquette, as it were, in prophesying. For example, he tells them that a man who prophesies must leave his head uncovered, whereas a woman who prophesies must cover her head (1 Cor 11:4–5). Spoken prophecy builds up the *ekklēsia*, and even when numerous people are compelled to prophesy there is room for all: "Let two or three prophets speak, and let the others weigh what is said. If a revelation is made to someone else sitting nearby, let the first person be silent. For you can all prophesy one by one, so that all may learn and all be encouraged" (1 Cor 14:29–31 NRSV). The ability to prophesy is a valuable divine gift worth striving for (1 Cor 14:1, 14:12). Finally, the prophets of the *ekklēsia*, if they are legitimate, will willfully acknowledge Paul as an authority (1 Cor 14:37–39).

One cannot dispute the prominence and importance of prophecy in Paul's letters. However, deserving of sustained attention is the manner in which prophecy is categorized so as to look quite distinct from other divinatory practices and the degree to which Paul's textual prophecy is privileged above and beyond even the other divinatory practices he himself engages in. That is, of all Paul's divinatory practices, his prophecy is the most consistently respected and examined by theologians, lay Christians, and New Testament scholars alike. In this book's Conclusion, we will return to the notion of modes of religiosity, but for the moment I suggest that prophecy has enjoyed such a status due, to some extent, to the privileging of text-based prophetic practices that have long overshadowed the practice of delivering, orally, the words of a god through a human mouthpiece who may very well be illiterate. While oral prophecy is prominent in 1 Corinthians, Paul engages in literary-based prophecy ubiquitously elsewhere, and

---

47. Martti Nissinen, "Prophecy and Omen Divination: Two Sides of the Same Coin," In *Divination and Interpretation of Signs in the Ancient World*, edited by Amar Annus (Chicago: University of Chicago Press, 2010), 341–351.

it is the preservation of this literate practice that has given credence to prophecy among intellectual theologians.

Use of Literary Texts or Written Symbols to Discern Divine Information, Plans, or Endorsements

The divinatory practice for which we have the most abundant evidence in Paul's letters is his literacy-dependent form of prophecy. Oral prophecy delivers divine information by means of the spoken word and can even read the physical world for signs that corroborate the prophet's message, whereas text-based prophecy communicates and corroborates by means of the written word. Thus, both the divine message and the *sēmeia* [signs] are conveyed in texts. Discussions of Paul's prophetic activities often conflate these two distinct kinds of practices— the literate and nonliterate. Linking literacy to prophecy introduces to divination a different avenue through which the words, intentions, or desires of a god may be interpreted and communicated, which Martti Nissinen refers to as the "literarization of prophecy."[48] Paul's reliance on written texts, in addition to oral recitation of teachings, is explicit. He repeatedly uses the phrase "As it was written . . . "[49] and queries rhetorically, "What does the writing say?"[50] He understands his role, in part, as revealing the meaning of *texts* to gentiles who are unfamiliar with them; he thanks God for strengthening the gentiles through his gospel message about Jesus Christ who, " . . . through the prophetic writings [γραφῶν προφητικῶν] is made known to all the gentiles."[51] Furthermore, Paul's own role as a gospel-bearing apostle was predetermined along with the message itself that "he promised beforehand through his prophets in the holy writings [γραφαῖς ἁγίαις] . . . ", which imbues the LXX texts with divinatory authority."[52] A textual approach to prophecy not only abounds in Paul letters—it is the only divinatory practice to appear in all letters except Philemon.

Broadly speaking, the varied use of texts in divination includes curse tablets, inscribed amulets, erotic spells, and apotropaic incantations. But in thinking about the divinatory interpretation of lengthy, preexisting texts, it is best to imagine a sliding scale: at one pole is the practice of opening (or unrolling) a text,

---

48. Nissinen, "Prophecy and Omen Divination," 344.

49. He uses this phrase fourteen times in Rom, three times in 1 Cor, and twice in 2 Cor.

50. Rom 4:3: "τί γὰρ ἡ γραφὴ λέγει;"

51. Rom 16:26.

52. Rom 1:2.

pointing to a random passage, and imagining that it delivers a prophetic message to or about an inquirer (often the reader). The practice, which we call bibliomancy, was widely known in antiquity, particularly with regard to passages of Homer [*sortes Homericae*] and, later, Vergil [*sortes Vergilianae*].[53] Augustine read Pauline epistles in this way; he altered the course of his life after randomly opening to Rom 13:13–14 (*Confessions* 8.12.29). The practice persisted through the Middle Ages and Renaissance to such a degree that Rabelais ridicules it in *Gargantua and Pantagruel*.[54] This kind of bibliomancy is quick, immediate, and can provide answers to a practical question, not unlike how Tarot cards are sometimes consulted today.

We certainly have evidence that Judeans used the LXX (or at least Torah) in such a manner, and according to Pieter Willem van der Horst, this usage coincides with the era in which Torah is reconceived of as divine by some readers—post exilic and later in the Hellenistic period. As van der Horst points out, the Letter of Aristeas is the earliest document we know of to call the LXX "holy" and "divine" [*hagnos* and *theios*].[55] We also see the notion that the HB/LXX are divine or holy in Jubilees, 4 Ezra, Philo, and Josephus. But we should not take for granted the notion that the Hebrew Bible texts were thought of as divine from the beginning; rather, they acquired this reading over time and under certain social conditions (religious and political reform; consolidation and centralization of religious practice; emergence of an empowered literate class; diaspora intellectuals). The canonized collection of Hebrew texts comes to be understood as "inspired"— "and it is in exactly the same period that we also see the beginnings of the use of the Torah as an oracle book."[56]

1 Maccabees 3:48 and 2 Macc 8:23 provide good examples of the oracular/bibliomantic usage of Torah by Judeans. In preparation for battle against Antiochus and his forces, Judas Maccabeus and his brothers retire to Mizpah to pray, strategize, and embolden themselves. They ritually sprinkle ashes on their heads, tear their clothes, make ritual offerings, rouse the Nazirites, and turn to Torah as an oracle book: "And they opened the book of the law to inquire into

53. Verdenius, *Homer* 17. On the other hand, Moa Ekbom's 2014 study, *The Sortes Vergilianae: A Philological Study*, argues that *sortes Vergilianae* were the invention of Renaissance scholars. See also Leonard Rutgers, ed., *The Use of Sacred Books in the Ancient World* (Leuven, Belgium: Peeters, 1998).

54. *Gargantua and Pantagruel* 3.10–12. See Theodore Ziolkowski, "'Tolle Lege': Epiphanies of the Book," *The Modern Language Review* 109.1 (2014): 1–14.

55. Pieter Willem van der Horst, *Japheth in the Tents of Shem: Studies on Jewish Hellenism in Antiquity* (Leuven, Belgium: Peeters, 2002), 161.

56. Ibid., 161.

those matters about which the Gentiles consulted the likenesses of their gods" (1 Macc 3:48 NRSV).[57] 2 Maccabees tells another version of the story described in 1 Maccabees, and we again see the oracular use of Torah. In 2 Maccabees, however, an oracular portion of Torah is used right at the beginning of the battle against Nicanor, in which the Maccabean forces prevail despite outrageous odds in favor of their defeat. The author recounts, "Besides, he [Judas Maccabeus] appointed Eleazar to read aloud from the holy book, and gave the watchword, 'The help of God'; then, leading the first division himself, he joined battle with Nicanor" (2 Macc 8:23).[58] Both instances appear to describe the random opening of Torah, with the expectation that God will lead the reader to a meaningful passage that communicates significant information regarding the immediate situation. Van der Horst observes that previously, such divination by random choice would happen by means of Urim and Thummim. With the slow process of reimagining Torah as itself divine, we see evidence of Judeans turning to the books in a divinatory manner.[59] It is entirely plausible that Paul used the LXX in this immediately bibliomantic manner; for us to assume that Paul refrained from such cut-and-dry bibliomantic uses of his holy *graphē* says more about us than about Paul or bibliomancy.

At the opposite pole is a more cognitively costly divinatory use of texts. That is, divinatory uses of texts also come in a form that employs a greater cognitive investment through intellectual concepts such as metaphor, allegory, theories about the cosmos and gods, complex textual interpretations, and even more complex reinterpretations. Paul frequently treats the holy writings in this kind of oracular way, which he alone can best interpret for his audiences. His sacred Judean *graphē* contain the key to all history and all futurity pertaining to ethnic Judeans as well as gentiles. As such, he regularly turns to various LXX texts from which he provides oracular readings to his followers.

Heidi Wendt's 2016 study contextualizes Paul's divinatory/prophetic use of texts vis-a-vis the way various religious specialists used the books of Bacis, the Sibylline Oracles, Chaldean Oracles, or Orphic texts such as the Derveni Papyrus.[60] While such a critical comparison is an important contribution, Paul's

---

57. καὶ ἐξεπέτασαν τὸ βιβλίον τοῦ νόμου περὶ ὧν ἐξηρεύνων τὰ ἔθνη τὰ ὁμοιώματα τῶν εἰδώλων αὐτῶν.

58. ἔτι δὲ καὶ Ελεαζαρον, παραναγνοὺς τὴν ἱερὰν βίβλον καὶ δοὺς σύνθημα θεοῦ βοηθείας τῆς πρώτης σπείρας αὐτὸς προηγούμενος συνέβαλε τῷ Νικάνορι.

59. This practice will persist well into the Middle Ages. Rabbi Ben Bag-Bag is said to have said of Torah, "Turn it, and turn it again, for everything is in it" (Mishnah, *Avoth* V 22).

60. Wendt, *At the Temple Gates*, 129–133.

use of the LXX is a shade different from these examples insofar as texts like Isaiah, Genesis, Exodus, Psalms, and Ezekiel provide extensive narrative frameworks uncharacteristic of the Sibylline Oracles or books of Bacis. Furthermore, Wendt's examples certainly benefited from the allure of the mystical and exotic in antiquity, but they did not occupy an authoritative or foundational position in Greek or Roman culture. Thus, an additional comparandum for understanding Paul's prophetic interpretation of Judean holy writings is to consider the widespread divinatory uses of Homer. Such divinatory usages include oral quotations recalled from memory, bibliomantic reinterpretations, and intellectualist allegory–prophecy.

The *Iliad* and *Odyssey* are as close as Greeks came to elevating any text to the status of "religious" canon.[61] Homer's importance, especially among Greek speakers, cannot be overstated; all schoolchildren memorized large swaths of the epic poems, and virtually all art, literature, and philosophy responded to Homer. As Anthony Long points out, "Throughout classical antiquity and well into the Roman empire, Homer held a position in Mediterranean culture that can only be compared with the position the Bible would later occupy."[62] As early as the sixth century BCE, Xenophanes of Colophon claims that, "From the beginning all have learned in accordance with Homer."[63] Not only was Homer the basis of Greek education, many took his words to be divine and oracular or prophetic. As Robert Lamberton observes in *Homer the Theologian*, many ancient interpreters understood that "Homer was a divine sage with revealed knowledge of the fate of souls and of the structure of reality, and that the Iliad and Odyssey are mystical allegories yielding information of this sort if properly read."[64]

---

61. For a brief but sweeping assessment of interpretations of Homer from the Archaic Age to the early Empire, see Margalit Finkelberg, "Homer as a Foundation Text." In *Homer, the Bible, and Beyond*, edited by Margalit Finkelberg and Guy G. Stroumsa (Leiden: Brill, 2003), 75–96.

62. Anthony A. Long, "Stoic Readings of Homer." In *Homer's Ancient Readers: The Hermeneutics of Greek Epic's Earliest Exegetes*, edited by Robert Lamberton and John Keaney (Princeton, NJ: Princeton University Press, 1992), 41–66, esp 44. G. R. Boys-Stones challenges comparisons between the place held by epic poetry and that of the Bible today by offering: "Homer simply did not have a claim to this kind of authority ex officio, as it were." Boys-Stones is correct if we are comparing Homer's place in antiquity to the Bible's place *today*. But in antiquity, both Homer and LXX texts occupied similarly authoritative places among Greeks and Judeans, respectively. See G. R. Boys-Stones, *Post-Hellenistic Philosophy: A Study of Its Development From the Stoics to Origen* (Oxford: Oxford University Press, 2001), 33.

63. Frag B10. (van der Horst, 177).

64. Robert Lamberton, *Homer the Theologian* (Los Angeles: University of California Press, 1986), 1. See also Lamberton's "The Neoplatonists and the Spiritualization of Homer." In *Homer's Ancient Readers: The Hermeneutics of Greek Epic's Earliest Exegetes*, edited by Robert Lamberton and John Keaney (Princeton, NJ: Princeton University Press, 1992), 115–133.

Despite his rejection of how poets portrayed the gods,[65] Plato contends with the notion that Homer possesses divine knowledge. In the *Republic*, Socrates presses Glaucon to consider the importance of scrutinizing Homer, who leads all poets in knowing everything that pertains to vice, virtue, and all things mortal and divine.[66] In the *Crito*, Socrates wakes in his prison cell to find Crito who has come to deliver unfortunate news: A ship from Delos will arrive imminently, and Socrates will therefore be executed the following day. Crito is confident in the accuracy of his information, but Socrates corrects him; the philosopher will die in three days' time. Evidence for this timeline is the dream that Socrates has just experienced, in which a beautiful woman dressed in white called to him, saying "Socrates, on the third day you will arrive in fertile Phthia."[67] This oracular statement delivered to Socrates in a dream is, in fact, a quote from *Iliad* 9.363. As Andromache Karanika suggests, this "dramatic device indicates the early usage of Homeric verses as divinatory device and suggests that these verses had the capacity to be recontextualized in connection with an individual's life" (257).[68]

In Aristophanes' *Pax*, an impromptu prophecy competition arises between Trygaeus and the "oracle-monger" [*chrēsomologos*] Hierocles. The two men hurl pithy and fearful oracular threats at one another until Trygaeus demonstrates his authority by applying the words of Homer:

> Hierocles: What oracle [χρησμὸν] ordered you to burn these joints of mutton in honor of the gods?
>
> Trygaeus: This grand oracle of Homer's: [1090] "Thus vanished the dark war-clouds and we offered a sacrifice to new-born Peace. When the flame had consumed the thighs of the victim and its inwards had appeased our hunger, we poured out the libations of wine." 'Twas I who arranged the sacred rites, but none offered the shining cup to the diviner.
>
> Hierocles: [1095] I care little for that. 'Tis not the Sibyl who spoke it.

---

65. *Rep.* 376e–378e, 381e, 379c–380a, 381e–382c.

66. *Rep.* 598d–598e.

67. *Crito* 44b.

68. Andromache Karanika, "Homer the Prophet: Homeric Verses and Divination in the *Homeromanteion*." In *Sacred Words: Orality, Literacy, and Religion*, edited by A. P. M. H. Lardinois et al. (Boston: Brill, 2011), 255–278. In addition to bibliomantic and prophetic uses of Homer, the epic verses were frequently employed in spells and incantations. See Gregg Schwendner, "Under Homer's Spell." In *Magic and Divination in the Ancient World*, edited by Leda Ciraolo and Jonathan Seidel (Leiden: Brill, 2002), 107–118; Derek Collins, "The Magic of Homeric Verses," *Classical Philology* 103 (2008): 211–236.

Trygaeus: Wise Homer has also said: "He who delights in the horrors of civil war has neither country nor laws nor home." What noble words![69]

Although *Pax* is a comedy, this short passage belies important information regarding the uses of Homer, allegorical interpretation, and prophecy. When asked about the oracular authority by which he sacrifices sheep parts, Trygaeus misquotes (or invents) a citation from Homer. He then quotes the *Iliad* 9.63–64 as a prophetic justification for establishing peace. Trygaeus is, *mirabile dictu*, bringing an end to the Peloponnesian War, and the play was staged just days before the Peace of Nicias, which was crafted to end the ten-year conflict between Athens and Sparta. The peace desperately needed in Homer, however, is that between the Achaeans and the Trojans. The words of *Iliad* 9.63–64, more specifically, are uttered by Nestor in an attempt to smooth over a dispute between Diomedes and Agamemnon. Thus, the Bronze Age circumstances narrated in Homer and those of Athens in 421 BCE are unrelated and separated by centuries, but Aristophanes' Trygaeus extracts a portion of Homer and repurposes it as divine authorization for his actions. Aristophanes does this knowing that Homer was widely thought to be divinely inspired and that the audience would connect the Homeric passage to the Peace of Nicias. Furthermore, Trygaeus' oracular use of Homer is not far-fetched and such usage persists for centuries; six hundred years after Aristophanes, Dio Cassius indicates that the oracle of Zeus-Belus at Apamea repurposes Homeric passages as prophetic utterances. For example, in his *Roman History* 79.8.6 and 79.40.4, the oracle quotes *Iliad* 2.478–479 and 8.102–103 to predict the rise of Septimius Severus and the defeat of Macrinus, respectively.[70]

In addition to the bibliomantic/sortilegium usage of Homer, for which we have extensive evidence, the philosophical and allegorical uses of Homer, tied to cosmic truths and divine revelation, also parallel Paul's use and interpretation of his holy *graphē*. This is particularly the case with Stoicism. From its founding, Stoicism understood allegory to be a fundamental part of philosophy, and numerous Stoic leaders produced allegorical commentaries on Homer in which the poet was

---

69. Aristophanes, *Pax* 1088–1098. In *The Complete Greek Drama*, trans. by Eugene O'Neill, Jr. (New York: Random House, 1938), vol. 2.

70. See also Ps. Plutarch, *de Homero* 2.218.4: "How could we fail to attribute all good things to Homer, when even things which he did not intend, later men have found in his poems. Some use Homer's words as an oracle [*manteion*], like the prophetic utterances of a god." Schwendner trans.

understood to reveal undeniable truths about the cosmos and divinity.[71] Allegory was not a literary practice, but a way to reach theological truths: Inasmuch as Homer contained the information necessary for learning about divinity, ethics, mortality, and virtue, allegory was a necessary means for unlocking that hidden information.[72] In that sense, a scholar/philosopher/allegorist like Chrysippus bore a similar divinatory burden as an exegete/allegorist/prophet like Paul.

Whereas allegory was a foundational part of Stoic philosophy (including their approaches to Homer), this was not the case for Platonism until Middle and Neoplatonism. This latter development can find its traces among scholars associated with Alexandria and those who come out of the Alexandrian tradition. Not coincidentally, Hellenistic Alexandria is also where the rabbis translated, organized, and undertook critical exegesis of the Hebrew Bible and Septuagint.[73] Maren Niehoff argues that by the first and second centuries, Philo and Plutarch are able to recover Homer as a theologian and teacher of Platonism by means of Aristotelian literary criticism developed and expanded in Alexandria.[74] By the Second Sophistic, the Platonist Maximus of Tyre "thought that Homer was the supreme voice of philosophical authority."[75] While Stoics (and eventually Platonists) approach Homer allegorically, we should note that such allegorical interpretations extend far beyond literary interests; both schools find in Homer evidence of divine wisdom and truths regarding how to understand God, what is the nature of the cosmos, and what is Virtue/the Good.

Recording anything as a text allows for its decontextualization, transportation, translation, and recontextualized reinterpretation. As a literary term, allegory supposes hidden symbolic ideas that are missed with superficial readings.[76]

---

71. Zeno of Citium, Chrysippus, Apollodorus of Athens, Crates of Mallus, and Cornutus all produced commentaries or treatises on Homer, Hesiod, and allegory. For more, see Boys-Stones, *Post-Hellenistic Philosophy*, 31–34; Andrew Laird, "Figures of Allegory From Homer to Latin Epic," In *Metaphor, Allegory, and the Classical Tradition*, edited by G. R. Boys-Stones (Oxford: Oxford University Press, 2003), 151–175.

72. To be sure, Stoics were also of the mind that epic poetry included untrustworthy nonsense (Cicero, *de Nat. Deo.* 2.63, 2.70).

73. Maren Niehoff, "Why Compare Homer's Readers to Readers of the Bible?" In *Homer and the Bible in the Eyes of Ancient Interpreters*, edited by Maren Niehoff (Leiden: Brill, 2012), 7.

74. For example, to fit Homer to his middle Platonist/monotheist theological agenda, Philo changes Homer's plural *theoi* to the neuter singular *to theion*. See Maren Niehoff, "Philo and Plutarch on Homer." In *Homer and the Bible in the Eyes of Ancient Interpreters*, edited by Maren Niehoff (Leiden: Brill, 2012), 127–153.

75. *Dissertation* 26.2–3; See also Boys-Stones, *Post-Hellenistic Philosophy*, 149.

76. Anthony Long distinguishes between strong and weak allegories: "A text will be allegorical in a strong [*sic*] sense if its author composes with the intention of being interpreted allegorically

When a text is decontextualized and repurposed such that it is thought to disclose cryptic *divine* information, however, the same reinterpretive allegorical practice becomes a kind of textual–intellectual divinatory exegesis. Both kinds of readings depend on divorcing a text from its original time, place, circumstances, authorial intention, and sometimes language (by means of translation). Allegory and prophecy are often connected; as Peter Struck has observed, "both allegorists and diviners are at root interpreters." He further suggests that "borrowing from divination into allegory" makes sense insofar as, "allegorists were highly sensitive to the capacity of fictive literature to carry multiple layers of significance."[77] We may say of Paul's *graphē* what Andrew Laird says of epic, namely, that it is "symbolic, enigmatic, polysemous, and instructive."[78]

Paul uses his holy Judean *graphē* in both ways—that is, literary–allegorical and prophetic–allegorical. For example, his use of the Sarah–Hagar story in Galatians 4 is clearly allegorical, as he describes it as such (Gal 4:24). Through the hermeneutic practice, Paul takes aspects of Gen 16–21 removes them from the surrounding text, alters the Genesis story to suit his allegorical needs, and repurposes the story in such a way that renders it crucial to gentiles pre- and post-Christ.[79] But Paul also widely uses texts prophetically without identifying them as the allegories they apparently are; that is, the texts are not considered in light of their original context, but refracted through the lens of prophecy and reapplied and repurposed to predict, explain, and/or underwrite the many things Paul tells his readers. His followers, largely unfamiliar with stories of

---

.... Such texts require their reader to take them allegorically; they are composed as allegories" (43). He gives examples of Dante's *Divine Comedy* and Bunyan's *Pilgrim's Progress*, and I would add Kafka's *Metamorphosis*. He continues, "A text will be allegorical in a weak [*sic*] sense if, irrespective of what its author intended, it invites interpretation in ways that go beyond its surface or so-called literal meaning" (43). See A. A. Long, "Stoic Readings of Homer." In *Homer's Ancient Readers: The Hermeneutics of Greek Epic's Earliest Exegetes*, edited by Robert Lamberton and John Keaney (Princeton, NJ: Princeton University Press, 1992), 41–66. Allegorical and mantic uses of texts often look like Andromache Karanika's description of the later Homeromanteion (PGM VII): " . . . verses are reproduced out of context and are re-contextualized in a manner that is not related to any internal textual narrative but are rather adjusted to external parameters" (256). In the case of Homeromanteion, Homeric lines are literally lifted out of the text and reassembled in a new way, sans context or narrative coherence. Paul also lifts passages of the LXX and reassembles them into a new document with new meaning applicable to the first-century Mediterranean world.

77. Peter Struck, "Divination and Literary Criticism?" In *Mantikê: Studies in Ancient Divination*, edited by Sarah Iles-Johnston and Peter Struck (Leiden: Brill, 2005), 147–165, esp. 150–151.

78. Laird, "Figures of Allegory," , 151–175, esp. 170.

79. See John Gager, *Reinventing Paul* (Oxford: Oxford University Press, 2000).

ancient Israel, appear to be none the wiser. In the interest of space I narrow
my focus to three examples, but there are numerous others in his letters. These
examples are not outstanding in any sense but, rather, typify the divinatory
usage I describe. Here, we see the blending of allegory and prophecy, not unlike how Stoics found divine secrets in Homer. Indeed, almost every instance
in his letters in which Paul borrows passages of LXX texts, he does so toward
allegorical–prophetic ends.

From Rom 9:25–33,[80] Paul quotes from Hos 1:10 and 2:23; Isa 10:22–23 and
1:9; and a combination of Isa 28:16 with 8:14. Thus, within the span of nine verses,
Paul extracts six phrases or full quotes from two books written hundreds of years
earlier and repurposes them toward a first-century Greek-speaking gentile audience. The original context of Hosea is an eighth-century conflict in northern
Israel over northern kingdom inhabitants' veneration of other deities in addition
to El. Israel is cast metaphorically as an unfaithful wife who must turn back to her
husband. This conflict pertains to circumstances of the eighth century BCE (later
edits notwithstanding) and not to the early Empire, but a prophetic repurposing
allows for timelessness and flexibility such that the text could, theoretically, be
applicable anywhere (if from eighth-century Hebrew to first-century Greek, why
not fifth-century Latin or twenty-first-century English?). The Isaiah passage Paul
uses in Rom 9:27–33 includes Isa 10:22–23, 1:9, and a combined Isa 28:16 with
8:14. The original text, of course, pertains to Israel and Judah and their loyalty to
Yahweh. Paul reuses the passages to demonstrate that Greek and Roman gentiles'
adoption into the family of Abraham presents a stumbling stone for Paul's contemporary Judeans, as does the central role of Christ as the *telos* of Torah. Such an
interpretation and textual repurposing would likely perplex the ancient Hebrew-
speaking author(s) of Isaiah and Hosea, who knew nothing of later Greeks,
Romans, or Jesus Christ.

---

80. Rom 9:25–33: "As indeed he says in Hosea, 'Those who were not my people I will call 'my
people,' and her who was not beloved I will call 'beloved.'" 26 "And in the very place where
it was said to them, 'You are not my people,' there they shall be called children of the living
God." 27 "And Isaiah cries out concerning Israel, 'Though the number of the children of Israel
were like the sand of the sea, only a remnant of them will be saved; 28 for the Lord will ex-
ecute his sentence on the earth quickly and decisively.'" 29 "And as Isaiah predicted, 'If the
Lord of hosts had not left survivors to us, we would have fared like Sodom and been made like
Gomorrah.'" 30 "What then are we to say? Gentiles, who did not strive for righteousness, have
attained it, that is, righteousness through *pistis*; 31 but Israel, who did strive for the righteousness that is based on the law, did not succeed in fulfilling that law." 32 "Why not? Because they
did not strive for it on the basis of *pistis*, but as if it were based on deeds. They have tripped
over the stumbling stone, 33 as it is written, 'See, I am laying in Zion a stone that will make
people stumble, a rock that will make them trip, and whoever trusts in him will not disgraced'"
(NRSV, modified).

A second example is the well-known passage of 1 Cor 15:54–55: "When this perishable body puts on imperishability, and this mortal body puts on immortality, then the saying that is written will be fulfilled: 'Death has been swallowed up in victory.' v55 'Where, O death, is your victory? Where, O death, is your sting?'" (NRSV). Here, Paul combines terminology and imagery from Isa 25:8 and Hos 13:14. Isaiah 25:6–10—haunting, dramatic, and hopeful—describes how God will prevail on Mt. Zion and prepare a sumptuous meal for his people, wipe away the tears from all faces, and swallow up death forever. If one continues reading, however, one realizes that the Moabites are the enemy to prevail upon after which Jerusalem will rejoice. The passage engages the conflict between Judahites and Moabites, yet Paul reapplies the image of "swallowing up death" (Isaiah 25:8) in victory to the receiving of Christ's *pneuma* by gentiles and their subsequent resurrection after death. Victory comes not on a mountaintop in Judah after the neighboring Moabites are crushed, but through the resurrection of Christ and his defeat of mortality. Hosea 13:14 is repurposed just as freely. Here the god of Israel admonishes Ephraim[81] for venerating other gods and their idols. God reminds Israel of his divine protection since the days of Egypt; Israel has become an unwise son who does not breach the womb at the appropriate time of birth and threatens death to himself and mother. God then rhetorically asks, "Should I save them from the power of Sheol? Shall I redeem them from death? O Death, where are your plagues? O Sheol, where is your destruction?" The Hosea passage clearly points to the prophet's condemnation of what he sees to be forbidden religious practices, disloyalty to the appropriate god, and the impending destruction that results from such rebellion. Paul alludes to the passage in 1 Cor 15:55, but like 15:54 the victory and appropriate veneration come in the form of the resurrected Christ and apply to Paul's faithful followers who have received Christ's divine *pneuma*. Again, if I may be so bold, the various ancient authors/editors who crafted Isaiah and Hosea would not recognize what Paul is talking about.

2 Corinthians 6:16–18 offers a third example: "What agreement has the temple of God with idols? For we are the temple of the living God; as God said, 'I will live in them and walk among them, and I will be their God, and they shall be my people. [17] Therefore come out from them, and be separate from them, says the Lord, and touch nothing unclean; then I will welcome you, [18] and I will be your father, and you shall be my sons and daughters says the Lord Almighty'" (NRSV). Like the earlier examples, Paul repurposes, reinterprets,

---

81. Ephraim is the most dominant tribe in the northern Kingdom of Israel. In Hosea, the prophet often uses "Ephraim" metonymically to account for all of Israel.

and reorders LXX passages. The "sources" for v16 are Lev 26:11–12 and Ezek 37:27; the sources for v17 are Isa 52:11 and Ezek 20:34; the sources for v18 are 2 Sam 7:14 and Isa 43:6. In Paul's three verses he borrows from six passages among three LXX texts as a prophecy revealing the Judean god's will to count Greek and Roman gentiles as his own people. Furthermore, all such borrowing serves Paul's immediate message that his gentile followers should not be partnered with the unfaithful [apistoi] lest they defile their bodies like unclean temples. But of the six passages Paul extracts and repurposes for prophetic authority, only Isa 52:11 pertains to purification and avoidance of pollution. We can count this as a prophetic use of texts insofar as Paul prefaces his teaching in v16b by the claim "As God said." As a prophetic teaching, this passage reveals the very words of the creator–God.

Space prohibits a more extensive survey, but these three examples demonstrate my larger point that Paul recycles earlier texts under the guise of the literate divinatory practice of prophecy. For Paul, such writings do not simply recount stories of a bygone era, nor are they ethnoreligious documents pertaining specifically to Judeans. Instead, they contain divine truths about the cosmos, god(s), human history, and world of gentiles in Paul's era. That Paul recombines numerous passages in this way is not lost on scholars; the annotations of study bibles regularly make note of Paul's textual references. But we should not take Paul's strategy as "natural" simply because Christians over the centuries have become accustomed to it. Instead, defamiliarizing Paul's textual–prophetic practices allows us to see how he reshuffles passages and invests older texts with new life, new context, and mysterious and idiosyncratic meanings. As texts written in response to specific political and social circumstances over the course of several centuries, Paul recontextualizes his *graphē* such that they possess special divine meaning about Christ's importance for Greek and Roman gentile salvation. Additionally, Paul's practice of choosing passages to interpret and apply to his contemporary era reflects broader textual practices that we see in divinatory and philosophical exegesis of the "Greek bible" that is, the Homeric epics. By the first century, Homer and the LXX occupy comparable status as texts to which others repeatedly turn for making sense of the world, the cosmos, and ethics, and for gleaning prophetic meaning hidden from the rest of the world. In terms of allegorical interpretive practices, there is little difference between reading Gen 16–21 as a mystery that is "actually" about gentile faithfulness and Christ, or reading Homer's description of Achilles' shield as "actually" revealing profound mysteries regarding the place of mortals in the cosmos. In both cases, the exegete–prophet provides meaning for those who cannot see it.

Conclusion

This chapter has looked closely at the range of divinatory practices for which we have evidence in Paul's letters. It would be unwise to assume that these practices account for all of Paul's divinatory expertise insofar as we do not have all of Paul's letters, nor is a small collection of letters likely to capture the full range of practices a person might engage in over the course of several years. But the seven undisputed letters give us great insight into his approach to divination, our understanding of which is greatly enriched when we contextualize Paul's letters in the first-century Mediterranean world. Furthermore, this chapter has offered a redescription and recategorization of Paul's divinatory practices insofar as they are reflected widely throughout the world he inhabited. I argue that Paul engages in three broad types of practices that channel divine information, through him, to those around him: (1) He identifies and interprets nonverbal signs from a divine source, (2) he channels verbal speech from a divine source, and (3) he uses texts in an oracular–prophetic way. Paul's verbal channeling includes indecipherable speech in the form of *glōssai*, as well as more conventional speech in the form of oral (nonliterate) prophecy. For his textual prophecies, Paul selects, reorders, repackages, and edits numerous passages from a Greek translation of the Hebrew Bible. This practice of allegorizing and repurposing culturally foundational texts toward prophetic ends reflects the allegorical and oracular uses of Homer that we see as early as the sixth century BCE.[82]

For each practice examined herein, we have solid comparanda among Greek, Roman, and Judean sources. This is an important point; while some scholars have denied Paul's deep and consistent engagement with divinatory practices, others have corralled Paul's practices into the unique category of "Christian." Indeed, there is nothing specifically Christian about Paul's divinatory practices, nor can we say that Christianity eschews divination. Rather, Paul's practices reflect and innovate upon widespread means of engaging with gods and other such beings, across the Mediterranean, without regard to ancient ethnic boundaries or modern scholarly interests. To be sure, without a deep and consistent participation in forms of divination, Paul would not be understood by his peers as an envoy from a god. His ability to divine information and teach that information to followers marks him as a type of deity specialist, regardless of whether modern readers approve of such practices. Finally, I observe that Paul's textual prophecy has tended to be the sole divinatory practice that traditionally finds comfort in scholarly studies; this partially results from

---

82. See Boys-Stones, *Post-Hellenistic Philosophy*, 31, n7.

the scholars' preference for literary practices and the privileging of intellectualist modes of religiosity. If there remain any doubts about Paul's self-presentation as a specialist in divinations and miracles, such doubts are laid to rest upon close examination of how he discusses his divine powers. To that, I turn my attention in the next chapter.

4

A Taxonomy of Paul's Wonderworking

FOR MANY PEOPLE in antiquity, divination and wonderworking (or so-called magic) are not inevitably associated. In his 2016 study *Divination and Human Nature*, Peter Struck notes that the two kinds of practices "have some relationship but it is not a bidirectional one."[1] That is, despite the common scholarly habit of tying the two together (Struck notes the number of studies by classicists and religion scholars with "magic and divination" in the title), the classes of practices are distinct, and one does not imply the other. Practitioners who claim to possess or channel divine power, and to be able to transform the material world by means of such power also typically claim the ability to communicate divine information and read divine signs, but diviners do not necessarily claim the ability to perform wonders, cast spells, heal, or channel divine power. He notes, "while on the one hand we have magicians who make rather indiscriminate claims about the range of their areas of expertise, the practitioners of the other specialties [medicine, divination, et al] tend to be more circumspect."[2] As an intrinsic feature of the reciprocity between gods and mortals, practices of *divinatio/mantikē* occupied a central role in ancient religiosity (insofar as basic communication was understood to be an essential feature of that reciprocal relationship). Miracle-performing practices, how-ever, were viewed with greater scrutiny and suspicion. Paul claims expertise in divination *and* miracle-working, and as such, he is distinct from the kinds of practitioners whose skills are limited to interpreting signs or translating divine communication.

---

1. Struck, *Divination and Human Nature*, 7.

2. Ibid., 7–8.

Wonderworking Practices
• Performance of unidentified wonders, powers, and abilities through the human agent of a god • Healings through the human agent of a god • Ritual transformation of material bodies into different material bodies

FIGURE 4.1   A taxonomy of Paul's wonderworking practices.

Because divination and wonderworking are so closely linked for Paul, a complete study cannot ignore these latter practices. This chapter, then, devotes attention to Paul's discussion of wondrous feats, divine abilities, and transformations through ritual power. First, I consider Paul's discussion of performing miracles, which begins with his use of the terms *dunameis* [powers] and *terata* [wonders]. Some scholars have argued that Paul (begrudgingly) discusses wondrous powers only with his Corinthian followers, but this chapter shows that he mentions such powers also in 1 Thessalonians, Galatians, and Romans. Second, the chapter looks at his claims to heal the diseases, illnesses, and pains of others, utilizing no expertise beyond the power invested in him from a deity. Whereas many physicians in antiquity sought natural explanations for illness and disease, Paul casts himself among healer–wonderworker figures who link illness and its resolution solely to a deity, with whose power he acts. Finally, the chapter examines Paul's discussion of baptism not as an initiation or purification ritual, but in light of ritual powers that purport to effect or change material bodies. The ritual transformation of material bodies is a sorely overlooked aspect of Paul's baptismal claims, and one that locates the practice among those frequently called *mageia* or *goēteia*. Figure 4.1 illustrates the taxonomy of practices addressed in this chapter.

Sorcery, Necromancy, and Magic

As a figure who specializes in the fate of the dead, who channels the power of a deity, and who transforms materials of one nature into materials of a different nature, Paul would be described by many an ancient Greek speaker using an assortment of words such as *goēs*, *pharmakos*, and *magos*. Such words roughly translate as sorcerer, magician, and spell-caster, respectively, but what all point to is a kind of ritual expertise that is simultaneously enlisted by others but is also suspect. In its early usages found in Archaic poetry, *goös* is associated with mourning for the dead—typically the singing and wailing of female survivors of the deceased. By the fourth century BCE the word has gained wider associations of interacting with the dead, and will quickly become associated with figures who conjure or solicit aid from the dead.[3] A cognate, *goēteia*, will for some time be understood as a kind of invoking and conversing with the souls of those who have died. Such figures succeeded in the *tekne* of dealing with souls—their knowledge, desires, intentions, needs, and afterlife whereabouts. Diogenes Laertius, for example, explains Empedocles' reputation as a *goēs*: He possessed the cures for old age and sickness, created rain during drought, and tamed fierce winds. Most important, he brought the dead back to life. Like Paul centuries later, Empedocles' reputed accomplishments intersect with multiple categories of practices, prompting his ancient interpreters to call him a *goēs, mantis*, physician, orator, and philosopher.[4] Claiming to wield the abilities of a god, his own lines of poetry boast: "Straightway as soon as I enter with these, men and women, into flourishing towns, I am reverenced and tens of thousands follow, to learn where is the path which leads to welfare, some desirous of oracles, others suffering from all kinds of diseases, desiring to hear a message of healing."[5] Although *goēteia* finds its roots in dealing with the dead, by the first century, it is frequently used interchangeably with *mageia*. Thus, by Paul's era it can mean *mageia*, but retains the association of interacting with the dead and practices pertaining to the afterlife.

Mageia, however, has a more tortuous past and, to this day, remains a category mired in polemic and vagueness. Although originally a term referring to the ritual and astrological specialists hailing from the Near East, the notion of the *magos* wends its way through a long Mediterranean history. Its nominative form, *mageia*, will come to denote practices and utterances outside civic religion—personal and private rituals that cannot be policed or controlled and are therefore suspected (rightly and wrongly) of malicious intentions and unsanctioned means of accessing divine power.[6] Because of its socially peripheral connotations, the term, in practice, becomes instrumental in discourses that belittle the rites

---

3. Sarah Iles-Johnston, *Restless Dead: Encounters Between the Living and the Dead in Ancient Greece* (Berkeley: University of California Press, 1999), 100–102.

4. Diogenes Laertius, *Lives* 8.58–64; see also Iles-Johnston, *Restless Dead*, 104–105.

5. Diogenes Laertius, *Lives of the Eminent Philosophers*. Translated by R. D. Hicks. Loeb Classical Library (Cambridge, MA: Harvard University Press, 1931), 8.62.

6. For a concise survey of *magos* and *mageia* related terms in Greek, see Fritz Graf, "Excluding the Charming: The Development of the Greek Concept of Magic." In *Ancient Magic and Ritual Power*, edited by Marvin Meter and Paul Mirecki (Boston: Brill, 2001), 29–42. For examination of the polemical use of the term magic, see Kimberly Stratton, *Naming the Witch: Magic, Ideology, and Stereotype in the Ancient World* (New York: Columbia University Press, 2007), esp. pp. 1–38.

and myths of others. The best example of this, of course, is the disparaging moniker, *magos*, attached to Simon Magus in canonical Acts and in the apocryphal *Acts of Peter*. Simon goes head-to-head with Peter in identical demonstrations of miracles. Yet the wondrous powers of Peter, Philip, and Paul are constructed as true and legitimate, and Simon's powers are taxonomically demoted to the illegitimate and dark realm of "magic."[7] Thus the problem of using the term *mageia*; it cannot easily be divorced from the history of suspicion and derision. Such a problem bankrupts the term of any meaning as an analytical category.[8] As David Frankfurter has pointed out, "Practically any practice . . . might be labelled 'magical' or 'sorcery' under certain conditions."[9]

Remaining, then, is the problem of how to compare and categorize practices in which human beings claim to perform outstanding feats with power derived from gods. Here, I justify my use of *mageia* not as an objective analytical term, but as a term that underscores how first-century observers would subjectively understand and categorize many of Paul's claims. I do not use the term in opposition to something scholars call "religion," but as a strategy of leveling the playing field in how scholarship has traditionally privileged and distinguished anything Pauline vis-à-vis the same kinds of practices his contemporaries engaged in. Paul claims to channel power from a divine realm. So did Empedocles. And Pythagoras. And Simon Magus. And Apollonius of Tyana. As did the unnamed religious practitioners who authored or fashioned the ancient amulets, incantations, magic bowls, curses tablets, ritual terra-cotta figurines, miracle accounts, and healing spells—which archaeologists have now excavated in the thousands. I do not suggest that the aforementioned figures are unanimously "the same," but rather, that their practices must be examined in light of the shared practical understandings of their era regarding power derived from gods and the specialists who professed to channel or direct that power. The features of such practices overlap in significant ways.

---

7. A similar distinction occurs with the term *pharmakos*. For example, in Exod 7:10–13, when Moses and Aaron best Pharaoh's "magicians" [*pharmakoi*], the feats they perform are identical, but the power of Pharaoh's team of ritual specialists are described as *pharmakoi*, magicians. See Chapter 2, "Prohibitions in the Hebrew Bible and its Greek Translation."

8. For *mageia* as an analytical category with little meaning or use, see Jonathan Z. Smith, "Trading Places." In *Ancient Magic and Ritual Power*, edited by Marvin Meyer and Paul Mirecki (Boston: Brill, 2001), 13–28.

9. David Frankfurter, "Dynamics of Ritual Expertise in Antiquity and Beyond: Towards a New Taxonomy of 'Magicians.'" In *Magic and Ritual in the Ancient World*, edited by Paul Mirecki and Marvin Meyer (Leiden: Brill, 2002), 159–178, esp. 159.

Performance of Unspecified Wonders, Powers, and Abilities Through the Human Agent of a God

Like Paul's use of *sēmeion*, which points directly to practices of divination, his use of the terms *dunamis* and *teras* point to practices of ritual power. Variations of *dunamis theou* [the power of god] appear countless times throughout the ancient Greek corpus, such as when the Chorus in Euripides' *Alcestis* exclaims, "the power [*dunamis*] of the gods is supreme."[10] Indeed, if gods have anything over humans, it is their power. Thus, for Greek speakers, any rhetorical or ritual practice that aims to channel, harness, or direct the superior power of a god through the medium of a mortal is subject to terms like *mageia* or *goēteia*.

Paul speaks frequently of *dunamis*, using variations of the term forty-four times in the undisputed letters. In most of these instances, *dunamis* refers to the power or force of the Judean deity. This is unsurprising considering that most all writers, when using the word in proximity to *theos* are typically referring to divine power that far surpasses that of humans. His usage in Rom 1:20, for example, reflects Euripides' usage in *Alcestis*: " . . . his eternal power and divine nature."[11] But on numerous occasions across in 1 Thessalonians, Romans, Galatians, as well as 1 and 2 Corinthians, Paul uses *dunamis* to express his own ability to channel or conduct that divine power. It is important to note that Paul writes of these practices in multiple letters. Lest we assume his hand is forced by one audience (Corinthian followers, for example), or that with only one audience he discusses magical–wondrous deeds, we see clearly that Paul engages in such practices over a span of time and among many audiences.

The first reference to Paul's wielding of divine powers is seen in 1 Thess 1:4–5: ". . . knowing, brothers beloved by God, that you have been chosen, because our message of good news came to you not in word alone, but also in power and in the divine pneuma and with great conviction." Years later, in Rom 15:19, Paul discusses the things Christ has accomplished through [*dia*] him. Such accomplishments have come about in "word and deed" [*logō kai ergō*] and "by the power of signs and wonders [*sēmeia kai terata*], by the pneuma of God." In Chapter 3 I contextualized Paul's ability to read signs and wonders as divinatory practices, but in these passages Paul also appears to remind his readers that his preaching came in tandem with actions that demonstrated superhuman powers—that he can manifest divine wonders "in deed" [*ergon*]. Such powers have the net effect of bringing wayward gentiles to heel in obedience [*hupakoē*].

---

10. *Alcestis* 220. "θεῶν γὰρ δύναμις μεγίστα."

11. Rom 1:20: "ἥ τε ἀΐδιος αὐτοῦ δύναμις καὶ θειότης."

If there is any ambiguity regarding how to interpret 1 Thess 1:4–5 or Rom 15:19, we find evidence in three other letters attesting to Paul's claim to work miracles and participate in practices of ritual power that reflect so-called magical practices in antiquity.

1 and 2 Corinthians contain multiple references to the performance of miraculous deeds. In 1 Cor 2:4–5, Paul writes, "My speech and my proclamation were not with plausible words of wisdom, but with a demonstration of the pneuma and of power [ἐν ἀποδείξει πνεύματος καὶ δυνάμεως), so that your *pistis* might not rest on wisdom but on the power of God." His use of ἀπόδειξις, or demonstration, points not to oral arguments or rhetorical methods of persuasion to gain his followers' faithfulness, but to a demonstration of divine power of some sort. This is, undoubtedly, some kind of action. He does not, however, identify what those demonstrations are. In 1 Cor 12:10 Paul again refers to his miraculous deeds of divine power. In listing the range of pneumatic gifts that the Judean deity bestows on faithful gentiles, Paul includes prophecy, healing, discernment of spirits, tongues, and "to another, the *energēmata dunameōn*"—the capability of powers. He reasserts this capability at the end of the chapter:

> 28 And God has appointed in the church first apostles, second prophets, third teachers; then deeds of power [ἔπειτα δυνάμεις], then gifts of healing, forms of assistance, forms of leadership, various kinds of tongues. 29 Are all apostles? Are all prophets? Are all teachers? Do all work miracles [μὴ πάντες δυνάμεις]? 30 Do all possess gifts of healing? Do all speak in tongues? Do all interpret? 31 But strive for the greater gifts. And I will show you a still more excellent way.
>
> 1 Cor 12:28–30 (NRSV)

Unequivocally, Paul refers to the performance of miraculous things whose ability is endowed from the world of divine beings. Still, if any doubt continues to linger, Paul refers explicitly to his host of wondrous powers in 2 Cor 12:12: "The signs of a [true] apostle were performed [*kateirgasthē*] among you with utmost patience, signs [*sēmeiois*] and wonders [*terasin*] and mighty works [*dunamesin*]" (NRSV). Again, I underscore his use of κατεργάζομαι—to achieve, effect by labor, to practice. Such practices include wondrous deeds and the manifestation of divine powers.

The final example demonstrating that Paul engages in practices that convey the superhuman powers of a god comes from Gal 3:5. To the Galatians he writes, "ὁ οὖν ἐπιχορηγῶν ὑμῖν τὸ πνεῦμα καὶ ἐνεργῶν δυνάμεις ἐν ὑμῖν ἐξ ἔργων νόμου ἢ ἐξ ἀκοῆς πίστεως." The NRSV renders this as "Well then, does God supply you with the Spirit and work miracles among you by your doing the works of the law, or by your believing what you heard?" The NRSV reflects most interpretations, in that God is presumed to perform miracles or powers that Paul's audience simply witnesses. Such an interpretation posits Paul's Galatian listeners as passive observers to God's miracles. However, *among you* is not the only possible translation for ἐν ὑμῖν, nor is it the best. In his reprimand to gentiles who might be more concerned for *nomos* [law] than *pistis* [faithfulness] in Gal 3:2, Paul reminds them that they received divine *pneuma* through *pistis* and not the *nomos*. By Gal 3:5, Paul is reminding his gentile readers that this *pneuma* enables them to perform *dunameis*. Rather than God working *dunameis* around them, God allows them to work *dunameis* themselves because they have received his *pneuma*, which is also the *pneuma* shared by Christ. I offer a more careful reading of 3:5: "Is it through works of the law or through faithfulness to what you hear,[12] that he supplies to you the *pneuma* and performs miracles in/through you?" The dative ὑμῖν paired with ἐν is more likely a dative of personal instrument, such as we see in Matt 9:34: "ἐν τῷ ἄρχοντι τῶν δαιμονίων ἐκβάλλει τὰ δαιμόνια" [". . . by the ruler of the daimones he casts out the daimonia"]. Paul's words also reflect the same phrase in *Odyssey* 10.69: "δύναμις γὰρ ἐν ὑμῖν" ["the power is in you"]. Thus, Gal 3:5 yields evidence that Paul has discussed the performing of divinatory powers with Galatians as well as with followers in Thessaloniki, Corinth, and Rome.

Because Paul does not identify the specific powers and miracles he performed for his many readers, we must take his words at face value and consider the range of things that ancient people thought of as miracles, powers, and wonders. That list is as broad and rich as the range of *sēmeia* we examined in Chapter 2 and includes casting spells, making the dead rise or speak, expelling *daimones*, facilitating divine bodily possession, healing through the power of a god, turning certain kinds of materials into other kinds of materials, and projecting the soul from the body and hastening its return. Although Paul refrains from naming his magical feats, we do have extensive evidence that such feats include practices from this aforementioned list: Paul trades in the fate of human souls; he practices the kind of miraculous healings derided by trained physicians like Hippocrates and Galen; he transforms the material nature of his faithful followers' bodies through baptism; also through baptism, he extends to the dead the opportunity to be transformed and to be led to a divine and blessed afterlife; he claims that

---

12. The translation of ἐξ ἀκοῆς πίστεως is also ambiguous. If the clause parallels ἐξ ἔργων νόμου [from works of the law], then the phrase could be rendered as "from hearing about the faithfulness." Thus, the sentence would be understood as, "Is it through works of the law or hearing about the faithfulness [of Abraham? of Christ?] that he supplies to you the *pneuma* and performs miracles in you?"

he traveled to the realm of God (although he is uncertain if he was in or out of his body). Without more evidence of Paul's *dunameis* than what I examine in this chapter, it is clear that his wondrous powers are far from unique; rather, they match, taxonomically, the practices of others in antiquity who were commonly called *magoi* and *goētes*. Given the negative inflection of such terms, we need not take a position regarding Paul's sincerity, earnestness, or authenticity. What we cannot ignore, however, is that Paul's practices themselves were widespread and he shared a historical and cultural context with others who performed them.

Thus, while Paul often refrains from naming outright the various wonders he has performed through the mighty power of a deity, he references such performances numerous times throughout his letters: 1 Thess 1:4–5; Rom 15:9; four instances in 1 Cor (2:4–5, 12:10, 12:12, 12:28–30), and in Gal 3:5. This is enough evidence for us to conclude that Paul's performance of miracles spans years and occupies a consistent feature of his itinerant preaching career.

Healings Through the Human Agent of a God

Paul's practice of divine healing is in keeping with the ways some understood healing to work in antiquity, but at odds with many trained physicians. That he claims to heal people through the power of a deity would have made him appear to others as either the human helpmate of a healer god or a suspicious traveling wonderworker. He explicitly mentions the practice of divine healing twice in his letters (1 Cor 12:9 and 12:28), and this is sufficient evidence for us to know that miracle healings were one of the many skills he claimed for himself and taught his followers that they too could acquire. Because he understands healing as a sign [*sēmeion*], a demonstration of divine power [*dunamis*], as well as one of the pneumatic gifts [*charismata iamatōn*], this suggests that each time Paul speaks of powers, signs, and gifts of the *pneuma* he implicitly includes the ability to heal by channeling the power of a deity. In terms of the specialized practices available to followers of Paul, the ability to heal ranks second only to the unnamed "deeds of power."[13] That Paul values miracle healing so highly and that it was bestowed on his followers as an elite pneumatic gift suggests it was not immediately available to everyone. To better understand Paul's claim to divine healing abilities it is helpful to consider etiologies of illness and disability in antiquity, methods

---

13. In 1 Cor. 12.27–31 Paul first ranks people: first *apostoloi*, second *prophētas*, and then *teachers* [*didaskaloi*]. He then ranks practices or skills: deeds of power [δυνάμεις], gifts of healing [χαρίσματα ἰαμάτων], forms of assistance [ἀντιλήμψεις], forms of leadership [κυβερνήσεις], and various kinds of tongues [γένη γλωσσῶν].

of healing or curing, and the types of figures who offered healing services, with whom Paul may be compared.

Theories of Sickness

Evidence suggests that opinions varied regarding the nature and origin of sickness, disability, and death.[14] In the early twentieth century, Shirley Jackson Case organized these positions into three categories of theory, which continue to be useful with some emendations: (1) an organic theory, (2) a moral theory, and (3) a "germ" theory.[15] By organic theory, Case points to those who understood sickness to be part of the natural occurrence of things; physical remedies provide the answers to predominately physical problems. This describes the intellectual disposition of ancient medicine, from the pre-Hippocratics to Galen.[16] But in a study that approaches ancient Mediterranean healing from the perspective of medical anthropology, John Pilch argues that most people in the ancient Mediterranean world "did not recognize secondary causality. Every event had to have a *personal* cause. If the problem was not caused by a human person, then one might suspect an other-than-human person."[17] Thus, the two remaining

---

14. Annette Weissenrieder's thorough study of illness in the Gospel of Luke begins with a critique of Western scholars' habit of analyzing ancient illnesses according to familiar (modern; Western) concepts of illness and health. She writes " . . . until very recent times, New Testament reports of illness and possession were interpreted as hysteria in the Freudian sense, mania, or epilepsy—or models such as those of 'dissociative disorder,' 'borderline syndrome' (personality disorder), or 'multiple personality' were applied to the New Testament texts" (8). My goal here is not to "translate" or interpret ancient descriptions of illness, but to consider the methods and claims to healing, and by whom healing was accomplished—regardless of the culturally situated construction of illness. See Annette Weissenrieder, *Images of Illness in the Gospel of Luke* (Tübingen, Germany: Mohr Siebeck, 2003).

15. Shirley Jackson Case, "The Art of Healing in Early Christian Times," *Journal of Religion* 3.3 (1923): 238–255.

16. This also describes the theoretical positions of many philosophers. In the *Timaeus*, for example, Plato suggests that physical and mental illness are due to discord (or disarrangement) of proper portioning of the four constituent elements of earth, fire, water, and air. It also describes the way many elite authors understood the interrelation between the body and its susceptibility to elements in the physical or natural world. For example, in his *Natural History*, Pliny demonstrates extensive knowledge regarding the medicinal effects of plants and minerals. *Nat. Hist.* 27.78–80. Weissenrieder, *Images of Illness in the Gospel of Luke*, 43–51, identifies three major eras of ancient medicine: The *Corpus Hippocraticum* dominated up to the first century CE and overlapped considerably with Alexandrian medicine, and finally, medicine of the Imperial Age built on previous eras.

17. John Pilch, *Healing in the New Testament: Insights From Medical and Mediterranean Anthropology* (Minneapolis: Fortress Press, 2000), 47.

notions of the origins and reasons for illness and disability (i.e. moral and/or germ theory) predominated in antiquity.

What Case calls the "moral theory" does not actually relate to morals, per se, but rather, to divine anger and punishment for human behavior. That is, the intervention of a god or one of the many intermediaries of gods was commonly thought to be the source of afflictions. Apollo sends a ten-day plague to kill the Greeks in book 1 of the *Iliad* for the abduction of Chryseis.[18] Plutarch complains that, "to the superstitious [τῷ δὲ δεισιδαίμονι] every infirmity of body, every loss of money or loss of children . . . is called plagues from god, and assaults of the demon. The individual does not venture to help himself, lest he should appear to fight against god . . . if sick, the physician is pushed away and the afflicted one exclaims 'let me alone to suffer my punishment, impious, accursed as I am, hateful to gods and demons.' "[19] The Hebrew Bible demonstrates this often, where affliction and death are meted as divine punishment for disobedience to Yahweh. The Egyptians are repeatedly struck with plagues because of Yahweh's anger.[20] In Num 12:9–15, Miriam's sudden onset of leprosy is attributed also to Yahweh. In Ezek 18:20–22 Yahweh explicitly states that the one who sins shall be punished with death, while he who follows his statutes will live. This understanding of divine anger and punishment persists among first-century Judeans. Philo (*Curses* 5) argues that those who ignore sacred laws will be afflicted with a horrible assortment of diseases of the body. As Michael Compton suggests, "Diseases were commonly regarded as the effects of the anger of heaven, and the restoration of the sick was felt to be dependent on the ceremonies and religious customs which pleased and obeyed the gods" (307).[21]

The third theory regarding the origin of sickness, especially in cases of what we today would call derangement or even mental illness, is the result of foreign invasion. While Case focuses specifically on "demon possession," this also includes the infiltration of foreign powers such as *baskania*, or the evil eye, and spells cast by enemies. Philo understands that illness is delivered by the intermediary figures

---

18. *Iliad* 1.1–300.

19. *On Superstition*, 16c. Jackson Case trans., 241.

20. Exod 12.29. Elsewhere in Exodus (e.g.15:26) Yahweh promises not to afflict Israelites with sickness as long as they obey him.

21. Michael Compton, "The Union of Religion and Health in Ancient Asklepieia," *Journal of Religion and Health* 37.4 (1998): 301–312. This is also seen in John 5:1–14, when Jesus cures a man who had been sick and unable to walk for thirty-eight years. When Jesus encounters the man later in the temple he says "Look, you are well; do not sin anymore so that nothing worse happens to you." This episode in John reflects the healing of the paralytic in Mark 2:1–12, but in Mark the explicit correlation between *hamartia* and sickness is not explicit. See also John 9:3.

of angels. He ascribes a special significance to the angels that the philosophers call "demons": "These are called 'demons' [δαίμονα] by the other philosophers, but the sacred record is wont to call them 'angels' or messengers [ἀγγέλους], employing an apter title, for they both convey the biddings of the Father to His children and report the children's need to their Father."[22] Peter's mother-in-law in Luke 4:38–39 has a demon named "Fever"—once identified, he can be cast out. When illness and injury are attributed to gods, healing is partially the domain of wonderworking and/or divinatory specialists with no medical training; because illness is connected to the divine, a specialist of the divine is consulted to cast it out or cure it.

But we must not forget that Paul's Judean deity is also a healing god. While the god frequently doles out punishment to mortals in the Sacred Writings [*graphē*], he is also identified explicitly as a god of healing.[23] In Exod 15:26, after promising the Israelites that he will not afflict them as he has the Egyptians, provided they listen to his voice, do what is right in his eyes, and keep his commandments, he states "For I, the Lord, am your healer." Likewise, in Sirach readers are told to value and respect physicians, but that "Healing comes from the most high" (38:2); "Pray to the lord and he will heal you" (38:9); and "Physicians, too will pray to the Lord to make diagnosis successful, and cause treatment to save life" (38:14).[24] While Philo demonstrates familiarity with the *Corpus Hippocraticum*, he also understands the source of all healing to derive from the Judean deity: "... health that comes by way of escape from illness he bestows both through medical science and through the physician's skill, letting both knowledge and practitioners enjoy the credit of healing, though it is He himself that heals alike by these means and without them" (*Leg. All.* 3.177).[25] Thus, while we may imagine Asclepius as the primary healing god for Greek speakers, Paul would understand the Judean god as a far greater healing god.

---

22. Philo, *On Dreams* 1.141. Translated by F. H. Colson and G. H. Whitaker. Loeb Classical Library (Cambridge, MA: Harvard University Press, 1934), vol. 5. Angels can infect people without being the etiology themselves (*Leg. All.* 1.252). Instead, the etiology of the illness stems from the transgressions of the person infected.

23. See, for example, Michael L. Brown, *Israel's Divine Healer* (Grand Rapids, MI: Zondervan, 1995).

24. NRSV. See Pilch, *Healing in the New Testament*, 62–63.

25. For examination of Philo's familiarity with the *Corpus Hippocraticum*, see Weissenrieder, *Images of Illness in the Gospel of Luke*, 348–355.

Healing and Healing Professionals

Howard Clark Kee observed that the various methods of healing often corresponded to a different theory of cause of illness.[26] The various methods of healing usually include some combination of *pharmakon*, ritual statements or prayers, touch, or the use of talismans or ritual texts.[27] Thus the distinctions between medicine and "magic" break down especially where pharmacology is concerned. An inscription from second-century BCE Crete (*IG* I, xvii, no.19) tells of a woman receiving a recipe from Asclepius to heal a malignant sore on her finger: "Asclepius ordered her to apply the shell of an oyster, burnt and ground down by her with rose ointment, and to anoint her finger with mallow, mixed with olive oil. And thus he cured her."[28] John Scarborough suggests that "Greek and Roman perceptions of the basic causes of pharmaceutical properties—in particular those of plants—continually fused religious with empirical data . . . . This pattern combined the conviction of divine powers of drugs—whether beneficial or deleterious—with deeply rooted observations gathered by farmers over hundreds of generations."[29]

Healing professionals operated in the early Roman Empire as physicians, agents of healing gods, or both.[30] Michael Compton describes the Asklepieion as "a

---

26. Howard Clark Kee, *Medicine, Miracle, and Magic in New Testament Times* (Cambridge: Cambridge University Press, 1986). Similar to Case's organization of etiologies of illness, Kee (3) identifies three ways that ancients understood illness and disability to originate: (1) functional disorders of the body, for which medicine was needed, (2) the work of demons or gods, for which a miracle was necessary, and (3) magical curse, for which counter-magic was needed.

27. Healing by means of the mixing of plants and minerals is found as early as Homer. In the *Iliad*, Agamemnon prays to "son of Asclepius" as he looks at bleeding Menelaus, who then receives soothing ointments on his arrow wounds (4.4.189–219). Jeffrey Pettis explores ancient knowledge of the healing properties of plants and minerals as they are combined with religious rituals, especially in the cult of Asclepius. See Jeffrey Pettis, "Earth, Dream, and Healing: The Integrations of *Materia* and Psyche in the Ancient World," *Journal of Religion and Health* 45.1 (2006): 113–129.

28. Pettis, "Earth, Dream, and Healing," 114.

29. John Scarborough, "The Pharmacology of Sacred Plants, Herbs, and Roots." In *Magika Hiera: Ancient Greek Magic and Religion*, edited by Christopher A. Faraone and Dirk Obbink (Oxford: Oxford University Press, 1991), 162.

30. By the first century CE, the primary healing gods were Asklepius, Isis, Serapis, and Yahweh. Diodorus Siculus says Egyptians believed Isis had discovered many remedies and was skilled in curative arts. The healing aspect of her cult was prominent at Rome. When Tibulus falls sick at Corcyra, he writes to "Delia," a devotee of Isis, at Rome, asking her to plead with Isis to restore his health (*Elegies* I.3). Strabo mentions a shrine to Asclepius at Canopus in Egypt which celebrated his curing of diseases.

vibrant center of devotion and thaumaturgical awe. Miracles abounded. Worship and cures melted into a unity as suppliants devoted themselves to the god whose grace was health."[31] Compton observes that the early centuries of Asklepieion medicine claim miraculous and incredible cures "directly enacted by the god" but that by the first and second centuries CE, the pharmacological knowledge and recuperative prescriptions of the temple priests became more important in treatment processes. This direct involvement included oracular dream interpretation. He states that, "In this later period, the records show that the treatments appear to have been as rational as the science of the age permitted . . . Cures became less miraculous but no less theurgical."[32] Thus, treatments came to include things such as sunlight, fresh air, pure water, music, medicinal remedies, exercise, special diets, baths, purgatives, bloodletting, and fumigation.

Yet, other kinds of healing do not depend on tested *pharmaka* administered by physicians widely considered legitimate. Some forms of healing rely only on the channeling of divine power through a god or the human agent of a god, and such agents were widely perceived as having (or claiming to have) "magical "powers. Jesus heals a deaf man with a speech impediment by placing his fingers in the man's ears and his spit on the man's tongue. Looking to the sky, he pronounces the word *Ephphatha* and the man's eyes open and his faculty of speech is restored.[33] In a move that reflects the growing association between emperors and gods and simultaneously extends divine authority to the new emperor, Suetonius attributes such healing powers to Vespasian. In a dream, Serapis promises a blind man and a lame man that they would be healed of their afflictions if Vespasian will touch the one's eyes with his spittle and the other's leg with his heel. Vespasian is incredulous that he should suddenly possess such abilities, yet the procedure works and both men are healed.[34] Prior to describing this event, Suetonius claims that because Vespasian had climbed up from lowly ranks and suddenly found himself emperor, he "wanted something which might clothe him with divine majesty and authority" [*"Auctoritas et quasi maiestas quaedam"*]. In Philostratus' biography of Apollonius of Tyana, a Neopythagorean and slightly younger contemporary of Paul from Asia Minor, we learn that the traveling philosopher–wonderworker healed a man from his limp and another man from blindness. Among his numerous miracles, Apollonius also restored one man's use of his hand and healed

---

31. Compton, "The Union of Religion and Health in Ancient Asklepieia," 303.

32. Ibid.

33. Mark 7:31–37.

34. Suetonius, *Vesp.* 7.

a woman from difficult labor pains.[35] These many examples, with their lack of *pharmaka* or a history of medical training, most resemble Paul's wondrous powers of healing.

Paul and Apollonius share a similar need for evidence that their authority is legitimate. Paul's healing is squarely in keeping with the wonderworking claims of those who were widely suspect in antiquity for having ulterior motives and fraudulent power. In *On the Sacred Diseases*, for example, Hippocrates (or a later editor) lambasts such figures when discussing the cure for epilepsy: "I think the first people to have projected this disease [epilepsy] as 'sacred' were men like those who are now mages [*magoi*] and purifiers [*kathartai*] and beggar–priests [*agurtai*] and vagrant charlatans [*alazones*]. These people purport to be extremely reverent of the gods and to know something more than the rest of us. They use the divine to hide behind and cloak the fact that they have nothing to apply to the disease and bring relief." He then proceeds to list a range of nonsensical methods for curing and treating epilepsy by such "charlatans," concluding: "Perhaps it is just that men trying to make a living invent all manner of things and make elaborate claims, especially with regard to this disease, and stick the blame for each form of the disease on a god."[36] Galen, too, is critical of such figures, and bemoans the fact that many people find a successful physician indistinguishable from a magician. In his treatise, *That the Best Physician is also a Philosopher*, he observes that the truly skilled doctor is denounced as a magician [*goēta*] or speaker of riddles [*paradoxologon*] when accurately predicting a hemorrhage or feverish sweat.[37]

Like many others, Paul associates illness as having a direct bearing on the sick person's relationship with a god or gods. In 1 Cor 11:30–32, he explains that sickness and death result from failing to observe the Lord's supper properly. Slightly more vague but also suggestive is his insistence in Rom 1:18–32 that God abandoned the gentiles to wallow in their passions for not venerating him exclusively and appropriately. By logical extension, the abandonment, while not an example of direct affliction, renders gentiles bereft of opportunities for divine healing. Paul leaves no evidence that he is offering medicinal skills from the position that observed pharmacological solutions heal physical problems. Rather, Paul offers the skills of a self-authorized agent capable of channeling the healing power of a god. This type of healing, performed by Paul, Apollonius of Tyana, Jesus, and the unnamed magician–healers criticized by Hippocrates and Galen is instantaneous and "empirical" in the sense that observers can witness a paralytic walk or

---

35. Philostratus, *Life of Apollonius* 3.39.

36. *On the Sacred Disease*, 1.10–11, 1.32. Daniel Ogden trans., 2009.

37. Galen, *That the Best Physician is also a Philosopher* 1.55.

a deaf man suddenly hearing. Healing, in such instances, is not a lengthy process requiring weeks or months at an Asklepieon, extended bed rest, or the consultation of medical manuals and tailored treatments. Instead, when sickness and disability result from divine punishment or need relief from a god, Paul's expertise in divine powers qualifies him to intervene and remove illnesses.

Baptism: The Ritual Transformation of Material Bodies Into Different Material Bodies

In 1 Cor 15:51–53, Paul writes, "Listen, I will tell you a mystery [μυστήριον]! We will not all die, but we will all be changed [ἀλλαγησόμεθα], in a moment, in the twinkling of an eye, at the last trumpet. For the trumpet will sound, and the dead will be raised imperishable [ἄφθαρτοι], and we will be changed. For this perishable body [τὸ φθαρτὸν] must put on imperishability, and this mortal body [τὸ θνητὸν] must put on immortality [ἀθανασίαν]" (NRSV). This remarkable claim appears in the context of his explanation for what a resurrected human body will be like ("How are the dead raised? With what kind of body do they come?").[38] Paul explains that once the mortal body has received the divine breathy *pneuma* of Christ, it will be transformed into a divine pneumatic body when it is raised up again. Similar to Plato's account in the *Timaeus*,[39] he teaches that there are different kinds of bodies and different kinds of flesh, such as the bodies of people, the bodies of animals, and the bodies of heavenly beings (1 Cor 15:39–41). These bodies not only look different, but their flesh is ontologically distinct: Some are sarx, or dumb flesh, whereas the divine ones are pneumatic. The bodies made of sarx are perishable, as is any organic compound that returns to dust (1 Cor 15:47–48). The divine pneumatic bodies are still material in nature, but their materiality is ethereal, divine, and everlasting; they do not perish and they do not decay. The mechanism through which this material transformation occurs is the ritual of baptism, which Paul discusses fourteen times throughout 1 Corinthians, Galatians, and Romans.

Typically, baptism is viewed in light of purification, initiation rites, or both.[40] Indeed, baptisms do function to initiate and to cleanse—literally and symbolically. But such approaches overlook an additional feature of Paul's baptism practice,

---

38. 1 Cor 15:35.

39. *Tim.* 39E–40A.

40. See, for example, Maxwell E. Johnson, *The Rites of Christian Initiation: Their Evolution and Interpretation, Revised and Expanded Edition* (Collegeville, MN: Liturgical Press, 2007); David Hellholm, Tor Vegge, Øyvind Norderval, and Christer Hellholm, eds., *Ablution, Initiation, and Baptism: Late Antiquity, Early Judaism, and Early Christianity* (Berlin: de

namely, the claim that a powerful physical change comes through channeling divine power. Thus, not every aspect of Pauline baptism can be contextualized vis-à-vis practices of so-called magic, theurgy, or "ritual power," but the prominent feature of Pauline baptism that claims to institute a physical transformation of the gentile body is best understood in such a way.[41] Paul's claims of material transformation are not intended to be symbolic, but literal changes that turn a gentile's regular body into something else, thereby releasing the initiate from the same eventual fate shared by all other gentiles.

He explains this physical transformation to readers in Corinth and later, in Rome (with a passing reference to the transformation in Phil 3:21). The gentile who is baptized into Christ thereafter "participates" in Christ. This means that such participants died with Christ, possess pneumatic divine bodies like Christ, and will resurrect with Christ (Rom 6:3–5). Juxtaposing a sarx-type body possessing a normal human *psuchē* [soul] with a pneumatic body, he writes, "It is sown in a psychic body [i.e. a regular body with a *psuchē*], it is raised in a pneumatic body [*sōma pneumatikon*]."[42] Elsewhere, Paul is more explicit about the sarcic/fleshy nature of such bodies and their opposition to the pneumatic.[43] Through baptism, gentiles are so thoroughly united with Christ's divine body that defilement of their bodies becomes a serious concern. Defiling the body through sexual relations with prostitutes, for example, is to defile Christ's own body since their bodies are now "members of Christ."[44] In Paul, we see a yoking of initiation rites with "magical" rites that involve wielding divine powers, such that the initiate is purported to transform into something new; what mortals call "death" is, in fact, the beginning of "real" life.[45]

This extraordinary claim of material transformation leading to a blessed afterlife is on par with the ritual offerings of many cult groups and mystery rites of the

---

Gruyter, 2011), esp. 3–40, "Rituals of Purification, Rituals of Initiation. Phenomenological, Taxonomical and Culturally Evolutionary Reflections" by Anders Klostergaard Petersen.

41. I would argue that that Pauline baptism confers two additional major changes upon gentile initiates: (1) a switch in ethnic lineage from gentile "outsiders" to descendants of Abraham (and therefore heirs), and (2) the bestowal of the divinatory gifts I discuss in this book. On the former point, see my Introduction as well as Hodge, *If Sons then Heirs*. On the relationship among divinatory powers, Christ's *pneuma*, and divine gifts, see Chapters 5 and 6.

42. 1 Cor 15:44. Many translations of 1 Cor 15:44, including the NRSV, render Paul's words as "It is sown a physical body, it is raised a spiritual body." The juxtaposition of physical vs. spiritual is misleading in the sense that the resurrected body is presented as something immaterial.

43. Cf. Rom 8:1–8; 1 Cor 3:1; Gal 3:3, 4:29, 5:16–18.

44. 1 Cor 6:15–16. Cf. Rom 8:9–11.

45. Cf. Phil 1:21; see also Cicero, *de Rep.* 6.9.14 (*Somnium Scipionis*).

ancient Mediterranean, and can be understood in the context of such offerings. Many Bacchic–Orphic initiates, for example, are buried with gold lamellae that provide the deceased initiate with a sort of narrative map through the underworld so they may reach the Elysian Fields:

> You will find in the house of Hades, on the right side, a spring, and standing by it a white cypress. Do not even approach this spring! Ahead you will find from the Lake of Memory, cold water pouring forth; there are guards before it. They will ask you by what necessity you have come. You, tell them the whole entire truth. Say, 'I am a child of Earth and starry Sky. My name is Starry. I am parched with thirst. But grant me to drink from the spring.'"[46]

The Orphic initiate is better off than the masses who will unknowingly drink from the River of Forgetfulness and languish forever in the Underworld as shades. But the initiate must die nonetheless. A similar afterlife is made possible in the Eleusinian Mysteries. According to the *Homeric Hymn to Demeter*, initiates enjoy a better fate in Hades than the uninitiated, but they, too, cannot escape Hades:

> She [Demeter] went to the lawgiver kings, Triptolemos and horse-goading Diocles, strong Eumolpos and Keleos leader of hosts, and taught them the sacred service, and showed the beautiful mysteries to Triptolemos, Polyxenos, and also Diocles—the solemn mysteries which one cannot depart from or enquire about or broadcast, for great awe of the gods restrains us from speaking. Blessed is he of men on earth who has beheld them, whereas he that is uninitiated in the rites [ἀτελὴς ἱερῶν], or he that has had no part in them, never enjoys a similar lot down in the musty dark [ὑπὸ ζόφῳ εὐρώεντι] when he is dead.[47]

46. Translated by Sarah Iles-Johnston, from Fritz Graf and Sarah Iles-Johnston, *Ritual Texts for the Afterlife: Orpheus and the Bacchic Gold Tablets* (New York: Routledge, 2007), 34–35. This example from central Greece dates in the fourth century BCE, but lamellae repeat similar images all the way through the third century CE. See also Yannis Zifopoulos, *'Paradise' Earned: The Bacchic-Orphic Lamellae of Crete* (Washington, DC: Center for Hellenic Studies, Hellenic Series 23, 2010).

47. *Homeric Hymn to Demeter* 473–483. Translated by Martin West. Loeb Classical Library 496 (Cambridge, MA: Harvard University Press, 2003).

Likewise, in Apuleius' *Metamorphoses*, we learn that initiation into the mystery rites of Isis may offer a prolonged life and guidance in an afterlife, but not escape from death itself. The goddess explains this to Lucius prior to his initiation:

> Moreover you will live in happiness, you will live in glory, under my guard-
> ianship. And when you have completed your life's span and travel down
> to the dead, there too, even in the hemisphere under the earth, you will
> find me, whom you see now, shining among the shades of Acheron and
> holding court in the deep recesses of the Styx, and while you dwell in the
> Elysian fields I will favour you and you will constantly worship me. But if
> by assiduous obedience, worshipful service, and determined celibacy you
> win the favour of my godhead, you will know that I—and I alone—can
> even prolong your life beyond the limits determined by your fate.[48]

Initiates into such rites enjoy a better post mortem existence compared with that of noninitiates, but they participate in the fate shared by all mortals—death of the body followed by descent to Hades. Once there, initiation will grant them special privileges and access to the Elysian Fields.

Because death is still inevitable for the aforementioned initiates, Paul's offerings of immortality surpass them, in a sense. Other groups appear to match the apostle's promises, however. Herodotus describes, for example, the Thracian Getae, whose belief in their own immortality "is as follows: they believe that they do not die, but that one who perishes goes to the deity Salmoxis, or Gebeleïzis, as some of them call him. Once every five years they choose one of their people by lot and send him as a messenger to Salmoxis, with instructions to report their needs."[49] A number of Orphic gold lamellae, instead of providing a description of

---

48. Apuleius, *Metamorp.* 11.6. Translated by J. Arthur Hanson. Loeb Classical Library (Cambridge, MA: Harvard University Press, 1989).

49. Herodotus, *Hist.* 4.94–96. Herodotus, with an English translation by A. D. Godley. (Cambridge, MA: Harvard University Press, 1920). Herodotus reports great suspicion regarding the origins of Salmoxis: "I understand from the Greeks who live beside the Hellespont and Pontus, that this Salmoxis was a man who was once a slave in Samos, his master being Pythagoras son of Mnesarchus; [2] then, after being freed and gaining great wealth, he returned to his own country. Now the Thracians were a poor and backward people, but this Salmoxis knew Ionian ways and a more advanced way of life than the Thracian; for he had consorted with Greeks, and moreover with one of the greatest Greek teachers, Pythagoras; [3] therefore he made a hall, where he entertained and fed the leaders among his countrymen, and taught them that neither he nor his guests nor any of their descendants would ever die, but that they would go to a place where they would live forever and have all good things. [4] While he was doing as I have said and teaching this doctrine, he was meanwhile making an underground chamber. When this was finished, he vanished from the sight of the Thracians, and went down into the underground chamber, where he lived for three years, [5] while the Thracians wished

how to navigate the underworld so as to reach the Elysian Fields, claim instead, "Happy and blessed, you will be a god instead of a mortal."[50] Such promises assuage the bitter fact of mortality, and Paul adds to this the promise of ritualized, whole-body transformation of his initiates. But unlike Herodotus' account or the gold lamellae, Paul offers an explanation, ever so brief, of just how immortality is made possible: through an instantaneous material-alchemical change delivered through the divine *pneuma* of Christ.

Resurrection stories are not entirely uncommon in antiquity. Zeus strikes dead and resurrects Asklepius on the battlefield of Troy (Pindar, *Pythian Ode* 3). Asklepius himself was the target of Zeus' ire for resurrecting a dead soldier (3.47–57). In Lucan's *Pharsalia*, Sextus Pompey visits the terrifying Thessalian necromancer, Erichtho, for her services in reanimating a decrepit corpse that delivers a prophecy regarding the civil war (*Phar.* 6.654–827). Jesus, of course, resurrects the daughter of Jairus in the synoptics (Mark 5:40–42; Matt 9:18–26; Luke 8:49–56) and Lazarus in John 11:43–44. In Lucian's *Philopseudes* (11–13) the gardener Midas dies suddenly by snake bite and a Babylonian magician resurrects him and drives the venom out by divine prayer and a rock shard from a dead virgin's grave.[51] We have numerous examples of the dead returning to life for varying lengths of time, including the widespread rumor that anticipated Nero's resurrection and return. *Nero redivivus*, as this rumor was called, gained notoriety in the first century and circulated as late as the fifth, and supposed that Nero either never actually died or that he would resurrect from the dead to rule again.[52]

While resurrection stories (though fantastic) were not uncommon, Paul offers more than the reanimation of his followers' bodies à la Erichtho or Midas; he offers the transformation of their bodies into divine pneumatic materiality, deathless and eternal. The verbs he uses to express this transformation, ἀλλαγησόμεθα (1 Cor 15:51) and μετασχηματίσει (Phil 3:21), denote both a transformation in nature and in shape or form. That is, they denote something other than resurrection of the dead (e.g. ἀνάστασις νεκρῶν in 1 Cor 15:12). In addition to the motion of "rising up," these additional terms suggest the radical material change that results in immortality for faithful initiates.

---

him back and mourned him for dead; then in the fourth year he appeared to the Thracians, and thus they came to believe what Salmoxis had told them. Such is the Greek story about him."

50. Graf and Iles-Johnston, *Ritual Texts*, 12–13.

51. Cf. Eleni Pachoumi, "Resurrection of the Body in the 'Greek Magical Papyri,'" *Numen* 58.5 (2011): 729–740.

52. Augustine, *City of God* 20.19.3.

That things transform into other things did not go unnoticed, especially by philosophers. In the *Physics*, for example, Aristotle uses the same word, μετασχημᾶτῖσις [change of form], to discuss natural and unmiraculous physical transformation of material things in the world: Plants emerge from seeds, bronze is forged into sculpture, construction materials are used to build a house, etc. Aristotle deliberates closely on the process by which things become other things either by emerging out of existing things or by being (re)shaped. Likewise, the verb is used in the *de Caelo* to discuss the emergence of elements from one another (e.g. how can water emerge out of air?) One possible solution is the "change of shapes" [μετασχηματίσει], in which materiality can be forged into different forms (*de Caelo* 305b).

This also rings true for the uses of ἀλλαγησόμεθα, which derives from ἀλλάσσω, *to change, barter, quit*, or *alter*. In relation to deities, however, the verb takes on the special tone of morphing in and out of mortal–immortal form, as shape-shifters who can manipulate themselves and others at will. In the *Bacchae*, Dionysus prepares to defend the rites of his Maenads, remarking, "On which account I have changed [ἀλλάξας] my form to a mortal one and altered my shape into the nature of a man."[53] The Orphic *Hymn to Proteus* begins, "I call upon Proteus, who holds the keys of the deep seas, First-born, you who have revealed the power of all nature, you who transforms divine matter [ὕλην ἀλλάσσων ἱερὴν] into manifold kinds of things."[54] Changing shape, form, and nature is the domain of the gods, which Paul extends to his mortal gentile followers through baptism. It is simply neither the right nor within the power of mortals to change the nature of materiality without the aid of a god, *daimon*, or other such invisible, powerful being. Calling on this aid or claiming to channel this divine aid is the practice of those whom Greek speakers called *goētes, magoi* or even *pharmakoi*.

Most of our examples of material transformations occur in fantastical literary accounts or religious myths. The divine powers of Moses and Aaron in Exodus for example, include turning Aaron's staff into a serpent (Exod 7:10) and turning the Nile to blood (Exod 7:15–24), followed by nine more divine plagues delivered through the magical commands of Moses and his brother (Exod 8–11). In the *Homeric Hymn to Demeter*, Demeter undertakes the process of turning young Demophoon into a god by covering him in ambrosia, exhaling her divine breath onto him, and burning off his mortality in the hearth fire, until the process is

---

53. " . . . ἀλλάξας ἔχω μορφήν τ' ἐμὴν μετέβαλον εἰς ἀνδρὸς φύσιν." Euripides, *Bacchae* 53. Euripides, *The Tragedies of Euripides*, translated by T. A. Buckley. *Bacchae*. (London: Henry G. Bohn, 1850).

54. *Hymn to Proteus* 1–3. My trans.

disrupted the boy's terrified mother, Metaneira (235–260). Jesus transforms water to wine in John 2:6–10. In Apuleius' *Metamorphosis*, the *saga*/sorcerer Mereo transforms one of her lovers into a beaver, an innkeeper into a frog, and a lawyer into a ram. Mereo's powers include transforming people, casting spells, and preventing her own stoning by magically locking all the townspeople in their homes (*Metam.* 1.8–9). Lucius himself is famously transformed into an ass in book 3 when he tries to replicate Pamphile after she transforms herself into an owl (3.22–25). He transforms back into human form only through the saving benefaction of Isis in book 11.

Such stories, from Moses to Meroe, are the ancient equivalent of Harry Potter fantasy magic—entertaining, alluring, propagandistic, and, in the case of Demeter, they function as part of the charter for the Eleusinian Mysteries. Yet in addition to such fantastic literary accounts, we have extensive evidence for actual practices in which materiality is assumed to change or come under the power of divine incantations, prayers, and rituals. The *Papyri Graecae Magicae* (*PGM*), for example, catalogues hundreds of spells from Greco-Roman Egypt that are intended to affect the behavior of others, change the weather, restrain animals, heal the body from illness and broken bones, coerce others into sexual desire, ensure business success, hobble enemies, and solicit divinatory abilities. Some spells promise the physical transformation of invisibility to the user, such as *PGM* 1.222–31 ("Indispensable invisibility spell"), which instructs thus:

> Take fat or an eye of a nightowl and a ball of dung rolled by a beetle and oil of an unripe olive and grind them all together until smooth, and smear your whole body with it and say to Helios: "I adjure you by your great name, BORKĒ PHOIOUR IŌ ZIZIA APARXEOUCH THYTHE LAILAM AAAAAA IIIII OOOO IEŌ IEŌ IEŌ IEŌ IEŌ IEŌ IEŌ NAUNAX AI AI AEŌ AEO ĒAO," and moisten in and say in addition: "Make me invisible, lord Helios, AEŌ ŌAĒ EIĒĒAŌ, in the presence of any man until sunset, IŌ IŌ Ō PHRIXRIZŌ EŌA."[55]

Similarly, *PGM* 1.247–62 empowers the user to move back and forth between visibility and invisibility, provided the ritual is performed correctly. *PGM* 3.612–32 provides the necessary prayer and combination of *pharmaka* so that the user may gain control over his own shadow, turning the shadow into a kind of servant. Although the earliest of the extant *PGM* date to the second century BCE, they

---

55. E. N. O'Neil, trans., in *The Greek Magical Papyri in Translation, Including the Demotic Spells*, 2nd ed., edited by Hans Dieter Betz (Chicago: University of Chicago Press, 1992).

reflect a range of on-the-ground practices referenced in much older literary accounts, such as Hades' "helm of darkness" [Ἄϊδος κϋνέη] donned by Perseus to render him invisible,[56] or the practices and practitioners targeted in the Hippocratic *On the Sacred Disease*: " . . . they claim to know how to draw down the moon and eclipse the sun, to make storms and fair weather, rain and drought, the sea impassable and the earth barren, and all other things of such kind."[57]

Pauline "Sympathetic Magic"

Morton Smith's voice stands almost alone in considering how Paul's baptism practices might be understood in terms of the "magical."[58] This is especially the case with baptism for the dead, which for Smith, "shows another magical notion—that ceremonies performed on a substitute for an intended object will affect the object." That Paul and his Corinthian followers baptized the dead is made clear in 1 Cor 15:29, when he chides them for questioning the likelihood of bodily resurrection: "Otherwise, what will those people do who receive baptism on behalf of the dead? If the dead are not raised at all, why are people baptized on their behalf?" Paul's practice of baptism is not simply an initiation rite or symbolic gesture toward hope for salvation, but a ritual in which the baptized are turned into something different and materially sublime, extending even to the bodies of those who have previously died.[59] Elsewhere in 1 Thessalonians, he

---

56. Hesiod, *Shield of Heracles* 227; Heraclitus, *De incredibilibus* 27.1.

57. *On the Sacred Disease* 1.29–30.

58. Morton Smith, "Pauline Worship as Seen by Pagans," *Harvard Theological Review* 73.1 (1980): 241–249.

59. For more on Pauline baptism for the dead, see Richard E. DeMaris, "Corinthian Religion and Baptism for the Dead (1 Corinthians 15:29): Insights From Archaeology and Anthropology," *Journal of Biblical Literature* 114.4 (1995): 661–682; Joel R. White, "'Baptized on Account of the Dead': The Meaning of 1 Corinthians 15:29 in Its Context," *Journal of Biblical Literature* 116.3 (1997): 487–499. As both authors point out, scholarly consensus is that we cannot determine what Paul refers to in this passage. I find that curious, considering that Paul seems to spell out what is going on: Followers are baptizing others in the name of the dead. 1 Thess 4:13–18 demonstrates some followers' concerns about what happens to their deceased loved ones prior to Christ's return, and it comes as no surprise, given that Paul is offering immortality through the material transformation of the body, that followers would also want to extend that offer of immortality to those who have died. Michael Hull argues that 1 Cor 15:29 does not refer to a proxy or substitutionary baptism for the dead, as there is no historical precedent for such a ritual. To reach such a conclusion, however, he must overlook extensive evidence for ancient sympathetic or substitutionary rituals. See Michael Hull, *Baptism on Account of the Dead (1 Cor 15:29): An Act of Faith in the Resurrection*, SBL Academia Biblica 22 (Atlanta, GA: Society of Biblical Literature, 2005).

reassures his readers that their loved ones will also be transformed, resurrected, and will live in the sky forever with Christ and his father, the Judean deity:

> But we do not want you to be uninformed, brothers and sisters, about those who have died, so that you may not grieve as others do who have no hope. [14] For since we believe that Jesus died and rose again, even so, through Jesus, God will bring with him those who have died [15] For this we declare to you by the word of the Lord, that we who are alive, who are left until the coming of the Lord, will by no means precede those who have died. [16] For the Lord himself, with a cry of command, with the archangel's call and with the sound of God's trumpet, will descend from heaven, and the dead in Christ will rise first. [17] Then we who are alive, who are left, will be caught up in the clouds together with them to meet the Lord in the air; and so we will be with the Lord forever.[60] (NRSV)

That the actions of the living have a direct impact on the dead was not a new idea; for centuries it was assumed that a dead person's shade wandered unhappily, unable to enter Hades until his or her body received proper funeral rites. As soon as funeral rites were conducted by the living, the necessary passage of the dead was assured. It was not far-fetched, then, for Paul or his readers to assume their actions might have an impact on those already dead. Furthermore, it is unsurprising that Paul's followers would want to baptize their dead, given that, "the dead were a vital part of the living community,"[61] that is, the dead could provide guidance for the living, the ancestors protected the family, and one's identity and place in the world were intimately tied to those who came before. What Paul adds to this long-standing assumption is the promise of material transformation of the dead through the baptism ritual enacted upon a substitutionary body.

Today we call this baptism by proxy, especially in discussions of its usage among Latter-Day Saints. But as Smith points out, this kind of ritual is "the basis for all substitutionary [or sympathetic] magic,"[62] wherein one object stands in for another object. Substitutionary magic, like other uses of the term magic, carries the polemical weight of derision and disbelief, but if we are able to suspend the sense of derision, we are free to find the similarities in ritual power between baptism by proxy and other substitutionary rituals. Originally theorized by James

---

60. 1 Thess 4:13–17. It is unclear in this passage if Paul refers to those who have been baptized and subsequently died or those who have been baptized by proxy; I will assume both.

61. Derek Collins, *Magic in the Ancient Greek World* (Malden, MA: Blackwell, 2008), 9.

62. Smith, "Pauline Worship as Seen by Pagans," 243.

Frazer, the notion of "sympathetic magic" entails that one object or body ritually acted upon can affect (materially or psychically) another, similar, object or body. Although much of Frazer's conclusions about magic have been reexamined and rejected since *The Golden Bough* (1890), the notion of "sympathy" (or even "substitution") resonates loudly when Pauline baptism for the dead is examined.

We have numerous examples of sympathetic ritual practices in antiquity, evidenced widely by ritual objects in the archaeological record. In one such example from third-century CE Egypt, now housed in the Louvre, the bronze figurine of a woman, pierced with pins, was discovered in a terra-cotta vase in the tomb of a young man, accompanied by an inscribed tablet with an erotic spell. The female figurine operated as a stand-in for an actual living woman whose sexual attention was sought by the ritual user.[63] Such figurines, often used in binding spells [*katadesmoi* or *defixiones*], have been discovered of wax, wool, terra-cotta, lead, bronze, and marble, and have been excavated from nearly every region of the ancient Mediterranean (North Africa, Egypt, Palestine, Greece, Anatolia, Italy, Sicily).[64] Such artifacts demonstrate the widespread practice of substitutionary rituals that seek to affect one object or person through the corresponding material of another object. Of course, a spell in which a proxy figurine is used to inflict erotic torment upon a love interest or vocal paralysis upon one's legal nemesis expresses different intentions than a spell in which one living body is used to cast the "spell" of immortality upon a dead body. Yet the two types of rituals draw from the same practical cultural understanding that ritual power can be applied to substitutionary bodies. More important, this demonstrates that Paul employed rituals in which divine power transformed the material nature of bodies, and used substitutionary or sympathetic bodies to extend that material transformation. Substitutionary or sympathetic rituals would be entirely familiar to Paul, who clearly refashioned such practices to ensure that even the dead bodies of his followers' loved ones could benefit from his ritual of baptismal–pneumatic transformation.

Smith defamiliarizes the reader from traditional understandings of baptism by associating Paul's baptism ritual with (often negatively inflected) magic terminology: "Such rites, beginning with an imitation death and ending with

---

63. See John J. Winkler, *The Constraints of Desire: The Anthropology of Sex and Gender in Ancient Greece* (New York: Routledge, 1990), 93–94; P. du Bourguet, "Ensemble magique de la periode romaine en Egypte," *La Revue du Louvre* 25 (1975): 255–257.

64. See, for example, Christopher Faraone, "The Agonistic Context of Early Greek Binding Spells." In *Magika Hiera: Ancient Greek Magic and Religion*, edited by Christopher Faraone and Dirk Obbink (Oxford: Oxford University Press, 1991), 3–32; see also Collins, *Magic in the Ancient Greek World*, 92–97.

resurrection by receipt of a divine spirit, to a new life, are familiar in magical material."[65] He is not wrong to do so; he points to *PGM* 4.154–220, for example, in which the initiate is instructed to lie naked and supine on a pure linen garment. He is then told to wrap himself like a corpse, close his eyes, and repeat a prayer three times to Typhon. After this, a sign of divine encounter will show itself—most likely in the form of a bird that will dive down and strike the initiate. The initiate is then instructed to rise, clothe himself in white, and burn incense while saying "I have been attached to your holy form. I have been given power by your holy name. I have acquired your emanation of the goods, Lord, god of gods, master, daimon."[66] The initiate imitates a death and rising to a new life through the god.[67] Given the ritualistic nature of baptism, it is entirely possible that Paul had his followers reenact the death and resurrection of Christ similar to the preceding example, with the result that the initiate shares the divine material nature of Christ (*pneuma*), is "in Christ" and has "put on Christ" (Gal 3:27).[68]

Paul, Psuchagōgos

Paul mentions death, the dead, resurrection of the dead, and dying almost forty times in the undisputed letters. It is no overstatement to observe that the dead factor heavily in his discourse. In this regard perhaps he is not unusual; death surrounded life in antiquity such that women had to birth an average of five

---

65. Smith, "Pauline Worship as Seen by Pagans," 242. He is particularly interested in Rom 6:3–11, and shared qualities found in the *PGM*, Isis worship, Mithras worship, and as rituals found as late as the Chaldean Oracles.

66. *PGM*, trans. Hans Deiter Betz. 6th ed., ed. K. Preisendanz; 2nd ed., ed. A. Henrichs (Leipzig, 1973–1974), 2 vols., cited by papyrus number (in this collection) and line. Here 4.154–220ff. Salvation by union with a god's form appears in 2 Cor 3:18; cf. Phil 2:6.

67. Smith points out, however, that in the *PGM*, the ritual was not understood as "participation in events previously experienced by the god. The death was symbolic of the initiate's present condition; union with the deity was attained only by/in resurrection. The Christian's god, however, had been executed, died, and been raised." ("Pauline Worship as Seen by Pagans," 243).

68. We know disappointingly little about the mechanics of Paul's baptism ritual. We can safely assume, I think, that the rite involved water or oil and some kind of spoken formula–prayer–incantation, during which the initiate receives the divine *pneuma* of Christ. How the baptismal liquid was applied (Was the initiate fully immersed? Sprinkled? Sprayed?), what incantations were spoken—we simply cannot say. Perhaps we can infer from gospel accounts and the *Didache* to fill in some blanks, and we can certainly draw conclusions about the baptism rituals of Christians from the third century onward. But we simply lack evidence for some of the precise details of Paul's baptismal rite.

children simply to end up with two who survive.[69] For those lucky enough to survive childhood, the estimated life expectancy in the first century was a dismal thirty to forty years. Absolutely everyone interacted with the dead in the form of visiting and maintaining cemeteries and in offerings at household shrines to the ancestors. Lacking a professionalized funeral industry, dead bodies were washed and prepared in the home. Thus, unlike inhabitants of the modern West, who are largely shielded by the messiness of death and its aftermath by a professionalized funeral industry, the reality of death and the presence of the dead were felt everywhere in antiquity. And yet, the ever-present possibility of death did not soften its blow; Cicero's despair at losing his beloved daughter, Tullia, reminds us that even in a world where death came early and mercilessly, grief still overwhelmed.[70]

Behind Paul's substitutionary or sympathetic rituals lies a concern for the souls of the dead. Indeed, in more general terms, it is fair to say that practices and discourses concerning the dead dominate Paul's teaching career. Paul's Lord, *Christos*, was counted among the dead for some time, if only briefly. Because of this proximity to death and the invocation of and sharing in the nature of a god who died and conquered death and resurrected, Morton Smith additionally draws comparisons between Pauline baptism and rituals of necromancy in antiquity. In particular, he looks at the recalling of spirits of executed criminals and those who died unmarried or childless to provide aid to the practitioner. He notes that Christ fit all three categories: death of an executed criminal who was both unmarried and childless. As Smith points out, such "spirits" acted as *paredroi*, or assistants, to living humans.[71] And if we accept Clint Tibbs' understanding of *pneumata* as "spirits" in Chapter 3,[72] we have clear evidence that Paul uses his divine powers to affect the world of the already-dead. As one who specializes in conjuring or altering the conditions or state of human souls, Paul would look quite like what Greek speakers called a *goēs* in the earlier sense of the term—a specialist in souls of the dead, often translated as "sorcerer." Such practices also resemble various *psuchagōgoi*, or "soul leaders" or "soul enchanters."

---

69. Ross Kraemer, "Typical and Atypical Jewish Family Dynamics: The Cases of Babatha and Berenice." In *Early Christian Families in Context: An Interdisciplinary Dialogue*, edited by David Balch and Carolyn Osiek (Grand Rapids, MI: Eerdmans, 2003), 141.

70. Cicero's *Consolatio*, a treatise on loss, grief, and consolation, has been lost, but he discusses his struggle with Tullia's death in letters with Atticus.

71. See Smith, *Jesus the Magician*, 243–244.

72. See Chapter 3, "Channeling Information from a Divine Source by Speech or Verbal Sound of a Human Agent."

The common portrayal of a psychagogue looks like Odysseus in Book 11 of the *Odyssey* insofar as the souls of the dead are ritually conjured, conversed with, and led to or from the Underworld. Yet we have many other images, such as the *Orpheotelestai*, the Orphic initiators, who thought that souls of the already-dead could be saved along with the souls of the living. Plato suggests as much in *Republic* 364e–365a:

> And they produce a bushel of books of Musaeus and Orpheus, the off-spring of the Moon and of the Muses, as they affirm, and these books they use in their ritual, and make not only ordinary men but states believe that there really are remissions of sins and purifications for deeds of injustice [*luseis te kai katharmoi adikēmatōn*], by means of sacrifice and pleasant sport for the living, [365a] and that there are also special rites for the defunct [*teleutēsasin*], which they call functions, that deliver us from evils in that other world, while terrible things await those who have neglected to sacrifice.[73]

In his commentary on the *Phaedo*, Olympiodorus interprets this to mean that such specialists offer post mortem initiation, thereby conjuring and saving the souls of those who have died.[74]

Such practitioners were often disparaged, yet their services were just as frequently sought. In addition to summoning the dead for prophetic purposes, *psuchagōgoi* were known to drive out spirits and to lay souls in their proper place. Sarah Iles-Johnston describes *psuchagōgoi* as "expert practitioners [who] lead ghosts away from one spot to another."[75] Daniel Ogden points to the contradictory roles of psychagogues and their relation to *goēteia*: "It seems that the *goos* and *goēteia* encompassed the same partly contradictory qualities as *psuchagōgia*: they both laid and roused the dead."[76]

Practitioners who claimed to perform rituals that might affect the behavior, fortune, or attitude of the dead were hardly new by the first century. Unsurprisingly, Plato had been highly critical of such figures:

---

73. Plato. *Plato in Twelve Volumes*, vols. 5 and 6 translated by Paul Shorey (Cambridge, MA: Harvard University Press; London: William Heinemann, 1969).

74. See Iles-Johnston, *Restless Dead*, 53–55; Ogden, *Greek and Roman Necromancy*, 124–25; Olympiodorus on *Phaedo* 87, 15 Novin.

75. See Iles-Johnston, *Restless Dead*, 21, also 82–123.

76. Daniel Ogden, *Greek and Roman Necromancy* (Princeton, NJ: Princeton University Press, 2001), 112.

Let us address those who take up the wild belief that the gods do not care or are placable, those who, in contempt for men, charm the souls [*psuchagōgousi*] of many of the living, by alleging that they charm the souls [*psuchagōgein*] of the dead. They undertake to persuade the gods, through the practice of sorceries [*goēteuontes*] with sacrifices and prayers and spells, and try to destroy root and branch individuals and entire houses for the sake of money.[77]

Paul, of course, frequently emphasizes his disinterest in money.[78] But he does so, to my mind, as a means of shielding himself from the type of suspicious gaze we find in Plato. It is not a stretch, then, to associate Pauline baptism with discourses and practices that pertain to material transformation of the initiate's body, interacting with spirits, and with conjuring the dead—if even to lead them from death to immortality.

The inheritance of Christian tradition over many centuries presents challenges when trying to view Pauline baptism in any light apart from that inherited tradition. But recalling that Christianity had not yet developed during Paul's lifetime, it is fruitful to enquire, "What does baptism of the dead resemble *without* Christianity?" That is, if we remove the layers of Christian familiarity, what else might Pauline baptism for the dead entail but a summoning and transforming of the souls of the dead? Although we have little information about the mechanics of the ritual, certainly the names of the dead were called, thus evoking them. In some instances, this may have happened at the actual grave. The dead, too, must have received the divine *pneuma* of Christ through the sympathetic or substitutionary body of a living follower. And finally, the material nature of the dead was assumed to transform, having received the divine "stuff" of Christ. If we disjoin this rite from scholarly expectations and assumptions about categorical differences between Christianity and so-called paganism, it becomes evident that Paul shares practical ritual understandings with ancient *psuchagōgoi/goētes*.

Conclusion

To be sure, Paul and his followers engaged in numerous practices for which we have no evidence. We cannot say, for example, if Paul encouraged the use of amulets or protective spells—practices that were widespread in his day and for which we

---

77. Plato, *Laws* 909a. Ogden trans.

78. Cf.1 Thess 4:11–12; 1 Cor 9:10–18; 2 Cor 9; Phil 4:10–20. Chapter 6 will look closely at Paul's discussion of material compensation for his mission to gentiles.

have abundant evidence (literary and archaeological) in the Christianity that will develop in the centuries after him. Nor can we say whether Paul claimed to raise the dead, as is supposed in Acts 20:7–12. But the evidence we do have, in Paul's first-person voice, confirms that many of his practices resemble the things that so-called *magoi* and *goētes* are reputed to have performed. Most important, Paul alludes to his divine powers in five of the seven undisputed letters: 1 Thessalonians, 1 and 2 Corinthians, Galatians, and Romans. While he often neglected to identify what his divine deeds were specifically, he mentions them frequently enough that we can understand them as a mainstay in his teaching and preaching practice.

Despite the many references to unnamed wonders, Paul is specific with regard to other wonders and powers. Like Apollonius of Tyana, Jesus Christ, and the unnamed magician–physicians criticized in the *Corpus Hippocraticum*, Paul's explanation for illness and for its resolution rests on divine power. He operates as the specially commissioned human agent of his deity, empowered to cure ailments and illnesses. Furthermore, Paul's understanding of baptism is such that the bodies of his faithful followers are transformed into new, divine material bodies that will stand up from their graves one day and live forever in the sky. While his afterlife offerings are on par with offerings we see in many of the mystery religions, Paul's promise of material transformation through ritual brings an even more magical–wondrous depth to his initiation practices. Rather than seeing baptism solely through the lens of initiation or purification, then, this feature of Pauline baptism is best characterized as the kind of ritual power that changes the nature of objects, people, and materials. Finally, and related to the baptism of living followers, Paul's baptism for the dead evokes association with widespread, albeit suspicious, practices of necromancers, psychagogues, *goētes*, as well as substitutionary or sympathetic magical practices.

5

Discursive Claims to Divine Authority

IN ADDITION TO the wondrous practices that Paul performs in front of others, he also engages in a number of practices whose power is generated through secrecy, inaccessibility, and publicly convincing others of things that happen in private. Such claims strategically position Paul in an intimate relationship with Christ and the Judean deity, to such a degree that he can mediate between the deities and his mortal, gentile followers. These assertions cast him as the handpicked representative of gods, and reflect widespread practices in the ancient Mediterranean that confer credibility and social capital to those making the assertions. This chapter examines those discursive claims to divine authority. While these features of Paul's self-presentation are examples neither of divination nor of wonderworking, they demand our attention insofar as they shore up his legitimacy as the kind of divinatory and wonderworking specialist demonstrated so far in this book. Furthermore, such a self-presentation strengthens the assertion that he is entrusted with the ability to extend miraculous powers to faithful gentile followers—a topic addressed in the next chapter.

Broadly speaking, Paul crafts his claims to divine authority in three ways. First, he professes to have visual divine encounters, including at least one trip to the third heaven. He does this four times. Second, he repeatedly self-describes as "called" [*klētos*] and "sent" [*apostolos*] by a god. Finally, on numerous occasions, he states that he possess secrets and mysteries, and that he comprehends special knowledge from and pertaining to gods. Each of the aforementioned claims has received treatment by scholars, but no link is drawn among them all so as to connect his overall self-portrait to a larger program of divinatory and wonderworking practice. Figure 5.1 illustrates Paul's discursive claims. The latter part of this chapter looks at what I call Paul's "divinatory pedagogy." That is, Paul is not simply performing wonders for his followers, but also teaching them how to value and practice their own divinatory and wonderworking gifts. His pedagogical approach is one of a mentor who schools novices on how to understand and contextualize their own newfound abilities.

Discursive Claims to Divine Authority

- Claims to have epiphanies or visitations by a god
- Claims to possess secrets, mysteries, and special knowledge from a divine source
- Claims to be commanded by a deity

FIGURE 5.1 Paul's discursive claims.

Discursive Claims to Divine Authority
Claims to Have Epiphanies or Visitations by a God

In 1 Cor 9:1 Paul rhetorically asks his readers, "Have I not seen [*heōraka*] Jesus our Lord?"[1] He poses the question in the context of verifying his authority and his "rights" as an apostle, from 1 Cor. 9:1–7.[2] Later, in 1 Cor. 15:8 Paul lists the humans who have seen the resurrected Christ: Cephas, the twelve, more than five hundred *adelphoi*, James, and then all of the apostles. Paul is the final person on this list: "Last of all, as to one untimely born, he [Christ] appeared also to me [*ōphthē k'amoi*]."[3] In Gal 1:11–17 Paul asserts that God revealed his son to him so that he [Paul] would announce Christ to the gentiles.[4] Finally, in 2 Cor 12:1–19 he claims not simply to have seen Christ, but to have been swept up to the abode of gods: "I will go to visions [*optasias*] and revelations [*apokalupsai*] of the Lord. I know a person in Christ who 14 years ago was caught up to the third heaven—whether in the body or out of the body I do not know."[5] Thus, on at least four occasions in three letters, Paul professes to have had visual if not physical contact with either Christ or the Judean god.

Paul is not speaking metaphorically, nor is he referring to a kind of intangible mental perception of Christ. While the verbs ὁράω and ἀποκαλύπτω do not exclusively refer to visual perception (they can also denote mental perception) Paul

---

1. οὐχὶ Ἰησοῦν τὸν κύριον ἡμῶν ἑώρακα;

2. In rapid fire, he asks a series of rhetorical questions whose affirmative answers are implied in their asking "Am I not free? Am I not an apostle? Have I not seen Jesus our lord? Are you not my work in the lord?" These questions are characteristic of the style of late Hellenistic diatribe. For more about the diatribe, see Stanley Stowers, *The Diatribe and Paul's Letter to the Romans*, SBL Dissertation Series, 57 (Missoula, MT: Scholars Press, 1981)].

3. "ἔσχατον δὲ πάντων ὡσπερεὶ τῷ ἐκτρώματι ὤφθη κἀμοί."

4. ". . . ἀποκαλύψαι τὸν υἱὸν αὐτοῦ ἐν ἐμοὶ ἵνα εὐαγγελίζωμαι αὐτὸν ἐν τοῖς ἔθνεσιν."

5. "ἐλεύσομαι δὲ εἰς ὀπτασίας καὶ ἀποκαλύψεις κυρίου. (2) οἶδα ἄνθρωπον ἐν Χριστῷ πρὸ ἐτῶν δεκατεσσάρων—εἴτε ἐν σώματι οὐκ οἶδα, εἴτε ἐκτὸς τοῦ σώματος οὐκ οἶδα, ὁ θεὸς οἶδεν."

claims actual visual encounters with the resurrected Christ. If he were referring to intellectual or mental perception, he would not provide his restricted list of those who had seen the god; the mental "perception" of Christ could certainly be claimed by more people than those on his list, including Paul's own followers. That the literalness of Paul's vision was understood from a very early period is evidenced in Luke's embellished account of one of these encounters on Paul's way to Damascus in Acts.[6]

Paul's descriptions make it difficult to determine if his encounters with a god happened numerous times or only twice (the occasion when the resurrected Christ first appeared to him and his trip to the third heaven). Regardless of whether he sees visions of a god on two occasions or multiple times over the course of several years, his statements are entirely in keeping with the ancient notion that gods appear to chosen mortals. But mortal brushes with gods, *daimones*, ghosts, and other inhabitants of the nonmortal world were not commonplace to the extent that such occurrences were unremarkable. Thus, when Paul speaks to his readers about seeing a god, they recognize what he is talking about, not because his claim was commonplace, but because the veracity of such a claim was understood to be within the realm of possibility. The claim would be intelligible and meaningful to Paul's readers, and would mark the apostle out as special in the eyes of the Judean deity. It does not, however, render Paul entirely unique in the larger landscape of the ancient Mediterranean.

When gods appear to mortals in antiquity, they usually do so in the guise of other mortals, as animals, in dreams, or in some form that masks or alters their exact features.[7] Stories of mortals who see gods face to face almost always result in damage or death to the viewer. As Pietro Pucci suggests, the "full manifestation [of gods] is intolerable for human senses and unutterable."[8] Tieresias is blinded by seeing Athena naked. The hunter Acteon stumbles upon Artemis while bathing, and the goddess turns him into a stag so that his hunting dogs tear him apart. Even though Moses sees Yahweh as a burning bush, he covers his face out of fear.[9] Later, when Moses asks to see the god in his full glory, Yahweh responds "You cannot see my face; for no one shall see me and

---

6. Acts 9.1–9.

7. There are numerous stories from antiquity of gods appearing to humans. For an overview of such events, see Robin Lane Fox, *Pagans and Christians in the Mediterranean World From the Second Century AD to the Conversion of Constantine* (London: Penguin Books, 1986), esp. 102–167 (chap. 4: Seeing the Gods).

8. Pietro Pucci, "Gods' Intervention and Epiphany in Sophocles," *The American Journal of Philology* 115.1 (1994): 15–46.

9. Exod 3.6.

live."[10] Isaiah is beside himself with fear for having seen Yahweh on his throne, until one of the seraphim cleanses his lips with a burning ember.[11] Sometimes when a god appears, only the select mortal can see it; such is the case in book 16 of the *Odyssey* when Athena appears only to Odysseus, in the guise of a mortal woman. Telemachus is also present but does not see her, "for in no wise do the gods appear in manifest presence to all" (16.160–161).[12]

Divine epiphanies and theophanies confirmed and/or conferred the link between a god and a place or god and a person. When applied to geographic locations, the appearance of a god consecrates that location and a shrine is inevitably built on the site. This is the case, for example, at the Asklepion at Epidaurus and the oracular site at Delphi. Such is also the case with the building of Solomon's temple in Jerusalem, as described in 2 Chronicles. Solomon chooses the site "where the Lord has appeared to his father David" (2 Chr 3:1). The temple, which will eventually compete with numerous other worships sites until Hezekiah, and later, Josiah, solidify and centralize worship in Jerusalem, is legitimated as "the" temple in 2 Chr 7:1–3, when the inner sanctum suddenly fills with fire so great that the priests cannot enter. God's glory [*Shekinah*] fills the sanctum and the consecration (i.e. authentication and legitimization) of the temple is complete. Lest any uncertainty remain, the author of Chronicles then tells us that God appears to Solomon in a dream to confirm that this, indeed, is his chosen house (2 Chr 7:12–18).

In addition to bestowing divine consecration on places, epiphanies confer divine authority upon people. In her study of ancient epiphanies, cult images, and religion, Verity Platt observes that, "epiphanies provided a means of both accessing the religiosity of the past and bypassing the established sources of authority in order to legitimise the new."[13] This observation is pertinent, given that from the Hellenistic period onward, we see "a productive tension between conservatism and innovation, in which the archaic and classical Greek past is treated on the one hand as a venerable source of identity and authority, and on the other as a toolbox for creative acts of transformation and modernization."[14]

---

10. Exod 33.20.

11. Isa 6.1–8. The potentially lethal effect of gazing on Yahweh is recurrent throughout the Hebrew Bible and LXX. See George Savran, *Encountering the Divine: Theophany in Biblical Narrative* (New York: T & T Clark, 2005), esp. 16–19.

12. Homer. *The Odyssey*, A.T. Murray trans (Cambridge: Harvard University Press, 1919).

13. Verity Platt, *Facing the Gods: Epiphany and Representation in Graeco-Roman Art, Literature, and Religion* (New York: Cambridge University Press, 2011), 124.

14. Ibid.

This is demonstrated, for example, in the number of kings who adopt the very title *Epiphanes*.[15] Paul, too, is able to assume this kind of divine authority when he claims to have seen the resurrected Christ, although the "venerable source of identity" that he innovates upon is more complex than simply the archaic or classical Greek past. The epiphany of Christ does not come to everyone, but a select few, and Paul is the last, and incidentally, the most relevant for his followers.

Thus, Paul's claim to have seen a resurrected god does not specifically identify him as a divinatory specialist, so much as it renders his divinatory authority inviolable. The relationship between epiphanies and power is undeniable. In her thorough and detailed 2015 study on such divine manifestations, Georgia Petridou identifies epiphanies as effective status-elevating mechanisms. That is, when an individual claims to perceive a deity, such an appearance, "is traditionally considered a sign of divine favouritism, a sign of *theophilia*—which in turn bestows upon him an exceptionally powerful position within his community."[16] The mythical and highly regarded seer–philosopher, Epimenides, for example, claims that in a decades-long sleep, he conversed with the gods and saw the throne of Zeus on Mt. Ida, along with the personifications of Truth [*Alētheia*] and Justice [*Dikē*].[17] He awoke from this sleep with the gift of prophecy. Moses, also, derives inviolable authority by interacting with God. We have numerous examples from antiquity of figures whose status and teachings are authorized by experiencing divine visitation. Like such figures, Paul's repeated insistence that he has the endorsement of a divine being means his authority comes from a plane that entirely surpasses the authority of mortals, be they official representatives of the Roman government, local established religious leaders, or his immediate competitors within the Jesus movement. Paul makes this clear in 1 Cor 14:37–38: "Anyone who claims to be a prophet, or to have spiritual powers, must acknowledge that what I am writing to you is a command of the Lord. Anyone who does not recognize this is not to be recognized" (NRSV).

Paul's claims to have divine visions and to be chosen personally by gods appeal most readily (but by no means exclusively) to divine call narratives of the sacred *graphē*, as many of them include a visual component.[18] In such cases, the ancient Israelite viewer is marked out as special by the deity and given important

---

15. From 205 to 295 BCE, various Eastern kings adopt the title, thereby claiming divine authorization: Ptolemy V, Antiochus IV, Antiochus VI, and Seleucas VI.

16. Georgia Petridou, *Divine Epiphany in Greek Literature and Culture* (Oxford: Oxford University Press, 2015), 334.

17. Maximus of Tyre, *Dialexeis* 10.1a–10.1d.

18. For analysis of theophanies in the Hebrew Bible, see Savran, *Encountering the Divine*, 2005.

instructions that, when fulfilled, will change the course of human events. Yahweh appears to Jacob in a dream and deeds the land around Bethel to him, instructing him to spread his people out and settle it.[19] When he appears as a burning bush to Moses he instructs Moses to lead the Israelites out of Egypt.[20] He appears to Gideon and instructs him to save Israel from the power of Midian.[21] This also holds true with the call of Isaiah, when the prophet sees Yahweh enthroned in the temple.[22] Like the appearances of all gods in antiquity, Christ's appearance to Paul is rare and unusual enough to indicate a favored status for those who claim the sighting. Yet, in each instance of a call narrative that includes a visual component, the mortal subsequently asserts divine authority to carry out an agenda or undertake a course of action. Paul's divine visions function similarly.

Even more remarkable than having a deity appear before his eyes, Paul claims in 2 Corinthians to have been swept up to the third heaven, where he hears and sees divine things. He writes:

> It is nothing to boast; nothing is to be gained by it, but I will go on to visions and revelations [ὀπτασίας καὶ ἀποκαλύψεις] of the Lord. I know a person in Christ who fourteen years ago was caught up [ἁρπαγέντα] to the third heaven [ἕως τρίτου οὐρανοῦ]—whether in the body or out of the body I do not know; God knows. And I know that such a person— whether in the body or out of the body I do not know; God knows—was caught up into Paradise [ἡρπάγη εἰς τὸν παράδεισον] and heard things that are not to be told, that no mortal is permitted to repeat [ἄρρητα ῥήματα ἃ οὐκ ἐξὸν ἀνθρώπῳ λαλῆσαι].[23]

In the middle of this account, Paul switches to the first person—a shift that has left commentators with much room for debate regarding the identity of the man "in Christ" who experienced this disorienting and awesome event. Most studies, the present one included, argue that Paul describes something that happened to him.[24] But perhaps because the passage is difficult to reconcile, it has frequently

---

19. Gen 28.10–15.

20. Exod 3.1–10.

21. Judg 6.

22. Isa 6.

23. 2 Cor 12.1–4

24. Schantz, *Paul in Ecstasy*, Stegman, *Second Corinthians*, Gooder, *Only the Third Heaven?*, Harris, *Second Epistle to the Corinthians*, Lambrecht, *Second Corinthians*, Barnett, *Second*

been examined in light of Paul's disdain for boasting (the passage is often named the *Fool's Speech*),[25] or in light of Jewish apocalyptic. In addition to looking at the passage in light of ethical prohibitions against boasting, I suggest the passage also be viewed vis-à-vis how it is linked or bundled with his numerous divinatory and wonderworking claims.

We have numerous comparanda for Paul's claim to a heavenly ascent. These include Cicero's *Somnium Scipionis*, 2 Enoch,[26] Poimandres,[27] the *Ascension of Isaiah*,[28] Lucian's *Icaromenippus*,[29] the Assyrian Dream Book,[30] and Parmenides'

Epistle to the Corinthians, Georgi, *The Opponents of Paul in Second Corinthians*, Tabor, *Things Unutterable*, Segal, "Heavenly Ascent," Barrett, *Signs of an Apostle*, and Hughes, *Second Epistle to the Corinthians*, all agree that Paul refers to his own experiences, though they propose various reasons for Paul's use of the third person. Barrett, for example, suggests Paul's use of the Rabbinic "this man" to mean "I" (307). Barnett suggests that Paul keeps "this man" at arm's length because the event Paul describes happened fourteen years earlier and thus cannot compete with his competitors' "more up-to-date claims" of ascent (562). As early as Pelagius and John Chrysostom, commentators have linked Paul's use of the third person to his desire not to claim something so magnanimous on his own behalf. Tabor agrees with these earlier assessments. Goulder, "Vision and Knowledge," argues that the "man in Christ" is a friend of Paul, while Morton Smith, "Prolegomena to a Discussion of Aretologies," argues that the man may be Jesus himself. Hermann, "Apollos" argues that the man is Apollos.

25. For examination of this passage as Paul's *Fool's Speech*, see Barnett, *Second Epistle to the Corinthians*, 551–566.

26. F. I. Andersen, "2 (Slavonic Apocalypse of) Enoch, A New Translation and Introduction." In *The Old Testament Pseudepigrapha*, edited by James Charlesworth (Garden City, NY: Doubleday, 1983–1985), vol. 1; Martha Himmelfarb, *Ascent to Heaven in Jewish and Christian Apocalypses* (New York: Oxford University Press, 1993).

27. Brian P. Copenhaver, *Hermetica: The Greek Corpus Hermeticum and the Latin Asclepius in a New English Translation, With Notes and Introduction* (Cambridge: Cambridge University Press, 1992); Roelof van den Broek and Cis van Heertum, eds., *From Poimandres to Jacob Böhme: Gnosis, Hermetism and the Christian Tradition* (Amsterdam: Bibliotheca Philosophica Hermetica, 2000); Jörg Büchli, *Der Poimandres: Ein Paganisiertes Evangelium; Sprachliche und Begriffliche Untersuchungen zum 1. Traktat des Corpus Hermeticum* (Tübingen, Germany: Mohr Siebeck, 1987).

28. Jonathan Knight, *The Ascension of Isaiah* (Sheffield, UK: Sheffield Academic Press, 1995); Enrico Norelli, "The Political Issue of the Ascension of Isaiah: Some Remarks on Jonathan Knight's Thesis, and Some Methodological Problems." In *Early Christian Voices: In Texts, Traditions, and Symbols: Essays in Honor of François Bovon*, edited by David H. Warren, Ann Graham Brock, and David W. Pao (Boston: Brill Academic, 2003), 267–282; Richard Bauckham, *The Fate of the Dead: Studies on Jewish and Christian Apocalypses* (Leiden: Brill, 1998), 363–390.

29. T. E. Page and W. H. D Rouse, *Lucian, With an English Translation by A. M. Harmon*. Loeb Classical Library (New York: Macmillan, 1915), vol. 2.

30. A. Leo Oppenheim, "New Fragments of the Assyrian Dream-Book," *Iraq* 31.2 (1969): 153–165; A. Leo Oppenheim, "The Interpretation of Dreams in the Ancient Near East. With a Translation of an Assyrian Dream-Book." *Transactions of the American Philosophical Society*, New Series 46.3 (1956): 179–373.

prooemium.[31] It may also be productive to consider the abduction myth of Ganymede, and even the later heavenly ascension passages of the Mithras Liturgy.[32] However, I would most readily add to the preceding examples the exploits of special philosopher–magicians who claimed to have left their bodies and returned with secret information, or to have caused others to leave their bodies. Proclus preserves an account of the Hellenistic Peripatetic Clearchus of Soli who proved that leaving the body was possible:

> Here is a proof that it is possible for the soul to leave the body and enter it again: the man in Clearchus who used a soul-drawing wand [*psuchoulkos rhabdos*] on a sleeping lad and persuaded the great Aristotle, as Clearchus says in his books *On Sleep*, that the soul separates from the body and enters it again and treats it as a sort of hotel. For the man struck the boy with his wand and drew out his soul. Leading the soul some distance from the body with the stick, he demonstrated that the body remained motionless and was preserved unharmed and was unable to feel anything when pricked, as if it were dead . . . . But when the wand brought it back into association with the body and it reentered it the boy described everything in detail.[33]

The account of Clearchus of Soli is matched by others, such as Maximus of Tyre's description of a man who would lie motionless while his soul "escaped his body and wandered through the ether like a bird." Once he returned to his body, he would report all the people, places, and things he claimed to have seen.[34] Apollonius' account of Hermotimus of Clazomenae relays a tragic tale of

---

31. Maja E. Pellikaan-Engel, *Hesiod and Parmenides: A New View on Their Cosmologies and on Parmenides' Proem* (Amsterdam: Adolf M. Hakkert, 1978); Lisa Atwood Wilkinson, *Parmenides and To Eon: Reconsidering Muthos and Logos* (New York: Continuum International Publishing, 2009); Patricia Curd, *The Legacy of Parmenides: Eleatic Monism and Later Presocratic Thought* (Princeton, NJ: Princeton University Press, 1998).

32. See also Alan Segal, "Heavenly Ascent in Hellenistic Judaism, Early Christianity and Their Environment," *ANRW* (1980): 1333–1394. James Tabor, *Things Unutterable*, has pointed out that early Christian commentators had no problem with the fact that Paul claimed heavenly ascent. John Chrysostom, Pelagius, and Gregory of Nazianzus, for example, did not even address the heavenly ascent, as they shared a similar ancient cosmology, as well as an understanding for how god(s) functioned in the world of humans. Like Gooder, Tabor, *Things Unutterable*, 4 criticizes scholarship that distinguishes Paul from the world in which he lived: "It is assumed, because Paul is Paul (i.e. great Christian theologian and apostle), he is somehow 'pure' of the magical-mystical elements associated with ascent to heaven in other materials of the period."

33. Proclus, *Commentary on Plato's Republic*. Ogden trans.

34. Maximus of Tyre 10.2.

soul-wandering: "They say his soul would wander from his body and stay away for many years. Visiting places, it would predict what was going to happen, for example torrential rains or droughts, and in addition earthquakes and pestilences and the suchlike."[35] Unfortunately for Hermotimus, his wife was unable to protect his motionless body during one of his soul-sojourns, and it was set aflame by intruders. The soul had no body to which it could return, and the people of Clazomenae dedicated a temple to him.

Given the abundance of ancient Greek, Roman, and Judean evidence for soul-flight, travel through the ether to espy one's neighbors, to take in the grandeur of the cosmos, or to visit the realm of the gods, Paul's claims are familiar enough that his readers would recognize them. Indeed, they fit within a genre of claims that confer authority to the person who has returned from such an astonishing voyage. In Paul's case, the claims posit a direct and intimate relationship with the Judean deity and his resurrected son, Jesus Christ. This direct line is of primary importance, given the fact that Christ is a deity no one has previously heard of. Thus, legitimacy is mutually conferred: Paul presents himself as the in-the-flesh representative of an undiscovered, foreign deity, and that deity has endowed the apostle with miraculous abilities that can be extended to faithful followers.

Claims to Possess Secrets, Mysteries, and Special Knowledge From a Divine Source

Paul's letters are thick with the promise of secret knowledge, mysteries to be revealed, and hidden things to which he has privileged access. On three occasions in Romans he refers to mysteries and his own knowledge of future events to be revealed to the world. In Rom 8:18 he writes of the future glory which awaits his followers " . . . the glory about to be revealed to us . . . the revealing of the children of God." He tells his readers that he wants them "to understand this mystery" (11:25). Later he refers to things that were secret in the past but are now disclosed: "according to the revelation of the mystery [ἀποκάλυψιν μυστηρίου] that was kept secret [σεσιγημένου] for aeons of time but is now revealed." (16:25). He uses the word *mustērion* eight times in the undisputed letters[36] (an additional thirteen usages occur in the deutero-Pauline and Pastorals, indicating that Paul was still associated with mysteries and secret things after his death).[37] In 1 Corinthians he speaks of hidden divine knowledge misunderstood by the rulers

---

35. Apollonius, *Historiae Mirabiles* 3. Ogden trans.

36. Rom 11:25, 16:25; 1 Cor 2:1, 2:7, 4:1, 13:2, 14:2, 15:51.

37. Eph 1:9, 3:3, 3:4, 3:9, 5:32, 6:19; Col 1:26, 1:27, 2:2, 4:3; 2 Thess 2:7; 1 Tim 3:9, 3:16.

of his age: "But we speak God's wisdom, secret and hidden, which God decreed before the ages for our glory. None of the rulers of this age understood this." (1 Cor 2:7). He tells his Corinthian readers to think of themselves as stewards of God's mysteries [οἰκονόμους μυστηρίων θεοῦ].[38] In 2 Corinthians Paul writes that the god of this world has blinded the minds of the *apistoi* [ἐτύφλωσεν τὰ νοήματα τῶν ἀπίστων] so that they cannot see the light of Paul's good news [τὸν φωτισμὸν τοῦ εὐαγγελίου].[39] By definition, those who are faithful to Paul's message are those whose minds are not blinded. Later, in his description of being swept up to the third heaven, he claims to have heard things "that are not to be told, that no mortal is permitted to repeat" ["ἄρρητα ῥήματα ἃ οὐκ ἐξὸν ἀνθρώπῳ λαλῆσαι"].[40] In Galatians Paul claims to have gone to Jerusalem because he was directed to do so through a revelation [κατὰ ἀποκάλυψιν].[41] In addition to mysteries, he speaks of things being "revealed" on seventeen occasions.[42]

Not only does Paul profess to have access to secret knowledge, mysteries, and instructions through revelation, his secret knowledge is frequently tied to the equally exclusive and powerful skills of reading and writing. As we saw in Chapter 3, reading and interpreting the ancient books of Moses in a divinatory capacity constituted a significant aspect of Paul's overall divinatory practice. In Rom 3:21 he states that "apart from the Law, the justice of God has been disclosed, and is attested by the law and the prophets." The law and prophets are books that Paul can read and interpret, but most of his followers cannot—both because they are predominantly illiterate and because they have no expertise in Judean sacred books. At every turn, Paul quotes and interprets his holy books to gentile listeners who are moderately familiar, at best, with such stories. In his hands, then, Paul habitually possesses the very mysteries to be revealed, and such possession imbues him with unique power vis-à-vis readers and followers.

The possession of secret and mysterious information is, likewise, linked to his ability to perform wondrous powers. In 1 Cor 2:1–4 he reminds them, "I did not come proclaiming the mystery [*to mustērion*] of God to you in lofty words or wisdom . . . but with a demonstration of the pneuma and of power [*dunamis*]." In 1 Cor 13 Paul weighs the value of love [*agapē*] against all the other qualities that a faithful follower may have: the ability to speak in tongues, the power to

---

38. 1 Cor 4:1.

39. 2 Cor 4:4.

40. 2 Cor 12:4.

41. Gal 2:2.

42. Rom 1:17, 1:18, 2:5, 8:18, 8:19, 16:25; 1 Cor. 1:7, 3:13, 14:6, 14:26, 14:30; 2 Cor 12:1, 12:7; Gal 1:12, 1:16, 2:2, 3:23.

prophesy, and to understand "all mysteries and all knowledge."[43] Without *agapē*, such things are meaningless, he teaches, but the passage reinforces Paul's own association of mysteries with divinatory powers. Perhaps his greatest secret of all, which he reveals to his readers, is the magical, mystical transformation of the body from 1 Cor 15:51, discussed in Chapter 4: "Listen, I will tell you a mystery! We will not all die, but we will all be changed, in a moment, in the twinkling of an eye, at the last trumpet. For the trumpet will sound and the dead will be raised imperishable, and we will be changed."[44]

In some ways, the content of Paul's secrets and mysteries is less important than the function of secrecy itself. As Hugh Urban suggests, "Secrecy is better understood ... not in terms of its content or substance—which is ultimately unknowable, if there even is one—but rather in terms of its forms or strategies— the tactics by which social agents conceal or reveal, hoard or exchange, certain valued information."[45] In his analysis of secrecy and esotericism in the Dead Sea Scrolls, Samuel Thomas expands on this notion, "Secret knowledge bestows certain advantages upon the knower, especially if it is a theological kind of knowledge that ties its legitimacy to divine provenance and to notions of special revelation."[46] This applies to Paul as much as it does to those who initiate into mysteries at places like Eleusis or Samothrace. Because of the oath to secrecy for initiates, we do not know what was "revealed" at Eleusis, for example, but some scholars suspect it may have been simply an ear of corn.[47] Regardless of the content of the mystery, the possession of something called a "secret" or a "mystery" increases the prestige and social capital of those in possession of the private but divine information; the one who possesses the information enjoys

---

43. "τὰ μυστήρια πάντα καὶ πᾶσαν τὴν γνῶσιν."

44. "ἰδοὺ μυστήριον ὑμῖν λέγω· πάντες οὐ κοιμηθησόμεθα, πάντες δὲ ἀλλαγησόμεθα, ἐν ἀτόμῳ, ἐν ῥιπῇ ὀφθαλμοῦ, ἐν τῇ ἐσχάτῃ σάλπιγγι· σαλπίσει γάρ, καὶ οἱ νεκροὶ ἐγερθήσονται ἄφθαρτοι, καὶ ἡμεῖς ἀλλαγησόμεθα."

45. Hugh Urban, "The Torment of Secrecy: Ethical and Epistemological Problems in the Study of Esoteric Traditions," *History of Religions* 37 (1998): 210.

46. Samuel Thomas, *The "Mysteries" of Qumran: Mystery, Secrecy, and Esotericism in the Dead Sea Scrolls* (Atlanta, GA: Society of Biblical Literature, 2009), 2. For further studies on secrecy in religious practice in antiquity, see Markus Mockmuehl, *Revelation and Mystery in Ancient Judaism and Pauline Christianity* (Tübingen, Germany: Mohr Siebeck, 1990); Hans G. Kippenberg and Guy G. Stroumsa, eds., *Secrecy and Concealment: Studies in the History of Mediterranean and Near Eastern Religions* (Leiden: Brill, 1995).

47. On the oath to secrecy, see Diogenes Laertius, *Vita Phil.* 7.7.186; that the secret revelation at Eleusis might be an ear of corn is suggested by Hippolytas of Rome in his *Refutation of all Heresies* (5.5).

the elevated status of gatekeeper–teacher vis-a-vis those who wish to acquire the knowledge.

The practice of concealing and divulging private and privileged divine information was a widely recognized practice in antiquity, especially among itinerant preacher–wonderworkers. In the *Phaedo*, for example, Socrates describes the important secret information possessed by founders of the mystery rites: "And I fancy that those men who established the mysteries were not unenlightened, but in reality had a hidden meaning when they said long ago that whoever goes uninitiated and unsanctified to the other world will lie in the mire, but he who arrives there initiated and purified will dwell with the gods. For as they say in the mysteries, 'the thyrsus-bearers are many, but the mystics few.'"[48] Strabo tells us of the presumed origins of Orpheus: "At the foot of Olympus lies the city of Dium. The village of Pimpeia is its neighbor. There they say Orpheus the Ciconian lived. A sorcerer [*goēs*]. He first lived the life of a beggar priest [*agurteuōn*] by means of music and divination [*mantikē*] and the celebration of the secret rites of mystery-initiation [*teletas*]. Later on he began to think more highly of himself and acquired for himself a troop of disciples and a degree of power."[49] The prominence of mystery-language in Paul's letters has prompted numerous scholars over the past century to query the similarities between Pauline *ekklēsiai* and so-called mystery religions.[50]

The notion of mysteries was so much a part of the fabric of ancient religiosity that numerous authors parody it. In the *Clouds*, Aristophanes' character Strepsiades knocks on the door of the Thinkery—a school that teaches wealthy but aimless gadabouts to turn mediocre arguments into foolproof ones. In knocking, he disrupts the thought of an advanced disciple, who initially refuses to divulge the sacred mysterious thoughts that were consuming him, saying, "It is not lawful to discuss it except to disciples." Strepsiades assures him of his own disciple status and the student relents, warning, "I will tell you, but you must

---

48. *Phaedo* 69c. Plato. *Plato in Twelve Volumes*, vol. 1 translated by Harold North Fowler; Introduction by W. R. M. Lamb. (Cambridge, MA: Harvard University Press; London: William Heinemann, 1966).

49. Strabo, frag. 19. Ogden trans.

50. Opinions on the matter range from equating Pauline groups to mystery cults, to claiming that Pauline groups are utterly unlike such groups. See H. A. A. Kennedy, *St. Paul and the Mystery-Religions* (London: Hodder & Stoughton, 1913); Stanley Stowers argues that such connections are weaker than those between Pauline groups resembling philosophical groups. See Stanley Stowers, "Does Pauline Christianity Resemble a Hellenistic Philosophy?" In *Redescribing Paul and the Corinthians*, edited by Ron Cameron and Merrill Miller (Atlanta, GA: Society of Biblical Literature, 2011).

regard these as mysteries"[*mustēria*].[51] The sacred mysteries revealed are that Socrates figured out how to measure the distance jumped by a flea by dipping its feet in wax, he learned the origin of buzzing sounds from a gnat (its posterior, he deduced, is like a tiny trumpet), and he secretly devised a metal compass-hook for stealing other people's cloaks at the public gymnasium. Once the doors fully open to the Thinkery school, Strepsiades and the disciple find Socrates foolishly swinging in the air from a basket, observing the heavens. Five hundred years after Aristophanes, Lucian will equally lampoon the notion of mysteries in his parody *Podagra*, or *Gout*. A man afflicted terribly by gout, thinking himself unfit for any deity, is initiated into the sacred mystery rites of the goddess, "Resistless Gout, the mistress of men's toils."[52] The mysteries that initiates encounter include foot, knee, ankle, hip, groin, and thigh pain. These divine mysteries are followed by others: inflammation and pain of the shoulder, arm, hand, elbows, and wrists (120–124). Lucian's Chorus exclaims, "Mighty Maid with heart of steel, Goddess dreadful in thy wrath, Hear the cries of thine own priests. Prosperous Gout, how great thy power!"[53]

For Aristophanes and Lucian, such profound, divine revelations are nothing short of absurdities. From the fourth century BCE to the height of the Roman Empire, discourses and practices pertaining to secret information and divine mysteries were so pervasive that even comedians took aim. When Paul claims to have returned from the third heaven with "things that are not to be told, that no mortal can repeat," he does so within a larger context in which his claims are nearly stereotypical for itinerant figures like him. Thus, Pauline mystery-language reflects similar language of its era—revered by many and satirized by others.

Claims to Be Commanded by a Deity or Other Divine Being

Paul's divine visions and possession of divine mysterious knowledge are simply evidence for a more common and more important claim that he makes of himself: that he has been commanded by a god to do what he does. His specific parlance includes claims of being chosen, being set apart, being called, and being sent. These images, as we will see, are largely derived from borrowing descriptions of prophets in his holy books. But more important, such claims are quite common in antiquity and, as such, Paul's rhetoric can be situated within a larger

---

51. Aristophanes, *Clouds* 143.

52. Lucian, *Podagra* 139. Translated by M. D. MacLeod. Loeb Classical Library (Cambridge, MA: Harvard University Press, 1967), vol. 8.

53. Ibid., 191–194.

milieu of those who ground their actions in divine authority. This is true of religious specialists, political figures, military leaders, and the founders of voluntary associations.

Beyond his divinations, his wonders, and his assertion of divine epiphanies, Paul is boldly explicit in his specialized role. His self-introduction in Rom 1:1–3 cannot be any clearer: "Paul, a servant of Jesus Christ, called as an apostle, set apart for the good news of God, whom he promised long ago according to his prophets in the holy writings concerning his son, who descended from the seed of David according to the flesh." He repeats this assertion in the introduction of 1 Corinthians: "Paul, called to be an apostle of Jesus Christ through the will of God." Two notions frame the conviction of his claim—being called [*klētos*] and being sent [*apostolos*].

The word *apostolos* has an unremarkable history prior to Paul's vigorous appropriation of it. A cognate of the verb *apostellein, to send out* or *to send forth*,[54] the earlier uses of *apostolos* generally denote expeditions or delegations—usually political or military in nature. Karl H. Rengstorf observes that *apostolos* is often paired with *ploion* [ship] and refers to specifically seafaring expeditions or delegations.[55] Thus, Lysias uses *apostolos* as simply the dispatching or commissioning of naval fleets (*On the Property of Aristophanes* 21.4, 43.3). Likewise, Demosthenes denotes the expedition of a specially commissioned fleet of ships as *apostolos* (3 *Olynthiac* 5.7; 1 *Philippic* 35.7; *On the Crown* 80.2). More rarely in its earlier

---

54. For a closer examination of the etymological aspects of *apostellein*, especially the distinction between *apostellein* and *pempein*, see Rengstorf, *Theological Dictionary of the New Testament*, 398–406; studies on the apostolate include A. A. Kennedy, "The Scope and Function of the Apostolate in the New Testament," *The Biblical World* 33.3 (1909): 160–170; Ernest D. Burton, "The Office of the Apostolate in the Early Church," *The American Journal of Theology* 16.4 (1912): 561–588; J. B. Lightfoot. "The Name and Office of an Apostle." In *Epistle of Saint Paul to the Galatians* (1865; reprint Grand Rapids, MI: Zondervan, 1957), 92–101; Kirsopp Lake, "The Twelve and the Apostles." In *The Beginnings of Christianity, Part 1, The Acts of the Apostles* (1933; reprint Grand Rapids, MI: Baker, 1979), vol. 5, 37–59; Sean Freyne, *The Twelve: Disciples and Apostles* (London: Sheed and Ward, 1968); Walter Schmithals, *The Office of Apostle in the Early Church* (New York: Abingdon, 1969); Jacques Dupont, "Le nom d'Apôtres: a-t-il été donné aux Douze par Jésus?" In *Études sur les évangiles synoptiques*, edited by Frans Neirynck (Leuven, Belgium: Peeters, 1985), 2.976–1018; Francis Agnew, "The Origin of the NT Apostle-Concept: A Review of Research," *Journal of Biblical Literature* 105 (1986): 75–96; Raymond Brown "The Twelve and the Apostolate," *New Jerome Biblical Commentary* 1377–1381 (135–157), 1989.

55. Rengstorf, *Theological Dictionary of the New Testament*, 407. Rengstorf links the common seafaring aspect of delegations with word's early usage to explain its near absence from the LXX and other Judean texts: "The Palestinians had no direct access to the sea and were thus under no necessity of equipping or even planning maritime expeditions" (413). Schmithals, *The Office of Apostle in the Early Church*, and Lightfoot, "The Name and Office of an Apostle," also document the early seafaring associations with *apostolos*.

usage, it describes an individual: Herodotus 1.21 uses *apostolos* interchangeably with *angelos* as the herald sent to broker a truce, and at 5.38 the Milesian leader Aristagoras is described as *apostolos* when he travels to Lacedaemon to forge an alliance. In the LXX, variations of the verb *apostellein* occur over seven hundred times, often when Yahweh personally sends out one of his heralds or commissions an Israelite with an important task. Thus, in Exod 23:20, God tells the Israelites "I am going to send [*ego apostellō*] an *angelos* in front of you, to guard you on the way as he brings you to the place that I have prepared."

Even more poignant for our purposes is Exod 3:10–15, in which variants of *apostellein* occur five times as Yahweh commissions Moses to go to Pharaoh and lead the Israelites out of Egypt. Moses is unconvinced of his own fitness for such a daunting task, and even less confident that the Israelites will acknowledge his authority. God responds by telling Moses "Thus you shall say to the Israelites, 'The Lord, the God of your ancestors, the God of Abraham, the God of Isaac, and the God of Jacob, has sent me [*apestalken me*] to you'" (3:15). As a noun *apostolos* appears only once in the LXX, when the blind prophet Ahijah bears terrible news on behalf of God, to be related to Jeroboam through his wife. She comes disguised to Ahijah's door and he says "Come in, wife of Jeroboam . . . . I am an *apostolos* with harsh news for you [lit. *I am a harsh apostolos for you*] (1 Kgs 14:6). Just prior to her arrival, God has informed Ahijah not only that the wife would be coming, but he also instructs Ahijah to tell her that, because God is dissatisfied with Jeroboam, disaster will come to all his kin. Josephus uses *apostolos* once, when he describes the Judean ambassadors sent to Rome to petition Caesar for Judean independence (*Judean Antiquities* 17.300). More often than not, he refers to the envoy as *hoi presbeis*, but the single time he does refer to them collectively as *apostolos* he makes a point of saying they were sent by the authority of the nation [οἱ ἀποσταλέντες γνώμῃ τοῦ ἔθνους].[56]

Paul seems to model his claim to a divine authorizing command most explicitly on the "call" of Jeremiah, however:

> Now the word of the LORD came to me saying, 5 "Before I formed you in the womb [*en koilia*] I knew you, and before you went out from your mother [*ek mētras*] I made you holy [*hēgiaka se*]; I appointed you a prophet to the nations" [*prophētēn eis ethnē*]. 6 Then I said, "Ah, Lord GOD! Truly I do not know how to speak, for I am only a boy." 7 But the LORD said to me, "Do not say, 'I am only a boy'; for you shall go to all

---

56. Philo does not use *apostolos*, but does on three occasions use *apostolē* to denote the "sending out" of an *angelos* and to interpret the name Methuselah as the sending out of death (*On the Posterity of Cain* 41.3, 44.2, 73.2; *On the Giants* 17.3).

to whom I send you [*exaposteilō se*], and you shall speak whatever I command you [*ean enteilōmai soi*]. 8 Do not be afraid of them, for I am with you to deliver you, says the LORD." 9 Then the LORD put out his hand and touched my mouth; and the LORD said to me, "Now I have put my words in your mouth.¹⁰ See, today I appoint you over nations [*ta ethnē*] and over kingdoms, to pluck up and to pull down, to destroy and to overthrow, to build and to plant." (Jer 1:4–10 NRSV, modified)

The author of Jeremiah crafts an authorizing moment that cannot be argued with or refuted. So utterly chosen by God, he is handpicked while in the womb [*en koilia*] of his mother [*ek mētras*], made holy [*hagios*], told that he will be sent out [*apostellein*], and appointed over the nations [*ta ethnē*]; the very words of God are placed into his mouth, rendering him an infallible prophet. Let us compare the divine authorizing account in Jeremiah with Paul's self-description in Gal 1:15–16:

But when God, who had set me apart [*aphorisas me*] from my mother's womb [*ek koilias mētros mou*] and called [*kalesas*] me through his grace, was pleased to reveal his Son to me so that I might proclaim him among the gentiles [*ta ethnē*], I did not confer with any human being, 17 nor did I go up to Jerusalem to those who were already apostles before me, but I went away at once into Arabia, and afterwards I returned to Damascus.

Combined with the frequent claims to be apostle [*apostolos*] to the gentiles [*ta ethnē*] and the use of *hagios* as a descriptor for himself and followers, the references to being selected while in his mother's womb closely match the divine authorizing technique of Jeremiah.

While his terminology may draw most directly from Jeremiah and other "divine call" narratives of the LXX,[57] the claim itself is entirely in keeping with the authorizing practices of Greeks, Romans, and Judeans more broadly. For example, Sarah Rollens has recently examined a number of strategies of divine authorization found in inscriptions affiliated with voluntary associations. Such inscriptions frequently claim that the deity appeared to someone and has commanded that person to undertake a certain course of action, thereby authorizing that course of action in the eyes of viewers or fellow participants. Rollens considers, for example,

---

57. Compare also Isa 44:2, 49:1, 49:5; Ps 22:9–10.

*SIG*³ 985, which dates to late second- or early first-century BCE Philadelphia in Asia Minor:

ἀγαθῆι τ[ύχηι]. | ἀνεγράφησαν ἐφ' ὑγιείαι κα[ὶ κοινῆι σωτηρίαι (?)] | καὶ δόξηι τῆι ἀρίστηι τὰ δοθέ [ντα παραγγέλμα]|τα Διονυσίωι καθ' ὕπνον π[ρόσοδον διδόν]||τ' εἰς τὸν ἑαυτοῦ οἶκον ἀνδρά[σι καὶ γυναιξὶν] | ἐλευθέροις καὶ οἰκέταις. Διὸς [γὰρ ἐν τούτωι] | τοῦ Εὐμενοῦς καὶ Ἑστίας τ[ῆς παρέδρου αὐ]|τοῦ καὶ τῶν ἄλλων θεῶν Σωτ[ήρων καὶ Εὐδαι]|μονίας καὶ Πλούτου καὶ Ἀρετῆς [καὶ Ὑγιείας] || καὶ Τύχης Ἀγαθῆς καὶ Ἀγαθοῦ [Δαίμονος καὶ Μνή]|μης καὶ Χαρίτων καὶ Νίκης εἰσὶν ἰδ[ρυμένοι βωμοί (?).] | τούτ[ωι] δέδωκεν ὁ Ζεὺς παραγγέλ[ματα τούς τε ἁ]|γνισμοὺς καὶ τοὺς καθαρμοὺς κ[αὶ τὰ μυστήρια (?) ἐπι]|τελεῖν κατά τε τὰ πάτρια καὶ ὡς νῦν [γέγραπται.

To good fortune! For health, . . . common salvation (?), and the best reputation, . . . the instructions (?) . . . which were given to Dionysios in his sleep were written down, . . . giving access (?) . . . into his house ([*oikos*]) to men . . . and women (?), free people and household slaves . . . . For in this house altars (?) . . . have been set up for Zeus Eumenes and Hestia . . . his consort (?), for the other Saviour gods, and for Eudaimonia [Prosperity], Ploutos [Wealth], Arete [Virtue], . . . Hygeia [Health] (?), (10) Agathe Tyche [Good Fortune], Agathos . . . Daimon [Good Spirit] (?), Mneme [Memory], the Charitai [the Graces], and Nike [Victory]. Zeus has given instructions to this man for the performance of the purifications, the cleansings, . . . and the mysteries (?) . . . in accordance with ancestral custom and in accordance with what has now . . . been written here (?).[58]

Following this introductory claim that Dionysios was issued a divine command to commence and perform the mystery rites in his *oikos*, *SIG*³ 985 proceeds to address the various rules and regulations of the household association: Sexual chastity of women is required; sexual seduction of others is anathema; spells, charms, and potions are forbidden; obedience to the god(s) is paramount. In return, it

58. Sarah Rollens, "The God Came to Me in a Dream: Epiphanies in Voluntary Associations as a Context for Paul's Visions of Christ," *Harvard Theological Review* 111.1 (2018) 41–65. Text and translation of *SIG*³ 985 taken from Philip Harland, "[121] Divine Instructions for the Household Association of Dionysios (late II–early I BCE)." In *Associations in the Greco-Roman World: An Expanding Collection of Inscriptions, Papyri, and Other Sources in Translation*, November 10, 2011. URL: http://philipharland.com/greco-roman-associations/divine-instructions-for-the-household-association-of-dionysios/. See also Gil H. Renberg, *"Commanded by the Gods": An Epigraphical Study of Dreams and Visions in Greek and Roman Religious Life*. PhD Dissertation, Duke University, 2003.

is hoped that the gods will extend mercy and bestow good rewards upon those who acquiesce. The final command of the inscription is to make physical contact with the divine command: "may those . . . men and (?) . . . women who have confidence in themselves touch this stone on . . . which the instructions of the god (?) . . . have been written, so that those who obey these instructions . . . and those who do not obey (?) . . . these instructions may become evident."[59] Touching the stone inscription would allow others to discern the obedient from the wayward; it would also separate those who accept the inscription as divine (and therefore authoritative) from those who do not.

Apuleius' *Metamorphoses* demonstrates how divine callings may have been presented in the cult of Isis. When she appears in person to Lucius, Isis commands him on the details of his participation in celebrations in her honor: "So therefore, pay careful attention to these commands [*istis imperiis*] of mine. The day which will be the day born from this night has been proclaimed mine by everlasting religious observance." She then provides him with clear instructions on how to join the procession so as to not appear as an outsider. After this "day of salvation" for him, she "calls" him as belonging to her for the rest of his life: "You will remember and keep forever sealed deep in your heart the fact that the rest of your life's course is pledged to me [*mihi reliqua vitae tuae curricula . . . vadata*] until the very limit of your last breath."[60] In his eagerness to finally undergo initiation into the rites of Isis, Lucius explains the divine calling which authorized and prepared him: "I had been long since announced and destined for the blessed ministry by a clearly visible and manifest mark of approval from the great deity." When Lucius is overcome with eagerness but still yet uninitiated, one of the priests of Isis beseeches him to be patient: "Besides, he said, there was no one in his company of priests with such corrupt character—or rather so determined to die—that he would dare to undertake this office thoughtlessly and sacrilegiously, without specific orders from the goddess [*seorsum iubente domina*], and thus incur fatal guilt."[61] According to Apuleius, the divine commands of Isis delineate every step of her worship by mortals: who, when, where, and how. It is for mortals, wisely, to understand why.

---

59. ὅσοι πιστεύσουσιν ἑα[υτοῖς ἄνδρες τε καὶ] | [γυ]ναῖκες τῆς γραφῆς ταύτης, ἐν [ἧι τὰ τοῦ θεοῦ παραγγὲλ]|[μα]τά εἰσιν γεγραμμένα ἵνα φαν[εροὶ γίνωνται οἱ κατα]|[κολου]θοῦ[ντ]ες τοῖς παραγγὲλ[μασιν καὶ οἱ μὴ κατακολου]|||[θοῦν]τες.

60. Apuleius, *Metamorphoses* 11.6. Translated by J. Arthur Hanson. Loeb Classical Library (Cambridge, MA: Harvard University Press, 1989).

61. Apuleius, *Metam.* 11.21.

We have numerous examples of gods calling or commanding people to do or act in certain ways in antiquity. Such claims are meaningful strategies for bolstering the credibility of any particular course of action, especially when that course of action may be viewed as questionable. Even among the already-powerful, such claims confer power and social capital. Plutarch recounts how Ptolemy Soter defended his theft of the colossal statue of Pluto from Sinope to Alexandria because the divine statue commanded him to do so in a dream, after which the statue took the name of Pluto in Egypt, namely, Serapis.[62] The presence of that colossal statue in Alexandria would only aggrandize Ptolemy's standing among Egyptians, and further emulsify the mythologies of Pluto–Serapis. In a historical moment when Alexander the Great's former generals compete ruthlessly for land, power, and the material and intellectual inheritance of Greek culture, Ptolemy's theft of the colossal statue from Asia Minor is blameless if demanded by the god. But among those who have comparatively little social capital, such as Paul, the assertion that a god is the true authority behind your actions and choices becomes much more instrumental. While Paul's language certainly reflects the imagery we see in Jeremiah, the Jeremiah account itself shares similar interests in validation and power that we see in the divine commands of Ptolemy Soter, Dionysios of Philadelphia, and Apuleius' Lucius.

Divinatory Pedagogy

I have established that Paul demonstrates expertise in interpreting signs and performing wonders. But he also offers his followers the opportunity to receive and to comprehend many of these same skills themselves. We ought not to underestimate the importance of this facet of Paul's teaching; while most of our evidence for specialists like Paul does not explicitly discuss the transmission of divinatory skills from expert to follower(s), we have sufficient evidence that developing these abilities was both desirable and sought. In Acts, Luke depicts Simon offering to buy from Peter and John the powers that divine *pneuma* has transmitted to them (Acts 8:18). Alexander of Abonoteichus learned many of his skills as a disciple of Apollonius of Tyana. Dio Cassius tells us that Tiberius became so proficient in *manteia* that he was able to determine that a *daimon* had been sent to him in his dreams, instructing him to give money to the man who had sent the *daimon* (57.15.7).[63] The emperor developed such proficiency in *manteia*

---

62. Plutarch, *On Isis and Osiris* 361F–362A.

63. "Tiberius, moreover, was forever in the company of Thrasyllus and made some use of the art of divination [μαντεία] every day, becoming so proficient in the subject himself, that when he

through long-term companionship with, trust in, and observation of his astrol-oger, Thrasyllus.[64] In 1 Cor 14:12 Paul calls his own readers "zealous for pneu-matic [abilities]" ["ζηλωταί ἐστε πνευμάτων"]. While many scholars have taken this to mean that Paul engages in such practices only to satisfy the demands of his Corinthian audience, my reading indicates that Paul is himself invested in such practices and goes to great lengths to teach his gentile audience the hierarchical value of each skill, as well as its appropriate usage. If nothing else, the assumption that the Corinthians influenced Paul's use of such practices admits that such skills and practices were highly valuable, and Paul's ability to train others would only increase his own appeal.

Paul's most thorough discussion of instructing followers in their divinatory abilities appears in 1 Corinthians. Yet, he makes a brief mention of this also in Gal 3:5 and Rom 1:11. As discussed in Chapter 4, Gal 3:5 demonstrates that Paul has taught this to his Galatian followers: "Is it through works of the law or through faithfulness to what you hear, that he [God] supplies to you the *pneuma* and performs miracles in/through you?" Paul reminds his Galatian readers that not only are they capable, through the power of his Judean deity, to possess *dunameis*, but that they do so enabled through the *pneuma* of Christ. At the beginning of his letter to the Romans, Paul writes that he is longing to see them so that he may share [*metadō*] some "spiritual gift" [*charisma humin pneumatikon*] to strengthen them.[65] Paul means this quite literally—*metadidōmi* means to dole out, transmit, or give a portion of something, and a *charisma pneumatikon*, as we have seen, is an actual divinatory ability such as healing, channeling divine speech, interpreting divine signs, or performing some other kind of wondrous act. Paul is not speaking metaphorically when he expresses eagerness to bestow such powers on potential gentile followers, but wishes in fact to instruct them in the usage and meaning of such powers. To borrow an observation from Brent Nongbri, Paul positions him-self as a "broker of divine benefaction."[66]

---

was once bidden in a dream to give money to a certain man, he realized that a spirit had been called up before him by deceit [ὅτι δαίμων τις ἐκ γοητείας], and so put the man to death. 8 But as for all the other astrologers and magicians [ἀστρολόγους καὶ τοὺς γόητας] and such as practised divination [ἐμαντεύετό] in any other way whatsoever, he put to death those who were foreigners [ξένους] and banished all the citizens that were accused of still employing the art at this time after the previous decree by which it had been forbidden to engage in any such business in the city; but to those that obeyed immunity was granted" (Dio Cassius, 57.15.7. Cary trans.).

64. Tacitus, *Ann.* 6.20–22; Suetonius, *Tib.* 14, 62, *Cal.* 19; Dio Cassius, 55.11, 57.15, 58.27.

65. Rom 1:11: "ἐπιποθῶ γὰρ ἰδεῖν ὑμᾶς, ἵνα τι μεταδῶ χάρισμα ὑμῖν πνευματικὸν εἰς τὸ στηριχθῆν αι ὑμᾶς."

66. Brent Nongbri, "Two Neglected Textual Variants in Philippians 1," *Journal of Biblical Literature* 128.4 (2009): 803–808.

In addition to references to divinatory skills in Galatians and Romans, the apostle outlines such skills in 1 Cor 12–14. As we have seen, Paul's organization and taxonomy of such powers provide scholars with a window into what he himself practiced, but we must remember that these passages are also didactic. Paul is training his readers to understand (1) the distribution of powers among followers, (2) the hierarchy of divine powers, and (3) the appropriate usage of such powers. In the event that they are uncertain about this knowledge, he assures them that Christ's divine *pneuma* is accompanied by the ability to understand the benefits of the *pneuma*: "For what human being knows what is truly human [τοῦ ἀνθρώπου] except the human spirit that is within? So also no one comprehends what is truly God's except the spirit of God [τὸ πνεῦμα τοῦ θεοῦ]. Now we have received not the spirit of the world, but the spirit that is from God, so that we may understand the gifts bestowed [χαρισθέντα] on us by God" (NRSV, modified).[67]

In terms of distribution, Paul teaches that all participants are apportioned the disclosure of pneuma for the common good.[68] Thereafter, skills are individually apportioned: utterance of wisdom, utterance of knowledge, *pistis*, the power to heal, the ability to perform miracles, discernment of *pneumata* or spirits, channeling types of divine speech (prophecy and tongues), and interpretation of tongues.[69] He exhorts them to understand such divinatory skills as coming from one and the same divine *pneuma*; he uses the metaphor of parts of a body to explain that diverse practices are akin to the diverse limbs and organs. Thus, to Paul, this repertoire of divinatory practices must cohere to his idea of a well-functioning unified body and must not include divinatory practices that might act as parasitic or autonomous limbs; instead, they are for "building up" the *ekklēsia*.

In addition to outlining the distribution of divinatory skills, Paul instructs his readers to understand the value and prestige of each skill. In 1 Cor 12:4–11 his distribution list appears to value each skill equally. Yet, he quickly establishes the rank of each power. He first ranks people who have the powers, followed by the powers themselves:

---

67. 1 Cor 2:11–12.

68. ἑκάστῳ δὲ δίδοται ἡ φανέρωσις τοῦ πνεύματος πρὸς τὸ συμφέρον (1 Cor 12.7).

69. Such abilities also include things like "knowledge" and "wisdom," which come upon them through divine benefaction rather than through technical training, apprenticeship, or education. Such abilities are not miraculous in and of themselves, but their method of acquirement renders them outstanding and miraculous.

And God has appointed in the *ekklēsia* first apostles, second prophets, third teachers; then deeds of power [δυνάμεις], then gifts of healing [χαρίσματα ἰαμάτων], forms of assistance, forms of leadership, various kinds of tongues [γένη γλωσσῶν]. Are all apostles? Are all prophets? Are all teachers? Do all work miracles [πάντες δυνάμεις]? Do all possess gifts of healing? Do all speak in tongues? Do all interpret [πάντες διερμηνεύουσιν]? But strive for the greater gifts [ζηλοῦτε δὲ τὰ χαρίσματα τὰ μείζονα]. And I will show you a still more excellent way [Καὶ ἔτι καθ᾽ ὑπερβολὴν ὁδὸν ὑμῖν δείκνυμι].

For Paul, not all followers have all the divinatory powers distributed through God's *pneuma*. And some powers are greater than others, inevitably reckoning some participants more powerful than others. Expertise in the full range of pneumatic powers appears relegated to the rank of apostles; Paul does not list practices in which he has no expertise. Likewise, his super-apostle rivals demonstrate similar expertise. Second to the apostles are prophets and teachers. He encourages them especially to engage in intelligible divine speech (prophecy) over unintelligible divine speech (tongues): "One who prophesies is greater than one who speaks in tongues, unless someone interprets, so that the *ekklēsia* may be built up" (14:5). He reminds readers that not everyone is an apostle, prophet, or teacher. Not everyone can work miracles or possess the ability to heal. Not all followers speak in tongues and interpret tongues. While claiming that not all people possess all such rarefied skills he exhorts them: "But strive for the greater gifts. And I will show you a still more excellent way." Paul claims initially that the ability to perform one wonder versus another is determined by the *pneuma* (1 Cor 1:11), but in encouraging them to "strive for the greater gifts" (12:31) he suggests that his followers can develop their skills with some kind of intention or training. He clarifies that this expansion and improvement of divinatory abilities can also come through petitioning God: "Therefore one who speaks in a tongue should pray for the power to interpret" (14:13). As we will see in Chapter 6, this also appears dependent on *pistis*.

Paul is clear with his readers regarding appropriate usage of their developing powers. He expresses frustration, even, at their misunderstanding and inferior execution of skills: "I thank God that I speak in tongues more than all of you" (14:18). His metaphor of the body is to convince them that the individual demonstration of divine power, for the sake of asserting the practitioner's superiority, is for naught: "Indeed, the body does not consist of one member but of many. If the foot would say 'Because I am not a hand, I do not belong to the body,' that would not make it any less a part of the body" (12:14). He argues that even the weakest parts of the body are indispensable, and then draws his metaphor back to the range of divine powers and their practitioners among his gentile readers: "Now you are the body of Christ and individually members of it" (12:27). While Paul frequently humbles himself to his readers,[70] his divinatory expertise strongly differentiates him from them. Paul is the foremost interpreter of Judean holy *graphē*, through which he practices much of his prophesying, and he appears to be the only one (besides his competitors) who can claim expertise in all of these divinatory skills. As *apostolos*, Paul wields more authority and possesses greater symbolic capital than one who prophesies or heals or interprets. His followers each share in a fraction of his entire divinatory repertoire.

Paul is not alone in claiming that his particular method to salvation is accompanied by a host of divine skills that are hierarchically arranged and attainable to initiates. Similar things are offered by Apollonius of Tyana, in his Letter 52. Apollonius' reputation as a wonderworking philosopher–magician only increased over time, especially by the time Philostratus wrote a biography of him in the early third century. In Letter 52, which was almost certainly fabricated after Apollonius' death, the Neopythagorean addresses a Stoic competitor and adversary, Euphrates, regarding the merits of Pythagoreanism. Apollonius outlines and hierarchizes the "selling points" of Pythagoreanism, much in the way Paul does when he lists and evaluates the specialness of divinatory abilities, according to the intensity of one's *pistis*. Apollonius asks Euphrates rhetorically, "If someone associates with a [true] Pythagorean, what will he get from him, and in what quantity?" He then answers his own inquiry with an extensive list that includes knowledge of things like statesmanship, astronomy, and harmonics, but also "medicine [*iatrikēn*], complete and god-given prophecy [*pasan theian mantikēn*], and also the higher rewards—greatness of mind, of soul ... piety, knowledge of the gods [*gnôsin theôn*] and not just supposition, but familiarity with blessed spirits [*daimonôn*] and not just faithfulness [*pistin*], but friendship with both gods and spirits ... health, cheerfulness, and immortality."[71] The qualities on Apollonius' list promise a life characterized by wisdom, equanimity, and knowledge, which culminates in intimacy with gods and the state of *athanasia* [immortality].

Both Apollonius' Letter 52[72] and 1 Cor 12 are good examples of the types of promises offered to those who join ranks and follow a divinatory expert who also claims philosophical knowledge. Apollonius was as much a Pythagorean

---

70. 1 Cor 15.9; 2 Cor 10.1, 11.16–21.

71. Letter 52, Jones trans., with modifications.

72. Working with the letters of Apollonius is challenging at best, given the problems of authenticity. In his authoritative commentary, Penella writes, "For most of the letters we must be content with stating probabilities and setting forth tentative lines of argumentation." See Robert Penella, *The Letters of Apollonius of Tyana: A Critical Text with Prolegomena* (Leiden: Brill,1979), 24.

philosopher as he was a miracle-worker, despite Philostratus' fantastic portrayal that leans heavily on the side of the miraculous. Paul is as much a divinatory specialist as he is an exegete of holy books and teacher of ethics (Paul's divinatory expertise pertains directly to his prophetic books, as we have seen). Apollonius promises immortality, as does Paul in the form of salvation and pneumatic resurrection. Both offer secret knowledge, healing skills, and prophecy. Apollonius does not offer wonderworking capabilities in his list of benefits to the Pythagorean, but Paul also makes it quite clear that wonderworking is at the top of the list of gifts and therefore unlikely to be attained by many. According to their respective letters, Apollonius and Paul share a number of practices, in fact: They claim to refuse money, they refer to healing, and refrain from boasting. To his "inveterate enemy" Euphrates, Apollonius defends and justifies hypothetical charges the latter would lay against him, including the practice of divination,[73] healing,[74] eating separate from others,[75] and the refusal to accept money and gifts.[76]

When using Letter 52 in discussions of Paul, the letter's date introduces complications. In his introduction to the Loeb Classical Library edition of the Letters of Apollonius, Christopher Jones suggests "It would not surprise if, in the feverish religious atmosphere of the Severan court, Philostratus had turned a remarkable but not exceptional Pythagorean teacher of the first century into a holy man for a new age."[77] No doubt, later writers tend to exaggerate the capabilities of those they seek to acclaim; this is seen extensively in the Apocryphal Acts and the Gospels. Yet, in *Alexander the False Prophet*, Lucian describes Alexander's pedigree in these terms: "This teacher and admirer of his was a man of Tyana by birth, one of those who had been followers of the notorious Apollonius, and who knew his whole bag of tricks."[78] We know that by the mid-second century Apollonius had developed the reputation for working wonders—a full seventy or eighty years prior to Philostratus' *Life*. Philostratus is hardly our only early source for information about Apollonius. The *Suda* tells us that Apollonius wrote *Initiations* or *On Sacrifices*, a *Will*, *Oracles*, *Letters*, a *Life of Pythagoras* (*Suda* A 3420) (*FGrHist* IV

---

73. 8.1.

74. 8.2.

75. 8.2.

76. 8.2.

77. *Letters of Apollonius*. Translated and edited by Christopher Jones. Loeb Classical Library (Cambridge, MA: Harvard University Press, 2006), 7.s.

78. *Alexander the False Prophet*, 5. A. M. Harmon, trans. Loeb Classical Library. (Cambridge, MA: Harvard University Press, 1925).

A 1064 T 9). Cassius Dio writes that Caracalla, "took such pleasure in magicians and charlatans [τοῖς δὲ μάγοις καὶ γόησιν] that he praised and honored Apollonius the Cappadocian, who flourished in the time of Domitian, though he was a complete magician and charlatan, and he built a heroic tomb for him."[79] In all, there are over fifty references to Apollonius prior to the sixth century, with a handful preceding Philostratus' *Life*.[80]

Apollonius' Letter 52 is useful in one of two ways. If we date it early, we have a meaningful, roughly contemporary comparandum for the way Paul elucidates the benefits he offers to potential followers (ethical improvement, divinatory and wonderworking abilities). If the letter is dated significantly later than Paul (the more likely possibility) it nevertheless gives us insight into how Paul's strategic claims might have been perceived one or two generations later. That is, if Letter 52 is read as a matter-of-fact list of practical benefits that might increase the appeal of Pythagoreanism, then what prevents us from reading Paul's claims the same way? In this sense, the date of the letter is immaterial to how we view similar claims in Pauline correspondence.

Conclusion

This chapter has demonstrated that Paul's practices of divination and wonderworking are framed and bolstered by strategic claims of divine authority. Who else better qualified to interpret divine signs or to transform the material nature of your body, than a figure who has been chosen, sent, and appointed by a deity to do so? Paul's discursive claims operate as a kind of rhetorical mortar, binding and stabilizing his numerous and disparate wonderworking and divinatory

---

79. Cassius Dio, 78.18.4. Jones trans.

80. All such references are collected in the Loeb Classical Library *Testamonia*, in the same volume edited by Jones. References to Apollonius that predate or are contemporaneous to Philostratus' *Life* include *Suda* A 3420; *Suda* 3421; Lucian, *Alexander the False Prophet* 5; Cassius Dio, *Histories* 67.18.1, 78.18.4; Philostratus of Athens, *Lives of the Sophists* 1.21, 2.5; Philostratus of Lemnos, *On the Correct Style of Writing Letters* 2.57; Origen, *Contra Celsum* 6.41. In the *Contra Celsum*, for example, Origen claims that, "About *mageia* we say that anyone wanting to know if philosophers are susceptible to *mageia* should read Moeragenes' memoirs of Apollonius of Tyana (the sorcerer and philosopher). There the man, not a Christian but a philosopher, said that not inconsiderable philosophers were beguiled by the sorcery in Apollonius after they had approached him as a quack magician; among these, I believe, he talked about the famous Euphrates and a certain Epicurean" (*Contra Celsum* 6.41, Jones trans LCL). Nevertheless, working with the letters of Apollonius is challenging, given the additional problems of authenticity. In his authoritative commentary, Robert Penella writes, "For most of the letters we must be content with stating probabilities and setting forth tentative lines of argumentation." See Robert Penella, *The Letters of Apollonius of Tyana: A Critical Text With Prolegomena* (Leiden: Brill,1979), 24.

practices, as well as his moral–ethical teachings. This authorization comes in many forms: divine visitations, a trip to the heavens, the possession of secret mysteries and knowledge, and the insistence that he has been especially selected and commanded by a god to accomplish the task of gentile salvation. And while Paul's claims function as a binding and stabilizing rhetorical strategy, they are rhetorical strategies that we commonly see elsewhere in the ancient world. These appear in descriptions of Orpheus, the parodies of Aristophanes and Lucian, the commissioning account of Jeremiah, and the inscription of Dionysios of Philadelphia—to name just a few of the comparanda examined.

Furthermore, as part of his larger rhetorical–divinatory practice, Paul engages in a divinatory pedagogy. He imparts to his followers how they, too, ought to contextualize, wield, develop, and understand their newfound divinatory and wonderworking abilities. Such outstanding abilities have not been visited upon his followers at random; on the contrary, they are to be understood as divine gifts extended from the faithful and rewarding Judean god to his faithful and obedient people. The following chapter will disentangle this complex relationship between gentile faithfulness and divinatory–wonderworking gifts.

6

Paul, Pistis, and Divine Powers

AN ECONOMY OF RECIPROCITY

THE PREVIOUS CHAPTERS redescribe the range of Paul's divinatory and wonderworking practices such that we can understand them in their ancient context. I have demonstrated that each practice has numerous ancient comparanda and that Paul's divinations and wonders are not specifically Christian or unique vis-à-vis his contemporaries. Nevertheless, how remarkable it must be to heal and cure the sick with no medical expertise and to be chosen by a god to channel divine speech; how indispensable to be a literate reader of divine signs; even more, how miraculous to attain immortality! While Paul defends his authority by frequently claiming to be called by and set apart by his deity, what of his followers? One might wonder how such extraordinary capabilities are bestowed upon regular people; how is it that Paul's followers, although they are largely non-Judeans, are able to accomplish such a range of unusual feats through the Judean deity? Moving forward, we will see how Paul links his repertoire of divinatory and wonderworking capabilities to the ethic of *pistis*, or faithfulness.

I argue that Paul frames these many divine gifts within a larger economy of reciprocity between gentile *pistis* and God's *charis*, delivered through the *pneuma* of Christ. That is, in an ongoing exchange of divine benefaction and human piety, divinatory and wonderworking skills constitute the "divine benefaction" bestowed on gentile followers, who offer their unwavering *pistis* in return. Furthermore, the greater a person's *pistis* toward the Judean deity, the more likely that person will be rewarded with concrete miracles and other benefits. Such gifts are delivered through Christ's *pneuma*, which interpenetrates the bodies of his followers, rendering them capable of the miracles and wonders examined in Chapters 3 and 4, and eventually transforming their flesh into something divine. This is not entirely surprising given that divinatory abilities were frequently understood to be gifts from gods; indeed, that is why Paul identifies them as such (that is, as *charismata*). Figure 6.1 illustrates this reciprocal exchange.

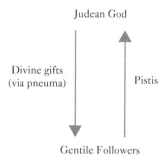

FIGURE 6.1 Divine gifts and gentile *pistis* in voluntary, reciprocal exchange.

Ample evidence demonstrates that divine benefaction [*charis*] is bestowed upon humans in return for their faithfulness, piety, and gratitude. This is unequivocally the case in Greek, Roman, and Judean religions, as it was in ancient Near Eastern religions (including Israelite). The mutual exchange of beneficence defines the ongoing reciprocal relations that mortals maintained with gods. Instead of critiquing reciprocity, as some New Testament scholars have claimed, Paul insists to his readers that their reciprocal relations are voluntary and that God's gifts are given "freely." Such discourse of willing participation, especially on the part of a powerful benefactor, is well within the bounds of ancient reciprocity. Some ancient philosophers (including Philo) oversimplified forms of reciprocity with gods as transactional exchange and then derided this as a crass and naïve understanding of the divine. But they do so in larger conversations that explore appropriate approaches to reciprocity, and not in a push to reject reciprocity overall. Curiously, many New Testament scholars reduce ancient reciprocity even more so to *do ut des* [I give so that you will give]—a kind of bribery or crude exchange of favors. In doing so, they tend to utilize this mischaracterization to demonstrate how Paul is distinct from and superior to the world that produced him.

This chapter first looks at how ancients understood the ethic of *pistis*, and its Latin equivalent, *fides*. It becomes clear that Paul does not introduce his readers to the importance of *pistis*, but rather, narrows its scope and redirects their *pistis* to his god exclusively. Second, I look at ancient practices of reciprocity and focus on Paul's strategy of situating gentile *pistis* within relations of reciprocity with his deity. I demonstrate that when Paul uses *charis*-related words (*charis, charites, charismata*) he is often referring to divinatory and wonderworking powers bestowed upon select mortals as rewards or as a show of divine favor. Paul stridently encourages the exclusive faithfulness of his followers and, as a show of favor and benefaction for such faithfulness, he promises that his deity will extend to them the various divinatory gifts in which Paul himself excels. Finally, the chapter addresses how and why New Testament scholarship has characterized Paul as rejecting reciprocity full-stop; such scholarship tends to craft an image of Paul that is distinct from and far surpasses that of his contemporaries. By addressing such arguments, we can see why it has been difficult to detect the correlation between gentile *pistis* and divinatory gifts.

My argument challenges the position of scholars such as James Harrison and John Barclay, then, in that I reject the reduction of ancient religiosity to *do ut des*, and argue that divine *charis* is not always a grandiose abstract concept (i.e. "grace") in Paul's letters, but a concrete position of benefaction toward gentiles for their faithfulness and loyalty. This benefaction consists of the miraculous ability to heal, to channel divine voices and messages, to read signs, and the like. The interchange of divinatory expertise-for-*pistis* hinges on the same kind of soft misrecognition we see in economies of gift exchange and generalized reciprocity. Thus, Paul presents the bestowal of divinatory power not as a divine obligation, but as God's willing and kind reward for gentile cultivation of *pistis* toward him. The *pneuma* of Christ functions as the medium through which Paul's *pistoi*—otherwise ordinary people—may be endowed with such extraordinary gifts. Thus, Paul describes such abilities not only as *charismata*, but as *pneumatic charismata*: gifts endowed and enabled through Christ's divine *pneuma*.

The Virtue of Pistis
Pistis in the Septuagint

Paul does not appear to encourage *pistis* as a general ethic, but rather, a specific *pistis* toward Christ and the Judean god, which he derives from portrayals of *pistis* in the LXX. That is, the *pistis* repeatedly enacted throughout the LXX is the model that Paul wants to see replicated among his gentile followers. While numerous scholars have rightly observed that Paul uses Abraham's faithfulness as a model for Christ's faithfulness (to be discussed shortly), the present analysis begins with a fuller picture: *Pistis* is a central feature governing much of the relationship between Israelites (later, Judeans) and their god. *Pistis* language pervades the LXX, with declensions and conjugations of *pistis, pistos* and *pisteuō* occurring hundreds of times throughout the texts. This broad constellation of *pistis* words pertains to loyalty, trustworthiness, and the type of solid commitment that binds oaths and shapes the contours of the relationship between Israelites and their deity, as well as Israelites and their neighbors. As Teresa Morgan suggests in her painstaking study on *pistis* and *fides*, "Human beings are required to practice *pistis* towards him [God] in order to avoid punishment and to maintain a just society."[1]

God's faithfulness is a constant theme in the LXX. His covenant with Abraham, his later covenant with Moses, as well as his constant demonstrations of protection, salvific power, and historic favor to Israel are refrains spanning Genesis to Daniel. God's *pistis* is so great that he clears the land of Israel of all previous inhabitants as a grant for those who have escaped slavery in Egypt. The Deuteronomist claims that the Israelites were chosen for this land not because they are greatest in number (in fact, they are the fewest), but because God faithfully keeps oaths and upholds promises made even long ago: "Know that the lord your God is this God, a faithful God [*theos pistos*], who guards the covenant agreement and has compassion for those who love him and for those who observe his commands to a thousand generations" (Deut 7:9, my trans.).[2] Century after century, God's faithfulness persists. This same *theos pistos* is the authority behind Moses' sharp rebuke of the Israelites for acting like "disgraceful children" [*tekna mōmēta*] in Deut 32:4. It is the Israelites who have faltered in their faithfulness to God. Psalm 18 celebrates God's decrees as *pistē* (LXX Ps 18.8; MT 19:7). Likewise, Ps 144 sings of God's greatness, perfection, and righteousness. God is, "faithful in all his words and fair in all his deeds" ["πιστὸς κύριος ἐν τοῖς λόγοις αὐτοῦ καὶ ὅσιος ἐν πᾶσι τοῖς ἔργοις αὐτοῦ) (LXX Ps 144.13a; MT 145:13). Faithfulness and gentleness please God [καὶ ἡ εὐδοκία αὐτοῦ πίστις καὶ πραότης.) (Sir 1:27). Of course, God is also angry, jealous, compassionate, and merciful—but insofar as his promises and commitments are concerned, God demonstrates *pistis* generation after generation.[3]

---

1. See Teresa Morgan, *Roman Faith and Christian Faith: Pistis and Fides in the Early Roman Empire and Early Churches* (Oxford: Oxford University Press, 2015), 195. Morgan's position, then, challenges some of the ideas in Dennis Lindsay's *Josephus and Faith: Πίστις and Πιστεύειν as Faith Terminology in the Writings of Flavius Josephus and the New Testament* (Leiden: Brill, 1993). Although Lindsay's book includes highly detailed philological data, his foundational categories are somewhat problematic, especially the term "secular" with reference to early Greek uses of *pistis*. That is, Lindsay uses the category "secular" uncritically for an era in which there is no social space exempt from the interest and involvement of gods. As Morgan points out, even when *pistis* is maintained between mortals, it is overseen by gods (or, a god).

2. "γνώσῃ ὅτι κύριος ὁ θεός σου, οὗτος θεός, θεὸς πιστός, ὁ φυλάσσων διαθήκην καὶ ἔλεος τοῖς ἀγαπῶσιν αὐτὸν καὶ τοῖς φυλάσσουσιν τὰς ἐντολὰς αὐτοῦ εἰς χιλίας γενεάς."

3. Paul's first-century contemporaries reiterate and discuss the faithfulness of God. For example, Philo tells us that God's faithfulness as an ally [πίστις δὲ τῆς ἐκ θεοῦσυμμαχίας] was demonstrated by Moses' small army defeating scores of myriads of "Arabians" without losing a man (*On the Virtues* 46). He claims that God does not swear oaths since he is the only faithful being [πιστὸς δὲ μόνος ὁ θεὸς] who exists. This absolute faithfulness renders all of God's words

Paul repeatedly teaches his readers about God's faithfulness, drawn from Septuagintal images.[4]

In addition to a faithful God, the LXX valorizes faithful people. Israel itself is sometimes *pistos* (or, as the case may be, *apistos*). The prophet Samuel is widely recognized as a faithful [πιστὸς] prophet of God, from Dan to Beersheba (1 Sam 3:20). The angel Raphael (in the guise of a person) in Tobit (Tob 5:3, 5:9, 10:6) is described as πιστὸς—reliable, trustworthy, or faithful.[5] In Deut 32:20, God threatens to abandon his children—a perverted generation [γενεὰ ἐξεστραμμένη]—because in them there is no faithfulness [οἷς οὐκ ἔστιν πίστις ἐν αὐτοῖς); the Israelites, gathered as an *ekklēsia*, are guilty of venerating other deities. Proverbs 3:3 instructs the listener to never waiver in this regard: "Let not mercy and faithfulness [ἐλεημοσύναι καὶ πίστεις] abandon you; fasten them to your neck and you will find good favor [χάριν] and enjoy a noble image before the Lord and men" (my trans). The author of 4 Maccabees provides an encomium for an unnamed mother who never falters in her loyalty toward God [διὰ τὴν πρὸς θεὸν πίστιν], despite watching the one-by-one brutal torture and murder of her seven sons (4 Macc 15:24). The horrifying sight of their severed toes and fingers, their burned flesh, and their cries fail to shake her faithfulness to God. 2 Samuel/2 Kings 23:1 offers David as an important precedent for Paul's notion of a faithful anointed one. Here, David is both πιστὸς and χριστὸς: "And these are the last words of David, faithful [πιστὸς] David son of Jesse, and faithful man whom the Lord raised up to the anointed one of Jacob's god [χριστὸν θεοῦ Ιακωβ], and seemly are the songs of Israel." 4 Kings/2 Kings 16:2 uses David as the exemplar against whom King Ahaz is compared, and fails. Ahaz, "did not do what was right in the eyes of the Lord his God, as his father David faithfully had [πιστῶς ὡς Δαυιδ ὁ πατὴρ]." Ahaz was guilty of observing religious rites toward other deities, and in locations besides Jerusalem—a miscarriage of the faithfulness demanded in LXX texts.

Of all the Israelites who provide examples of faithfulness, Paul makes greatest use of Abraham.[6] In Rom 4 and Gal 3–4 Abraham's *pistis* undergirds the

---

oaths (*Allegorical Interp.* 3.204). And in his *On the Changing of Names* (182), he reasserts the image of God as *pistos* from Deut 32:4.

4. Rom 3:3; 1 Cor 1:9, 10:13; 2 Cor 1:18; 1 Thess 5:24.

5. Tobit's own faithfulness to God and ancestral customs are equally unequivocal in the text, although not identified in those terms.

6. Paul is not the only later author to make such use of Abraham. In 1 Maccabees, Mattathias exhorts his sons to remain steadfast in their commitment to their god and ancestral customs: "Was not Abraham found faithful [πιστός] when he was tested, and it was reckoned to him as righteousness?" (1 Macc 2:52). In describing the bereft mother whose faithfulness

possibility of gentile salvation. Quoting Gen 15:6, Paul writes, "Abraham trusted [Ἐπίστευσεν] God and it was reckoned to him as righteousness" (Rom 4:3). He goes on to explain that because Abraham's *pistis* rendered him righteous in God's eyes prior to circumcision and prior to the Law, Abraham's gentile descendants are capable of being righteous through *pistis*, apart from circumcision and the Law (Rom 4:9–12). Paul's theology rests not on generic *pistis*, but on the *pistis* of Abraham as an originary, Ur-*pistis*: "For this reason it is out of faithfulness [ἐκ πίστεως], that it [the promise] be in accordance with *charis*, so that the promise be steadfast for all his seed—not only to the one out of the Law, but also to the one out of faithfulness [ἐκ πίστεως] of Abraham who is the father of us all." (Rom 4:16).[7]

Paul (re)interprets the Genesis Abraham story as the explanation for how and why gentiles are saved by receiving the *pneuma* of Christ. In Galatians 3:7–9 Paul tells his readers that because Abraham was justified by *pistis*, prior to circumcision and Mosaic Law, those who share in Abraham's *pistis* are legitimate descendants of Abraham: "And the Writing [*graphē*], foreseeing that God would justify the gentiles out of faithfulness [*ek pisteōs*] announced the good news to Abraham beforehand: 'All the gentiles will be blessed in you.'" The story of Sarah, Hagar, Isaac, and Ishmael provides the framework for Paul's notion of lineage and inheritance, such that gentiles who received the *pneuma* of Christ and demonstrate

---

is punished by losing her seven sons, the author of 4 Maccabees writes, "but as a daughter of God-fearing Abraham, she remembered his patient endurance [καρτερίας]" (4 Macc 15:28). When Philo lists the generations from Abel to Moses, Abraham receives the epithet: "Ἀβραὰμ ὁ πιστός" (*de Posteritate Caini* 173). For more on the trope of faithful Abraham see Frederick Holmgren, "Faithful Abraham and the 'Amana Covenant Nehemiah 9: 6–10: 1." *Zeitschrift für die Alttestamentliche Wissenschaft* (*ZAW*) 104 (1992): 249–254; Bradley Gregory, "Abraham as the Jewish Ideal: Exegetical Traditions in Sirach 44:19–12." *Catholic Biblical Quarterly* 70 (2008): 66–81.

7. Stanley Stowers has argued this point persuasively: "The fact that Gen 15:6 has God accepting Abraham as righteous when the patriarch first hears the promise and before he could act out his faith meant that trust/faithfulness toward God was the primary generative act that ensured Abraham's paternity, making him the father of Jews and gentiles. Romans 4 does not put Abraham's trust and his circumcision into opposition but simply stresses that the trust came first. In this way, Paul makes God's miracle and Abraham's commitment to God's promise generative of Abraham's work of circumcision rather than making the circumcision the basic generative act." Stanley Stowers, *A Rereading of Romans: Justice, Jews, and Gentiles* (New Haven, CT: Yale University Press, 1994), 228. Echoing Stowers, Stephen Young observes that *ek pisteos* is a means by which gentiles gain access to the benefactions of the Judean god. Young points out, "Paul depicts him [Abraham] not as a proto-example for Christ followers of 'Justification by Faith,' but rather as the patriarchic head of a lineage specifically based upon and defined by his law-dissociated faithfulness" (41). See Stephen L. Young, "Paul's Ethnic Discourse on 'Faith': Christ's Faithfulness and Gentile Access to the Judean God in Romans 3:21–5:1," *Harvard Theological Review* 108 (2015): 30–51. See also John Gager, *Reinventing Paul* (New York: Oxford University Press, 2000).

the faithfulness of Christ (which is modeled on the faithfulness of Abraham) are adopted into the lineage of the ancient patriarch. Stowers offers a more likely translation for Rom 1:16–17: "for I am not ashamed of the good news, because it is a power which God has to save all who are faithful, the Jew first and afterwards also the Greek. For it [the good news] makes known God's merciful justice as a consequence of [Jesus'] faithfulness which leads to faithfulness [like Jesus']. As it is written, 'The righteous one [that is, Jesus] shall live as a consequence of faithfulness.'"[8]

Paul establishes three parallel relationships of allegiance and mutual trust, which gentiles are required to demonstrate in their own behavior and thinking: Abraham's faithfulness to God, Christ's faithfulness to his father, and God's faithfulness to those who are faithful to him.[9] Each of these figures

---

8. Stowers, *A Rereading of Romans*, 199.

9. I concur with scholars who translate *pistis Christou* as "faithfulness of Christ," instead of the traditional "faith in Christ" [Rom 3:22, 3:26; Gal 2:16 (x2), 2:20 ("son of God"), 3:22, 3:26; Phil 3:9]. The traditional translation has largely been defended by scholars with deep theological investments in the phrase. The anxiety that such scholars have regarding the threat of a subjective genitive translation (i.e. faithfulness of Christ) is expressed succinctly by Roy Harrisville, "Before ΠΙΣΤΙΣ ΧΡΙΣΤΟΥ," 357: "If the subjective rendering is accepted and becomes the translation of choice in our modern English versions of scripture, the reader will be left wondering as to what personal connection should exist between herself and Christ other than the ritual of baptism and a vague notion of 'participation.'" Harrisville's concerns reflect the position of many academic theologians insofar as contemporary Christian concerns drive the questions and interpretations about Paul and his followers. Resituating Paul's letters in the first century allows us to ask important historical questions that do not entertain anxieties over one's twenty-first-century relationship to Christ any more than they entertain one's twenty-first-century relationship to Orpheus or Mithras. See Roy A. Harrisville, "Before ΠΙΣΤΙΣ ΧΡΙΣΤΟΥ: The Objective Genitive as Good Greek," *Novum Testamentum* 48 (2006): 353–358. For a summary of the so-called *pistis Christou* debate, see Matthew Easter, "The *Pistis Christou* Debate: Main Arguments and Responses in Summary," *Currents in Biblical Research* 9 (2010): 33–47; Richard Hays, *The Faith of Jesus Christ: The Narrative Substructure of Galatians 3:1–4:11* (Grand Rapids, MI: Eerdmans, 2002). I. G. Wallis, in *The Faith of Jesus Christ*, traces the history of how *pistis Christou* was read among early Christian theologians, and concludes that the phrase was read as "faithfulness of Christ" until theological problems related to Arianism (Easter, "The *Pistis Christou* Debate," 36). Through Wallis' work, we find a traceable history of how "faith in Christ" becomes a mainstay in Christian discourse. See I. G. Wallis, *The Faith of Jesus Christ in Early Christian Traditions*, Society for New Testament Studies Monograph Series 84 (Cambridge: Cambridge University Press, 1995). Teresa Morgan's thorough and extensive examination of *pistis* and its Latin equivalent, *fides*, offers a great deal to this conversation. Morgan explores the range of usages for both words among Greeks, Romans, and Judeans, from the Septuagint to Imperial Rome. She points out that New Testament scholars and theologians have largely taken "faith" for granted, as if the concept has no history and demands no explanation, often stretching "the meaning of *pistis* in the New Testament beyond what is historically plausible" (4). As Morgan points out, "If *pistis* and *fides* occur occasionally in non-Christian contexts to refer to human attitudes to the divine, they mean no more than the divine-human equivalent of the loyalty people normatively offer to more powerful members of their human community, and not what Christians, for instance, mean by

demonstrates a degree of *pistis* that Paul valorizes, but gentiles benefit most directly from the faithfulness of Christ; it is through sharing in Christ's faithfulness and in receiving his *pneuma* that they are adopted into the family of Abraham and receive the eternal benefactions of the patriarch's ancient, elected lineage. Like Abraham and Christ, Paul's gentile Christ-initiates must exhibit unequivocal faithfulness. Teresa Morgan calls this an economy of *pistis*: "A faithful God calls his apostle to *pistis*; the faithful apostle, acting as God's intermediary, calls others to *pistis* towards God, who may themselves inspire yet others, by their example if not by active preaching . . . . *Pistis* can therefore been seen as circling, from God, through the apostle, to other people, and back to God" (217). This circle of faithfulness, loyalty, and mutual trust is a closed system that excludes unacceptable practices, thoughts, or sympathies for the ancestral deities of Paul's gentile Greek and Roman followers (e.g. Gal 4:8–11; 1 Thess 1:9; Rom 1:23, 10:14–22; 1 Cor 8, 12:2).

Pistis *and* Fides *Among Greeks and Romans*

Whether Paul draws exclusively from Septuagintal notions of *pistis* and *pistos* might not have been entirely evident to his followers, as they too shared in notions of loyalty and faithfulness between humans and gods. As early as sixth-century Greece, Theognis writes of *Pistis* as a personified deity who oversees honest, reliable human interactions (*Eleg.* 1.1137). By the early Principate, the deified virtue *Fides* appears on numerous coins, among them, Fides Augusta, Fides Maxima, and Fides Publica.[10] The goddess sponsors faithfulness and trustworthiness across numerous fields of social activity, and her temple on the Capitoline dates originally to the third century BCE. Cicero claims that "the mind without *fides*" cannot be relied upon for friendship (*Inv* 1.47).[11] In his *Orations*, Dio claims that the worst evil in a city is failure to maintain *pistis* toward its most noble and honorable benefactors (31.25). Plutarch argues that justice [*dikaiosunē*] is the most envied

---

faith" (126). For a full catalogue of scholarship on this debate, see Morgan, *Roman Faith and Christian Faith*, 12, n53.

10. Morgan, *Roman Faith and Christian Faith*, 129–130. Cicero, *de Nat. Deo.* 2.61, 2.79; on the equivalence of *pistis* and *fides*, see Morgan, *Roman Faith and Christian Faith*, 2–3, and Suzan Agteres, "Pistis and Fides as Civic and Divine Virtues: A Pauline Concept Through Greco-Roman Eyes." In *Paul's Greco-Roman Context*, edited by Cilliers Breytenbach, Bibliotheca ephemeridum theologicarum lovaniensium 277 (Leuven, Belgium: Peeters), 541–559.

11. For more on Roman attitudes toward *fides* as a divine quality that becomes deified, see Anna J. Clark, *Divine Qualities: Cult and Community in Republican Rome* (Oxford: Oxford University Press, 2007).

of virtues because of its reputation for excellence [*aretēs doxa*] and its trustworthiness [*pistis*], which cultivates *pistis* in others. Indeed, as Suzan Agteres points
out, *pistis/fides* is the "ultimate civic virtue" (529), tied to good citizenship, moral
order, and stable relations between people.

Among philosophers, *pistis* is vital to moral development. Especially among
Stoics, *pistis* is simultaneously a divine quality endowed to humans by gods, a
quality that humans must strive to perfect, and a quality that gods themselves
possess. Epictetus identifies *pistis* as one of the two most noble virtues, along-
side moral respect [*aidos*]. As Keith Seddon claims, Epictetus views *aidos* and
pistis as, "aspects of a perfected moral character [*prohariesis*] that is brought fully
into harmony with nature."[12] In the *Discourses*, Epictetus discusses two types of
people: the miserable, wretched men who cleave to their mortal flesh and concern
themselves with trivial, ephemeral earthly matters, and those who by their birth
are inclined toward intelligence, logic, and, "are called to fidelity [*pros pistin*],
to self-respect, and to unerring judgement in the use of external impressions."[13]
He likens many of the former to wolves; unfaithful and treacherous and hurtful
[*apistoi kai epibouloi kai blaberoi*]. Elsewhere, he argues that men are born *pros
pistin*, such that fidelity is our natural state (2.4.1) and any deviation from that
(i.e. designs on a neighbor's wife or plots to swindle) is akin to cracks in an
earthen vessel—rendered useful to no one. Elsewhere he rhetorically asks, "Do
we not have a sense of *pistis*, by nature" [*ouk echomen phusei ti piston*]? (My trans.,
Disc. 2.10). In the *De natura deorum*, Cicero's Quintus Licilius Balbus argues that
Fides, along with *Mens, Virtus*, and *Concordia*, is a divine quality—the capacity
for which is passed down from gods to humans (*de Nat.* 2.79).

Greeks, Romans, and Judeans assumed the gods would reward mortals for
their faithfulness and piety. Hippolytas, for example, is rewarded by Artemis for
his loyalty in Euripides' eponymous play; the goddess gives to him the reward
[χάριν] of great honors [τιμὰς μεγίστας] by young girls of Trozen who will forever
shear their hair in honor of him prior to marriage, compose poetry of him, and
never let his honor go unsung.[14] In book 8 of Ovid's *Metamorphoses*, the hero Lelex

---

12. Epictetus, *Encheiridion* 24; Keith Seddon, *Epictetus' Handbook and the Tablet of
Cebes: Guides to Stoic Living* (New York: Routledge, 2006), 98.

13. Epictetus, *Discourses* 1.3.4. Translated by W. A. Oldfather. Loeb Classical Library
(Cambridge, MA: Harvard University Press,1925).

14. Euripides, *Hippolytas* 1418–1430. In the case of Greek and Roman religion, exclusive faithfulness may earn you rewards from that deity, but punishment from other gods, who also de-
serve veneration. Thus, we do not frequently find exclusive forms of veneration (*pistis, eusebeia,*
etc.) directed at gods. Indeed, even in the case of Hippolytas, he is rewarded by Artemis but
punished by Aphrodite.

recounts the tender story of Baucis and her husband Philemon, who are rewarded for their generosity and obedience to the gods, by becoming eternal caregivers to the temple of Jupiter and Mercury at Tyana. As Lelex finishes recounting the story of the elderly faithful couple, he declares, "cura deum di sint, et qui coluere colantur" ("Let those beloved of the gods be gods; let those who have worshipped be worshipped.").[15] The island of Delos and its inhabitants are rewarded with an oracular temple to Apollo for agreeing to let Leto give birth to Far-Shooting Phoebus on the island. While poor in soil, the island will be rewarded not only with a temple site of primary significance, but it will also become enriched by the perpetual aroma of sacrificed meats and worshippers donating hecatombs (*Homeric Hymn to Apollo* 3.45–88).

Divine reward for human *pistis* is much more frequent in Israelite and Judean texts, as worshippers of Yahweh were expected to demonstrate a singularity in divine loyalty. Insofar as it may be relevant to Paul and his thinking, such recompense for *pistis* is best exemplified in 1 Sam 26:23: "the Lord will return to each one his righteousness and his faithfulness" ["καὶ κύριος ἐπιστρέψει ἑκάστῳ τὰς δ ικαιοσύνας αὐτοῦ καὶ τὴν πίστιν αὐτοῦ"]. We find a similar promise made in Ps 100: "My eyes [will be] on the faithful [τοὺς πιστοὺς] of the land, so that they might be seated with me" (Ps 100:6/MT 101:6). Sirach 46:15 describes Samuel the prophet as "perfect in his faithfulness" [ἐν πίστει αὐτοῦ ἠκριβάσθη], and links his legitimacy as a prophet to his *pistis*. According to 1 Macc 14:35, Simon's faithfulness [τὴν πίστιν τοῦ Σίμωνος]) and justice are so great that the people make him high priest and leader. In that brief passage, *pistis* is twice identified as the rationale for choosing Simon as the most outstanding among them. In Jer 5:1 God promises to treat propitiously [ἵλεως] the rare person who truly strives for faithfulness [ζητῶν πίστιν].

In the same way that Paul calls his groups of followers *ekklēsiai*, thereby reviving the image of God's people at Sinai/Horeb,[16] he also draws on Septuagintal notions of *pistis* and *pistos* in reimagining gentile followers as newly minted latter-day Israelites. Turning to the LXX texts is helpful for understanding Paul's specific references and revivalist goals. Yet, we must also understand that, across the Mediterranean, *pistis/fides* was already long touted as a valuable ethic worthy of cultivating in one's character. It was indispensable among soldiers in war

---

15. Ovid, *Metamorphoses*, vol. I, books 1–8. Translated by Frank Justus Miller; revised by G. P. Goold. Loeb Classical Library 42 (Cambridge, MA: Harvard University Press, 1916). I thank Timothy Haase for this reference.

16. Jennifer Eyl, "Semantic Voids, New Testament Translation, and Anachronism: The Case of Paul's Use of Ekklēsia," *Method & Theory in the Study of Religion* 26 (2014): 315–339, esp. 321–325.

(Polybius 8.36), necessary for stable friendships, and also terribly important in the human–god relationship. Indeed, gods reward mortals for their *pistis*. Paul does not introduce his followers to the notion of *pistis*, but rather, he attempts to redirect and narrow their *pistis* toward his specific deity, his understanding of Christ, and his overall message regarding gentile salvation. His frequent emphasis on *pistis* offers a corrective to gentile disobedience toward the Judean god (Rom 1). Furthermore, he uses *pistis* as a means by which to shore up the permeable and unstable boundaries between followers and nonfollowers[17] by narrowing the scope of a virtue already widely esteemed.

Pistis in the Economy of Reciprocity

For Paul, *pistis*/faithfulness is not a stand-alone moral quality—the cultivation of which results in the betterment of his followers' characters. Rather, *pistis* is a key factor in a relationship of reciprocity between Paul's god and Paul's followers. This relationship of reciprocity promises to endow followers with special divine abilities such as prophesying, miracle healing, and speaking in tongues—skills that are not shared by the general population and for which his followers appear to have no prior training. While the vast majority of theologians and translators have ubiquitously understood *pistis* as "faith," such an understanding divorces Paul from his first-century context, in which *pistis* typically refers to mutual trust and faithfulness in relationships of reciprocity. Paul's innovative contribution to this kind of relationship is his forceful and repetitive emphasis on *pistis* as the human demonstration of piety—to the exclusion of many other common demonstrations of piety such as observation of holy days, animal offerings, and temple upkeep—in that ongoing relationship of reciprocity.

Although inhabitants of the ancient Mediterranean certainly had contracts, leases, trade, and market prices, networks of reciprocity predominated. As Pseudo-Aristotle observes, "the giving and interchange of favors holds together the lives of men."[18] From the fifth century onward, Greek and Roman philosophers generated a number of treatises that address practices of reciprocity and the ethics of exchange, most notably, Theophrastus' *On Gratitude* (D. L. 5.48); Chrysippus' *On Duties* and *On Favors* (*SVF* 3.674, 2.1081); Epicurus' *On Gifts and Gratitude* (D. L. 10.28); Cicero's *De Officiis*; Seneca's *De Officiis* and *De Beneficiis*. Reciprocity

---

17. 1 Cor 6:6, 7:12–16, 10:27, 14:22–24; 2 Cor 6:14–7:1.

18. Pseudo-Aristotle, frag. 3, in Marian Plezia, ed., *Aristotelis Epistularum Fragmenta cum Testamento* (Warsaw: Panstwowe Wydawnictwo Naukowe, 1961), 44–45. Griffin, "De Beneficiis and Roman Society," trans. l

not only predominated in political and other social relations, it characterized the relationships that mortals maintained with gods. It is difficult to overstate the importance of reciprocity in ancient Mediterranean religions: Gods give everything, and mortals routinely and perpetually offer gratitude, honor, and respect.[19] These returns include material goods and social goods.

Human–Divine Relationships of Reciprocity

Reciprocity entails relationships of mutual beneficence that are separate from and cannot be reduced to commercial transactions. Reciprocity exists in all known human societies and is an example of the prosocial tendencies of our species.[20] Reciprocal bonds keep people—individuals, families, clans, states, etc.— tied to one another as reliable partners in the face of danger, need, loss, and in times of abundance. Such relationships are generated and maintained through practices of doing favors and exchanging gifts.[21] Daniel Ullucci characterizes this as a "system of different and deferred return."[22] That is, a favor or gift is not expected to be identical to the gift or favor that originated the relationship. Furthermore, a period of time typically elapses before a gift or favor is returned, thereby perpetuating the reciprocal exchange and the relationship of reciprocity itself. The appropriate amount of return is culturally determined, but becomes intuitive to members of a society. For example, we know when someone has given a gift that is too expensive, too cheap, or too thoughtless. We recognize the difference between a person extending herself kindly and extending herself excessively. Likewise, we know when gratitude is lacking or when kindnesses are not

---

19. I include Judean religion in the larger category of "Mediterranean." Aaron Glaim demonstrates persuasively the great degree to which Judean religion was rooted in reciprocity with God. See Aaron Glaim, *Reciprocity, Sacrifice and Salvation in Judean Religion at the Turn of the Era.* PhD dissertation, Brown University, 2014.

20. For studies on human cognition that leans toward prosociality, cooperation, and empathy, see Frans de Waal, *Primates and Philosophers: How Morality Evolved* (Princeton, NJ: Princeton University Press, 2015); Marco Iacoboni, "Imitation, Empathy, and Mirror Neurons," *Annual Review of Psychology* 60 (2009): 653–670.

21. Marcel Mauss. *The Gift; Forms and Functions of Exchange in Archaic Societies* (Glencoe, IL: Free Press, 1954); J. Parry, "The Gift, the Indian Gift, and the 'Indian Gift,'" *Man* 21 (1986): 453–473; Miriam Griffin, "De Beneficiis and Roman Society," *Journal of Roman Studies* 93 (2003): 92–113; Jason Whitlark, *Enabling Fidelity to God: Perseverance in Hebrews in Light of the Reciprocity Systems of the Ancient Mediterranean World* (Milton Keynes, UK: Paternoster, 2008), 17–54.

22. Daniel Ullucci, *The Christian Rejection of Animal Sacrifice* (New York: Oxford University Press, 2012), 26.

reciprocated. Although it is bad manners to assess the financial value of favors and gifts to the drachma, denarius, or dollar, favors and gifts of somewhat equal value (according to one's means) are expected in return if the relationship of trust and interdependence is to continue. Exact equivalence is never possible, however, and the inexactness helps to perpetuate the relationship. Such a clinical description of reciprocity allows us to recognize how such relationships operate, but on the ground people tend to "misrecognize" the mechanics of reciprocity.[23] Real life is significantly messier, and the extension of favors or bestowal of gifts is simply a universal means to create and maintain cooperative, mutually important relationships in which beings can rely upon one another as trusted familiars, confidants, allies, partners, and kin.

Contrary to the contractual obligation of market exchange or barter, reciprocity lacks enforcement, obligation, or coercion. While parties may feel obligated on a social level to return a favor for a favor, whether they do so is up to their discretion. Failing to return a kindness with gratitude, or a favor with some other kind of favor, will likely terminate the reciprocal relationship, or at least upset it, until it has been set aright by the offending party who did not demonstrate the appropriate amount of gratitude or reciprocal giving. Thus, "parties in reciprocal exchange conceive of their actions as voluntary (even when they are in fact highly constrained)."[24] Perceived voluntary participation is crucial to reciprocity, as "compulsion" turns the relationship into something else entirely. If one party unexpectedly recasts reciprocity in terms of obligation, the trust is disturbed. For example, if your neighbor insists to you, "Last fall I helped you rake the leaves in your yard. Tomorrow you are required to come help me paint my house," you intuitively sense that the voluntary nature of your mutual exchange is manipulated and betrayed. This would be akin to the neighbor unexpectedly saying, "Last fall I helped you rake leaves in your yard. Today, four months later, you have to pay me for that." Reciprocity and barter/market exchange are mutually exclusive, and voluntary participation is central to the operations of reciprocity. Through misrecognition, the neighbor may ask for a favor, and you may recollect what the neighbor once did for you. You may ask yourself, "Do I want to maintain a warm mutually beneficial relationship with this person? If so, I should help him tomorrow." Most likely, you will not have a logical flowchart in your mind, but will intuitively volunteer to help, or not. If you do not want to maintain such a relationship, you may decline to help. Thus, either party may damage

---

23. Pierre Bourdieu, *Outline of a Theory of Practice*, 5–6. See also Ullucci, *The Christian Rejection of Animal Sacrifice*, 26.

24. Ullucci, *The Christian Rejection of Animal Sacrifice*, 162, n64.

the reciprocal relationship by (1) violating the terms of volition by introducing obligation, or (2) refusing to return a benefaction/kindness with some other kind of benefaction/kindness. This is an important observation, since many New Testament scholars have insisted that Paul conceives of God differently than his contemporaries, insofar as Paul insists that God gives freely. Such a position lacks the understanding that in reciprocity, everyone must "give freely."

Market exchange, on the other hand, seeks precise equivalence between goods or services. For example, in 64 CE Nero set a price ceiling for wheat being sold at Rome, at three *sestertii* per modius (about 6.5 kg).[25] A buyer must offer that amount of money to obtain that amount of wheat. As Ullucci points out, "Because of these direct equivalences, economic exchange produces a relationship between commodities exchanged, not people exchanging them" (25). With market exchange and bartering, a relationship is permitted to end the moment the transaction is completed. Indeed, future obligation is sometimes discouraged, so that sellers and buyers are free to find better deals. Such transactions are cut and dry, and contractual in the sense that parties agree to fair prices for specific goods. Thus, market exchange involves obligation and the potential for enforcement, insofar as the buyer is obligated to pay and the seller is expected to deliver on the goods; should one party fail to fulfill her end of the agreement, there may be legal consequences. Jennifer Larson has observed that commercial exchange does not depend on trust in the way that ongoing relations of reciprocity depend on trust,[26] and this is precisely because commercial exchange involves obligations that are enforceable.

Because reciprocity is messier than market exchange, and because an exact equivalence between exchanged favors or gifts is not possible, reciprocity can establish relationships of power not produced in market exchange. Vast disparities of wealth, status, and power can exist between the parties involved, rendering impossible the "return" of a favor or gift of remotely similar proportion. In such arrangements "social goods" are returned.[27] Loyalty, allegiance, respect, gratitude, and honor operate as appropriate responses to generosity that cannot be recompensed. This may render the lower-status person symbolically indebted to the benefactor. In such cases, as Hans van Wees points out, "generosity is not

25. Peter Temin, *The Roman Market Economy* (Princeton, NJ: Princeton University Press, 2013), 33.

26. Jennifer Larson, *Understanding Greek Religion: A Cognitive Approach* (New York: Routledge, 2016), 41.

27. Glaim, *Reciprocity, Sacrifice and Salvation in Judean Religion at the Turn of the Era*, 18, articulates well the usefulness of both "material goods" and "social goods" in reciprocal exchange.

meant to be repaid in kind at all, but to be reciprocated with long term subordination to the benefaction" (41).[28] Intractable disparity in reciprocal relations will eventually become codified in the patron–client relationship at Rome.[29] As Seneca points out, such relationships are not governed by contracts or legal enforcement, but by *fides* (*de Ben.* 3.7.1, 3.15.1).

Whatever asymmetry may exist between rich and powerful benefactors and their poorer, less powerful counterparts, is only exaggerated between gods and humans.[30] The god–mortal relationship for Greeks, Romans, Judeans, and others, is one characterized by profound asymmetry.[31] Stowers has pointed out that deities are more than the powerful and invisible patrons of humans—they are better understood as "interested parties."[32] Yet, the reciprocal relationship and disparity in power and status do share features of patronage. In no way can mortals match divine generosity. (How could we thank a god for our lives? For our children? For prosperity? For our health? For our safety?) This problem of asymmetry inspires LXX Ps 115 (MT Ps 116): "What shall I return to the Lord for all he has returned to me?" In part, humans cannot reciprocate such generosity because gods do not "need" anything. Yet, the one thing humans always owe to gods is honor, and to fail in that regard is consistently met with divine vengeance.

---

28. Hans Van Wees, "The Law of Gratitude: Reciprocity in Anthropological Theory." In *Reciprocity in Ancient Greece*, edited by Christopher Gill, Norman Postlethwaite, and Richard Seaford (Oxford: Oxford University Press, 1998), 13–49. This problem generated anxiety among some recipients of favors at Rome, lest they be demeaned by becoming indebted (Cicero, *de Off.* 2.69; Seneca, *de Beneficiis* 2.23.2–23.3).

29. Richard Saller identifies four features consistent to the patronage relationship: (1) reciprocal exchange of goods and services, (2) a personal relationship that extends over time, (3) asymmetry in power and status, and (4) voluntary participation. See Richard Saller, *Personal Patronage Under the Early Roman Empire* (1982); Andrew Wallace-Hadrill, ed., *Patronage in Ancient Society* (New York: Routledge, 1989).

30. Seth Schwartz rejects the notion that ancient Israelites (and later, Judeans) participate in widespread patronage and reciprocity networks. He writes, " . . . the Jews were heirs to a set of strongly antireciprocal cultural imperatives" (10). While I do not agree entirely with Schwartz's argument, there is no doubt that Israelites and Judeans constructed their relationships with God(s) (*Elohim*) as based on reciprocity. See Seth Schwartz, *Were the Jews a Mediterranean Society?* (Princeton, NJ: Princeton University Press, 2010), 7–44. See also Glaim, *Reciprocity, Sacrifice and Salvation in Judean Religion at the Turn of the Era*.

31. A major difference being the language used to speak of the asymmetrical relationship. Romans would often use the term *amicitia* or *amicus* even between unequals, thereby politely obfuscating the disparity between social superior and inferior. When speaking of the reciprocity between gods and humans, the vertical relationship is clear. See Griffin, "De Beneficiis and Roman Society," 97.

32. See Chap 1 "Modes of Religiosity and Paul"; Stowers, "The Religion of Plant and Animal Offerings," 37.

As Plato's Euthyphro claims, "Of course the gods do not need our gifts—it is all a matter of honor and recognition and gratitude [*charis*]."[33] Euripides affirms this notion: "the gods relish being honored by mortals."[34] Literary and archaeological demonstrations of this notion abound. For example, a second-century Greek herm currently in the Istanbul Archeological Museum (Inv 3891 T) bears the following inscription:

> *For a beneficient god*
> *For good fortune*
> *For a fine season*
> *For rain-bearing winds*
> *For a prosperous summer*
> *For an autumn*
> *For a winter*[35]

While the precise original location of this herm is unknown, it is likely that, as with most herms, it was placed in a public space—at a crossroads, a property boundary, or in front of a house, tomb, library, or public bath. Herms protected through apotropaic power, but they are simultaneously demonstrations of veneration and gratitude. Herm 3891 T both venerates and solicits the protection of a beneficient deity who will deliver practical seasonal needs that enable human flourishing. This coheres with basic relations of reciprocity between human and deities insofar as the humans best offer honor and gratitude, while powerful deities bestow the very things that make life possible. Lack of respect, however, is precisely what got gentiles into the moral (and mortal) dilemmas that Paul offers to resolve: Long ago, gentiles turned their backs on God (thereby upsetting reciprocity), and in return he abandoned them to sickness, death, and devastation. Paul writes, "for though they knew God, they did not honor him as God or give thanks to him" (Rom 1:21).

The anger that Paul's god feels after being disrespected and dishonored by lowly, ungrateful mortals is seen repeatedly throughout Mediterranean myths. Those who do not venerate Dionysus as a deity in Euripides' *Bacchae* are afflicted with madness and death. Whole cities can be wiped out from a god's anger if the inhabitants have failed to show proper veneration, as eventually happens to

---

33. Parker, "Pleasing Thighs: Reciprocity in Greek Religion," 121.

34. Ibid., 125.

35. *"Agatho daimon/Agathēi tuchēi/Kaloi kairōi/Ombris anemois/Ksari* (or *eari*?) *therei/ Metopono/Xeimoni."*

Troy after the judgment of Paris (in favor of Aphrodite). Theognis bemoans the tragic condition when all the gods except Hope have fled the world in response to human disrespect. Without the gods, there are no honest oaths, no laws, no kindness: "Gone, O Friend, are the Charites" ["Χάριτές τ', ὦ φίλε, γῆν ἔλιπον"]. Gone, too, according to Theognis, is *Pistis*. Because there are no pious men who respect the gods anymore, mortals have been abandoned and the world is in disarray (*Eleg.* 1.1135–1150).

Divine anger and vengeance as a response to mortal disrespect and disloyalty is often individualized. Odysseus, for example, is beleaguered with seafaring problems for a decade, partially because of his offense against Poseidon (*Od.* 9.525). Individuals can be targeted with divine wrath for just a hint of dishonor. Plutarch tells us that the gods become angry with Camillus when he thoughtlessly reneged on his vow to Apollo after sacking Veii. He brings upon himself the punishment for neglecting this vow: He must now re-collect a percentage of the spoils already distributed among the citizenry to offer as his promised tithe. This generates great anger among the population, impoverished by years of war. But the seers determined that the gods demand appropriate offerings [χαριστηρί ων δεομένην] (Plutarch, *Camillus* 7.7), and Camillus has brought a twofold vengeance upon himself. By failing to respect the gods as promised, he incurs their anger. In remedying divine anger, he suffers a backlash for taking back what was given to Roman citizens. Thus, disrespect for gods can bite a person from several directions at once. While some stories of disrespect may be read by moderns as lighthearted etiologies (Arachne forever transformed into the hated spider, for example), the perceived gravity of disrespecting deities in antiquity ought not to escape our attention. Indeed, primordial disrespect for God is the very basis of Paul's theology.

Respect for gods can come in numerous ways: demonstrations of gratitude (offerings in the form of ritually slaughtered animals, first fruits of a crop, oil or wine, incense, and terra-cotta figurines); dedication of children; prayers and promises; upkeep of the god's house or temple or shrine; observation of days that are special to a god; and following special patterns of behavior demanded by a god. Included in this list is demonstration of loyalty and faithfulness, or *pistis*.[36] Paul sees little need for gentile participation in one of the most common and widespread practices of honor and respect toward his god—animal sacrifice.[37] Additionally, we have little clear evidence of other types of offerings made among

---

36. In the *de Nat. Deo.*, for example, Cicero includes *fides* in his taxonomy of deified qualities that constitute *religio* (*de Nat. Deo.* 2.36.79; 3.18.47).

37. Ullucci, *The Christian Rejection of Animal Sacrifice.*

Pauline groups, outside of the things they may have contributed to their communal meals, or what appears to be a reference to an incense or perfume offering in Phil 4:18. Consistently, he emphasizes moral qualities such *pistis, elpis,* and *agapē* (2 Cor 13:13) in the hearts and minds of his followers. Although Paul claims that *agapē* is the greatest of these three, it is their unwavering *pistis* that may enable followers to perform wondrous feats and enjoy newly discovered divinatory abilities.

Paul clearly understands *pistis* as an "offering" to God, like a libation or animal sacrifice. Philippians 2:17–18 makes this explicit: "But even if I am being poured as an offering [σπένδομαι] over the sacrifice [ἐπὶ τῇ θυσίᾳ] and the offering of your faithfulness [τῆς πίστεως ὑμῶν], I am delighted and rejoice with all of you— likewise, you should also be glad and rejoice [συγχαίρετέ] with me." Here, Paul understands himself as a sacrificial libation, and the *pistis* of his followers is an offering made to God at the altar. [38] *Thusia* [sacrifice] and *spendein* [the pouring of libation offerings] are two of the most frequent words that accompany discussions of ritualized reciprocity among ancient Greek speakers. For Paul, *pistis* is such an offering.

Paul and Reciprocity

Paul's letters are shot through with references to the exchange of mutually beneficial gifts, kindnesses, and favors. I focus on three passages to demonstrate my argument, although there are more. Throughout these passages Paul speaks of mutual benefits, mutual gift giving, mutual emboldening or strengthening, gratitude, and indebtedness. His understanding of reciprocity is native such that when the language is not explicit, it is subtle and indirect. That is, Paul operates so thoroughly within the conventions of reciprocal relations that such conventions are not always named outright but are obvious with any close examination. Furthermore, as the evidence demonstrates, Paul's engagement with reciprocity involves other Christ followers, as well as reciprocal relations between mortals and God. This is an important point, as some scholars have suggested that Paul may participate in intrahuman reciprocity, but rejects reciprocal relations with God.

In the opening of Rom 1:8–15, Paul does not hesitate to establish what he hopes will be a reciprocal relationship with the readers:[39]

---

38. See also Glaim, *Reciprocity, Sacrifice and Salvation in Judean Religion at the Turn of the Era,* 170–171.

39. Translations in this chapter are my own unless otherwise noted.

8 First, I am thankful to my God through Jesus Christ for all of you, because your faithfulness [πίστις] is proclaimed through the whole world. 9 For God—whom I serve in my spirit [ἐν τῷ πνεύματί μου] in the good news of his son—is my witness that I incessantly make mention of you, always in my prayers, 10 asking that by the will of God, by any means and at any time, I may be successful and come to you. 11 For I am longing to see you so that I may share with you some pneumatic gift to strengthen you [ἵνα τι μεταδῶ χάρισμα ὑμῖν πνευματικὸν]—12 or rather, to be mutually encouraged [συμπαρακληθῆναι] by one another's faithfulness [τῆς ἐν ἀλλήλοις πίστεως], both yours and mine. 13 I do not want you to be unaware, brothers, that many times I have intended to come to you (but have been hindered until now), so that I may harvest some returns [τινὰ καρπὸν] among you as I have among the rest of the gentiles. 14 I am a debtor [ὀφειλέτης] both to Greeks and to barbarians, both to the wise and to the senseless 15—thus my eagerness to proclaim the good news also to you who are in Rome.

He opens the letter to the Romans with a salutation that speaks of warm reciprocal wishes for their relationship, expressing eagerness to share the kind of divine gifts that he has brought to others (1:11), which will strengthen their resolve. Their shared *pistis* will be mutually beneficial (1:12). Lest they wonder why he has not visited earlier, Paul makes it clear that they have always been on his mind, that he has consistently spoken to God on their behalf (1:9), and that, finally, he would like to reap some benefits for his efforts (1:13). He has already done so among "the rest of the gentiles." His language of reciprocity is sometimes explicit and sometimes subtle. The use of words such as *metadō, charisma, tina karpon,* and *opheiletēs,* generate the overall picture of interdependence, reciprocity, and mutual beneficence. Paul places himself and his readers on each end of a reciprocal relationship: He shares divine pneumatic gifts, talks to God on their behalf, and seeks the profits [*karpon*]. Yet, he is also indebted to them and feels the need to defend his tardy arrival to their city. They, in turn, strengthen him with their world-renowned *pistis,* but stand as recipients of his divine gifts and, presumably, will offer some kind of return [*karpon*] for Paul's efforts. Rom 1:8–15 is almost entirely concerned with ingratiating himself into a reciprocal relationship with potential Pauline followers in Rome.[40]

---

40. For examination of Paul himself operating as a sort of benefactor, see Stephen Joubert, *Paul as Benefactor: Reciprocity, Strategy, and Theological Reflection in Paul's Collection.* Wissenschaftliche Untersuchungen zum Neuen Testament 2.124 (Tübingen, Germany: Mohr Siebeck, 2000).

As an example of reciprocity, Rom 15:25–27 has received more attention from scholars. Here, Paul discusses the reciprocal relationship that his gentile readers ought to have with the Jesus people in Jerusalem. He tells them that if gentiles are now sharing in the pneumatic benefactions of those in Jerusalem, then the gentiles should not balk at helping the Jerusalem people out, materially:

> Currently, however, I am going to Jerusalem to serve the needs of the holy people; 26 for Macedonia and Achaia have been pleased to make contributions [κοινωνίαν τινὰ] to the poor among the holy people at Jerusalem. 27 They did this consensually [ηὐδόκησαν], and indeed they are indebted [ὀφειλέται] to them; for if the gentiles have come to share [ἐκοι νώνησαν] in their pneumatic [benefactions] [τοῖς πνευματικοῖς], they [the gentiles] are obliged to be of service [ὀφείλουσιν λειτουργῆσαι] to them in material things [ἐν τοῖς σαρκικοῖς]).

Here, Paul is quite explicit about the reciprocal relationship between those who share in pneumatic benefactions (which include divinatory and wonderworking abilities) and those who return the favor with material support. To point this out does not suggest that Paul is hoodwinking his readers, but rather, that Paul is situated squarely in a world that operates on reciprocal relations. This passage also prepares Roman readers for Paul's visit; despite claims earlier in the letter that he is indebted to Greeks and barbarians (1:14), it is actually the recipients of pneumatic benefactions who are indebted to Paul. When he eventually arrives in Rome, his readers will certainly be expected to reflect the (materially generous) example of other followers in Macedonia and Achaia. Paul is not merely suggestive of a desire to see materially generous followers—he explicitly declares them *indebted* [ὀφείλουσιν].[41]

The Romans passages echo what Paul has earlier told readers in 1 Corinthians regarding generosity, reciprocity, and a return for one's labor. In discussing his own self-sufficiency and unwillingness to take advantage of the material support owed him, Paul wonders, "Who plants a vineyard and does not eat any of its fruit [τὸν καρπὸν]? Or who tends a flock and does not get any of its milk?" (1 Cor 9:7). He continues, asking, " . . . the ploughman is obliged to plow in hope and whoever threshes must thresh in hope [of a share in the crop]. 11 If we have sown pneumatic [benefactions] [τὰ πνευματικὰ ἐσπείραμεν] among you, is it too great if we harvest material benefits [τὰ σαρκικὰ θερίσομεν] from you? 12 If others share in this license [ἐξουσίας] over you, do we not still more?" (1 Cor 9:10–12). Paul's

---

41. See also Phil 4:15–20; 1 Cor 16:1–4; 2 Cor 8.

comments here push even beyond even the normal conventions of reciprocity, in that he likens humans to animals, fruit-bearing trees, and pastures that have been sown and harvested. This is more reliable than human reciprocity—which is perpetuated by learned behaviors of give, take, and appropriate demonstrations of gratitude—insofar as Paul likens his peripatetic labor and his followers' reciprocal obligations to the natural and inevitable returns involved in agriculture and animal husbandry. He seems to suggest that expecting anything less than reciprocal returns from his followers would be nonsensical.

More important, however, is the central role that pneumatic gifts play in Paul's understanding of reciprocity. In the Romans and 1 Corinthians passages it is clear that the extensive list of abilities Paul frequently describes as χάρισμα πνευματικὸν (tongues, miracles, healings, prophecy, etc.) constitute the types of things for which one ought rightfully offer a return. But whereas such reciprocal return is inevitable, expected, and obligated, Paul refuses to demand it. Instead, he expresses his own disinterest in monetary returns (1 Cor 9:15–18), lauds the example of other generous givers (2 Cor 8), and allows his readers to "figure out" the appropriate demonstrations of reciprocal exchange. The fact that Paul allows followers to figure out how to give in return renders their mutual relationship ever more reciprocal and ever more voluntary. Likewise, for Paul's faithful followers, such gifts *are* the fruits of their fidelity; wondrous powers and divinatory skills are a return for something offered by them. This ongoing to-and-fro of mutual beneficence, allegiance, and support is precisely how reciprocity works.

Gentile Faithfulness and Divine Gift Giving

When used to describe human actions and sentiments, *charis* points to offerings, gifts, and gestures of gratitude or thanksgiving toward gods. When used to describe the actions of gods, *charis* refers to a wide array of benefactions bestowed upon humans: health, wealth, rescue from danger, a stroke of luck, personal attractiveness, answer to a specific request or prayer, etc. For example, Athena is said to "pour out" *charis* [χάριν κατέχευεν] onto Telemachus in the form of strength, beauty, and majesty in *Odyssey* 2.11. Such benefactions include divinatory skills and powers of wonder. *Mantikē* is a *charis*. The ability to discern signs is a *charis*. In the *Cyropedia*, Xenophon links the reading of signs with human *charis*: "Zeus of my forefathers and you, Sun, and all gods, accept this not only as a finale of my numerous and splendid actions but also as a ritual of thanksgiving; for in sacrifices, heavenly signs, birds, and sayings you have always indicated to me what I should do or not do" (*Cyr.* 8.7.3).

The ability to prophesy, in particular, is understood as one of the divine gifts that gods bestow on mortals. That skill begins as a *charis* at the top, even among the gods themselves. Zenobius, the second-century Sophist and collector of pro-verbs, recounts a saying at Delphi, "Many are seer-stone soothsayers [*thrioboloi*], but few are prophets." Zenobius goes onto explain that true prophecy (at Delphi) was understood to be a divine favor from Zeus to Apollo [*ton Dia charizomenon tō Apollōni*], distinguishable from the ineffective imitation of pebble-stone divina-tion.[42] Zenobius reaffirms what Apollo himself claims in *Homeric Hymn* 3— that the ability to ascertain the thoughts and intentions of the gods is a gift in ex-change for human piety (*Homeric Hymn to Apollo* 480–485). Callimachus' *Hymn* 5, *The Bath of Pallas*, retells the story of renowned seer Teiresias. Callimachus' ver-sion claims that Teiresias went blind after stumbling upon Athena bathing nude (like Acteon). Tiresias' mother Chariklo, a devotee of Athena, laments her son's loss of vision. Athena promises as *charis* to Chariklo that Teiresias will become a powerful seer [*mantin*], more prodigious than any other [*hē mega tōn allōn dē ti perissoteron*], with the ability to accurately read the flight of birds (both good and bad omened), and utter many oracles [*polla de theopropa*] (120–125). In Pindar's *Isthmian Ode* 6, Heracles beseeches Zeus to give Telemon a great son. Zeus sends the sign of a great eagle, just as, "pleasant *charis* provoked him within and he spoke up like a seer [*mantis anēr*]." (*IO* 6.50–51). For Heracles to suddenly speak pro-phetically regarding Telemon's progeny, divine *charis* must jostle and move him.

Paul's terminology would be recognizable to followers and naysayers alike, even when he vacillates between forms of *charis* and *charisma*. Of all our ancient sources, he is among the most consistent and explicit in identifying divinatory and wonderworking powers as special rewards from a deity. His consistent use of *charis* (in addition to *charisma* and *charismata*) squares with how all Greek speakers would describe kindnesses, benefactions, gifts, and aid from gods: They are not skills developed through education or arduous training, but powers that arrive directly from a divine source. It has not escaped the attention of scholars that Paul calls these powers "gifts," but many scholars have neglected to realize that *charismata* are the things that all sorts of ancient gods give to people and that such gifts are bestowed in relationships of reciprocity.

Thus, in addition to demonstrating general reciprocity among himself and his followers, Paul consistently participates in the same kind of human–divine reciprocity seen throughout antiquity. And while Greeks, Romans, Judeans, and others, offered innumerable types of things to deities, Paul emphasizes gentile *pistis* as the most important offering his followers can submit. In exchange for

---

42. Zenobius, 75.5, my trans.

such faithfulness, gentiles are the beneficiaries of divine gifts [*charis*]. We see how Paul connects gentile loyalty and divine gift giving in a relationship of reciprocity, in 1 and 2 Corinthians, Galatians, and Romans. It is important to note that these examples occur throughout his letters, thereby clarifying for readers (ancient or modern) that Paul asserts a *pistis–charis* relationship over many years of writing to different audiences. That is, Paul does not make this association merely once, which would provide only meager evidence for my argument. On multiple occasions in the undisputed letters, *pistis* and *charis* are integral halves of a human—divine reciprocal dynamic.

In 2 Cor 4 Paul writes of the various afflictions he and his co-ministers have suffered; they are perplexed but not despairing; beaten but not destroyed.[43] They carry in their bodies the death of Christ, which means they also carry in their bodies the eternal life of Christ. He then tells his readers (2 Cor 4:13–16):

> But just as we have the same spirit of faithfulness [πνεῦμα τῆς πίστεως] that is in accordance with what has been written—"I trusted, so I spoke"— we also trust, and so we speak, 14 knowing that the one who raised the Lord Jesus will also raise us with Jesus, and will place us beside him, along with you. 15 For, all these things are for your sake so that the benefaction [χάρις], as it as it extends to more and more people, will make gratitude [εὐχαριστίαν] abound for the glory [δόξαν] of God.

Here, Paul quotes the first line of LXX Ps 115, "Ἐπίστευσα, διὸ ἐλάλησα."[44] The line is often translated as "I believed, therefore I spoke," but such a translation occludes the larger sentiment of the Psalm, as well as the larger point that Paul makes. That larger sentiment, as well as Paul's purpose in drawing from Ps 115, is the strong reciprocal relationship of mutual trust, loyalty, and reliability that the psalmist cultivates with God (and vice versa). Such mutual trust includes the ongoing exchange of divine favors and unwavering human loyalty and praise. Psalm 115 asks, "What will I return [ἀνταποδώσω] to the Lord, for all that he has returned [ἀνταπέδωκέν] to me?" There is no accounting for who "gave first" as the same verb, "to return," [ἀνταποδίδωμι] is used for both parties. The psalmist then describes what is given and returned: "A cup of deliverance [ποτήριον σωτηρίου] I will take, and [in return] I will watch over the name of the Lord" (115.4). He details the manner in which he will watch over the name of the Lord—with

---

43. Paul frequently switches between the first person singluar and plural. Thus, the "we" of 2 Cor is often ambiguous and can inlcude Paul, his co-ministers, and their Corinthian followers.

44. Cf. MT Ps 116.10–19.

loyalty, prayers, and praise. The sacrifice that the psalmist will offer to God is not in animal parts or grains, but a sacrifice of praise [σοὶ θύσω θυσίαν αἰνέσεως] (115.8). He will also offer his vows [τὰς εὐχάς] to God in front of all the people, and become god's slave [δοῦλος]. This, in exchange for divine σωτήριος [deliverance]. In light of the repeated imagery of loyalty, exclusive belonging, and reciprocity, "I believed" may satisfy later Protestant notions that *pistis* and belief (or faith) are correlates when it comes to Christianity and its Jewish precursors, but such a translation neglects the deep roots of reciprocal relations between God and his people in the LXX, Paul's letters, and in the ancient Mediterranean more generally.

Paul identifies himself and his followers as sharing the same "spirit of *pistis*" found in Ps 115: mutual giving, and a return for God's beneficence with human praise, loyalty, exclusive dedication and enslavement to God. While the psalmist describes a warm gratitude for divine reciprocity, Paul explicitly links gentile *pistis* to God's *charis* in a reciprocal exchange. In v 15, Paul seems to imply that as God extends his various *charites* to wider numbers of people, their *eucharistia*, or gratitude, will accordingly abound. That gratitude, if it looks anything like the gratitude of Ps115, will necessarily include praise, exclusive belonging, and veneration—which we may also call *pistis*. Some readers may take a strong interest in whether God gives first, or gives freely, but my interest here is in the consistency, ubiquity, and perpetual nature of the reciprocity itself. Regardless of whether God's *charis* demands gratitude, or whether *pistis* and *eucharistia* inspire God's *charis*, an ongoing reciprocal relationship is simply assumed to exist.

Like 2 Cor 4, Gal 2 introduces the notion that a faithful follower dies with Christ and subsequently has Christ living within the body. Paul first discusses his fourteen-year sojourn in Syria that led him eventually to Jerusalem (2:1). There he experienced some degree of conflict with the "supposed leaders" (2:2–10). Paul, however, proved that God entrusted him with the responsibility of preaching to gentiles, by showing those leaders the divine gift [*charis*] God extended to him (2:9). He does not specify what that divine *charis* consisted of, but in light of Paul's other claims, it likely included the performance of some kind of wonder. The conflict with the Jerusalem people continues in Antioch (2:11–14). Paul then writes (2:19–21):

> For through the law [διὰ νόμου] I died to the law, so that I might live to God. I have been crucified together with Christ; 20 and I no longer live, but Christ lives in me. And the life I now live in the flesh [ἐν σαρκί] I live in the faithfulness [ἐν πίστει] of the son of God [τῇ τοῦ υἱοῦ τοῦ θεοῦ], who loved me and gave himself on my behalf. 21 I do not reject [οὐκ ἀθετῶ]

God's benefaction [τὴν χάριν τοῦ θεοῦ]; for if justification is through the law, then Christ died for nothing.

Paul again links *pistis* and *charis* in a relationship of reciprocity. If Christ is indwelling, then so too, is the indwelling of Christ's *pneuma* and the benefits of Christ's *pistis* toward God. It is as if Christ's faithfulness enshrouds and interpenetrates the very life of a faithful follower (in this instance, Paul). Such *pistis* results in the *charis* of God. Thus, Christ gives Paul and his gentile followers access to *pistis, pneuma*, and to the array of divine benefactions Paul teaches. That Christ is the gentile access point to God's divine gifts is a claim Paul will repeat in Rom 5:2.

In Gal 2:21, Paul's allusions are dramatic ones. To refute the *charis* of another is grounds for long-term feelings of enmity, distrust, and suspicion. Polybius, for example, uses the phrase "*charin kai philian athetein*" to describe the treacherous massacre of a protective Achaean envoy whom the Mantineans turned over to Spartans (*Hist.* 2.58.5). Elsewhere, the verb *athetein* is associated with severe examples of broken treaties, betrayals of good faith, rebellion, and treachery (LXX 1 Kgs 2:17; Is 1.2; Polybius 9.36). All such examples pertain to maintaining or breaking the faithfulness between trusting parties. Subtly alluding to the shock of broken faithfulness, Paul starkly rejects such behavior, and reifies the reciprocity of *pistis–charis*.

Later in the letter, Paul claims that gentile followers who seek to be justified through Torah have cut themselves off from Christ and "cast aside [divine] benefaction [τῆς χάριτος]" (Gal 5:4). He continues, "For we eagerly await the hope of righteousness, by the pneuma [πνεύματι] out of faithfulness [ἐκ πίστεως]" (Gal 5:5). Paul has already established a dual roadmap to salvation with the Judean god—one for Judeans (the Law) and one for gentiles (Christ).[45] In light of his earlier arguments, it makes sense that gentiles who tread the path of Torah have, indeed, cut themselves off from the other path. Yet, by extension, they have also refused God's gifts, which they should be entitled to through *pneuma* and *pistis*. Thus, Gal 5:4–5 adds to his earlier argument regarding dual lineages and paths to salvation: the law on one hand, and Christ (through *pneuma* and *pistis*) on the other. This secondary but parallel path is a reciprocal one, in which divine *charis* and gentile *pistis* are mutually offered and demonstrated.

Paul's letter to the Romans sometimes expounds on and clarifies ideas he has discussed in prior letters. For example, Romans explains in greater detail the parallel paths to salvation with the Judean god—the Law for ethnic Judeans, and the

---

45. Gal 3:1–4:7.

path of Christ for gentiles. Receiving the *pneuma* of Christ and emulating the faithfulness of Christ will effectively "graft" gentiles into the family of Abraham.[46] Such reiteration and expansion is also the case for Paul's ideas about the reciprocal relationship involving God's *charis* and gentile *pistis* (modeled on Christ's *pistis*). I look at three examples from Romans that, though perhaps redundant, demonstrate that Paul does not equivocate on the mutual exchange of *charis* and *pistis*.

Chapter 4 of Romans discusses how and why righteousness was reckoned to Abraham. As one who trusted God prior to the giving of the Law, Abraham is blessed with the promise of being the father of many nations; he is given a land grant; he is declared righteous in God's eyes.[47] Paul explains to his readers why trusting God, outside of "works," is of value. He then tells his readers (4:16):

> For this reason, it is out of faithfulness [ἐκ πίστεως], that it may be according to [God's] benefaction [κατὰ χάριν]; to the end that the promise [τὴν ἐπαγγελίαν] be secure to all the seed; not to that only which is of the law, but also to that which is of the faithfulness of Abraham [ἐκ πίστεως Ἀβραάμ], who is the father of us all."

Paul repeats similar claims made in Galatians regarding Abraham and gentile inheritance, but here he also reiterates the connection between *pistis* and *charis*. It appears that fulfillment of the promise to Abraham now includes some reciprocal relationship between gentile *pistis* (modeled on Abraham's *pistis*) and the extension of God's *charis* to gentiles. To be clear, however, this comes out of [ἐκ] the faithfulness, and not the other way around. Paul suggests here that God has long awaited gentile *pistis* to bestow divine favor to them—an idea that he also suggests, indirectly, when he claims that gentile disloyalty prompted God to abandon the gentiles (Rom 1:18–32, especially 1:21 and 1:28) in the primordial past.

Romans 5:1–2 offers another example of the interdependence of God's divine favor and gentile faithfulness. Again, Paul claims justification out of faithfulness [ἐκ πίστεως], but adds to that: ". . . we have peace [εἰρήνην] with God through our Lord Jesus Christ, through whom and by faithfulness [τῇ πίστει] we have gained access to this benefaction [τὴν χάριν] in which we stand; and we boast in our hope for the splendor of God." Paul's declaration of "peace" [εἰρήνην] with God through *pistis* is reminiscent of the peace found through other forms of *pistis*: faithful treaties and reliable allies, for example. Plutarch uses the two concepts in proximity, related to brokering peace treaties and the *pistis* necessary

---

46. Rom 11:17–24.

47. Gen 15–21.

for such relations to be successful (*Phocion* 26.3; *Aemilius* 4.3) as do Herodian (*Hist.* 3.15.6) and Cassius Dio (*Hist.* 11.43, 69.15, 71.3). More important, it is reminiscent of the close relationship between *Fides* and *Concordia* in Roman civic religion.[48] The peace brokered between gentiles and God is dependent on mutual trust and fidelity. With that fidelity secured, gentiles now have gained access to the range of divine *charismata* Paul details in 1 and 2 Corinthians. Paul speaks as if the faithful Christ functioned as an envoy, demonstrating to an alienated ethnicity how to also show fidelity and obedience to the only appropriate God.

Perhaps the most telling and explicit passage in which Paul links *pistis* and the bestowal of divine favor, comes in Rom 12:3–8:

> For by the *charis* given to me I say to all among you not to think of yourself more highly than you ought to think, but to think with temperate mind, each according to the measure of faithfulness [μέτρον πίστεως] that God has apportioned [ὁ θεὸς ἐμέρισεν]. 4 For just as in one body we have many members, and not every limb has the same function, 5 so we, who are many, are one body in Christ, and we are individual members of one another. 6 We have gifts [χαρίσματα] that differ according to the benefaction [τὴν χάριν] given to us, whether that be prophecy in proportion to faithfulness [προφητείαν κατὰ τὴν ἀναλογίαν τῆς πίστεως] or service [διακονίαν] in proportion to ministration; whether that be the teacher in teaching, or the summoner in invoking; the one who gives, in generosity; the leader, in zeal; the one who is compassionate, in cheerfulness.

Paul's argument here is somewhat circular: One's *charisma* is in proportion to the measure of *charis* in that specific arena; thus, the divinatory practice of prophecy is successful in proportion to one's *pistis*, and yet, *pistis* appears to be something that God himself can apportion. That God ultimately apportions *pistis*, and thus

---

48. See Morgan, *Roman Faith and Christian Faith*, 128–129; Freyburger, 2009, 29–306. *Pistis/ Fides* is also associated with justice [*iustitia/dikaiosynē*], in the LXX as well as Greek and Roman texts (Cicero, *Repub.* 2.2; Plutarch, *Mor.* 275a, 278a; *Cato Minor* 44.7–8; Morgan, *Roman Faith and Christian Faith*, 118–120). New Testament scholars have looked closely at *pistis* and righteousness in the LXX, because of Paul's reliance on Abraham's righteousness and his quoting of Habakkuk 2:4 (Rom 1:17; Gal 3:11), but the scholarship tends to neglect the close association of faithfulness and justice more generally. Desta Heliso's detailed study, for example, focuses exclusively on biblical and Second Temple explanations for Rom 1:17. See Desta Heliso, *Pistis and the Righteous One: A Study of Romans 1:17 Against the Background of Scripture and Second Temple Jewish Literature.* Wissenschaftliche Untersuchungen zum Neuen Testament 235 (Tübingen, Germany: Mohr Siebeck, 2007). Morgan observes, ". . . to a Greek speaker of the late Hellenistic world or early principate *dikaiosynē*, and even more the juxtaposition of *dikaiosynē* and *pistis*, have unmistakably social, political and legal overtones" (181).

can determine the pizazz of one's pneumatic skills, is a reminder that his readers ought not to grow braggadocious in their demonstration of powers or abilities. This, in some ways, contradicts other statements with regard to "striving" for better gifts (e.g.1 Cor 12:31, 14:1, 14:12;), but coheres still with other claims that God apportions the skills out in a way he sees fit (1 Cor 4:7, 7:7, 12:4–11). The two claims—that one can develop and strive for certain abilities, but that God ultimately determines the extent of such abilities—is perhaps a contradiction, but not a problematic one. Such claims are made on a regular basis in antiquity and today, as when an ascetic trains herself to practice detachment from material possessions, but prays to a god for the strength and wisdom to achieve detachment. Thus, Paul simultaneously teaches his followers that a person's measure of faithfulness (to God) will set the limits of their ability to prophesy, while God also enables varying degrees of faithfulness. Indirectly, then, *pistis* too is a divine gift—an idea we have already seen in Cicero's *de Nat. Deo.* 2.79, but also in Epictetus (2.8.23) and Plutarch (*Mor.* 550d).[49]

The final example brings us back to Paul's Corinthian correspondence. In 1 Corinthians, Paul's language of reciprocal divine favor and faithfulness is also central, but this time it is God who is *pistos*. He writes (1 Cor 1:4–9):

> I give thanks to my God always for you because of the gift of God [τῇ χάριτι τοῦ θεοῦ] that has been given you in Christ Jesus, 5 for in every way you have been made wealthy [ἐπλουτίσθητε] in him, in all speech [ἐν παντὶ λόγῳ] and every kind of knowledge [πάσῃ γνώσει]—6 just as the testimony of Christ has been established securely among you—7 so that you are not lacking in any [pneumatic] gift [χαρίσματι] as you wait for the revealing [τὴν ἀποκάλυψιν] of our Lord Jesus Christ. 8 He will also strengthen you so that in the end you may be blameless on the day of our Lord Jesus Christ. 9 God is faithful [πιστὸς], through whom you were called into the fellowship of his son, Jesus Christ our Lord.

As part of his epistolary salutation, Paul reminds his followers in Corinth that their pneumatic powers have been granted to them as gifts from God. While those abilities include things like wisdom, knowledge, teaching, and improved ethics, they also include the range of divinatory and wonderworking powers he will detail later in the letter (as discussed in Chapters 3 and 4). This time, however, God's enrichment of faithful followers and bestowal of divine abilities is evidence of God's own faithfulness in their reciprocal relationship.

---

49. See also Morgan, *Roman Faith and Christian Faith*, 132–134.

As I have demonstrated, the *pistis* of Paul's followers constitute the gentile contribution to a reciprocal relationship with Paul's Judean god. The divine contribution is *charis*, in its most abstract sense, with specific and concrete instantiations of that *charis* in the form of *charismata*. Through Christ's *pneuma*, Paul's gentiles are adopted into the family of Abraham and receive the benefaction of a range of concrete goods: resolution to their moral and ethical failings, membership in what is (to them) an exotic and ancient lineage, and most important for this study, access to extraordinary divinatory abilities not enjoyed by the average person, and, ultimately, immortality. One's expertise in prophecy, for example, is in proportion to one's *pistis*. Yet, the route is not immediate or direct; gentiles both participate in Christ's faithfulness, by means of receiving his *pneuma*, and demonstrate their own "human" version of Christ's faithfulness. Furthermore, receiving the benefactions is not guaranteed, as God cannot be compelled by anyone or anything. The exchange is not crafted as a crass this-for-that; rather, faithfulness-rewarded-with-*charis* operates on deeply held, traditional notions of divine reciprocity whose boundaries are woolly and ambiguous.

New Testament Scholars Reject Reciprocity

To claim that Paul engages in reciprocity with God, especially linking faithfulness to powers of divination and wonderworking, is distasteful to many scholars of early Christianity. Ben Witherington III, for example, shields Paul even from basic reciprocity, claiming that grace [*charis*] is wholly unlike anything Paul's followers would understand: "The relationship between a human being and a god in Greco-Roman religion was perceived to involve reciprocity. The god gave blessings and the human being responded or petitioned with prayers, sacrifices, verbal or written praise (gratitude), and the like. With such a background, the concept of grace must itself have been quite difficult for the Gentile Corinthians to grasp, but the idea of God as benefactor to whom one was obligated to respond would not be difficult to grasp."[50] James Dunn would agree with Witherington: "The idea of mutuality which was attached to human *chesed* in the OT, and the importance of reciprocity which was such a central feature of the benefaction ideology of the Greco-Roman world, are both left behind in Paul." (322–323).[51] Indeed, some New Testament scholars seem to reduce the richness and complexity of ancient Mediterranean religiosity to a simple relationship of

---

50. Ben Witherington III, *Conflict and Community in Corinth: A Socio-Rhetorical Commentary on 1 and 2 Corinthians* (Grand Rapids, MI: Eerdmans, 1995), 420, n28.

51. James Dunn, *The Theology of the Apostle Paul* (Grand Rapids, MI: Eerdmans, 1998).

mutual back-scratching, in a larger attempt to demonstrate that Paul heroically rejects such a crass practice. To address this common position in New Testament scholarship, I look at two studies in particular—not because they are especially egregious in any way, but because they conform to the opinion that Paul does not operate within a framework of reciprocal relations with God. Indeed, both studies are precise and detailed scholarly endeavors, but both are vexing insofar as they stand entrenched in the notion that Christian texts and practices warrant unique interpretations.

James Harrison's 2003 study, *Paul's Language of Grace in its Graeco-Roman Context*, focuses primarily on the language of benefaction, or euergetism, found in inscriptions in the Greek East (although he also looks closely at Philo, Josephus, and epistolary handbooks).[52] He argues that such inscriptions constitute the most important evidence for the immediate context of Paul's language of benefaction; in contrast to ideas produced in the "aristocratic literary grid,"[53] inscriptions would have been publicly accessible, located everywhere, and therefore shared a much wider audience than elite literary circles. Honorific decrees and votive dedications were ubiquitous in antiquity, and the durability of such evidence (compared with wax or papyrus) provides a more widespread sample. Because New Testament scholarship has often overlooked inscriptional evidence, Harrison's analysis was much needed.[54] Harrison concludes that Paul rejects reciprocity with God by introducing what he calls God's "reign of grace," which is unilateral and simply cannot be repaid.[55] This reign of grace competes with and far outstrips the civic beneficence of the Caesars. However, important conceptual problems beleaguer Harrison's otherwise important study.

The reduction of ancient religiosity to *do ut des* is a favorite among conservative scholars who wish to distance Paul from the widespread ancient assumptions that people and gods share mutual interests and care. Harrison's assessment is likewise reductive and mischaracterizes the flexibility of and diverse approaches to reciprocity with the gods in antiquity.: "The *do ut des* mentality of Graeco-Roman religion reduced human piety to a mere business transaction."[56] While

---

52. James Harrison, *Paul's Language of Grace in Its Graeco-Roman Context.* Wissenschaftliche Untersuchungen zum Neuen Testament 172 (Tübingen: Mohr Siebeck, 2003).

53. Ibid., 26.

54. Ibid., 35.

55. Harrison, *Paul's Language of Grace*, writes, "Christ's death is an act of God's patronage that inaugurates the reign of grace" (226). In addition to the basic reign of grace, "The gift of Christ's righteousness (Rom 5:18–19) heralds the eschatological reign of grace, in the present age and at the eschaton" (226).

56. Harrison, *Paul's Language of Grace*, 284.

we certainly have evidence of mortals demanding things from *daimones* and even threatening them, the overwhelming evidence suggests that people knew gods could not be forced and were not unilaterally placed under obligation to humans in exchange for sacrifices, honor, or praise. People may have hoped or assumed that gods would reciprocate with generosity and care, but it was also widely assumed that one could not always count on reciprocity. On the contrary, gods could be terribly unpredictable, and they were never obligated in the sense that humans were, because gods were so far superior to humans in power and knowledge.[57]

This mischaracterization of *do ut des*, as well as divine obligation, is evident in the way Harrison reads some ancient material related to ritual devotion.[58] Especially curious is his analysis of epistolary correspondence between two twin brothers, Thaues and Gaous (who held service roles at the Sarapeion at Memphis), and the house of Ptolemy and Cleopatra between 168 and161 BCE.[59] The correspondence concerns sesame and kiki oil needed as a libation offering in the temple, which had previously been withheld. The royal couple restored the oil offerings

---

57. Abundant evidence points to the coexistence of two mutually exclusive attitudes: Gods would respond kindly to various types of actions and demonstrations of devotion, but a person could do nothing to alter fate. Thus, the same person could attempt to persuade Poseidon to let her survive a terribly tumultuous journey by sea, and at the same moment accept that the Fates had already determined the length of her life, which Poseidon could not change. These two things may be contradictory, but the contradiction is apparently not significant enough to prevent people (both ancient and modern) from thinking or behaving this way.

58. By mischaracterizing the *do ut des* of ancient religions, Harrison can present Paul and Paul's god as profoundly unique. Such claims are frequent and grandiose: "Again, that unilateral understanding of God's grace in early Christianity—where God was not obligated to anyone by way of gratitude of favor (Rom 11:25; 1 Cor 4:7)—must have fallen on many uncomprehending ears in view of the prevailing ethos of reciprocity" (56–57). Elsewhere, "God's infinite generosity simply cannot be requited" (321) (cf. Rom 11:35; 1 Cor 4:7; 1 Thess 3:9). Harrison's explanation for this profound uniqueness is as follows: "Undoubtedly, in reflecting on his radical experience of grace on the Damascus road (2 Cor 4:1; Gal 1:15–16), Paul felt that all such views [of reciprocity] stripped the Abrahamic covenant of grace of its unilateral and unmerited aspect (Rom 4:1–25; Gal 3:6–25, 4:21–31) and obscured its fulfillment in the glorious Covenant of the Spirit (Rom 7:6; 2 Cor 3:4–18; Gal 3:14)" (346). Again Harrison, writes " . . . divine recompense is either a matter of God's free grace or His retributive justice" (321–322) (but not rooted in reciprocity). Harrison is able to formulate his argument because he ignores the actual *charismata* that Paul enumerates. I argue that God's "grace" is, in fact, a gift within relations of reciprocity—and Paul spells out those gifts even when he claims that God's beneficence is free and voluntary. Harrison mentions the *charismata* only briefly, and refrains from examining the individual gifts themselves. This oversight brings us back to the problems addressed in my Introduction—namely, that New Testament scholars are uncomfortable with Paul's wonderworking and divinatory practices and find much greater comfort in the abstract notion of "Grace."

59. *UPZ* I, nos. 34, 35, and 36. See Ulrich Wilcken ed., *Urkunden Der Ptolemäerzeit I* (Leipzig: de Gruyter, 1927).

out of piety to Sarapis and "care for the brothers."[60] Harrison's translation of the brothers' correspondence with the royal financial manager reads as follows: "For this Sarapis and Isis Anmut may now give to you favor [χάρειν] and satisfaction in regard to the King and Queen, on account of your holy relations to the divinity."[61] Harrison provides another similar example, wishing divine favor for the pious care of temple offerings. In light of this correspondence, Harrison queries, "What picture of the grace of Sarapis emerges in this correspondence? It is singularly cultic. The gods dispense χαριτὲς to those who ensure that the correct drink offerings are regularly provided. Furthermore, the gods themselves are placed under obligation by correct ritual: they reciprocate with gratitude."[62] He then observes that thinking the gods are obligated to reciprocate for mortal offerings and praise, "was at odds with the Christian understanding [of divine grace] that emphasized that god exercised genuine χάρις precisely because He was *not* under obligation."[63] Not only does Harrison assume that Sarapis cannot extend "genuine *charis*" to his devotees, his ability to assume so depends on the notion of divine obligation. The correspondence is better translated as, "For this, may Sarapis and Isis Anmut now give you favor," as the Greek verb διδοῖ is not a future indicative but the subjunctive of δίδωμι, and this mood is regularly used in prayers and petitions toward God, not as commands but in the manner of a request. The brothers *wish* for the king and queen that they will be recompensed for their generosity, but there is certainly no guarantee or unequivocal obligation from Sarapis or Isis. Because word order largely determines meaning in English, the placement of "may" in Harrison's translation reads as permissive or even prescriptive, whereas the Greek implies neither. The brothers are not allowing Sarapis to grant favors, nor are they demanding it, nor can they ensure it. Harrison's translation hides what I will call the "subjunctive nature" of reciprocity with gods, and this misreading opens the door to the scholar's overemphasis on divine obligation. While not as tentative as the optative mood, the subjunctive still communicates uncertainty. The brothers express gratitude and good wishes to the royal house and chief financial officer. It is unclear how this sentiment of grateful well-wishing is any different from Paul in Rom 16:20: "May the *charis* of our Lord Jesus Christ be with you."[64]

---

60. Harrison, *Paul's Language of Grace*, 86.

61. Ibid., 87.

62. Ibid., 87.

63. Ibid., 87.

64. Indeed, Paul regularly wishes that god will bless his followers with *charis*, although he typically drops the verb from such statements: Rom 1:7; 1 Cor 1:3; 2 Cor 1:2, 13:13; Gal 1:3, 6:18; Phil 1:2, 4:23; 1 Thess 1:1, 5:28; Phil 3;25.

Harrison's claim that Paul rejects reciprocity rests on shaky evidence. First, he notes Paul's lack of "reciprocity" language typical in inscriptions of civic euergetism: The apostle does not use words like *axios, kataxios*, or *ameibein* to describe mutual giving.[65] Thus, what Paul doesn't say may tell us as much as what he does say. Yet, Paul's lack of vocabulary drawn from civic euergetism does not indicate a lack of reciprocal relations, nor does it indicate a Pauline critique of reciprocity full-stop. Harrison's argument also turns on his interpretation of 2 Cor 8–9, in which Paul discusses the Jerusalem collection. Paul clearly has expectations of reciprocity, as he compares the generosity and voluntary giving of the Macedonians, benevolently delivers his good news, and then "tests" the genuineness of the Corinthians' love (i.e. generosity in giving) against the Macedonians' (2 Cor 8:18). But to Harrison, 2 Cor 8–9, "is best explained by Paul's perception that the Corinthians were in danger of operating on the basis of reciprocity (2 Cor 9:5–11), rather than from divine love, as regards the Jerusalem collection. For Paul, it is love that subverts the dynamics of the Graeco-Roman reciprocity system (Rom 13:8–10; 2 Cor 8:8, 24; 1 Cor 13:3)."[66] Again, Harrison mischaracterizes reciprocity as bribery or compulsion, as Paul does not seek to warn them against reciprocity, but to encourage them to give voluntarily and not be taken advantage of [μὴ ὡς πλεονεξίαν]. In particular, one must read 2 Cor 9:6–9 with strange lenses to miss the language of mutual beneficence: "The one who sows sparingly [φειδομένως] will reap a harvest sparingly, and the one who sows bountifully [ἐπ' εὐλογίαις] will reap bountifully. Each one [must give] as he prefers in his heart, not from strain or force—for God loves a cheerful giver. And God has the power to make every gift [πᾶσαν χάριν] abound for you, so that as you always have everything you need, you make good deeds [ἔργον ἀγαθόν] abound everywhere." Mutual giving and abundance are ideals in reciprocity; the language of voluntary participation is what distinguishes reciprocity from bribery or extortion.

Harrison's final piece of evidence that Paul rejects reciprocity is, "the social relations between believers."[67] That is, "the honorific titles and privileges of the associations are to be absent from the body of Christ. The hierarchical structure of the honor system is radically overturned: all believers are endowed with χαρίσματα; the weak, not the strong, are to be given the first place of honor; all believers are slaves of Christ who must serve each other."[68] No doubt, Paul speaks

---

65. Harrison, *Paul's Language of Grace*, 348.

66. Ibid., 349.

67. Ibid., 349.

68. Ibid., 349.

openly of challenging conventional notions of rich–poor and free–slave in a way that is strikingly similar to popular philosophy of his day,[69] but again, that he fails to include the exact honorific titles seen in public inscriptions is not evidence that Paul eschews reciprocity. Indeed, Paul replaces such honorifics with his own: saints, prophets, teachers, brothers, and "the faithful." With Paul's terminology we simply see some of the traditional vocabulary of reciprocity repackaged, reimagined, and renamed.

The displeasure in looking at Paul in terms of ancient reciprocity is further reflected in the very language that scholars use to categorize divine favors. When used to describe something that gods do for mortals, *charis* refers always to a benefaction of some sort and is typically translated as gift, favor, kindness, or benefaction. *Charis* is not a particularly complex notion in antiquity and can account for innumerable things: emancipation from slavery, survival of a shipwreck, birth of a child, a financial gain, recovery from an illness, the failure of one's enemies, pleasant weather after days of rain, rainy days after a drought, a good meal, a lasting friendship, a house, an education, a successful crop yield, etc. The list is literally endless, insofar as the positive events of a human life are often attributed to the benevolent hand of a deity. Yet, when some scholars of early Christianity discuss that very same Greek word (*charis*) in relation to the god of Paul or Jesus, they forego the typical translation and instead speak of the *grace* of God. "Grace" imbues *charis* with a gravitas that the word does not inherently possess. Perhaps it is assumed that the *grace of God* is more dignified and legitimate than a *gift from Poseidon.*

This switch in terminology is seen most prominently in John Barclay's detailed and extensive *Paul and the Gift*.[70] Barclay's tome is a thorough examination of gift exchange and reciprocity as it is discussed among Judean texts and authors (e.g. *Wisdom of Solomon*, Philo, Ps. Philo), in Seneca's *de Beneficiis*, and later Christian interpreters of Paul (Augustine, Luther, Badiou, et al.). Barclay argues that the Christ-event is the gift God extends to gentiles despite their unworthiness. This gift is not outside the realm of reciprocity, but is incongruous in the sense that gentiles are not deserving of benefits from the Judean god, and cannot actually repay the gift. Thus, such a gift constitutes what he calls "incongruous grace." Christ is the instantiation of incongruous grace. Astutely, he warns against a return to the "theologically pernicious contrasts between Pauline grace and Jewish works-righteousness," (572)[71] yet he inadvertently reinscribes the

---

69. Abraham Malherbe, *Paul and the Popular Philosophers.*

70. John Barclay, *Paul and the Gift* (Grand Rapids, MI: Eerdmans, 2015).

71. The conversation regarding Paul, *pistis*, and *charis* has long revolved around "grace versus works" and "faith versus works." Such discussions construct ancient Judean religion ("Judaism")

misconception that Paul dissolves ethnic differences and introduces a Christian universalism delivered through the Grace of God.[72]

Barclay's study makes important points. He is careful to remind the reader against assuming that "gift" in antiquity means a benefaction or favor with no strings attached (562). As he points out, a gift can be *unconditioned* without being *unconditional* (562). This matters because of long-standing theological claims that God gives absolutely "freely" (which suggests divine giving takes place outside of reciprocity). As he points out, however, the notion of the "unreciprocated gift" develops only in modernity. To many interpreters the "free gift" is "free from obligation, and unreciprocated, given *without a return*" (52)—a position we saw in Harrison's study. To Barclay, such a notion is colored by contemporary concerns with altruism. In antiquity, both market exchange and gift giving existed, in some sense, within relations of reciprocity. He clarifies, "A distinction between sale and gift is no modern phenomenon . . . but the distance between these two transactional modes has arguably increased to the extent that they have become not just differentiated but ideologically polarized" (55). All of this is to say that when Paul speaks of gifts from God or, especially, a "free gift" from God (e.g. Rom 5:15–17), he is most definitely speaking within a framework of reciprocity. This is also the case when Seneca and Philo (*Virt.* 83) discuss free gifts: For all such authors, the free gift is a voluntary one, but not external to expectations of a reciprocal, mutually beneficial relationship of some duration.[73]

---

as an archaic works-based legalist relationship with God, superseded by a Christianity founded on faith and grace. Christian supersessionist interests ignore the widespread usage of words like *charis* and *pistis* as the common terms to describe reciprocal relationships with gods and fellow humans. Following E. P. Sanders (whose approach James Dunn has dubbed "the New Perspective" on Paul), many scholars have addressed and drawn back the curtain on deeply seated theological interests that dominated scholarship on early Christianity.

72. For example, Barclay writes, "Paul we have found, explores the incongruity of grace, which he relates to the *Christ-event* as the definitive enactment of God's love for the unlovely, and to *the Gentile mission*, where the gifts of God ignore ethnic differentials of worth and Torah-based definitions of value ('righteousness')" (565–566). He continues, "Paul declares that the ethnic distinction between Jew and Gentile, which was foundational to his 'ancestral traditions,' has been dissolved by the incongruous gift of Christ" (*Paul and the Gift*, 567).

73. Barclay, *Paul and the Gift*, 39–45, is likewise critical of Seth Schwartz's argument that the Jews rejected reciprocity, because of the abundant evidence demonstrating reciprocal relations in ancient Jewish texts, and because he finds Schwartz's notion of the "pure" gift questionable. He argues, "Jewish giving to the poor is fully enmeshed in the expectation of reciprocity, and its distinctive elements are justified not by an 'anti-reciprocal' ethos but by the modulation of the reciprocity-ethos into the expectation of reciprocity from God" (44). Furthermore, he points out, the Hebrew Bible abounds with examples of reciprocity with God. See Seth

Despite his contributions to the discussion of Paul and reciprocity, Barclay is beleaguered by the same terminological problems we see throughout New Testament scholarship. When discussing the history of anthropological studies on gift giving and reciprocity, he employs the term "gift." When discussing Seneca's *de Beneficiis*, he uses the term "gift." But as his attention turns toward Paul and Christian interpreters of Paul, his terminology changes to *grace*. There are intermediate occasions where he discusses the combined term "gift/grace"— as if the former term passes its baton to the latter—but eventually the transfer in terminology is complete. The title of his well-researched study indicates perhaps where he wants to stand, but not where he is compelled to go, if he is to contend with so many theologians and scholars who write about "grace." *Charis* is simply categorized differently when it appears in relation to the god(s) of Abraham, Jesus, or Paul.

More important, because he limits his examination to Romans and Galatians, Barclay omits two of the most important letters in Paul's discussion of *charis*, namely, 1 and 2 Corinthians. Romans uses *charis* language twenty-nine times, whereas the Corinthian correspondence offers a combined thirty-six instances (seventeen in 1 Corinthians; nineteen in 2 Corinthians). Romans is certainly indispensable to this discussion, but in Galatians, Paul speaks of *charis* only eight times. The omission of 1 and 2 Corinthians, where frequency of the gift far outstrips that of Galatians, generates a striking lacuna in thinking about Paul's participation in reciprocity and God's gift giving. But what Paul has to say about gifts in 1 and 2 Corinthians would, inevitably, take Barclay's argument in an unwanted direction. In addition to an ineffable and ethereal "grace" that is widely theorized in Christian theology, Barclay would be forced to contend with the reality of Paul and his followers thinking they can heal one another, attain immortality, channel the indecipherable words of a god (or one among a god's retinue), and perform all sorts of strange, wondrous feats. Indeed, one can formulate an abstract argument regarding incongruous grace only if one ignores how Paul speaks of practical divinatory gifts in 1 and 2 Corinthians. Harrison's study also ignores such practices. Furthermore, in a study that looks in detail at Paul's language of the gift in Romans and Galatians, Barclay skips over the first mention of pneumatic gifts in Romans, where Paul expresses eagerness to see them so that he may share pneumatic gifts with them (1:11). His chapter on Romans examines Rom 1:1–7, omits verses 8–15 and resumes its examination at Rom 1:16. To be sure, one cannot examine absolutely every passage of every text, but in an impressive 582-page tome that largely functions as a commentary on

Schwarz, *Were the Jews a Mediterranean Society? Reciprocity and Solidarity in Ancient Judaism* (Princeton, NJ: Princeton University Press, 2010), esp. 21–44.

"the gift," this oversight is more than just curious. If Barclay were to address Rom 1:11, he would need to reconcile the passage with Paul's list divinatory gifts in 1 and 2 Corinthians.

Ancient Critiques of Reciprocity?

Numerous scholars have rejected outright the simplistic reduction of ancient reciprocity with gods to transactional *do ut des*. Jan Bremmer, for example, notes, "All this 'traffic' between god and man should not be seen in a framework of contract (*do ut des*), but in one of goodwill and friendship."[74] G. S. Kirk adds, "Scholars are usually content to reduce the whole business of . . . gifts to the over-simple and much-distorted legal principle of *do ut des*, a tag which serious discussions of divine ritual could well do without."[75] Despite this growing critique especially among classicists, it is a mainstay in the kind of New Testament scholarship whose interests lie in distinguishing Paul from his unevolved contemporaries. Ancient authors occasionally appear to help in that endeavor.

A cursory glance would suggest that even some Greeks, Romans, and Judeans critiqued or rejected reciprocity. At best, ritual reciprocity with gods ran the risk of being a mislabeled commercial transaction or (at worst) a misguided and crass exchange of favors. We have numerous examples of orators and philosophers deriding and dismissing some of the basic practices of mutual beneficence. Fairly consistently, such figures reiterate the same general arguments: Gods are so effusive and powerful in their giving that mortals cannot possibly recompense; an offering toward a god is, in reality, an attempt to trick, bribe, or buy the favor the god; the gods are not salesmen and cannot be bribed; to think a god can be persuaded or bribed is to misapprehend the nature of a god. Not coincidentally, these are the same arguments of many Christian theologians and New Testament scholars. However, the ancient writers do not reject reciprocity, but show concern for how it is maintained.

In the *de Beneficiis*, for example, Seneca commends the gods for their daily efforts of benefaction and scoffs at the notion that humans could ever possibly do anything to reciprocate. He argues that it is our role to follow the example of the gods [*deorum exemplum*], who benefit in no way from human offerings and

---

74. Jan Bremmer, "Greek Normative Animal Sacrifice." In *Companion to Greek Religion*, edited by Daniel Ogden (Oxford: Blackwell, 2007), 132–144, esp. 133.

75. G. S. Kirk, "Some Methodological Pitfalls in the Study of Ancient Greek Sacrifice (in Particular)." In *Le sacrifice dans l'antiquité*. (Vandouvres, Geneva: Fondation Hardt, 1980), 74–75; M. Lambert, "Ancient Greek and Zulu Sacrificial Ritual," *Numen* 40 (1993): 293–318. See also Lännström, "A Religious Revolution?" 266, n13.

who give without reward. As such, it is also our role to never undertake a virtuous
act in hopes of repayment. He exclaims, "We should be ashamed to set a price
on any benefit whatsoever—the gods are ours for nothing!" (*de Ben.* 4.25.1–3).[76]
Likewise, Philo frequently comments on God's effusive giving and lack of need.
While he calls God a "lover of gifts" [*philodoros*] dozens of times in his treatises,
he also claims that God has no need for gifts, and that the only meaningful thing
mortals can give to God is their virtuous action. In his *On the Cherubim,* he
writes:

> Therefore, if you consider the matter, you will find that all men, and es-
> pecially those who have been alluded to as giving gratuitously [χαρίζεσθαι
> πιπράσκοντας], sell rather than give; and that they, who we fancy are re-
> ceiving favours [λαμβάνειν χάριτας], are, in reality, purchasing the benefits
> [χαρίζεσθαι πιπράσκοντας] which they derive; for they who give, hoping
> to receive a requital, such as praise or honour, and seeking for a return of
> the favour which they are conferring, under the specious name of a gift,
> are, in reality, making a bargain [κυρίως πρᾶσιν]. Since it is usual, for those
> who sell, to receive a price in return for what they part with; but they who,
> receiving presents, feel anxiety to make a return for them, and make such
> a return in due season, they in reality perform the part of purchasers; for
> as they know how to receive, so also do they know how to requite. But
> God distributes his good things, not like a seller [πωλητὴρ] vending his
> wares at a high price, but he is inclined to make presents of everything,
> pouring forth the inexhaustible fountains of his graces [χαρίτων], and
> never desiring any return; for he has no need of anything, nor is there any
> created being competent to give him a suitable gift in return [ἀντιδοῦναι
> δωρεάν]. (122–123)[77]

Here, Philo reduces reciprocal kindnesses between humans to commercial transaction. He has, of course, a model fueling his cynicism, insofar as benefaction
practices in the Empire were frequently abused. But Philo flattens the multilay-
ered landscape of human gift giving so that he can craft a deity entirely immune to
bribery and manipulation (against which humans are expressly not immune). This
does not mean God is exempt from reciprocity, however; in *On Abraham* Philo is
clear that piety, honor, and obedience to God are human offerings for which God
offers a reward (*On Abraham* 177). Nor does Philo rail against sacrificial offerings,

---

76. "Pudeat ullum venale esse beneficium: gratuitos habemus deos!" Loeb trans.

77. Yonge trans.

depending on the intention behind them. Instead of petitioning God for a favor (when God cannot be bribed, bought, or persuaded), sacrifices and offerings simply offer back to God the things that belong to God to begin with, "through the excess of his beneficence to our race."[78] Sacrifices ought to be demonstrations of gratitude and honor, never attempts to influence or cajole. Furthermore, in addition to the gratitude of sacrificial offerings, humans honor God through their cultivation of virtue [ἀρετή]. Virtue, indeed, is the greatest thing humans can offer God, as virtue is perfect [ὁλόκληρος] and one ought not offer to God anything imperfect (*The Sacrifices of Cain and Abel* 57–58). Philo's comments conform to common philosophical claims that gods do not need "things" from people, and that gratitude and virtue are the most venerable kinds of human offering.

Josephus is equally critical of people who think they can wheedle their way into a god's heart through offerings and promises. In *Against Apion* he links this to ethnicity. That is, such practices are characteristic of non-Judeans. In a veritable tirade against Greeks and their human-like gods, Josephus criticizes "the most famous poets and most celebrated legislators" (2.239) for the outlandish portrayals of gods who behave like overgrown, spoiled children; gods who are young, and others who are old; gods who live in the sea, and gods who live on mountains; gods who connive, and gods who are not powerful enough to save the lives of their own children. He refrains from identifying specific gods, but any reader familiar with the Greek pantheon would recognize his ridicule for Zeus, Poseidon, Athena, the nymphs, Pan, and others. Given the unpredictability of divine temperament, he claims, the Greeks

> . . . have been absolutely compelled to regard some of the gods as givers of blessings [δοτῆρας ἀγαθῶν] and to call others "(gods) to be averted" [ἀποτροπαίους]. They then rid themselves of the latter, as they would of the worst scoundrels of humanity, by means of favours and presents [χάρισι καὶ δώροις], expecting to be visited by some serious mischief if they fail to pay them their price. Now, what is the cause of such irregular [ἀνωμαλίας] and erroneous [πλημμελείας] conceptions of the deity? For my part, I trace it to the ignorance of the true nature of God [τὴν ἀληθῆ τοῦ θεοῦ φύσιν] with which their legislators entered on their task, and to their failure to formulate even such correct knowledge of it as they were able to attain and to make the rest of their constitution conform to it. (2.249–250).[79]

---

78. *On the Unchangeableness of God* 7, Yonge trans.

79. Josephus. *Against Apion*. Trans. H. St. J. Thackeray. Loeb Classical Library 186. (Cambridge, MA: Harvard University Press, 1926).

Josephus goes on to claim that instead of theologians educating people on the "true nature of God," the task of imparting proper veneration and proper theology was left to the least qualified lot of Greek society: the poets who love to spin a good yarn, those who live beholden to their passions, orators seeking the approval of the people, painters and sculptors at liberty to make gods look like persons, and the craftsmen whose professional self-interest made them eager to use materials like ivory and gold in the statuary (2.251–252). In short, to Josephus, the very people equipped to teach the "true nature of God" (i.e. intellectual theologians) were the very ones left out. The result, then, is a litany of ridiculous and unbecoming stories of divine intrigue, adultery, incest, and impassioned emotions invented and propagated by Greek *hoi polloi.*

Josephus and Philo reduce mutual beneficence between mortals and gods to an unflattering and ethically impoverished system of self-interested gifts that is characteristic of the Greeks. And yet it is in Plato, a Greek, that we find a voice most carefully deconstructing this kind of approach to gods. In the *Euthyphro* 14b–15b, Plato's Socrates steers his unsuspecting interlocutor toward the realization that the veneration typically showed to gods is little more than trade [*emporikē*]. The extended passage warrants citing in full:[80]

EUTHYPHRO: I told you a while ago, Socrates, that it is a long task to learn accurately all about these things. However, I say simply that when one knows how to say and do what is gratifying [κεχαρισμένα] to the gods, in praying and sacrificing, that is holiness [τὰ ὅσια], and such things bring salvation [σώζει] to individual families and to states; and the opposite of what is gratifying to the gods is impious [ἀσεβῆ], and that overturns and destroys everything.

SOCRATES: You might, if you wished, Euthyphro have answered much more briefly the chief part of my question. But it is plain that you do not care to instruct me. For now, when you were close upon it you turned aside; and if you had answered it, I should already have obtained from you all the instruction I need about holiness. But, as things are, the questioner must follow the one questioned wherever he leads. What do you say the holy, or Euthyphro holiness [τὴν ὁσιότητα], is? Do you not say that it is a kind of science of sacrificing and praying [οὐχὶ ἐπιστήμην τινὰ τοῦ θύειν τε καὶ εὔχεσθαι]?

EUTHYPHRO: Yes.

SOCRATES: And sacrificing is making gifts [τὸ θύειν δωρεῖσθαί] to the gods and praying is asking from them?

80. Plato, *Euthyphro.* Translated by Harold North Fowler. Loeb Classical Library 36 (Cambridge, MA: Harvard University Press, 1914).

EUTHYPHRO: Exactly, Socrates.

SOCRATES: Then holiness, according to this definition, would be a science of giving and asking ['Επιστήμη ἄρα αἰτήσεως καὶ δόσεως].

EUTHYPHRO: You understand perfectly what I said, Socrates.

SOCRATES: Yes, my friend, for I am eager for your wisdom, and give my mind to it, so that nothing you say shall fall to the ground. But tell me, what is this service [ἡ ὑπηρεσία] of the gods? Do you say that it consists in asking [αἰτεῖν] from them and giving [διδόναι] to them?

EUTHYPHRO: Yes.

SOCRATES: Would not the right way of asking be to ask of them what we need from them?

EUTHYPHRO: What else?

SOCRATES: And the right way of giving, to present them with what they need from us? For it would not be scientific giving to give anyone what he does not need.

EUTHYPHRO: You are right, Socrates.

SOCRATES: Then holiness would be an art [τέχνη] of barter ['Εμπορική] between gods and men?

EUTHYPHRO: Yes, of barter ['Εμπορική], if you like to call it so.

SOCRATES: I don't like to call it so, if it is not true. But tell me, what advantage [ἡ ὠφέλεια] accrues to the gods from the gifts [τῶν δώρων] they get from us? For everybody knows what they give, since we have nothing good which they do not give. But what advantage do they derive from what they get from us? Or have we so much the better of them in our bartering [τὴν ἐμπορίαν] that we get all good things from them and they nothing from us?

EUTHYPHRO: Why you don't suppose, Socrates, that the gods gain any advantage from what they get from us, do you?

SOCRATES: Well then, what would those gifts of ours to the gods be?

EUTHYPHRO: What else than honour [τιμή] and praise [γέρα], and, as I said before, gratitude (χάρις)?

SOCRATES: Then, Euthyphro, holiness is grateful [Κεχαρισμένον] to the gods, but not advantageous [οὐχὶ ὠφέλιμον] or precious [φίλον] to the gods?

EUTHYPHRO: I think it is precious [φίλον], above all things.

SOCRATES: Then again, it seems, holiness is that which is precious to the gods.

EUTHYPHRO: Certainly.

Plato's *Euthyphro* is a go-to text for those who want to imagine ancient Greek religion in terms of *do ut des*. But Anna Lännström makes the important observation that Socrates is the one who collapses Euthyphro's understanding of mutual *charis* into *emporikē*: "Socrates omits *charis* from consideration completely when he revises Euthyphro's definition, turning it into a trade" (265).[81] Barter is expressly not what Euthyphro describes or how he understands the reciprocal relations with gods, yet that is precisely where he ends up through Socrates' coaching.

Socrates' position contradicts what most other ancient authors have to say about the various purposes for sacrifice and other forms of reciprocity. Theophrastus, for example, claims at least three purposes: to show honor, to express gratitude, and to petition for benefits (*On Piety* frag. 12), but in reality the purposes are innumerable (and ultimately inaccessible to us). Socrates reduces sacrificial reciprocity, in particular, to the exchange of materially equivalent goods, in a larger dialogue the goal of which is to investigate the nature of piety and impiety. Contrary to rejecting reciprocity itself, Socrates (and thus Plato) desire to understand the correct manner in which mortals can please the gods. But more important, Socrates' translation of sacrificial reciprocity to barter violates the divide that makes them mutually exclusive to begin with. Socrates' rhetorical maneuver reflects the maneuvers of many New Testament scholars insofar as the complexity and richness of reciprocity is subject to being hammered flat and commercialized. If reciprocity were no more than trade, Lännström rightly argues, "the gods' willingness to participate would seem utterly mysterious because they get so little out of it" (267). This is why, when Socrates reduces sacrificial offerings to a commercial transaction, it *doesn't* make sense to him, to Euthyphro, or to the reader. He himself points out that the gods don't "need" anything. By reducing such practices to *do ut des*, one is free to reject this form of reciprocity as absurd and impiously belittling to gods.

The majority of ancients simply did not reject reciprocity as the fundamental way of engaging with and relating to god(s). The arguments of intellectuals such as Seneca, Philo, Josephus, and Plato are framed by larger concerns about appropriate forms of exchange between mortals and gods, not by questioning whether gods ought to be honored and thanked for their benefactions to begin with and not by questioning whether gods bestow rewards. No doubt, some people did present offerings to gods in hopes of procuring a special favor, as when people today bargain with a god to ensure a loved one's recovery from disease or so that the airplane won't crash. But instead of rejecting reciprocal care and honor between gods and people, these ancient authors question how such relations ought to work, whether gods are subject to obligation in the way that people can be rendered beholden, and whether material offerings, alone, get the job done. These questions do not constitute critical rejection, but careful deliberation on the ideal human responses for all that the gods give. This is true for Judeans like Philo and

---

81. Lännström, "A Religious Revolution?" 261–274.

Josephus as much as it is for non-Judean Greeks and Romans. Across the board, the deliberations of such intellectuals lambast human attempts at coercion and insist on the fact that gods give voluntarily. In that broad sense, Paul offers little new, nor is there anything uniquely "Christian" about his position.

Conclusion

At first blush, the topic of reciprocity may seem far afield from divination and wonderworking. But as we have seen in this chapter, Paul brings them quite close insofar as the former relationship of mutual beneficence leads to the latter set of gifts. The previous chapters have demonstrated Paul's own claim to divinatory and wonderworking expertise, but here I explain how and why such abilities are extended to his gentile followers. *Pistis* (and its Latin equivalent, *fides*) was a widely valued ethic throughout the LXX, as well as numerous Greek and Latin gentile texts. And with the unwavering reorientation of their *pistis* toward Christ and the Judean deity, Paul's gentile followers are likely to be endowed with miraculous abilities that are unavailable to the "unfaithful" person. Such abilities include reading God's messages as they appear imprinted on the physical world in the form of *sēmeia*, the ability to prophesy, to channel divine voices and sounds, to interpret such voices, and to heal the sick and injured. Such gifts also include the performance of wondrous miracles that, to our chagrin, remain unspecified in the letters. All such abilities are divine gifts, *charismata*, delivered through the *pneuma* of Christ. While these gifts are free and voluntary on the part of Paul's god, they occur within the context of reciprocity. As I have shown, voluntariness is required in reciprocity lest it become transactional, contractual, and obligatory.

Reducing ancient religiosity, and ancient reciprocity, to a mere *do ut des* erases the richness and complexity of ancient relations among humans, as well as the relations between humans and their gods. Contrary to rejecting reciprocity, Paul's discussion of pneumatic gifts delivered to gentiles fits squarely within the bounds of ancient reciprocal relations and cannot fully be understood outside of such a context. To extract Paul's pneumatic gift discourse from its reciprocity context is to reinscribe the kinds of taxonomic and methodological problems addressed in Chapter 1. According to Paul, though, these abilities are gifted in proportion to gentile *pistis*, by a god who extends kindness to those do not deviate from him, but "who continue in his kindness" (Rom 11:22).

Conclusion

MANTIKĒ, MODES, AND MILIEU

THIS STUDY SINGLES out the divinatory and wonderworking practices in Paul's letters because such practices constituted an important and consistent aspect of his career, but have long been neglected in Pauline studies. In discussing this project, I have occasionally encountered subtle derision for a portrait of Paul as the early Empire's version of a backwoods Pentecostal preacher who handles snakes and heals through laying on hands, or a flashy televangelist—full of bombast and fraudulent magical promises while he swindles you out of your last dollar. Ironically, this study offers no such portrait. Rather, the book argues that Paul and his practices are best understood within their historical milieu. That milieu was diverse, rich, complex, and encompassed a broad range of ways that people interacted with their gods—almost all of which were organized around basic practices of reciprocity.

As Jonathan Z. Smith understands the term, "redescription, at the level of data, is neither a procedure of substitution nor of synonymy; it is the result of comparison across difference, taking cognitive advantage of the resultant mutual distortion" (27).[1] This project has not taken into consideration the varied studies of divinatory practices by modern anthropologists, and therefore the comparative scope is somewhat narrowed. But the redescriptive framework offered here allows us to view Paul's practices in a new and more historically realistic light. Rather than focus on categories and constructs that do not get us closer than we already are to understanding Paul, I have resisted traditional language and categories (such as *charismatic* or *grace*), as they serve only to reinscribe

---

1. Jonathan Z. Smith, "Re: Corinthians." In *Redescribing Paul and the Corinthians*, edited by Ron Cameron and Merrill Miller (Atlanta, GA: Society of Biblical Literature, 2011), 17–34.

anachronistic understandings of this material. Instead, this study considers Paul's practices in light of how ancient Greek speakers would have understood them— as types of *mantikē, prophēteia, teratoskopeia, mageia, goēteia,* and others.

Paul's vocabulary is at times distinct: He alone refers to this bundling of skills and abilities as "pneumatic gifts." But the distinctiveness of his terminology does not tell us much about the distinctiveness of the practices themselves. Rather, they point to a strategy of repackaging recognizable doings and sayings, which may or may not include some innovative aspects to their performance. Combined with Paul's narrative of gentile history and future, such practices appear simultaneously novel and ancient. The recombining of practices and teachings points again to Letter 52 of Apollonius; the "true" Pythagorean will eventually attain intimacy and friendship with gods, accurate and true prophetic abilities, and immortality. Both Paul and Apollonius offer followers benefits that include ethics, righteousness, and divinatory expertise.

The palpability and involvement of the gods in human affairs was simply a given for most people in antiquity. The world was legible as a place through which gods communicated important information to humans: admonishments and endorsements, warnings of danger and encouragement, divine intention or will, verification of the legitimacy of those who could properly "read" the signs. Innumerable examples survive—texts, inscriptions, artifacts, oracular shrines— demonstrating the creative and complex ways in which Greeks, Romans, and Judeans ascertained such information through practices of divination. Such practices included interpreting the flight of birds, earthquakes, and dreams, as well as the utterances of oracles, prophets, summoning the dead, etc. We cannot understand Paul's engagement with divination outside this historical and cultural context; it is the only context he knew.

When Paul writes about the things he has accomplished "through the power of signs and wonders" (Rom 15:19), his readers or listeners know exactly what he is talking about, as they hold in common an understanding about the semiotic nature of the world and the hands-on involvement of gods/God. For Paul, these signs and wonders include a panoply of divinatory practices such as uttering indecipherable divine speech, channeling intelligible divine words in the form of prophecy, and employing his ancient mysterious Judean books to deliver divine messages. Such practices are not original to Paul, nor are they specifically "Christian": We see them elsewhere in the many accounts of divine possession, oracular utterances, and in the divinatory–allegorical uses of texts including Homeric verses.

Likewise, when Paul speaks of enacting feats of divine powers [*dunameis*], his followers understand what that entails. He does not reluctantly stoop to the level of divinatory or wonderworking tricks to sway those of his listeners who have been seduced by the powers of his competitors. Rather, such practices reappear consistently throughout his letters and constitute a fundamental aspect of his teaching career. Paul's letters are so thick with divinatory and wonderworking claims that one would be hard-pressed to argue convincingly that his hand is forced. Such practices generate symbolic capital for those who claim them, and Paul is no different; he is one example from the array of religious specialists who operated and innovated in the early Roman Empire.

As this book demonstrates, for every divinatory or wonderworking practice evidenced in Paul's letters, we have numerous meaningful comparanda throughout Greek, Roman, and Judean texts and inscriptions. In a complex and sometimes ad hoc fashion, Paul, like all people, performs, adopts, recycles, and innovates upon the practices he already knows and recognizes. These practices, in turn, are meaningful and intelligible to observers and new followers because of the widespread shared practical understanding regarding how to communicate with gods, how gods empower special people, and how to maintain relations of mutual beneficence with gods. These shared practical understandings are so pervasive that they appear to be intuitive. Rather than constructing his practices and ethical teachings anew, then, Paul simply redirects gentile faithfulness, emphasizes voluntary participation in reciprocity, and zeros in on particular ways that the Judean god prefers to communicate by extending signs and miraculous powers.

To imagine a god who utterly ignores the offerings, devotion, and petitions of his or her devotees is to imagine a god with an unimaginable psychology. Cicero suggests as much when he queries, "For how can holiness [*sanctitas*] exist if the gods pay no heed to a man's affairs? What is the meaning of an animate being that pays no heed to anything?" *(de Nat* 1.123).[2] It is this basic assumption of divine interest—an intuitive and unreflective assumption—that undergirds ancient practices of reciprocity with deities. This fundamental assumption also propels divinatory practices and the ability for mortals to claim that they wield powers of divine origin. Gods take an interest in human affairs; gods communicate with humans; gods are inclined to reward the faithful and the pious. Gods send gifts for demonstrable, persistent human veneration. Sometimes, gods even bestow gifts for reasons that cannot be deduced by human observers.

Nevertheless, Paul's claim to perform miracles and wonders (or things his ancient observers might call *mageia*) tend to make Pauline scholars shift uncomfortably in their seats. The way to exculpate Paul from accusations of magic is to emphasize that his power comes from God. Graham Twelftree, for example, does

---

2. Loeb Classical Library, Rackham trans.

precisely this: "For Paul, God is the author of these miracles . . . nowhere does Paul lay claim to conducting the miracles himself or suggest that he is directly involved in their performance."[3] Indeed, Paul does attribute his magical–wondrous power to the Judean deity. But what Twelftree and other scholars neglect to see is that almost all ancient wonderworkers claim to be channeling the power of a deity. With the exception of those who are portrayed as gods themselves (e.g. Jesus in the gospels or Empedocles' grandiose self-description), such figures harness or facilitate the power of a god and not the power of themselves. Attributing miraculous power to a deity is simply a practitioner's way of saying, "I myself am not a god, but I have privileged access to the power of a god." That Paul attributes his divine powers to a deity only underscores his resemblance to other diviners and wonderworker–magicians.

Additionally, many New Testament scholars have argued that Paul rejected ancient relations of reciprocity, thereby presenting a supreme deity liberated from the *do ut des* obligations of giving. Such a position not only misunderstands and mischaracterizes reciprocity, it introduces faulty critiques of so-called paganism as well as Judean religion. As Jennifer Larson observes, "Traditionally, the Christian West has looked back upon interactions with 'pagan' gods as examples of an inferior kind of relationship with the divine. From the viewpoint of Christian theologians, the very nature of pagan worship was suspect because it involved the exchange of one grace or favor [*charis*] for another, whereas the apostle Paul had taught that charis was unidirectional rather than reciprocal."[4] As the present study has shown, Paul's giving is a mutual exchange of piety, reverence, and faithfulness, rewarded voluntarily and generously with a host of *charismata* in the form of divinatory and wonderworking abilities.

The claim that Paul rejects reciprocity is also a subtle critique of ancient Judean religion. That is, the added dimension of "works righteousness" depictions of Judaism supposes a Christianity in which ritual offerings, good deeds, and adherence to Mosaic Law, are surpassed in favor of the ideal of "faith"—but in such a way that is divorced from reciprocal relations. The Christian deity gives entirely freely, and no amount of good behavior or generosity can prompt that deity to reward humans. Such a notion, of course, will be articulated fully by John Calvin (reading Luther). But we must be wary of reading Lutheran or Calvinist theology back into Paul. "Works righteousness" has long served Christian supersessionist interests, but such a position overlooks many versions of God's divine justice in

---

3. Twelftree, *Paul and the Miraculous*, 191.

4. Larson, *Understanding Greek Religion*, 40.

the Hebrew Bible, while also misunderstanding how Paul crafts reciprocal beneficence between God and faithful gentiles.

It is important to underscore the practical and specific associations of
charis(mata), or gifts. When gods bestow gifts upon people, such benefactions
are evidenced: They are real, tangible, and denote some kind of favored status
or reward. The Christian theological category of "grace" distances Paul from
reciprocity insofar as grace is more ethereal, abstract, and intangible. While
Paul certainly speaks regularly in abstracts (indeed, *mysteries*), he also speaks
in specifics—money, imprisonment, ethical choices, and practical benefactions
from God. Unlike Philo, Paul never says, "you cannot bribe God"—though he
would very likely agree with Philo. But reciprocity is not bribery and that is why
scholars call it reciprocity and not bribery. As Larson points out, ". . . coercion
is inconsistent with reciprocity."[5] It is likely that Paul sometimes conceptualizes
charis in abstract or theoretical ways, but he also understands it literally and practically, and as part of a reciprocal relationship.

At one extreme in antiquity is the Epicurean assertion that human behavior
has no effect on divine participation in human life because gods simply have no regard for the affairs of mortals (thus their eternal bliss). At the other extreme is the
notion that mortals can "control" or strongarm deities through rituals, offerings,
promises, and demands. In the middle, however, are a number of positions that
operate within some kind of framework of reciprocity: gods can have a soft heart,
gods can be begged, gods can be just, gods can be faithful, etc. Paul lands squarely
in this rich middle area—he understands the Judean deity as neither prone to
bribery or coercion nor to abject indifference. It is abundantly clear that Paul's
relationship with his followers involves reciprocal exchange, care, beneficence,
and mutual support. Likewise, Paul strives to establish such reciprocal relations
among followers themselves. Most important, however, Paul establishes clear
dynamics of reciprocal exchange between gentile followers and the Judean god,
which entails *pistis* as the human contribution and *charis(mata)* as the divine return. *Charis* is even bestowed prior to the promise of gentile *pistis*. To claim that
Paul rejects reciprocity is to imagine a Paul who lives in a radically different place
and time from the first-century Mediterranean.

It is no coincidence that many scholars dismiss the centrality of divinatory
and wonderworking practices in Paul's letters. Likewise, it is no coincidence that
many have oversimplified reciprocity to something like *do ut des*—not unlike the
position taken by ancient philosopher–theologians like Plato, Seneca, or Philo.
The lack of coincidence is due to the shared mode of religiosity in which such

5. Ibid., 43.

philosopher–theologians operate. That is, both bodies—ancient philosophers and contemporary New Testament scholars—overlap in their intellectualist interests and in practices oriented toward the abstract. The shared mode of religiosity, that of the *literate cultural producer*, favors the cerebral, the allegorical, and the conceptual. And most important, this mode tends to critique, police, or feign rejection of aspects of the more primary mode of *everyday social exchange*. Thus, in the same way that Cicero cannot imagine that the lofty gods would linger under your bed at night so as to send you encrypted messages in dreams,[6] it might strike a theologian–scholar as unlikely that God would empower Paul to teach his followers to discern whether a fellow tongue-speaker has been possessed by a good spirit or a bad one.[7] If anything is scrutinized in the mode of the literate cultural producer it is the literal, the practical, and the material.[8]

The intellectualist mode of religiosity often takes as its object of critique the practices and ideas of the mundane, practical world. This includes mundane, practical interactions between people, and between people and their gods. For some, it is simply more intellectually satisfying to theorize about the ethereal grace of the divine, than to think of the gods rewarding for good behavior with actual "gifts." As Larson, again, observes, "The view that offerings were bribes or commercial exchanges is a reflective critique of intuitive belief and practice. Although regularly renewed since ancient times, this critique misrepresents the actual dynamics of worship."[9] Thus, ancient theologians critiqued relations of mutual exchange and beneficence with gods, in a similar way that contemporary theologians do, and Paul's theological and ethical claims are afforded a deeper gravitas than that extended to his contemporaries and predecessors.

One problem with this picture is that Paul moved between modes of religiosity, even though he may have had an affinity for the mode of the literate cultural producer. No doubt, he engaged in the more cognitively costly practices of theologizing, teaching ethics, and presenting complex, counterintuitive ideas. But operation in this secondary mode is never the result of disavowing or exorcising the primary, mundane mode. If Whitehouse and Stowers are correct, the primary mode of religiosity is a ubiquitous feature of human cognition and no amount of

---

6. *De Div.* 2.63; see also Chapter 2, "Dreams and Dream Interpretation."

7. 1 Cor 12:10.

8. This is to not reinscribe an unhelpful dichotomy between elite vs. popular religion. See Stanley Stowers, "Why Expert Versus Nonexpert is not Elite Versus Popular Religion: The Case of the Third Century." In *Religious Competition in the Greco-Roman World*, edited by Nathanial DeRosiers and Lily C. Vuong. (Atlanta, GA: SBL, 2016), 139–153.

9. Larson, *Understanding Greek Religion*, 47.

critiquing will expunge it. Indeed, it is not for expunging, insofar as it develops directly from intuitive, mundane social relations between people. Paul is hardly alone in operating in more than one mode; this is why Cicero can guffaw at the notion of gods sending dreams as divine messages in his *de Divinatione* (2.63), but elsewhere wonder what kind of god could ever be immune to human petitions, human piety, or human suffering (*de Nat. Deo.* 1.123). No matter how abstractly or loftily he envisions deities, he always returns to the default position of relating to them in practical and social ways—they react to humans and take an interest in human life.

This book does not refute the prominence of intellectualist and theological interests in Paul's thinking and practice. Rather, I bring to the fore other kind of practices that are equally prominent, but have been ignored or dismissed in traditional analyses of Paul. Such practices, which ancient observers would understand as types of *mantikē, teratoskopeia, mageia*, etc. involve tangible and practical demonstrations of the presence of a deity in the midst of humans. Such practices, whether performed by a purported quack or a trusted prophet, underscore the assumed semiotic nature of the world. Furthermore, the redescriptive framework I have provided allows us to contextualize Paul's divinatory and wonderworking practices within this historical milieu. In such a light, we can understand him vis-a-vis others who claimed to deliver divine messages, interpret divine texts, heal the sick, possess mysteries, and confer blessed afterlives.

Bibliography

Achtemeier, Paul. "Jesus and the Disciples as Miracle Workers in the Apocryphal New Testament." In *Aspects of Religious Propaganda in Judaism and Early Christianity*, ed. Elisabeth Schüssler Fiorenza, 148–186. Notre Dame, IN: Notre Dame Press, 1976.

Adanson, Michel. *Familles des Plantes*. Paris: Vincent, 1763.

Agnew, Francis. "The Origin of the NT Apostle-Concept: A Review of Research," *Journal of Biblical Literature* 105 (1986): 75–96.

Agteres, Suzan. "Pistis and Fides as Civic and Divine Virtues: A Pauline Concept Through Greco-Roman Eyes." In *Paul's Greco-Roman Context*, ed. Cilliers Breytenbach, BETL 277, 541–559. Leuven, Belgium: Peeters, 2015.

Aldershot, Hants. *Magic and Divination in Early Islam*. Burlington, VT: Ashgate, 2004.

Allen, James. *Inference From Signs: Ancient Debates About the Nature of Evidence*. Oxford: Clarendon, 2001.

Alvar Ezquerra, Jaime. *Romanising Oriental Gods. Myth, Salvation and Ethics in the Cults of Cybele, Isis and Mithras*. Leiden: Brill, 2008.

Andersen, F. I. "2 (Slavonic Apocalypse of) Enoch, A New Translation and Introduction." In *The Old Testament Pseudepigrapha*, ed. James Charlesworth, vol.1, 91–21. Garden City, NY: Doubleday, 1983–1985.

Annus, Amar, ed. *Divination and Interpretation of Signs in the Ancient World*. Chicago: University of Chicago Oriental Institute, 2010.

Ashton, John. *The Religion of the Apostle Paul*. New Haven, CT: Yale University Press, 2000.

Asirvatham, Sulochana R. "Olympias' Snake and Callisthenes' Stand: Religion and Politics in Plutarch's Life of Alexander." In *Between Magic and Religion: Interdisciplinary Studies in Ancient Mediterranean Religion and Society*, ed. Sulochana Asirvatham et al., 93–125. New York: Rowman & Littlefield, 2001.

Atran, Scott. *In Gods We Trust: The Evolutionary Landscape of Religion*. Oxford: Oxford University Press, 2002.

Aune, David, ed. *Apocalypticism, Prophecy, and Magic in Early Christianity*. Tübingen, Germany: Mohr Siebeck, 2006.

Aune, David. *Prophecy in Early Christianity and the Ancient Mediterranean World*. Grand Rapids, MI: Eerdmans, 1983.

Bailey, Kenneth. "Constructing Monothetic and Polythetic Typologies by the Heuristic Method," *The Sociological Quarterly* 14.3 (1973): 291–308.

Baker, Cynthia. "A 'Jew' by Any Other Name?" *Journal of Ancient Judaism* 2.2 (2011): 153–180.

Balty, Jean. "Apamea in Syria in the Second and Third Centuries A.D.," *Journal of Roman Studies* 78 (1988): 91–104.

Barclay, John. *Paul and the Gift*. Grand Rapids, MI: Eerdmans, 2015.

Barnett, Paul. *The Second Epistle to the Corinthians*. Grand Rapids, MI: Eerdmans, 1997.

Barr, James. "Paul and the LXX: A Note on Some Recent Work," *Journal of Theological Studies* 45 (1994): 593–601.

Barrett, C. K. *The Signs of an Apostle*. Philadelphia: Fortress Press, 1972.

Barrett, James. *Staged Narrative. Poetics and the Messenger in Greek Tragedy*. Berkeley: University of California Press, 2002.

Barrett, Justin. *Why Would Anyone Believe in God?* Walnut Creek, CA: AltaMira Press, 2004.

Barrier, Jeremy. *The Acts of Paul and Thecla: A Critical Introduction and Commentary*. Tübingen, Germany: Mohr Siebeck, 2009.

Bascom, William. *Ifa Divination: Communication Between Gods and Men in West Africa*. Bloomington: Indiana University Press, 1982.

Bauckham, Richard. *The Fate of the Dead: Studies on Jewish and Christian Apocalypses*. Leiden: Brill, 1998.

Beard, Mary. "Cicero and Divination: The Formation of a Latin Discourse," *Journal of Roman Studies* 76 (1986): 33–46.

Beard, Mary, John North, and Simon Price. *Religions of Rome: A History*. Cambridge: Cambridge University Press, 1998.

Beare, Frank. "Speaking with Tongues: A Critical Survey of the New Testament Evidence," *Journal of Biblical Literature* 83.3 (1964): 229–246.

Beck, Roger. *A Brief History of Ancient Astrology*. Malden, MA: Blackwell, 2007.

Beck, Roger. *The Religion of the Mithras Cult in the Roman Empire: Mysteries of the Unconquered Sun*. New York: Oxford University Press, 2006.

Beck, Roger. "Ritual, Myth, Doctrine, and Initiation in the Mysteries of Mithras: New Evidence From a Cult Vessel," *Journal of Roman Studies* 90 (2000): 145–180.

Beckner, Morton. *The Biological Way of Thought*. New York: Columbia University Press, 1959.

Berchman, Robert M., ed. *Horizons of Prophecy, Divination, Dreams, and Theurgy in Mediterranean Antiquity*. Atlanta, GA: Scholars Press, 1998.

Berchman, Robert M., ed. *Mediators of the Divine: Horizons of Prophecy, Divination, Dreams, and Theurgy in Mediterranean Antiquity*. Atlanta, GA: Scholars Press, 1998.

Bering, Jesse. "Intuitive Conceptions of Dead Agents' Minds: The Natural Foundations of Afterlife Beliefs as Phenomenological Boundary," *Journal of Cognition and Culture*, 2.4 (2002): 263–308.

Berkowitz, Beth. "A Short History of the People Israel From the Patriarchs to the Messiah," *Journal of Ancient Judaism* 2.2 (2011): 181–207.

Bernard, J. H. "Prophets and Prophecy in New Testament Times," *The Biblical World* 25.2 (1905): 117–124.

Betz, Hans Dieter, trans. *The Greek Magical Papyri in Translation, Including the Demotic Spells*, 2nd ed. Chicago: University of Chicago Press, 1992.

Betz, Hans Dieter. *Der Apostel Paulus und die sokratische Tradition*. Tübingen, Germany: Mohr Siebeck, 1972.

Blackburn, Barry. *Theios Anēr and the Markan Miracle Traditions: A Critique of the "Theios Anēr" Concept as an Interpretative Background of the Miracle Traditions Used by Mark*. Tübingen, Germany: Mohr Siebeck, 1991.

Blass, Rachel B. *The Meaning of the Dream in Psychoanalysis*. Albany: State University of New York Press, 2002.

Gideon. Bohak, Gideon. *Ancient Jewish Magic: A History*. New York: Cambridge University Press, 2008.

Bohak, Gideon. "Prolegomena to the Study of the Jewish Magical Tradition," *Currents in Biblical Literature* 8 (2009): 107–150.

Bolyki, Janos. "Miracle Stories in the Acts of John." In *The Acts of John*, ed. Jan Bremmer, 15–36. Kampen, The Netherlands: Kok Pharos Publishers, 1995.

Bonfim, Evandro. "Glossolalia and Linguistic Alterity: The Ontology of Ineffable Speech," *Religion and Society: Advances in Research* 6 (2015): 75–80.

Bouché-Leclercq, A. *Histoire de la divination dans l'antiquité*, vols. 1–4. Paris: E. Leroux, 1879.

Bourdieu, Pierre. *The Field of Cultural Production*. Edited by Randal Johnson. New York: Columbia University Press, 1993.

Bourdieu, Pierre. *The Logic of Practice*. Translated by Richard Nice. Stanford, CA: Stanford University Press, 1990.

Bourdieu, Pierre. *Distinction: A Social Critique of the Judgement of Taste*. Cambridge, MA: Harvard University Press, 1984.

Bovon, François. "Miracles, magie, et guérison dans les Actes Apocryphes des Apôtres," *Journal of Early Christian Studies* 3 (1995): 45–59.

Bovon, François and E. Junod. "Reading the Apocryphal Acts of the Apostles," *Semeia* 38 (1986): 165–166.

Bowden, Hugh. "Before Superstition and After: Theophrastus and Plutarch on *Deisidaimonia*," *Past & Present* 199.3 (2008): 56–71.

Bowers, Paul. "Paul and Religious Propaganda in the First Century," *Novum Testamentum* 22.4 (1980): 316–323.

Boyarin, Daniel. *Border Lines: The Partition of Judeo-Christianity*. Philadelphia: University of Pennsylvania Press, 2006.

Boyer, Pascal. *Religion Explained: The Evolutionary Origins of Religious Thought*. New York: Basic Books, 2001.

Boys-Stones, G. R. *Post-Hellenistic Philosophy: A Study of its Development From the Stoics to Origen*. Oxford: Oxford University Press, 2001.

Bremmer, Jan N. "Greek Normative Animal Sacrifice." In *Companion to Greek Religion*, ed. Daniel Ogden, 132–144. Oxford: Blackwell, 2007.

Bremmer, Jan N., ed. *The Apocryphal Acts of Andrew*. Leuven, Belgium: Peeters, 2000.

Bremmer, Jan N., ed. *The Apocryphal Acts of Peter. Magic, Miracles and Gnosticism* (Studies on the Apocryphal Acts of the Apostles 3). Leuven, Belgium: Peeters, 1998.

Bremmer, Jan N., ed., *The Apocryphal Acts of John*. Kampen, The Netherlands: Kok Pharos Publishers, 1995.

Brenk, Frederick. "'A Most Strange Doctrine.' *Daimon* in Plutarch," *The Classical Journal* 69.1 (1973): 1–11.

Brouwer, H. H. J. *Bona Dea: The Sources and a Description of the Cult*. Leiden, New York: Brill, 1989.

Brown, Michael L. *Israel's Divine Healer*. Grand Rapids, MI: Zondervan, 1995.

Brown, Raymond. "The Twelve and the Apostolate." In *The New Jerome Biblical Commentary*, 1377–1381. Englewood Cliffs, NJ: Prentice-Hall, 1990.

Bruce, F. F. "Is the Paul of Acts the Real Paul?" *Bulletin of the John Rylands University Library* 58 (1976): 282–305.

Büchli, Jörg. *Der Poimandres: Ein Paganisiertes Evangelium; Sprachliche und Begriffliche Untersuchungen zum 1. Traktat des Corpus Hermeticum*. Tübingen, Germany: Mohr Siebeck, 1987.

Bultmann, Rudolph. 'Evangelien', *Religion in Geschichte und Gegenwart*, 2nd ed.Vol. 2. 419. Tübingen: Mohr Siebeck, 1928.

Burkert, Walter. "Signs, Commands, and Knowledge: Ancient Divination Between Enigma and Epiphany." In *Mantikê: Studies in Ancient Divination*, ed. Sarah Iles Johnston and Peter Struck, 29–49. Boston: Brill, 2005.

Burton, Ernest D. "The Office of the Apostolate in the Early Church," *American Journal of Theology* 16.4 (1912): 561–588.

Cameron, Ron and Merrill P. Miller. "Introducing Paul and the Corinthians." In *Redescribing Paul and the Corinthians*, ed. Ron Cameron and Merrill P. Miller, 1–16. Atlanta, GA: Society of Biblical Literature, 2011.

Carlyle, May. "A Survey of Glossolalia and Related Phenomena in Non-Christian Religions," *American Anthropologist* 58.1 (1956): 75–96.

Cartledge, Mark. *Charismatic Glossolalia: An Empirical-Theological Study*. Burlington, VT: Ashgate, 2002.

Cary, Earnest, trans. *Roman History by Cassius Dio*. Loeb Classical Library, vol. 7. Cambridge, MA: Harvard University Press, 1924.

Casadio, Giovanni and Patricia Johnson. *Mystic Cults in Magna Graecia*. Austin: University of Texas Press, 2009.

Cavadini, John, ed. *Miracles in Jewish and Christian Antiquity: Imagining Truth.* Notre Dame, IN: Notre Dame Press, 1999.

Charlesworth, James H., ed. *The Old Testament Pseudepigrapha.* London: Darton, Longman & Todd, 1983.

Ciraolo, Leda and Jonathan Seidel. *Magic and Divination in the Ancient World.* Leiden: Brill, 2002.

Clark, Anna J. *Divine Qualities: Cult and Community in Republican Rome.* Oxford: Oxford University Press, 2007.

Clark Wire, Antoinette. *The Corinthian Women Prophets: A Reconstruction Through Paul's Rhetoric.* Minneapolis: Fortress, 1990.

Clauss, Manfred. *The Roman Cult of Mithras: The God and His Mysteries.* New York: Routledge, 2000.

Cleveland, Ingrid T. *The Egyptian Cults in Ancient Rome: A Study of the Diffusion and Popularity of the Cults in Roman Society.* Ann Arbor: UMI, 1987.

Cohen, Shaye. *Beginnings of Jewishness: Boundaries, Varieties, Uncertainties.* Berkeley: University of California Press, 1999.

Collins, Derek. "The Magic of Homeric Verses," *Classical Philology* 103 (2008): 211–236.

Collins, Derek. *Magic in the Ancient Greek World.* Malden, MA: Blackwell, 2008.

Collins, Derek. "Mapping the Entrails: The Practice of Greek Hepatoscopy," *American Journal of Philology* 129.3 (2008): 319–345.

Compton, Michael. "The Union of Religion and Health in Ancient Asklepieia," *Journal of Religion and Health* 37.4 (1998): 301–312.

Conway, Colleen. *Behold the Man: Jesus and Greco-Roman Masculinity.* Oxford: Oxford University Press, 2008.

Copenhaver, Brian P. *Hermetica: The Greek Corpus Hermeticum and the Latin Asclepius in a New English Translation, With Notes and Introduction.* Cambridge: Cambridge University Press, 1992.

Cramer, Frederick H. *Astrology in Roman Law and Politics.* Philadelphia: American Philosophical Society, 1954.

Cryer, Frederick H. *Divination in Ancient Israel and Its Near Eastern Environment.* Sheffield, UK: Sheffield Academic Press, 1994.

Curd, Patricia. *The Legacy of Parmenides: Eleatic Monism and Later Presocratic Thought.* Princeton, NJ: Princeton University Press, 1998.

Davies, Stevan L. *Jesus the Healer: Possession, Trance, and the Origins of Christianity.* New York: Continuum, 1995.

de Grummond, Nancy Thomson, and Erika Simon, eds. *The Religion of the Etruscans.* Austin: University of Texas Press, 2006.

DeMaris, Richard E. "Corinthian Religion and Baptism for the Dead (1 Corinthians 15:29): Insights From Archaeology and Anthropology," *Journal of Biblical Literature* 114.4 (1995): 661–682.

de Waal, Frans. *Primates and Philosophers: How Morality Evolved.* Princeton, NJ: Princeton University Press, 2015.

Bibliography

Dicks, D. R. "Astrology and Astronomy in Horace," *Hermes* 91.1 (1963): 60–73.

Dillon, M. P. J. "The Didactic Nature of Epidaurian Iamata," *Zeitschrift für Papyrologie und Epigraphik* 101 (1994): 239–260.

Dodson, Derek S. *Reading Dreams: An Audience-Critical Approach to the Dreams in the Gospel of Matthew*. New York: T & T Clark, 2009.

Domhoff, William G. *The Scientific Study of Dreams: Neural Networks, Cognitive Development, and Content Analysis*. Washington, DC: American Psychological Association, 2003.

Drews, Robert. "Pontiffs, Prodigies, and the Disappearance of the *Annales Maximi*," *Classical Philology* 83.4 (1988): 289–299.

Duboisson, Daniel. *The Western Construction of Religion: Myths, Knowledge and Ideology*. Translated by William Sayers. Baltimore: Johns Hopkins University Press, 2003.

du Bourguet, P. "Ensemble magique de la periode romaine en Egypte," *La Revue du Louvre* 25 (1975): 255–257.

Dunn, James. *Jesus and the Spirit: A Study of the Religious and Charismatic Experience of Jesus and the First Christians as Reflected in the New Testament*. Grand Rapids, MI: Eerdmans, 1997.

Dunn, James. *The Theology of the Apostle Paul*. Grand Rapids, MI: Eerdmans, 1998.

Dupont, Jacques. "Le nom d'Apôtres: A-t-il été donné aux Douze par Jésus?" In *Études sur les évangiles synoptiques*, ed. Frans Neirynck, 2.976–2.1018. Leuven, Belgium: Peeters, 1985.

Easter, Matthew. "The *Pistis Christou* Debate: Main Arguments and Responses in Summary," *Currents in Biblical Research* 9 (2010): 33–47.

Edinow, Esther. *Oracles, Curses, and Risks Among the Ancient Greeks*. New York: Oxford University Press, 2007.

Edmonds, J. M., ed. and trans. *The Characters of Theophrastus*. Cambridge, MA: Harvard University Press, 1961.

Eisenbaum, Pamela. "Paul as the New Abraham." In *Paul and Politics: Ekklesia, Israel, Imperium, Interpretation*, ed. Richard Horsley, 130–145. Harrisburg, PA: Trinity Press International, 2000.

Ekbom, Moa. *The Sortes Vergilianae: A Philological Study*. PhD Thesis. Uppsala: Uppsala University, 2013.

Elliott, J. K., ed. *The Apocryphal New Testament: A Collection of Apocryphal Christian Literature in an English Translation*. Oxford: Clarendon, 1993.

Ellis, Earle E. *Prophecy and Hermeneutic*. Tübingen, Germany: Mohr Siebeck, 1978.

Engberg-Pedersen, Troels. *Cosmology and Self in the Apostle Paul: The Material Spirit*. New York: Oxford University Press, 2010.

Engberg-Pedersen, Troels. *Paul and the Stoics*. Louisville, KY: Westminster John Knox Press, 2000.

Epp, Elden. *Junia: The First Woman Apostle*. Minneapolis: Fortress Press, 2005.

Epstein, David. "Cicero's Testimony at the 'Bona Dea' Trial," *Classical Philology* 81 (1986): 229–235.

Eyl, Jennifer. "Semantic Voids, New Testament Translation, and Anachronism: The Case of Paul's Use of Ekklēsia," *Method & Theory in the Study of Religion* 26 (2014): 315–339.

Faraone, Christopher. "The Agonistic Context of Early Greek Binding Spells." In *Magika Hiera: Ancient Greek Magic and Religion,* ed. Christopher Faraone and Dirk Obbink, 3–32. Oxford: Oxford University Press, 1991.

Fee, Gordon. *God's Empowering Presence: The Holy Spirit in the Letters of Paul.* Peabody, MA: Hendrickson, 1991, 581–584.

Finkelberg, Margalit. "Homer as a Foundation Text." In *Homer, the Bible, and Beyond*, ed. Margalit Finkelberg and Guy G. Stroumsa, 75–96. Leiden: Brill, 2003.

Flannery-Dailey, Frances. *Dreamers, Scribes, and Priests: Jewish Dreams in the Hellenistic and Roman Eras.* Leiden: Brill, 2004.

Forbes, Christopher. *Prophecy and Inspired Speech in Early Christianity and Its Hellenistic Environment.* Tübingen, Germany: Mohr Siebeck, 1995.

Forman, Paul. "The Astrophysics of Berossos the Chaldean," *Isis* 59.1 (1968): 91–94.

Fox, Robin Lane. *Pagans and Christians in the Mediterranean World From the Second Century AD to the Conversion of Constantine.* London: Penguin Books, 1986.

Frankfurter, David. "Dynamics of Ritual Expertise in Antiquity and Beyond: Towards a New Taxonomy of 'Magicians.'" In *Magic and Ritual in the Ancient World*, ed. Paul Mirecki and Marvin Meyer, 159–178. Leiden: Brill, 2002.

Frankfurter, David. *Religion in Roman Egypt: Assimilation and Resistance.* Princeton, NJ: Princeton University Press, 1998.

Freeman, Charles. *Holy Bones, Holy Dust: How Relics Shaped the History of Medieval Europe.* New Haven, CY: Yale University Press, 2011.

Freyburger, Gérard. *Fides: étude sémantique et religieuse depuis les origines jusqu'à l'époque augustéenne.* Paris: Les Belles Lettres, 2009.

Freyne, Sean. *The Twelve: Disciples and Apostles.* London: Sheed and Ward, 1968.

Foster, R. V. "Hebrew Prophets and Prophecy," *Old Testament Student* 6.6 (1897): 166–170.

Frueh, Edward. "*Sinistra ut Ante Dextra*: Reading Catullus 45," *The Classical World* 84.1 (1990): 15–21.

Gager, John. *Moses in Greco-Roman Paganism.* New York: Abingdon, 1972.

Gager, John. "Moses the Magician: Hero of an Ancient Counter-Culture?" *Helios* 21 (1994): 179–188.

Gager, John. *Reinventing Paul.* Oxford: Oxford University Press, 2000.

Geller, Mark. "Deconstructing Talmudic Magic." In *Magic and the Classical Tradition*, ed. C. Burnett, W. Ryan, 1–18. London: Warburg Institute, 2006.

Georgi, Dieter. *The Opponents of Paul in Second Corinthians.* Philadelphia: Fortress Press, 1986.

Gillespie, T. W. *The First Theologians: A Study in Early Christian Prophecy.* Grand Rapids, MI: Eerdmans, 1994.

Gillespie, T. W. "A Pattern of Prophetic Speech in First Corinthians," *Journal of Biblical Literature* 97.1 (1978): 74–95.

Glaim, Aaron. "Reciprocity, Sacrifice and Salvation in Judean Religion at the Turn of the Era." PhD Dissertation, Brown University, 2014.

Gnuse, Robert. *Dreams and Dream Reports in the Writings of Josephus.* New York: Brill, 1996.

Gnuse, Robert. "The Temple Experience of Jaddus in the Antiquities of Josephus: A Report of Jewish Dream Incubation," *Jewish Quarterly Review* 83.3–4 (1993): 349–368.

Gooder, Paula. *Only the Third Heaven?: 2 Corinthians 12:1–10 and Heavenly Ascent.* New York: T & T Clark, 2006.

Goodman, Felicitas D. *Speaking in Tongues: A Cross-Cultural Study of Glossolalia.* Chicago: University of Chicago Press, 1972.

Goulder, Michael D. "Vision and Knowledge," *Journal for the Study of the New Testament* 56 (1994): 53–71.

Gourinat, Jean-Baptiste. "*Akrasia* and *Enkrateia* in Ancient Stoicism: Minor Vice and Minor Virtue?" In *Akrasia in Greek Philosophy: From Socrates to Plotinus*, ed. Christopher Bobonich and Pierre Destrée, 215–248. Leiden: Brill, 2007.

Graf, Fritz. "An Oracle Against Pestilence From a Western Anatolian Town," *Zeitschrift für Papyrologie und Epigraphik* 92 (1992): 267–279.

Graf, Fritz. "Excluding the Charming: The Development of the Greek Concept of Magic." In *Ancient Magic and Ritual Power*, ed. Marvin Meyer and Paul Mirecki, 29–42. Boston: Brill, 2001.

Graf, Fritz and Johnston, Sarah Iles. *Ritual Texts for the Afterlife: Orpheus and the Bacchic Gold Tablets.* New York: Routledge, 2007.

Grammatiki, Karla A., ed. *Fiction on the Fringe: Novelistic Writing in the Post-Classical Age.* Leiden: Brill, 2009.

Green, Steven. "Malevolent Gods and Promethean Birds: Contesting Augury in Augustus' Rome," *Transactions of the American Philological Association* 139 (2009): 147–167.

Greene, John. *The Role of the Messenger and Message in the Ancient Near East; Oral and Written Communication in the Ancient Near East and in the Hebrew Scriptures: Communicators and Communiqués in Context.* Atlanta, GA: Scholars Press. 1989.

Gregory, Bradley. "Abraham as the Jewish Ideal: Exegetical Traditions in Sirach 44:19–12," *Catholic Biblical Quarterly* 70 (2008): 66–81.

Griffin, Miriam. "De Beneficiis and Roman Society," *Journal of Roman Studies* 93 (2003): 92–113.

Griffiths, J. Gwyn. "Some Claims of Xenoglossy in the Ancient Languages," *Numen* 33.1 (1986): 141–169.

Grudem, W. A. *The Gift of Prophecy in 1 Corinthians*. Washington, DC: University Press of America, 1982.

Gunther, John J. *St. Paul's Opponents and Their Background: A Study of Apocalyptic and Jewish Sectarian Teachings*. Leiden: Brill, 1973.

Guthrie, Stewart. *Faces in the Clouds: A New Theory of Religion*. Oxford: Oxford University Press, 1995.

Gutzwiller, Kathryn. "Seeing Thought: Timomachus' Medea and Ecphrastic Epigram," *American Journal of Philology* 125.3 (2004) 339–386.

Haack, Marie-Laurence. *Les haruspices dans le monde romain*. Pessac, France: Ausonius, 2003.

Hachlili, Rachel. "The Zodiac in Ancient Jewish Synagogal Art: A Review," *Jewish Studies Quarterly* 9.3 (2002): 219–258.

Haenchen, Ernst. *Die Apostelgeschichte*. Göttingen, Germany: Vandenhoeck & Ruprecht, 1968.

Halliday, W. R. *Greek Divination: A Study of Its Methods and Principles*. Chicago: Argonaut, 1967.

Halliday, W. R. "'The Superstitious Man' of Theophrastus," *Folklore* 41.2 (1930): 121–153.

Hamilton, W. "The Myth in Plutarch's *De Genio* (589F–592E)," *Classical Quarterly* 28.3 (1934): 175–182.

Hankinson, R. J. "Stoicism, Science and Divination," *Apeiron: A Journal for Ancient Philosophy and Science, 21.2, Method, Medicine and Metaphysics: Studies in the Philosophy of Ancient Science* (Summer 1988): 123–160.

Hansen, William, ed. *Anthology of Ancient Greek Popular Literature*. Bloomington: Indiana University Press, 1998.

Harrisville, Roy A. "Before ΠΙΣΤΙΣ ΧΡΙΣΤΟΥ: The Objective Genitive as Good Greek," *Novum Testamentum* 48 (2006): 353–358.

Harland, Philip. "Divine Instructions for the Household Association of Dionysios (Late II–Early I BCE)," *Associations in the Greco-Roman World: An Expanding Collection of Inscriptions, Papyri, and Other Sources in Translation*, November 10, 2011. URL: http://philipharland.com/greco-roman-associations/divine-instructions-for-the-household-association-of-dionysios/.

Harnack, Adolf von. *Die Mission und Ausbreitung des Christentums in den ersten drei Jahrhunderten*. Leipzig: J. C. Hinrichs, 1902.

Harris, Murray J. *The Second Epistle to the Corinthians: A Commentary on the Greek Text*. Grand Rapids, MI: Eerdmans, 2005.

Harris, William. *Dreams and Experience in Classical Antiquity*. Cambridge, MA: Harvard University Press, 2009.

Harris, William, trans. and ed. "Heraclitus: The Complete Fragments." In *Ancient Philosophy and New Thoughts* (June 2011). URL: http://community.middlebury.edu/~harris/Philosophy/heraclitus.pdf.

Harrison, James. *Paul's Language of Grace in its Graeco-Roman Context.* Wissenschaftliche Untersuchungen zum Neuen Testament 172. Tübingen, Germany: Mohr Siebeck, 2003.

Hays, Richard. *The Faith of Jesus Christ: The Narrative Substructure of Galatians 3:1–4:11.* Grand Rapids, MI: Eerdmans, 2002.

Hays, Richard. *Echoes of Scripture in the Letters of Paul.* New Haven, CT: Yale University Press, 1989.

Heliso, Desta. *Pistis and the Righteous One: A Study of Romans 1:17 Against the Background of Scripture and Second Temple Jewish Literature.* Wissenschaftliche Untersuchungen zum Neuen Testament 235. Tübingen, Germany: Mohr Siebeck, 2007.

Hellholm, David, Tor Vegge, Øyvind Norderval, and Christer Hellholm, eds. *Ablution, Initiation, and Baptism: Late Antiquity, Early Judaism, and Early Christianity,* Beihefte zur Zeitschrift für die neutestamentliche Wissenschaft 176. Berlin: de Gruyter, 2011.

Herczeg, Pál. "Sermons in the Acts of John." In *The Apocryphal Acts of John,* ed. Jan Bremmer, 153–170. Kampen, The Netherlands: Kok Pharos Publishers, 1995.

Herczeg, Pál. "*Theios aner* Traits in the Apocryphal Acts of Peter." In *The Apocryphal Acts of Peter: Magic, Miracles, and Gnosticism,* ed. Jan Bremmer, 29–38. Leuven, Belgium: Peeters, 1998.

Hermann, L. "Apollos," *Revue des sciences religieuses* 50 (1976): 330–336.

Hill, David. *New Testament Prophecy.* Atlanta, GA: John Knox Press, 1979.

Hillard, Tom W. "Scipio Aemilianus and a Prophecy from Clunia," *Historia: Zeitschrift für Alte Geschichte* 54.3 (2005): 344–348.

Himmelfarb, Martha. *Ascent to Heaven in Jewish and Christian Apocalypses.* New York: Oxford University Press, 1993.

Hirst, Margaret E. "The Portents in Horace *Odes* I.2.1–20," *The Classical Quarterly* 32.1 (1938): 7–9.

Holmes, Michael. *The Apostolic Fathers: Greek Texts and English Translations,* 3rd ed. Grand Rapids, MI: Baker Academic, 2007.

Holmgren, Frederick. "Faithful Abraham and the 'Amana Covenant Nehemiah 9: 6–10: 1," *Zeitschrift für die Alttestamentliche Wissenschaft (ZAW)* 104 (1992): 249–254.

Holowchak, M. Andrew. *Ancient Science and Dreams: Oneirology in Greco-Roman Antiquity.* New York: University Press of America, 2002.

Horsley, Richard. *1 Corinthians.* Nashville, TN: Abingdon, 1998.

Hovenden, Gerald. *Speaking in Tongues: New Testament Evidence in Context.* London: Sheffield Academic Press, 2002.

Hughes, Philip. *The Second Epistle to the Corinthians.* Grand Rapids, MI: Eerdmans, 1962.

Hull, Michael. *Baptism on Account of the Dead (1 Cor 15:29): An Act of Faith in the Resurrection.* SBL Academia Biblica 22. Atlanta, GA: Society of Biblical Literature, 2005.

Hutchinson, Valerie J. *Bacchus in Roman Britain: Archaeological Evidence for His Cult.* Ann Arbor: University of Michigan Press, 1983.

Iacoboni, Marco. "Imitation, Empathy, and Mirror Neurons," *Annual Review of Psychology* 60 (2009): 653–670.

Jackson, Robert. *At Empire's Edge: Exploring Rome's Egyptian Frontier*. New Haven, CT: Yale University Press, 2002.

Jackson Case, Shirley. "The Art of Healing in Early Christian Times," *Journal of Religion* 3.3 (1923): 238–255.

Jacobus, Helen. *Zodiac Calendars in the Dead Sea Scrolls and Their Reception: Ancient Astronomy and Astrology in Early Judaism*. Leiden: Brill, 2014.

Jannot, Jean- René. *Religion in Ancient Etruria*. Translated by Jane K. Whitehead. Madison: University of Wisconsin Press, 2005.

Jaquith, James. "Toward a Typology of Formal Communicative Behaviors: Glossolalia," *Anthropological Linguistics* 9.8 (1967): 1–8.

Jeanmarie, Henri. *Dionysos: Histoire du culte de Bacchus: L'oorgiasme dans l'antiquité et les temps modernes, origine du théâtre en Grèce, Orphisme et mystique Dionysiaque, èvolution du Dionysisme après Alexandre*. Paris: Payot, 1970.

Jeffers, Ann. *Magic and Divination in Ancient Palestine and Syria*. New York: Brill, 1996.

Jeffers, Ann. "Magic and Divination in Ancient Israel," *Religion Compass* 1 (2007): 628–642.

Jefford, Clayton. *The Apostolic Fathers and the New Testament*. Peabody, MA: Hendrickson, 2006.

Jeyes, Ulla. "The 'Palace Gate' of the Liver: A Study of Terminology and Methods in Babylonian Extispicy," *Journal of Cuneiform Studies* 30.4 (1978): 209–233.

Johnson Hodge, Caroline. *If Sons, Then Heirs: A Study of Kinship and Ethnicity in the Letters of Paul*. Oxford: Oxford University Press, 2007.

Johnson, Lee A. "Women and Glossolalia in Pauline Communities: The Relationship Between Pneumatic Gifts and Authority," *Biblical Interpretation* 21 (2013): 196–214.

Johnson, Maxwell E. *The Rites of Christian Initiation: Their Evolution and Interpretation*, revised and expanded edition. Collegeville, MN: Liturgical Press, 2007.

Johnston, Sarah Iles. *Hekate Soteira: A Study of Hekate's Roles in the Chaldean Oracles and Related Literature*. Atlanta, GA: Scholars Press, 1990.

Johnston, Sarah Iles. *Restless Dead: Encounters Between the Living and the Dead in Ancient Greece*. Berkeley: University of California Press, 1999.

Johnston, Sarah Iles. *Ancient Greek Divination*. Oxford: Wiley-Blackwell, 2008.

Johnston, Sarah Iles and Fritz Graf. *Ritual Texts for the Afterlife: Orpheus and the Bacchic Gold Tablets*. New York: Routledge, 2007.

Jones, Christopher, ed. and trans. *Letters of Apollonius*. Loeb Classical Library. Cambridge, MA: Harvard University Press, 2006.

Joubert, Stephen. *Paul as Benefactor: Reciprocity, Strategy, and Theological Reflection in Paul's Collection*. Wissenschaftliche Untersuchungen zum Neuen Testament 2.124. Tübingen, Germany: Mohr Siebeck, 2000.

Joyce, Richard. "Early Stoicism and *Akrasia*," *Phronesis* 40.3 (1995) 315–335.

Kalinowski, Marc. *Divination et société dans la Chine médiévale: Etude des manuscrits de Dunhuang de la Bibliothèque Nationale de France et de la British Library.* Paris: Bibliothèque Nationale de France, 2003.

Karanika, Andromache. "Homer the Prophet: Homeric Verses and Divination in the *Homeromanteion*." In *Sacred Words: Orality, Literacy, and Religion*, ed. A. P. M. H. Lardinois et al., 255–278. Boston: Brill, 2011.

Kearsley, Rosalind. "Octavian and Augury: The Years 30–27 B.C.," *Classical Quarterly* 59.1 (2009): 147–166.

Kee, Howard Clark. *Medicine, Miracle, and Magic in New Testament Times.* Cambridge: Cambridge University Press, 1986.

Kee, Howard Clark. *Miracle in the Early Christian World: A Study in Sociohistorical Method.* New Haven, CT: Yale University Press, 1983.

Kennedy, A. A. "The Scope and Function of the Apostolate in the New Testament," *The Biblical World* 33.3 (1909): 160–170.

Kennedy, A. A. *St. Paul and the Mystery-Religions.* London: Hodder & Stoughton, 1913.

King, Charles. "The Organization of Roman Religious Beliefs," *Classical Antiquity* 22.2 (2003): 275–312.

Kippenberg, Hans G. and Stroumsa, Guy G., eds. *Secrecy and Concealment: Studies in the History of Mediterranean and Near Eastern Religions.* Leiden: Brill, 1995.

Kirk, G. S. "Some Methodological Pitfalls in the Study of Ancient Greek Sacrifice (in Particular)." In *Le Sacrifice dans l'antiquité*, 74–75. Vandouvres, Geneva: Fondation Hardt, 1980).

Kitz, Anne Marie. "Prophecy as Divination," *Catholic Biblical Quarterly* 65 (2003): 22–42.

Knight, Jonathan. *The Ascension of Isaiah.* Sheffield, UK: Sheffield Academic Press, 1995.

Kollman, Bernd. "Images of Hope: Towards an Understanding of New Testament Miracle Stories." In *Wonders Never Cease: The Purpose of Narrating Miracle Stories in the New Testament and its Religious Environment*, ed. Michael Labahn and Jan Liertaert Peerbolte. New York: T & T Clark, 2006.

Kraemer, Ross. "Typical and Atypical Jewish Family Dynamics: The Cases of Babatha and Berenice." In *Early Christian Families in Context: An Interdisciplinary Dialogue*, ed. David Balch and Carolyn Osiek, 130–156. Grand Rapids, MI: Eerdmans. 2003.

Kraemer, Ross and Jennifer Eyl, "Translating Women: The Perils of Gender-Inclusive Translation of the New Testament." In *Celebrate Her for the Fruit of Her Hands: Studies in Honor of Carol L. Meyers*, ed. Charles Carter, 295–318. Winona Lake, IN: Eisenbrauns, 2015.

Kuhlmann, Klaus. *Das Ammoneion: Archäologie, Geschichte und Kultpraxis des Orakels von Siwa.* Mainz: P. von Zabern, 1988.

Kuhrt, A. "Assyrian and Babylonian Traditions in Classical Authors: A Critical Synthesis." In *Mesopotamien und seine Nachbarn, Berliner Beiträge zum Vorderen Orient*, ed. H. J. Nissen and J. Renger, 539–540. Berlin: Reimer, 1982.

Laird, Andrew. "Figures of Allegory From Homer to Latin Epic." In *Metaphor, Allegory, and the Classical Tradition*, ed. G. R. Boys-Stones, 151–175. Oxford: Oxford University Press, 2003.

Lake, Kirsopp. "The Twelve and the Apostles." In *The Beginnings of Christianity, Part 1, The Acts of the Apostles*, ed. F. J. Foakes Jackson and Kirsopp Lake, 5: 37–59. Grand Rapids, MI: Baker, 1979.

Lambert, M. "Ancient Greek and Zulu Sacrificial Ritual," *Numen* 40 (1993): 293–318.

Lamberton, Robert. *Homer the Theologian*. Los Angeles: University of California Press, 1986.

Lamberton, Robert. "The Neoplatonists and the Spiritualization of Homer." In *Homer's Ancient Readers: The Hermeneutics of Greek Epic's Earliest Exegetes*, ed. Robert Lamberton and John Keaney, 115–133. Princeton, NJ: Princeton University Press, 1992.

Lambrecht, Jan. *Second Corinthians*. Sacra Pagina Series, 8. Collegeville, MN: Liturgical Press, 1999.

Lange, Armin. "The Essene Position on Magic and Divination." In *Legal Texts and Legal Issues: Proceedings of the Second Meeting of the International Organization for Qumran Studies*, ed. Moshe Bernstein et al., 377–345. New York: Brill, 1997.

Lange, Armin. "Greek Seers and Israelite-Jewish Prophets," *Vetus Testamentum* 57 (2007): 461–482.

Lännström, Anna. "A Religious Revolution? How Socrates' Theology Undermined the Practice of Sacrifice," *Ancient Philosophy* 31 (2011): 261–274.

Larson, Jennifer. *Understanding Greek Religion: A Cognitive Approach*. New York: Routledge, 2016.

Lattimore, Richmond. "Portents and Prophecies in Connection With the Emperor Vespasian," *The Classical Journal* 29.6 (1934): 441–449.

Levene, Dan. *A Corpus of Magic Bowls: Incantation Texts in Jewish Aramaic From Late Antiquity*. New York: Keegan Paul, 2003.

Lhote, Eric. *Les lamelles oraculaires de Dodone*. Geneva: Droz, 2006.

Lietaert Peerbolte, Jan. "Paul the Miracle Worker: Development and Background of Pauline Miracle Stories." In *Wonders Never Cease: The Purpose of Narrating Miracle Stories in the New Testament and Its Religious Environment*, 180–199. London: T&T Clark, 2006.

Lightfoot, J. B. "The Name and Office of an Apostle." In *Epistle of Saint Paul to the Galatians*, 92–101. Grand Rapids, MI: Zondervan, reprint, 1957.

Lightfoot, J. L. *The Sibylline Oracles, With Introduction, Translation, and Commentary on the First and Second Books*. Oxford: Oxford University Press, 2007.

Lincoln, Bruce. *Discourse and the Construction of Society: Comparative Studies of Myth, Ritual, and Classification*. Oxford: Oxford University Press, 2014.

Lincoln, Bruce. *Holy Terrors: Thinking About Religion After September 11*. Chicago: University of Chicago Press, 2006.

Lindsay, Dennis. *Josephus and Faith: Πίστις and Πιστεύειν as Faith Terminology in the Writings of Flavius Josephus and the New Testament*. Leiden: Brill, 1993.

Litwa, M. David. *Iesus Deus: The Early Christian Depiction of Jesus as a Mediterranean God*. Minneapolis: Fortress Academic, 2014.

Lombard, Emile. *De la glossolalia chez les premiers chrétiens et des phénomènes similaires*. Lausanne: Bridel, 1910.

Long, Anthony A. "Stoic Readings of Homer." In *Homer's Ancient Readers: The Hermeneutics of Greek Epic's Earliest Exegetes*, ed.Robert Lamberton and John Keaney, 41–66. Princeton, NJ: Princeton University Press, 1992.

Lutes, Chris. "First Church of Signs and Wonders: Do We Want Magic or God?" *Christianity Today* 45.1 (2001): 81.

MacDonald, Dennis. "Apocryphal and Canonical Narratives About Paul." In *Paul and the Legacies of Paul*, ed. William Babcock, 55–70. Dallas: Southern Methodist University Press, 1990.

MacDonald, Margaret Y. "Reading Real Women Through the Undisputed Letters of Paul." In *Women and Christian Origins*, ed. Ross Kraemer and Mary Rose D'Angelo, 199–220. New York: Oxford University Press, 1999.

Mack, Burton, *A Myth of Innocence: Mark and Christian Origins*. Philadelphia: Fortress Press, 1988.

MacMullen, Ramsay. *Enemies of the Roman Order: Treason, Unrest, and Alienation in the Empire*. Cambridge, MA: Harvard University Press, 1966.

Majercik, R. *The Chaldean Oracles, Text, Trans. and Commentary* (Studies in Greek and Roman Religion v). Leiden: Brill, 1989.

Malherbe, Abraham. *Paul and the Popular Philosophers*. Minneapolis: Fortress Press, 2006.

Malony, Newton H. *Glossolalia: Behavioral Science Perspectives on Speaking in Tongues*. New York: Oxford University Press, 1985.

Manetti, Giovanni. *Theories of the Sign in Classical Antiquity*. Translated by Christine Richardson. Bloomington: Indiana University Press, 1993.

Martin, Dale. "Tongues of Angels and Other Status Indicators," *Journal of the American Academy of Religion* 59.3 (1991): 547–589.

Martin, Ira. *Glossolalia, The Gift of Tongues*. Cleveland, TN: Pathway Press, 1970.

Mason, Steve. "Jews, Judeans, Judaizing, Judaism: Problems of Categorization in Ancient History," *Journal for the Study of Judaism* 38 (2007): 457–512.

Masuzawa, Tamoko. *The Invention of World Religions*. Chicago: University of Chicago Press, 2005.

Matthews, Roger and Cornelia Roemer, eds. *Ancient Perspectives on Egypt*. London: University College London, 2003.

Mauss, Marcel. *The Gift; Forms and Functions of Exchange in Archaic Societies*. Glencoe, IL: Free Press, 1954.

May, Carlyle. "A Survey of Glossolalia and related Phenomena in Non-Christian Religions," *American Anthropologist* 58.1 (1956): 75–96.

McCasland, Vernon S. "Signs and Wonders," *Journal of Biblical Literature* 76.2 (1957): 149–152.

McCulloch, Harold Y. Jr., "Literary Augury at the End of 'Annals' XIII," *Phoenix* 34.3 (1980): 237–242.

McCurry, Justin. "Tokyo Governor Apologises for Calling Tsunami 'Divine Punishment.'" *The Guardian*, March 15, 2011. URL: http://www.guardian.co.uk/world/ 2011/mar/15/tokyo-governor-tsunami-punishment.

McDonough, Christopher. "The Swallows on Cleopatra's Ship," *The Classical World* 96.3 (2003): 251–258.

Meier, John P. "The Circle of the Twelve: Did it Exist During Jesus' Public Ministry?" *Journal of Biblical Literature* 116.4 (1997): 635–672.

Mendonsa, Eugene. *The Politics of Divination: A Processual View of Reactions to Illness and Deviance Among the Sisala.* Berkeley: University of California Press, 1982.

Mills, Watson E. *Speaking in Tongues: A Guide to Research on Glossolalia.* Grand Rapids, MI: Eerdmans, 1986.

Milner, N. P. "Notes and Inscriptions on the Cult of Apollo at Oinoanda," *Anatolian Studies* 50 (2000): 139–149.

Mockmuehl, Markus. *Revelation and Mystery in Ancient Judaism and Pauline Christianity.* Tübingen, Germany: Mohr Siebeck, 1990.

Morgan, Teresa. *Roman Faith and Christian Faith: Pistis and Fides in the Early Roman Empire and Early Churches.* Oxford: Oxford University Press, 2015.

Mosshammer, Alden. "Thales' Eclipse," *Transactions of the American Philological Association* 111 (1981): 145–155.

Mount, Christopher. *Pauline Christianity: Luke-Acts and the Legacy of Paul.* Leiden: Brill, 2002.

Najda, Andrzej Jacek. *Der Apostel als Prophet: Zur Prophetischen Dimension des Paulinischen Apostolats.* Frankfurt: Lang, 2004.

Nasrallah, Laura. *An Ecstasy of Folly: Prophecy and Authority in Early Christianity.* Cambridge, MA: Harvard University Press, 2003.

Needham, Rodney. "Polythetic Classification: Convergence and Consequences," *Man* 10.3 (1975): 349–369.

Nichols, Shaun. "Imagination and Immortality: Thinking of Me," *Synthese* 159.2 (2007): 215–233.

Niehoff, Maren. "Why Compare Homer's Readers to Readers of the Bible?" In *Homer and the Bible in the Eyes of Ancient Interpreters*, ed. Maren Niehoff, 1–14. Leiden: Brill, 2012.

Niehoff, Maren, "Philo and Plutarch on Homer." In *Homer and the Bible in the Eyes of Ancient Interpreters*, ed. Maren Niehoff, 127–153. Leiden: Brill, 2012.

Nigosian, S. A. *Magic and Divination in the Old Testament.* Brighton, UK: Sussex Academic Press, 2008.

Nissinen, Martti. "Prophecy and Omen Divination: Two Sides of the Same Coin." In *Divination and Interpretation of Signs in the Ancient World*, ed. Amar Annus, 341–347. Chicago: Oriental Institute of the University of Chicago, 2010.

Nock, Arthur Darby. "Alexander of Abonuteichos," *Classical Quarterly* 22 (1928): 160–162.

Nongbri, Brent. *Before Religion: A History of a Modern Concept.* New Haven, CT: Yale University Press, 2013.

Norelli, Enrico. "The Political Issue of the Ascension of Isaiah: Some Remarks on Jonathan Knight's Thesis, and Some Methodological Problems." In *Early Christian Voices: In Texts, Traditions, and Symbols: Essays in Honor of François Bovon*, ed. David H. Warren, Ann Graham Brock, and David W. Pao, 267–282. Boston: Brill Academic, 2003.

Novakovic, Lidija. *Messiah, the Healer of the Sick: A Study of Jesus as the Son of David in the Gospel of Matthew.* Tübingen, Germany: Mohr Siebeck, 2003.

Ogden, Daniel. *Magic, Witchcraft, and Ghosts in the Greek and Roman Worlds.* Oxford: Oxford University Press, 2009.

Ogden, Daniel. *Greek and Roman Necromancy.* Princeton, NJ: Princeton University Press, 2001.

Oppenheim, A. Leo. "New Fragments of the Assyrian Dream-Book," *Iraq* 31.2 (1969): 153–165.

Oppenheim, A. Leo. "The Interpretation of Dreams in the Ancient Near East. With a Translation of an Assyrian Dream-Book," *Transactions of the American Philosophical Society*, New Series 46.3 (1956): 179–373.

Pachoumi, Eleni. "Resurrection of the Body in the 'Greek Magical Papyri,'" *Numen* 58.5 (2011): 729–740.

Palmer Bonz, Marianne. "The Jewish Donor Inscriptions from Aphrodisias: Are They Both Third Century, and Who are the Theosebeis?" *Harvard Studies in Classical Philology* 96 (1994): 281–299.

Parke, H. W. *Sibyls and Sibylline Prophecy in Classical Antiquity.* London: Routledge, 1988.

Parker, Robert. "Pleasing Thighs: Reciprocity in Greek Religion." In *Reciprocity in Ancient Greece*, ed. Christopher Gill, Norman Postlethwaite, and Richard Seaford, 105–126. Oxford: Oxford University Press, 1998.

Parry, J. "The Gift, the Indian Gift, and the 'Indian Gift,'" *Man* 21 (1986): 453–73.

Pease, Arthur Stanley. "The Omen of the Sneeze," *Classical Philology* 6.4 (1911): 429–443.

Peek, Philip M., ed. *African Divination Systems: Ways of Knowing.* Bloomington: Indiana University Press, 1991.

Pellikaan-Engel, Maja E. *Hesiod and Parmenides: A New View on Their Cosmologies and on Parmenides' Proem.* Amsterdam: Adolf M. Hakkert, 1978.

Penella, Robert. *The Letters of Apollonius of Tyana: A Critical Text With Prolegomena.* Leiden: Brill, 1979.

Persuitte, David. *Joseph Smith and the Origins of the Book of Mormon.* Jefferson, NC: McFarland, 2000.

Pervo, Richard. *Profit with Delight: The Literary Genre of the Acts of the Apostles.* Philadelphia: Fortress Press, 1987.

Petridou, Georgia. *Divine Epiphany and Greek Literature.* Oxford: Oxford University Press, 2015.

Pettis, Jeffrey. "Earth, Dream, and Healing: The Integrations of *Materia* and Psyche in the Ancient World," *Journal of Religion and Health* 45.1 (2006): 113–129.

Pilch, John. *Healing and Visions in the Acts of the Apostles*. Collegeville, MN: Liturgical Press, 2004.

Pilch, John. *Healing in the New Testament: Insights From Medical and Mediterranean Anthropology*. Minneapolis: Fortress Press, 2000.

Platt, Verity. *Facing the Gods: Epiphany and Representation in Graeco-Roman Art, Literature, and Religion*. New York: Cambridge University Press, 2011.

Pogrebin, Robin. "It Seems the Cards Do Lie; A Police Sting Cracks Down on Fortunetelling Fraud." June 30, 1999. URL: http://www.nytimes.com/1999/06/30/nyregion/it-seems-the-cards-do-lie-a-police-sting-cracks-down-on-fortunetelling-fraud.html?scp=3&sq=astrologer%20fraud&st=cse.

Porter, James. "Philo's Confusion of Tongues: Some Methodological Observations," *Quaderni Urbinati di Cultura Classica*, New Series 24.3 (1986): 55–74.

Porter, Stanley, ed. *Paul and His Opponents*. Leiden: Brill, 2005.

Porterfield, Amanda. *Healing in the History of Christianity*. New York: Oxford University Press, 2005.

Potter, David. *Prophets and Emperors: Human and Divine Authority From Augustus to Theodosius*. Cambridge, MA: Harvard University Press, 1994.

Praeder, Susan Marie. "Miracle Worker and Missionary: Paul in Acts of the Apostles." In *SBL 1983 Seminar Papers*. ed. K. H. Richards, 107–129. Chico: Scholars Press, 1983.

Prieur, Jean-Marc. *Acta Andreae*. Turnhout: Brepols, 1989.

Pucci, Pietro. "Gods' Intervention and Epiphany in Sophocles," *American Journal of Philology* 115.1 (1994): 15–46.

Pyysiäinen, Ilkka. *Supernatural Agents: Why We Believe in Souls, Gods, and Buddhas*. Oxford: Oxford University Press, 2009.

Ramsey, John T. "'Beware the Ides of March!': An Astrological Prediction?" *The Classical Quarterly* 50.2 (2000): 440–454.

Rankin, H. D. "Heraclitus on Conscious and Unconscious States," *Quaderni Urbinati di Cultura Classica*, New Series 50.2 (1995): 73–86.

Rajak, T. "Was There a Roman Charter for the Jews?" *Journal of Roman Studies* 74 (1984): 107–123.

Rawson, Elizabeth. "Caesar, Etruria and the *Disciplina Etrusca*," *Journal of Roman Studies* 68 (1978): 132–152.

Reimer, Andy. *Miracle and Magic: A Study in the Acts of the Apostles and the Life of Apollonius of Tyana*. New York: Sheffield Academic Press, 2002.

Reiner, Erica. "Astral Magic in Babylonia," *Transactions of the American Philosophical Society*, New Series 85.4 (1995): i–150.

Reiner, Erica. *Babylonian Planetary Omens*. Malibu, CA: Undena Publications, 2005.

Remus, Harold. *Jesus as Healer*. Cambridge: Cambridge University Press, 1997.

Remus, Harold. *Pagan Christian Conflict Over Miracle in the Second Century.* Cambridge, MA: Philadelphia Patristic Foundation, 1983.

Renberg, Gil H. "'Commanded by the Gods': An Epigraphical Study of Dreams and Visions in Greek and Roman Religious Life." PhD Dissertation, Duke University, 2003.

Rengstorf, K. H. "Apostolos." In *Theological Dictionary of the New Testament*, ed. G. Kittel, 407–447. Grand Rapids, MI: Eerdmans, 1964.

Ribeiro, René. "Projective Mechanisms and the Structuralization of Perception in Afrobrazilian Divination," *Revue Internationale d'Ethnopsychologie Normale et Pathologique* 1.2 (1956): 3–23.

Richardson Jr., L. "Trimalchio and the Sibyl at Cumae," *The Classical World* 96.1 (2002): 77–78.

Richter, Daniel S. "Plutarch on Isis and Osiris: Text, Cult, and Cultural Appropriation," *Transactions of the American Philological Association* 131.1. (2001): 191–216.

Ricks, Stephen. "The Magician as Outsider in the Hebrew Bible and the New Testament." In *Ancient Magic and Ritual Power*, ed. Marvin Meyer and Paul Mirecki, 131–143. Boston: Brill, 2001.

Riemer, Ulrike. "Miracle Stories and Their Narrative Intent in the Context of the Ruler Cult of Classical Antiquity." In *Wonders Never Cease: The Purpose of Narrating Miracle Stories in the New Testament and Its Religious Environment*, ed. Michael Labahn and L. J. Lietaert Peerbolte, 32–47. New York: T & T Clark, 2006.

Riley, Mark. "The Purpose of Plutarch's *De Genio Socratis*," *Greek, Roman, and Byzantine Studies* 18.3 (1977): 257–273.

Ripat, Pauline. "Expelling Misconceptions: Astrologers at Rome," *Classical Philology* 106.2 (2011): 115–154.

Ripat, Pauline. "Roman Omens, Roman Audiences, and Roman History," *Greece and Rome* 53 (2006): 155–174.

Ripat, Pauline. "The Language of Oracular Inquiry in Roman Egypt," *Phoenix* 60.3 (2006): 304–328.

Rochberg-Halton, F. "Elements of the Babylonian Contribution to Hellenistic Astrology," *Journal of the American Oriental Society* 108.1 (1988): 51–62.

Rollens, Sarah. "The God Came to Me in a Dream: Epiphanies in Voluntary Associations as a Context for Paul's Visions of Christ," *Harvard Theological Review* 111.1 (2018): 41–65.

Romberg, Raquel. *Healing Dramas: Divination and Magic in Modern Puerto Rico.* Austin: University of Texas Press, 2009.

Römer, T. "Competing Magicians in Exodus 7–9: Interpreting Magic in Priestly Theology." In *Magic in the Biblical World. From the Rod of Aaron to the Ring of Solomon*, ed. T. Klutz, 12–22. New York: T & T Clark International, 2003.

Rutgers, Leonard, ed. *The Use of Sacred Books in the Ancient World.* Leuven, Belgium: Peeters, 1998.

Saller, Richard. *Personal Patronage Under the Early Roman Empire*. Cambridge: Cambridge University Press, 1982.

Savran, George. *Encountering the Divine: Theophany in Biblical Narrative*. New York: T & T Clark, 2005.

Scarborough, John. "The Pharmacology of Sacred Plants, Herbs, and Roots." In *Magika Hiera: Ancient Greek Magic and Religion*, ed. Christopher A. Faraone and Dirk Obbink, 138–174. Oxford: Oxford University Press, 1991.

Schantz, Colleen. *Paul in Ecstasy: The Neurobiology of the Apostle's Life and Thought*. Cambridge: Cambridge University Press, 2009.

Schatzki, Theodore. "Introduction: Practice Theory." In *The Practice Turn in Contemporary Theory*, ed. Theodore Schatzki et al. New York: Routledge, 2001.

Scherrer, Steven J. "Signs and Wonders in the Imperial Cult: A New Look at a Roman Religious Institution in the Light of Rev 13:13–15," *Journal of Biblical Literature* 103.4 (1984): 599–610.

Schilbrack, Kevin. *Philosophy and the Study of Religions: A Manifesto*. Malden, MA: Wiley Blackwell, 2014.

Schmithals, Walter. *The Office of Apostle in the Early Church*. New York: Abingdon, 1969.

Schnabel, Paul. *Berossos und die Babylonisch-Hellenistische Literatur*. Leipzig: Teubner, 1923.

Schofield, Malcolm. "Cicero for and Against Divination," *Journal of Roman Studies* 76 (1986): 47–65.

Schreiber, Stefan. *Paulus als Wundertäter: Redaktionsgeschichtliche Untersuchungen zur Apostelgeschichte und den authentischen Paulusbriefen*. New York: de Gruyter, 1996.

Schütz, John. *Paul and the Anatomy of Apostolic Authority*. Louisville, KY: Westminster John Knox, 2007 (reprinted).

Schwartz, Daniel. *Studies in the Jewish Background of Christianity*. Tübingen, Germany: Mohr Siebeck, 1992.

Schwartz, Michael. "Divination and Its Discontents: Finding and Questioning Meaning in Ancient and Medieval Judaism." In *Prayer, Magic, and the Stars in the Ancient and Late Antique World*, ed. Scott Noegel et al., 155–168. University Park: Pennsylvania State University Press, 2003.

Schwarz, Seth. "How Many Judaisms Were There?: A Critique of Neusner and Smith on Definition and Mason and Boyarin on Categorization," *Journal of Ancient Judaism* 2.2 (2011): 208–238.

Schwarz, Seth. *Were the Jews a Mediterranean Society? Reciprocity and Solidarity in Ancient Judaism*. Princeton, NJ: Princeton University Press, 2010.

Schweitzer, Albert. *The Mysticism of the Apostle Paul*. New York: Holt, 1931.

Schwendner, Gregg. "Under Homer's Spell." In *Magic and Divination in the Ancient World*, ed. Leda Ciraolo and Jonathan Seidel, 107–118. Leiden: Brill, 2002.

Scurlock, JoAnn. "Prophecy as a Form of Divination; Divination as a Form of Prophecy." In *Divination and Interpretation of Signs in the Ancient World*, ed. Amar Annus, 277–316. Chicago: University of Chicago Press, 2010.

Seddon, Keith. *Epictetus' Handbook and the Tablet of Cebes: Guides to Stoic Living*. New York: Routledge, 2006.

Seel, Otto, ed. *M. Juniani Justini Epitoma Historiarum Philippicarum Pompei Trogi*. Leipzig: Teubner, 1956.

Segal, Alan. "Heavenly Ascent in Hellenistic Judaism, Early Christianity and Their Environment," *ANRW* (1980): 1333–1394.

Seow, C. L. "The Syro-Palestinian Context of Solomon's Dream," *Harvard Theological Review* 77.2 (1984): 141–152.

Shantz, Colleen. *Paul in Ecstasy: The Neurobiology of the Apostle's Life and Thought*. New York: Cambridge University Press, 2009.

Sharf, Robert. "Experience." In *Critical Terms for Religious Studies*, ed. Mark C. Taylor. Chicago: University of Chicago Press, 1998: 94–116.

Slingerland, Edward. *What Science Offers the Humanities: Integrating Body and Culture*. Cambridge: Cambridge University Press, 2008.

Slingerland, Edward. *Creating Consilience: Integrating the Sciences and the Humanities*. New York: Oxford University Press, 2011.

Smith, Jonathan Z. "On Comparison." In *Drudgery Divine: On the Comparison of Early Christianities and the Religions of Late Antiquity*, 36–53. Chicago: University of Chicago Press, 1990.

Smith, Jonathan Z. "*Dayyeinu*." In *Redescribing Christian Origins*, ed. Ron Cameron and Merrill Miller, 483–488. Atlanta, GA: Society of Biblical Literature, 2004.

Smith, Jonathan Z. "Religion, Religions, Religious." In *Relating Religion: Essays in the Study of Religion*, ed. Jonathan Z. Smith, 179–196. Chicago: University of Chicago Press, 2004.

Smith, Jonathan Z. "When the Chips Are Down." In *Relating Religion: Essays in the Study of Religion*, ed. Jonathan Z. Smith, 1–60. Chicago: University of Chicago Press, 2004.

Smith, Jonathan Z. "Trading Places." In *Ancient Magic and Ritual Power*, ed. by Marvin Meyer and Paul Mirecki, 13–28. Boston: Brill, 2001.

Smith, Morton. *Jesus the Magician*. Berkeley, CA: Ulysses Press, reprint 1998.

Smith, Morton. "Pauline Worship as Seen by Pagans," *Harvard Theological Review* 73.1 (1980): 241–249.

Smith, Morton. "Prolegomena to a Discussion of Aretologies, Divine Men, the Gospels and Jesus," *Journal of Biblical Literature* 90 (1971): 174–199.

Sneath, Peter. "The Construction of Taxonomic Groups." In *Microbial Classification*, ed. G. C. Ainsworth and P. Sneath. Cambridge: Cambridge University Press, 1962.

Sokal, Robert and Peter Sneath. *Principles of Numerical Taxonomy*. San Francisco: Freeman, 1963.

Speyer, Wolfgang. "The Divine Messenger in Ancient Greece, Etruria and Rome." In *The Concept of Celestial Beings—Origins, Development and Reception*, ed. Friedrich Reiterer et al., 35–50. Berlin: de Gruyter, 2007.

Stegman, Thomas. *Commentary on Second Corinthians*. Grand Rapids: Baker Academic, 2009.

Stowers, Stanley. "Why Expert Versus Nonexpert is not Elite Versus Popular Religion: The Case of the Third Century." In *Religious Competition in the Greco-Roman World*, ed. Nathanial DeRosiers and Lily C. Vuong, 139–153. Atlanta: SBL, 2016.

Stowers, Stanley. "The Religion of Plant and Animal Offerings Versus the Religion of Meanings, Essences, and Textual Mysteries." In *Ancient Mediterranean Sacrifice*, ed. Jennifer Wright Knust and Zsuzsanna Várhelyi, 35–56. New York: Oxford University Press, 2011.

Stowers, Stanley. "What Is Pauline Participation in Christ?" In *Redefining First-Century Jewish and Christian Identities: Essays in Honor of Ed Parish Sanders*, ed. Fabian E. Udoh, 352–371. Notre Dame, IN: University of Notre Dame Press, 2008.

Stowers, Stanley. "Paul and Self-Mastery." In *Paul in the Greco-Roman World: A Handbook*, ed. J. Paul Sampley, 524–550. Harrisburg, PA: Trinity Press International, 2003.

Stowers, Stanley. "Does Pauline Christianity Resemble a Hellenistic Philosophy?" In *Paul Beyond the Judaism/Hellenism Divide*, ed. Troels Engberg-Pedersen, 81–102. Louisville, KY: Westminster John Knox Press, 2001.

Stowers, Stanley. *A Rereading of Romans: Justice, Jews, and Gentiles*. New Haven, CT: Yale University Press, 1994.

Stowers, Stanley. "Comment: What Does *Unpauline* Mean?" In *Paul and the Legacies of Paul*, ed. William Babcock, 70–78. Dallas, TX: Southern Methodist University Press, 1990.

Stowers, Stanley. *The Diatribe and Paul's Letter to the Romans*, SBL Dissertation Series, 57. Missoula, MO: Scholars Press, 1981.

Stratton, Kimberly. *Naming the Witch: Magic, Ideology, and Stereotype in the Ancient World*. New York: Columbia University Press, 2007.

Struck, Peter. *Divination and Human Nature: A Cognitive History of Intuition in Classical Antiquity*. Princeton, NJ: Princeton University Press, 2016.

Struck, Peter. "Divination and Literary Criticism?" In *Mantikê. Studies in Ancient Divination*, ed. Sarah Iles Johnston and Peter Struck, 147–165. Leiden: Brill, 2005.

Struck, Peter. *Birth of the Symbol: Ancient Readers at the Limits of Their Texts*. Princeton, NJ: Princeton University Press, 2004.

Struck, Peter. "Reading Symbols: Traces of Gods in the Ancient Greek-Speaking World." PhD Dissertation, University of Chicago, 1997.

Sweet, J. P. M. "A Sign for Unbelievers: Paul's Attitude to Glossolalia," *New Testament Studies* 13.3 (1967): 240–257.

Swerdlow, N. M. *Ancient Astronomy and Celestial Divination.* Cambridge, MA: MIT Press, 1999.

Swidler, Ann. "What Anchors Cultural Practices." In *The Practice Turn in Contemporary Theory*, ed. Theodore Schatzki et al., 74–92. New York: Routledge, 2001.

Tabor, James. *Things Unutterable: Paul's Ascent to Paradise in Its Greco-Roman, Judaic, and Early Christian Contexts.* Lanham, MD: University Press of America, 1986.

Takács, Sarolta Anna. *Isis and Sarapis in the Roman World.* Leiden: Brill, 1995.

Tatum, Jeffrey W. "Cicero and the 'Bona Dea' Scandal," *Classical Philology* 82 (1990): 85–202.

Taves, Ann. *Religious Experience Reconsidered: A Building Block Approach to the Study of Religion and Other Special Things.* Princeton, NJ: Princeton University Press, 2009.

Temin, Peter. *The Roman Market Economy.* Princeton, NJ: Princeton University Press, 2013.

Thiselton, Anthony. "The 'Interpretation' of Tongues: A New Suggestion in the Light of Greek Usage in Philo and Josephus," *Journal of Theological Studies* 30 (1979): 15–36.

Thomas, Christine. *The Acts of Peter, Gospel Literature and the Ancient Novel.* Oxford: Oxford University Press, 2003.

Thomas, Samuel. *The "Mysteries" of Qumran: Mystery, Secrecy, and Esotericism in the Dead Sea Scrolls.* Atlanta, GA: Society of Biblical Literature, 2009.

Tibbs, Clint. *Religious Experience of the Pneuma: Communication With the Spirit World in 1 Corinthians 12 and 14.* Tübingen, Germany: Mohr Siebeck, 2007.

Tucker, C. Wayne. "Cicero, Augur, De Iure Augurali," *The Classical World* 70.3 (1976): 171–177.

Twelftree, Graham. *Paul and the Miraculous: A Historical Reconstruction.* Grand Rapids, MI: Baker Academic, 2013.

Twelftree, Graham. "Signs, Wonders, Miracles." In *Dictionary of Paul and His Letters*, ed. Gerald F. Hawthorne et al., 875–877. Downers Grove, IL: InterVarsity Press, 1993.

Ullucci, Daniel. *The Christian Rejection of Animal Sacrifice.* New York: Oxford University Press, 2012.

Urban, Hugh. "The Torment of Secrecy: Ethical and Epistemological Problems in the Study of Esoteric Traditions," *History of Religions* 37 (1998): 209–248.

Van Dam, Cornelis. *The Urim and Thummim: A Means of Revelation in Ancient Israel.* Winona Lake, IN: Eisenbrauns, 1997.

Van den Broek, Roelof and Cis van Heertum, eds. *From Poimandres to Jacob Böhme: Gnosis, Hermetism and the Christian Tradition.* Amsterdam: Bibliotheca Philosophica Hermetica, 2000.

van der Horst, Pieter Willem. *Japheth in the Tents of Shem: Studies on Jewish Hellenism in Antiquity.* Leuven, Belgium: Peeters, 2002.

Van Seters, J. "A Contest of Magicians? The Plague Stories in P." In *Pomegranates and Golden Bells: Studies in Biblical, Jewish, and Near Eastern Ritual, Law, and Literature in Honor of Jacob Milgrom*, ed. D. P. Wright et al., 569–580. Winona Lake, IN: Eisenbrauns, 1995.

Van Wees, Hans. "The Law of Gratitude: Reciprocity in Anthropological Theory." In *Reciprocity in Ancient Greece*, ed. Christopher Gill, Norman Postlethwaite, and Richard Seaford, 13–49. Oxford: Oxford University Press, 1998.

Veenstra, Jan. *Magic and Divination at the Courts of Burgundy and France: Text and Context of Laurens Pignon's Contre les Devineurs* (1411). Leiden: Brill, 1998.

Verbrugghe, G. P. and Wickersham, J. M. *Berossos and Manetho Introduced and Translated: Native Traditions in Ancient Mesopotamia and Egypt.* Ann Arbor: University of Michigan Press, 2000.

Verheyden, Joseph et al., eds. *Prophets and Prophecy in Jewish and Early Christian Literature.* Tübingen, Germany: Mohr Siebeck, 2010.

Versluys, M. J. and Malaise, Michel. *Isis on the Nile: Egyptian Gods in Hellenistic and Roman Egypt: Proceedings of the IVth International Conference of Isis Studies, Liege, November 27–29, 2008.* Leiden: Brill, 2010.

Walker, Ronald W. "The Persisting Idea of American Treasure Hunting," *BYU Studies* 24 (1984): 429–459.

Wallace-Hadrill, Andrew, ed. *Patronage in Ancient Society.* New York: Routledge, 1989.

Wallis, I. G. *The Faith of Jesus Christ in Early Christian Traditions*, Society for New Testament Studies Monograph Series 84. Cambridge: Cambridge University Press, 1995.

Walton, Francis R. "The Messenger of God in Hecataeus of Abdera," *Harvard Theological Review* 48.4 (1955): 255–257.

Walsh, Robyn and David Konstan. "Civic and Subversive Biography in Antiquity." In *Writing Biographies in Greece and Rome: Narrative Technique and Fictionalization*, ed. K. de Temmerman and Kristoffel Demoen, 26–43. Cambridge: Cambridge University Press, 2016.

Wasserman, Emma. "Paul Among the Philosophers: The Case of Sin in Romans 6–8," *Journal for the Study of the New Testament* 30.4 (2008): 387–415.

Wasserman, Emma. *The Death of the Soul in Romans 7: Sin, Death, and the Law in Light of Hellenistic Moral Psychology.* Wissenschaftliche Untersuchungen zum Neuen Testament 2.56. Tübingen, Germany: Mohr Siebeck, 2008.

Weissenrieder, Annette. *Images of Illness in the Gospel of Luke.* Tübingen, Germany: Mohr Siebeck, 2003.

Wendt, Heidi. *At the Temple Gates: The Religion of Freelance Experts in the Roman Empire.* New York: Oxford University Press, 2016.

White, Joel R. "'Baptized on Account of the Dead': The Meaning of 1 Corinthians 15:29 in Its Context," *Journal of Biblical Literature* 116.3 (1997): 487–499.

Whitehouse, Harvey. *Modes of Religiosity: A Cognitive Theory of Religious Transmission.* New York: AltaMira Press, 2004.

Whitlark, Jason. *Enabling Fidelity to God: Perseverance in Hebrews in Light of the Reciprocity Systems of the Ancient Mediterranean World.* Milton Keynes, UK: Paternoster, 2008.

Wildfang, Robin Lorsch. "The Propaganda of Omens: Six Dreams Involving Augustus." In *Divination and Portents in the Roman World*, ed. Robin Lorsch Wildfang and Jacob Isager, 443–456. Odense, Denmark: University of Odense Press, 2000.

Wilkinson, Lisa Atwood. *Parmenides and To Eon: Reconsidering Muthos and Logos*. New York: Continuum International, 2009.

Williams, Margaret. *The Jews Among the Greeks and Romans: A Diaspora Sourcebook*. Baltimore: Johns Hopkins University Press, 1998.

Winkler, John J. *The Constraints of Desire: The Anthropology of Sex and Gender in Ancient Greece*. New York: Routledge, 1990.

Witherington, Ben III. *Conflict and Community in Corinth: A Socio-Rhetorical Commentary on 1 and 2 Corinthians*. Grand Rapids, MI: Eerdmans, 1995.

Witmer, Stephen E. *Divine Instruction in Early Christianity*. Tübingen, Germany: Mohr Siebeck, 2008.

Wittgenstein, Ludwig. *Preliminary Studies for the "Philosophical Investigations", Generally Known as The Blue and Brown Books*. Oxford: Blackwell, 1958.

Wood, James. "Between God and Hard Place," *New York Times,* January 23, 2010. URL: http://www.nytimes.com/2010/01/24/opinion/24wood.html?scp=4&sq=pat%20robertson%20haiti%20earthquake&st=cse.

Wright, N. T. "Paul, Arabia, and Elijah (Galatians 1:17)," *Journal of Biblical Literature* 115.4 (1996): 683–692.

Young, Elizabeth Marie. "Inscribing Orpheus: Ovid and the Invention of a Greco-Roman Corpus," *Representations* 101.1. (2008): 1–31.

Young, Serenity. "Buddhist Dream Experience: The Role of Interpretation, Ritual, and Gender." In *Dreams: A Reader on the Religious, Cultural, and Psychological Dimensions of Dreaming*, ed. Kelly Bulkeley, 9–28. New York: Palgrave, 2001.

Young, Stephen L. "Paul's Ethnic Discourse on 'Faith': Christ's Faithfulness and Gentile Access to the Judean God in Romans 3:21–5:1," *Harvard Theological Studies* 108 (2015): 30–51.

Zeev, Miriam Pucci Ben. *Jewish Rights in the Roman World*. Tübingen, Germany: Mohr Siebeck, 1998.

Zifopoulos, Yannis. *'Paradise' Earned: The Bacchic-Orphic Lamellae of Crete*, Hellenic Series 23. Washington, DC: Center for Hellenic Studies, 2010.

Ziolkowski, Theodore. "'Tolle Lege': Epiphanies of the Book," *Modern Language Review* 109.1 (2014): 1–14.

Index